S0-AIR-747

VOLUME FIFTY ONE

International Review of
RESEARCH IN
DEVELOPMENTAL
DISABILITIES

SERIAL EDITORS

ROBERT M. HODAPP
Vanderbilt Kennedy Center for Research on Human Development, Department of Special Education, Peabody College, Vanderbilt University, Nashville, TN, USA

DEBORAH J. FIDLER
Professor of Human Development and Family Studies, Colorado State University, Fort Collins, CO, USA

BOARD OF ASSOCIATE EDITORS

PHILIP DAVIDSON
University of Rochester School of Medicine and Dentistry

ELISABETH DYKENS
Vanderbilt University

MICHAEL GURALNICK
University of Washington

RICHARD HASTINGS
University of Warwick

LINDA HICKSON
Columbia University

CONNIE KASARI
University of California, Los Angeles

WILLIAM McILVANE
E. K. Shriver Center

GLYNIS MURPHY
University of Kent

TED NETTELBECK
Adelaide University

MARSHA MAILICK
University of Wisconsin-Madison

JAN WALLANDER
Sociometrics Corporation

VOLUME FIFTY ONE

INTERNATIONAL REVIEW OF
RESEARCH IN
DEVELOPMENTAL
DISABILITIES

Edited by

ROBERT M. HODAPP
*Vanderbilt Kennedy Center for Research on Human
Development, Department of Special Education,
Peabody College, Vanderbilt University, Nashville, TN, USA*

DEBORAH J. FIDLER
*Professor of Human Development and Family Studies,
Colorado State University, Fort Collins, CO, USA*

ELSEVIER

AMSTERDAM • BOSTON • HEIDELBERG • LONDON
NEW YORK • OXFORD • PARIS • SAN DIEGO
SAN FRANCISCO • SINGAPORE • SYDNEY • TOKYO
Academic Press is an imprint of Elsevier

Academic Press is an imprint of Elsevier
50 Hampshire Street, 5th Floor, Cambridge, MA 02139, United States
525 B Street, Suite 1800, San Diego, CA 92101-4495, United States
125 London Wall, London EC2Y 5AS, United Kingdom
The Boulevard, Langford Lane, Kidlington, Oxford OX5 1GB, United Kingdom

First edition 2016

Copyright © 2016 Elsevier Inc. All rights reserved.

No part of this publication may be reproduced or transmitted in any form or by any means, electronic or mechanical, including photocopying, recording, or any information storage and retrieval system, without permission in writing from the publisher. Details on how to seek permission, further information about the Publisher's permissions policies and our arrangements with organizations such as the Copyright Clearance Center and the Copyright Licensing Agency, can be found at our website: www.elsevier.com/permissions.

This book and the individual contributions contained in it are protected under copyright by the Publisher (other than as may be noted herein).

Notices
Knowledge and best practice in this field are constantly changing. As new research and experience broaden our understanding, changes in research methods, professional practices, or medical treatment may become necessary.

Practitioners and researchers must always rely on their own experience and knowledge in evaluating and using any information, methods, compounds, or experiments described herein. In using such information or methods they should be mindful of their own safety and the safety of others, including parties for whom they have a professional responsibility.

To the fullest extent of the law, neither the Publisher nor the authors, contributors, or editors, assume any liability for any injury and/or damage to persons or property as a matter of products liability, negligence or otherwise, or from any use or operation of any methods, products, instructions, or ideas contained in the material herein.

ISBN: 978-0-12-804785-9
ISSN: 2211-6095

For information on all Academic Press publications
visit our website at https://www.elsevier.com

Working together
to grow libraries in
developing countries

www.elsevier.com • www.bookaid.org

Publisher: Zoe Kruze
Acquisition Editor: Kirsten Shankland
Editorial Project Manager: Hannah Colford
Production Project Manager: Vignesh Tamil
Cover Designer: Maria Ines Cruz

Typeset by TNQ Books and Journals

CONTENTS

CONTRIBUTORS

L.G. Anthony
Children's National Health System, Washington, DC, United States; George Washington University School of Medicine, Washington, DC, United States

M.M. Burke
University of Illinois at Urbana-Champaign, Champaign, IL, United States

C. Corr
Vanderbilt University, Nashville, TN, United States

E. Dlugi
George Washington University, Washington, DC, United States

A.J. Esbensen
Cincinnati Children's Hospital Medical Center, Cincinnati, OH, United States

M.H. Fisher
Michigan State University, East Lansing, MI, United States

M. Godfrey
Drexel University, Philadelphia, PA, United States

L.J. Hahn
University of Illinois, Champaign, IL, United States

L. Kenworthy
Children's National Health System, Washington, DC, United States; George Washington University School of Medicine, Washington, DC, United States

C. Lee
University of Illinois at Urbana-Champaign, Champaign, IL, United States

M. Maiman
Drexel University, Philadelphia, PA, United States

L. Morin
Michigan State University, East Lansing, MI, United States

K.A. Patton
University of Illinois at Urbana-Champaign, Champaign, IL, United States

C. Peng
George Washington University, Washington, DC, United States

N. Raitano Lee
Drexel University, Philadelphia, PA, United States

J.E. Roberts
University of South Carolina, Columbia, SC, United States

A.J. Schwichtenberg
Purdue University, West Lafayette, IN, United States

B.L. Tonnsen
Purdue University, West Lafayette, IN, United States

G.L. Wallace
George Washington University, Washington, DC, United States

B.E. Yerys
Children's Hospital of Philadelphia, Philadelphia, PA, United States; University of
Pennsylvania, Philadelphia, PA, United States

PREFACE

Following *IRRDD*'s milestone 50th anniversary volume earlier this year, Volume 51 begins the next chapter in scientific integration in intellectual and developmental disabilities (IDDs) research. Coming directly after such an auspicious volume, we struggled with the challenge: How best to represent the future of IDD research as we begin the next 50 years?

Our answer was to look toward a new cohort of scholars, to focus Volume 51 on scientific integrations from scholars who are at earlier points in their careers. These colleagues, each of whom is making important contributions in their respective areas, were invited to synthesize work in new ways or to update previous scientific understandings that reflect the latest findings in their subfields. As a result, Volume 51 enriches the field with new ideas, new frameworks for generating hypotheses, and new calls for scientific innovation in the decades to come. The volume thus reflects a range of important topics at this particular moment—including more basic scientific examinations of early intersubjectivity and dysregulation in neurogenetic syndromes, the neuropsychology of IDD and autism spectrum disorder (ASD), and more applied issues of victimization and parent advocacy in IDD.

Volume 51's second theme relates to the contexts in which these new careers are being launched. As the training to become an academic scientist becomes increasingly complicated and multidisciplinary, no researcher can exist in a vacuum. Instead, each new scientific career is a result of, and perpetuates, an ongoing, multiple-person conversation, involving formal and informal training, discussions, reviews, collaborations, and other interactions and events. Most significantly, every new scientific career reflects tireless mentoring by more senior scholars. This theme of mentoring and collaboration emerges as well in the present volume, in which some authors collaborated with more senior mentors on their contributions, while others included their own new generation of graduate students and trainees in the work presented.

The volume begins with Nancy Raitano Lee, Moshe Maiman, and Mary Godfrey exploring how recent understandings of neuropsychology may shed light on the nature of IDD. They address this relationship by comparing and contrasting neuropsychological profiles associated with three neurogenetic syndromes: Down syndrome, fragile X syndrome, and Williams syndrome. In contrast to many cross-syndrome studies published in IDD outlets, Lee and colleagues use these neuropsychological profiles to identify commonalities, rather than differences. Based on these commonalities, they hypothesize about which neuropsychological domains may contribute to IDD in general and how this knowledge may help the field develop a richer understanding of the nature of IDD, regardless of underlying etiology.

The theme of innovative theoretical frameworks then continues with Bridgette Tonnsen and Jane Roberts' exploration of the emergence of anxiety in fragile X syndrome. In this work, the authors carefully examine the dynamic nature of the early development of anxiety in this neurogenetic syndrome and identify precursors that predispose young children to develop co-occurring anxiety symptoms. The authors also use fragile X syndrome as a case study to elucidate the development of anxiety more generally, as well as to explore the clinical implications that can be drawn from the dynamics presented in the syndrome.

Gregory Wallace, Benjamin Yerys, Cynthia Peng, Elizabeth Dlugi, Laura Anthony, and Lauren Kenworthy then provide an important update for our current understanding of executive function in individuals with ASD. Although this team published a comprehensive review of the topic in 2008, a great deal of new work has been published since that time. Wallace and colleagues provide a helpful summary of the new scientific and clinical insights. They focus on information regarding laboratory and ecologically valid assessment of executive function in ASD and explore the implications of comorbid attention deficit and hyperactivity disorder on executive function profiles in ASD.

The issue of early emergence of developmental profiles is revisited in a different way in the next contribution, as Laura Hahn examines the issue of early intersubjectivity in children with different neurogenetic disorders. Again comparing Down syndrome, fragile X syndrome, and Williams syndrome, Hahn identifies early competencies and early disruptions in the development of foundational social behaviors, particularly in the area of joint attention. She then examines hypothetical downstream effects of syndrome-specific disruptions in joint attention that may lead to more pronounced social and social cognitive profiles in each of these groups. Hahn concludes by highlighting the challenges that lie ahead for early development work in neurogenetic syndromes, as well as by making a case for the future importance of this work.

In another critical area of regulation in IDD diagnostic groups, Anna Esbensen and Amy Schwichtenberg provide a comprehensive, up-to-the-minute review of sleep-related research and its implications for evidence-based treatments in IDD. The authors provide an in-depth review of sleep research across a range of syndromes, including Angelman syndrome, Cornelia de Lange syndrome, 5p-(Cri-du-chat) syndrome, Down syndrome, fragile X syndrome, Prader–Willi syndrome, Smith–Magenis syndrome, Williams syndrome, ASD, and idiopathic IDD. By discussing as well the difficulties in measuring sleep problems and other methodological issues in sleep research, the reader begins to glimpse the next wave of scientific innovation in this area.

Volume 51's final two contributions take the discussions in more applied settings. In Chapter 6, Meghan Burke, Kimberly Patton, and Chung eun Lee address the applied IDD issue of parental advocacy and its role in obtaining appropriate services across the lifespan for individuals with IDD. They describe why there is a pressing need for parental advocacy, how parents advocate for their children, and the effects of advocacy for early childhood services, school services, transition services, and adult services. Although critical to parents throughout the lives of their offspring, this topic has only begun to receive sustained research attention.

In the final contribution to this volume, Marisa Fisher, Catherine Corr, and Lindsay Morin present a compelling account of the lifelong challenges associated with susceptibility to victimization that begins during early development and continues into adulthood. By focusing on pressing issues across the lifespan and considering together different types of abuse and vulnerability, Fisher and colleagues are able to identify both common and specific prevention and intervention strategies across the lifespan.

As shown by Volume 51's seven chapters, then, IDD research has strong momentum for the next 50 years, even if the amount of work that remains is vast. And yet, from the work presented in this volume, a final unifying theme emerges—a call to use science and practice to improve the lives of individuals with IDD, their caregivers, and communities. This volume launches IRRDD into its next era toward meeting that ideal—and though the work ahead will demand new innovation and insight—these seven contributions suggest that we are well equipped with new cohorts of talented scholars dedicated to IDD research. We thank each of Volume 51's contributors for their dedication and continuing hard work in service to the field of IDD research and practice.

Deborah J. Fidler, Coeditor
Robert M. Hodapp, Coeditor

CHAPTER ONE

What can Neuropsychology Teach Us About Intellectual Disability?: Searching for Commonalities in the Memory and Executive Function Profiles Associated With Down, Williams, and Fragile X Syndromes

N. Raitano Lee[1], M. Maiman, M. Godfrey
Drexel University, Philadelphia, PA, United States
[1]Corresponding author: E-mail: nrl39@drexel.edu

Contents

Abstract

In the current chapter, we begin to answer the question of what neuropsychology can teach us about intellectual disability (ID) by closely examining similarities and

International Review of Research in Developmental Disabilities, Volume 51
ISSN 2211-6095
http://dx.doi.org/10.1016/bs.irrdd.2016.07.002

© 2016 Elsevier Inc.
All rights reserved.

differences in memory and executive function skills in youth with three genetic syndromes associated with ID — Down (DS), Williams (WS), and Fragile X (FXS) syndromes. In particular, we provide a detailed description of the research literature on short-term, long-term, and working memory as well as inhibition, and cognitive flexibility/shifting in these three groups. In our review, we identify cognitive domains that have the most consistent evidence for impairment (i.e., performance below mental age expectations) across the groups, in an effort to begin to shed light on key cognitive deficits that may underlie ID regardless of etiology. Our review of the literature revealed evidence for impairments in all of the cognitive domains reviewed in at least two of the three ID groups. However, somewhat more consistent support for impairments across groups was found for studies of long-term and working memory. Thus, in the chapter's discussion, we conceptualize long-term and working memory impairments in relation to the neuroanatomical phenotypes associated with these syndromes in an attempt to begin to bridge relations between brain and cognition in these groups, and thus, advance our understanding of the neuropsychology of ID. We conclude the chapter by identifying limitations in the existing literature and directions for future research.

What can neuropsychology teach us about the causes and treatment of intellectual disability (ID)? How can studying ID through the lens of neuropsychology help us to understand the core cognitive processes that characterize the disorder? In the current chapter, we begin to answer these questions by reviewing research on the neuropsychology of three genetic disorders associated with ID — Down (DS), Williams (WS), and Fragile X (FXS) syndromes. In particular, we focus on two broad areas of neuropsychological function — memory (explicit short- and long-term memory) and executive function (working memory, inhibition, and shifting) — in an effort to highlight shared deficits across three distinct causes of ID that may be central to the development and treatment of the disorder.

While the current chapter's focus is on memory and executive function, ultimately our goal is to understand the causes and correlates of ID at multiple levels of analysis. These include etiology (e.g., genetic, epigenetic, environmental influences), the neural phenotype, cognition, behavior, and development. This multi-level conceptual framework draws upon the work of Morton and Frith (1995, pp. 357—389) and Pennington (1999, 2006) in which 'causal models' are discussed as tools for theorizing about and testing relations among the different factors that may contribute to the development of complex behavioral disorders. The model we utilize in our laboratory is illustrated in Fig. 1.

In this review, we will attempt to touch on each level of our model. We start by providing an operational definition of ID (behavioral level). Then

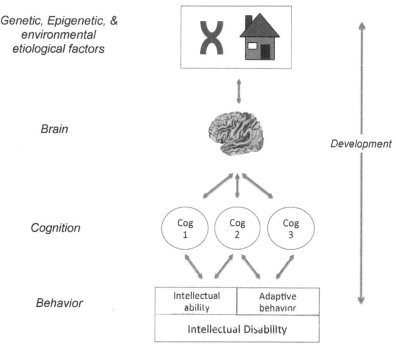

Figure 1 *Theoretical model for conceptualizing intellectual disability.* This schematic, which draws upon the work of Morton and Frith (1995, pp. 357–389) and Pennington (1999, 2006) on causal models in developmental neuropsychology, provides a framework for theorizing about and testing relations among the different factors that may contribute to a complex behavioral disorder such as ID.

we briefly provide background on the etiology of these syndromes and what is known about their neuroanatomical and cognitive phenotypes. Next we examine memory and executive function profiles in these groups. We elected to focus our review on these two multifaceted cognitive domains, as different aspects of memory and executive function have been tied to general learning capacity and adaptive function skills in youth with both typical and atypical development (e.g., Conway, Kane, & Engle, 2003; Edgin, Pennington, & Mervis, 2010; Pennington, Moon, Edgin, Stedron, & Nadel, 2003). Thus, these skills may represent core cognitive deficits that contribute to the development of ID. When possible, we note findings in the literature that relate to the developmental trajectories that characterize these syndromes. Lastly, we end the chapter with a synthesis of the literature, looking for similarities and differences in the neural and cognitive atypicalities associated with the ID syndromes we review.

1. ID DEFINITION

Historically, the terminology utilized to label what we now refer to as ID has changed considerably (see Schalock, Luckasson, & Shogren, 2007 for a review). Despite these changes, including the recent change from the term mental retardation to that of ID (American Psychiatric Association, 2013; Schalock et al., 2010), definitions and/or diagnostic criteria for ID remain largely unchanged and are fairly consistent across sources. For example, the American Association on Intellectual and Developmental Disabilities defines ID as "...a disability characterized by significant limitations in both intellectual functioning and in adaptive behavior, which covers many everyday social and practical skills" and that "...originates before the age of 18" (Schalock et al., 2010, p. 1). The DSM-5 adopts a very similar definition (American Psychiatric Association, 2013).

2. SELECTION OF ID SYNDROMES TO REVIEW

In order to identify whether there are shared memory and executive function impairments that characterize ID regardless of etiology, we deemed it important to review neuropsychological and neuroanatomical findings for several groups with ID due to differing etiologies. Specifically, we focused on youth with three genetic syndromes — DS, WS, and FXS. These disorders were selected for two primary reasons: (1) the literature on the neuropsychology of these syndromes is much richer than for other genetic ID syndromes, such as Smith-Magenis or Cornelia de Lange syndromes, for example, and; (2) while all three disorders are associated with ID, they vary with regard to their relative profile of cognitive strengths and weaknesses. Thus, they permit an examination of the shared neuropsychological features that may underlie ID regardless of etiology as well as permit the examination of syndrome-specific cognitive profiles.

3. DS, WS, AND FXS: ETIOLOGY AND NEUROANATOMICAL PHENOTYPES

DS is the most common genetic cause of ID occurring at a rate of 1/691 live births (Parker et al., 2010). It is due (in most cases) to nondisjunction during meiosis, resulting in three rather than two copies of chromosome 21; hence, it is also referred to as Trisomy 21. WS is a rare genetic disorder. Though rates were once thought to be close to 1/20,000, the work of Stromme, Bjornstad, and Ramstad (2002) suggests that it occurs in closer to 1/7500. It is due to a hemizygous deletion of between 26 and 28 genes on chromosome 7 (7q11.23; Peoples et al., 2000). FXS is the most common inherited genetic ID syndrome (Sherman, 2002). While the exact prevalence is unknown (Hagerman, 2008), it is generally thought to occur at a rate of ~1/4000 to 1/8000 (Hagerman, 2008), with one recent estimate reporting a rate of ~1/5000 males (Coffee et al., 2009). The genetic mutation responsible for FXS is an expansion of CGG repeats in the 5′-UTR section of the FMR1 gene. A full mutation involves >200 repeats, resulting in silencing of the FMR1 gene.

DS, FXS, and WS present with shared and unique neuroanatomical features that are likely to underlie some of the overlapping and specific characteristics of their cognitive-behavioral profiles. Both DS and WS are characterized by reduced total cerebral volume (for reviews, see Lee et al., 2016; Martens, Wilson, & Reutens, 2008). Results of studies with FXS are mixed, with some studies suggesting similar volume to controls (e.g., Eliez, Blasey, Freund, Hastie, & Reiss, 2001) and others suggesting larger cerebral volume (e.g., Meguid et al., 2012). Research examining the thickness and surface area of the cortex in these groups has identified increases in cortical thickness (at least in some regions) in all three syndromes (Lee et al., 2016; Meguid et al., 2012; Thompson et al., 2005), regional reductions in cortical surface area in DS and WS (Lee et al., 2016; Thompson et al., 2005), and reports of similar surface area measurements to typically developing controls in FXS (Meguid et al., 2012).

With regard to more localized anatomical differences, DS is associated with decreased hippocampal and cerebellar volume (after adjustments for total brain or intracranial volume) across multiple reports and reduced frontal and temporal volumes in most reports (Jernigan & Bellugi, 1990; Pinter, Brown et al., 2001; Pinter, Eliez, Schmitt, Capone, & Reiss, 2001; Raz et al., 1995; for a review, see Lee et al., 2016). Moreover, atypicalities in both the thickness and surface area of much of the frontal lobe have been noted in youth with DS (Lee et al., 2016).

WS is associated with specific reductions in parietal and occipital lobe gray matter (Boddaert et al., 2006) alongside relative increases in the volume of the amygdala and medial orbital frontal cortex (after adjustments for total brain or intracranial volume) at least in some reports (e.g., Reiss et al., 2004). The few studies that have examined the hippocampal formation in WS suggest atypicalities, with one study noting that the hippocampus is relatively larger after adjusting for intracranial volume (Sampaio et al., 2010) and another reporting localized shape differences in the hippocampal formation (Meyer-Lindenberg et al., 2005).

Lastly, like DS, FXS is also associated with cerebellar abnormalities, including reductions in the volume of the cerebellar vermis (Mostofsky et al., 1998; Reiss, Aylward, Freund, Joshi, & Bryan, 1991). In addition, the amygdala is reported to be smaller, while the hippocampus is noted to be larger (Reiss, Lee, & Freund, 1994). The caudate is reported to be larger in both cross-sectional (e.g., Eliez et al., 2001; Hoeft et al., 2011) and longitudinal studies (Bray et al., 2011; Hazlett et al., 2012). In contrast, longitudinal studies suggest that structures of the prefrontal cortex become more aberrant in teens with FXS over time (Bray et al., 2011). Based on the neuroanatomical anomalies across these three syndrome groups, hypotheses can be generated about domains of neuropsychological function that are likely to be most impacted. Relations between neuroanatomical and neuropsychological abnormalities in these groups will be touched upon in the chapter's discussion.

4. THE DS, WS, AND FXS COGNITIVE-BEHAVIORAL PHENOTYPES

In the sections that follow, we will provide a brief overview of intellectual and adaptive functioning, verbal and visual spatial skills, and socioemotional functioning in youth with DS, WS, and FXS.

4.1 Down Syndrome

On average, IQs for adults with DS fall into the moderate range of ID; however, IQ scores range from mild to profound ID (Carr, 2012). Intellectual abilities falling into the average range of functioning have also been reported in some exceptional cases (Epstein, 1989). For individuals with DS, IQ scores in adulthood are lower than those reported in infancy and early childhood, as research suggests that there is a progressive reduction in IQ in DS during infancy and childhood, such that mental age does not keep pace with chronological age (Carr, 1970; Hodapp & Zigler, 1990). This decrease in IQ, however, appears to taper and plateau in early adulthood with relative stability in IQ scores reported from young adulthood into the mid 40s (Carr, 2012). This stability precedes a mid-to-later life decline in cognitive functioning for some individuals with DS due to precocious-onset Alzheimer's disease (Lott, 1982; Zigman, Schupf, Urv, Zigman, & Silverman, 2002).

Impairments in adaptive functioning in children with DS are evident from an early age and, similar to their intellectual abilities, these skills develop at a slower pace than typically developing peers (Dykens, Hodapp, & Evans, 1994, 2006; Jacola, Hickey, Howe, Esbensen, & Shear, 2014). As reviewed by Martin, Klusek, Estigarribia, and Roberts (2009), language impairment is a prominent feature of the DS cognitive-behavioral phenotype. In particular, speech intelligibility in DS is quite poor and reported to be below mental age expectations (Barnes et al., 2009; Chapman, Seung, Schwartz, & Kay-Raining Bird, 1998). Findings on tests of receptive vocabulary abilities in DS are mixed with some studies reporting levels that are similar to mental age or greater than nonverbal mental age (Chapman et al., 1998; Laws & Bishop, 2003) and others reporting scores below mental age expectations (Caselli, Monaco, Trasciani, & Vicari, 2008; Hick, Botting, & Conti-Ramsden, 2005). One well-documented area of deficit for individuals with DS is syntax. Research shows that syntactic abilities are below mental age expectations (Abbeduto et al., 2003; Caselli et al., 2008; Chapman, Schwartz, & Bird, 1991; Laws & Bishop, 2003) as well as below expectations based on vocabulary abilities (Abbeduto et al., 2003; Berglund, Eriksson, & Johansson, 2001; Chapman et al., 1991; Laws & Bishop, 2003).

Yang, Conners, and Merrill (2014) recently provided an extensive review of visuospatial processing skills in DS in order to evaluate whether visuospatial abilities are really an area of strength for the group as has been suggested in the literature. They reviewed the domains of visuospatial memory, construction, closure, mental rotation, and wayfinding (i.e., the ability to orient oneself and navigate in space to get from one point to another). Counter to common perception, they reported that the data across studies indicate that visuospatial abilities are not a relative strength in DS. If anything, these skills are commensurate with mental age expectations and in some cases they are below mental age expectations.

Briefly, with regard to social and psychiatric functioning, on average, young children with DS are reported to have relative strengths in social functioning when compared to mental age expectations (Fidler, Most, Booth-LaForce, & Kelly, 2008). Consistent with this, significant emotional or behavioral disturbances are less common in children with DS than in children with other developmental disorders (Dykens, 2007). However, there is emerging evidence that heightened rates of depression and psychosis may occur for individuals with DS (relative to other groups with ID) during adolescence and adulthood (Dykens et al., 2015). Lastly, like most (if not all) ID syndromes, DS is associated with heightened rates of autism spectrum disorders (ASD; DiGuiseppi et al., 2010; Warner, Moss, Smith, & Howlin, 2014) relative to estimates in the general population; however, these rates appear lower than those reported for a number of ID syndromes, particularly FXS.

4.2 Williams Syndrome

Overall intellectual functioning in WS is thought to fall in the mild to moderate range of ID. While there is considerable variability in the IQ scores reported for individuals with WS in the literature, IQ scores of greater than 70 are thought to be rare (for a review, see Martens et al., 2008). Unlike DS and FXS (described next), longitudinal investigations of IQ across childhood and into young adulthood in WS suggest relative stability in scores (Fisch et al., 2010). Individuals with WS have well-documented impairments across all areas of adaptive functioning (Davies Howlin, & Udwin 1997; Kirchner, Martens, & Andridge, 2016). However, they have relative strengths (i.e., relative to other groups with developmental disabilities or when different adaptive function skills are compared to one another) in socialization and communication and relative weaknesses in motor, daily living, and self-care skills (Greer, Brown, Pai, Choudry, & Klein, 1997; Hahn, Fidler, & Hepburn, 2014; Kirchner et al., 2016; Mervis & Klein-Tasman, 2000).

As reviewed by Mervis (2009), early reports of WS in the literature suggested that language was an island of exceptional ability within the WS profile. However, more recent reports suggest that strengths observed in language in this group are *relative* to other cognitive skills that are especially problematic (e.g., visuospatial processing; for a review, see Martens et al., 2008) and/or groups with ID with significant language impairments, such as DS. Mervis (2009) notes that the strongest language domain for individuals with WS appears to be concrete vocabulary skills. On average, scores on tests of both receptive and expressive vocabulary, like the Peabody Picture Vocabulary Test and the Expressive Vocabulary Test, fall into the low average range, with the majority of participants scoring above 70 on these tests (Mervis & John, 2010). In contrast, relational vocabulary (i.e., the ability to identify how two or more words are related) is particularly weak. In fact, Mervis (2009) notes that she and her colleagues found that performance on the Test of Relational Vocabulary was almost as low as performance on a visuospatial construction task (Block Design), a task that taps the hallmark cognitive deficit associated with WS (Mervis &

John, 2008). With regard to other language domains, research suggests that syntactic abilities are relatively commensurate with or slightly below mental age expectations (e.g., Grant, Valian, & Karmiloff-Smith, 2002) and narrative abilities are thought to be lower than mental age expectations (Reilly, Losh, Bellugi, & Wulfeck, 2004). Thus, while some language skills are relatively strong for WS relative to their visuospatial abilities or groups with significant language impairments, most language skills are below chronological age expectations and some are actually lower than mental age expectations.

Of the syndromes included in the current chapter, WS is probably best known for impaired visuospatial abilities. As reviewed by Martens et al. (2008), there have been many reports of impaired (i.e., below mental age expectations) visuospatial processing and visuospatial construction in WS. In addition, there are several reports that suggest that individuals with WS tend to have difficulties with global visual processing and instead they preferentially focus on local or detailed components of visual displays (e.g., Bihrle, Bellugi, Delis, & Marks, 1989; Porter & Coltheart, 2006).

With regard to social and psychiatric functioning, WS is associated with hypersociability, an interest in engaging socially with others that exceeds that of individuals with typical development of a similar mental ability level (for a review, see Jarvinen, Korenberg, & Bellugi, 2013). In addition, WS is thought to be associated with high rates of anxiety (Leyfer, Woodruff-Borden, Klein-Tasman, Fricke, & Mervis, 2006). Similar to DS and FXS, elevated rates of ASD symptoms have been noted in WS (Klein & Mervis, 1999; Lincoln, Searcy, Jones, & Lord, 2007); however, to the best of our knowledge, large scale prevalence studies of ASD in individuals with WS have not been published.

4.3 Fragile X Syndrome

Like DS, mean IQ scores in adolescence and adulthood for males with FXS fall into the moderate range of ID. For females, scores are higher and tend to fall somewhere in the low average range (for a review, see Bennetto & Pennington, 2002). Also similar to DS, IQ scores for males with FXS decline over the course of childhood and adolescence, perhaps with the steepest declines occurring early in childhood (Fisch et al., 1999, 1992). Impairments in adaptive function have also been reported in males with FXS, with relative strengths in daily living and interpersonal skills and a relative weakness in communication skills (i.e., relative to mental age; Dykens, Leckman, Paul, & Watson, 1988). In addition, recent research suggests that adaptive functioning skills decline for males with FXS over the course of childhood and adolescence. Similarly, for females with FXS, communication skills (but not other adaptive function skills) decline across childhood and adolescence (Klaiman et al., 2014).

In a review by Finestack, Richmond, and Abbeduto (2009), the authors note that less is known about the language skills of youth with FXS than other ID syndromes. This may be due to the fact that certain structural language skills (e.g., articulation, vocabulary, grammar) are not as impaired in FXS as they are in other ID groups, such as DS. As Finestack and colleagues review, reports on the speech of individuals with FXS indicate that although intelligibility is below chronological age expectations, it is relatively commensurate with mental age (Roberts et al., 2005). Existing reports of vocabulary and syntactic abilities are mixed, with some studies suggesting that these skills are below mental age expectations (Price, Roberts, Vandergrift, & Martin, 2007) and others reporting that they are relatively commensurate with mental age expectations (Abbeduto et al., 2003; Roberts, Price, et al., 2007). While pragmatic language presents as a problem for youth with a variety of ID syndromes, some aspects of pragmatic language standout for FXS. Specifically, FXS in males is characterized by very repetitive language (Sudhalter, Scarborough, & Cohen, 1991) as well as impairments in conversational skills, including conversational turn taking and the ability to engage in clear, coherent discourse (Roberts, Martin, et al., 2007).

Results of studies on visuospatial processing skills in individuals with FXS are mixed. While there is some suggestion that egocentric spatial learning (Kogan et al., 2009) is a relative strength, visuo-construction and visuo-motor skills have been reported to be lower than peers with DS (Cornish, Munir, & Cross, 1999). Perhaps some of the inconsistency in findings relates to (a) the inclusion of only males or both males and females with FXS in the study, (b) the comparison group used, and (c) the age at which visuospatial skills are examined. Related to the age of evaluation, Quintin et al. (2015) found that perceptual organization skills (as measured by the Wechsler scales) began to deviate from verbal abilities in adolescence and worsen for individuals with FXS. These authors reported that it was in adolescence that a verbal over visuospatial advantage began to emerge. Thus, it appears that more research is needed to clarify the nature of visuospatial processing skills in FXS both with regard to patterns of performance relative to typically developing mental age matched peers but also with regard to the developmental trajectory of these skills.

With regard to psychiatric functioning, males with FXS have significant difficulties with inattention and hyperactivity (Baumgardner, Reiss, Freund, & Abrams, 1995; Hatton et al., 2002) that exceed those observed in other groups of children with ID (Turk, 1998). In addition, FXS is characterized by very high rates of anxiety disorders, particularly social anxiety disorder and specific phobia (Cordeiro, Ballinger, Hagerman, & Hessl, 2011). Moreover, of the ID syndromes reviewed here, FXS consistently has the highest rates of ASD reported in the literature, with estimates of 25–50% (for a review, see Bailey, 2004).

5. MEMORY AND EXECUTIVE FUNCTION PROFILES IN DS, WS, AND FXS

In the sections that follow, we turn to the focus of our review, research on memory and executive function in DS, WS, and FXS. We first define the constructs of interest, which include short-term and long-term memory as well as the executive function constructs of working memory, inhibition, and cognitive flexibility/shifting. We then summarize the relevant literature on these constructs in the three ID groups.

5.1 Memory

Memory is a multifaceted system that can be divided into multiple cognitive processes with differing neural underpinnings. In the current review, we focus on explicit, retrospective memory systems exclusively. (For a review of implicit memory in ID syndromes, see Vicari, 2004.) Retrospective memory is the process of recalling previously learned information, and may be divided into short- or long-term memory. Information that is actively upheld and preserved for a matter of seconds is known as short-term memory (STM), while long-term memory (LTM) refers to information that is stored and can be retrieved for later use (Jarrold, Nadel, & Vicari, 2009). With regard to the neuroanatomy of these memory systems, short-term memory encoding and retrieval are thought to invoke a network of cortical and subcortical structures; these include regions of the frontal lobes, superior regions of the temporal lobes, inferior regions of the parietal lobes, and at the subcortical level, the hippocampus (Baldo, Katseff, & Dronkers, 2012; Finke et al., 2008; Konkel & Cohen, 2009; Piekema, Kessels, Mars, Petersson, & Fernández, 2006; Wildgruber, Kischka, Ackermann, Klose, & Grodd, 1999). Both human and animal models have clearly demonstrated that long-term memory relies upon medial temporal lobe structures, most notably the hippocampus (for a review, see Squire, Stark, & Clark, 2004).

Significant short- and long-term memory impairments are seen across DS, WS, and FXS, and there is evidence to suggest that these impairments relate to intellectual ability and adaptive function levels (at least in DS and WS; Edgin, Pennington, et al., 2010; Pennington et al., 2003). However, the exact profile of memory impairments appears to vary across disorders. Moreover, performance differs in some studies based on the presentation modality of the material to be remembered (i.e., verbal versus nonverbal presentation), given differences in the three disorders in their relative verbal and nonverbal/visuospatial strengths and weaknesses as reviewed above.

5.1.1 Short-Term Memory

Research has long established significant verbal short-term memory (STM) deficits in youth with DS. In comparison to mental age matched peers, adolescents with DS perform significantly worse on verbal STM tasks such as digit span and word list recall (e.g., Jarrold & Baddeley, 1997; Jarrold, Baddeley, & Hewes, 2000; Jarrold, Baddeley, & Phillips, 2002; Lee, Pennington, & Keenan, 2010; Mackenzie & Hulme, 1987; Marcell & Weeks, 1988; McDade & Adler, 1980; Pennington et al., 2003; Vicari, Bellucci, & Carlesimo, 2000). This impairment has also been found in young, early school-aged children. Specifically, Næss, Lervåg, Lyster, and Hulme (2015) conducted a longitudinal study, annually assessing verbal STM abilities of 6-year-old children with DS, and typically developing children matched on nonverbal mental abilities. Typically developing children performed significantly better on sentence memory and nonword repetition tasks at each time point over the course of three years and the gap between the DS and control groups widened with time. Similar findings of significantly slower improvement across development have been found for adolescents and young adults with DS as well (Frenkel & Bourdin, 2009; Mackenzie & Hulme, 1987). Furthermore, a body of research has examined the verbal STM skills of children with DS relative to a variety of ID groups. While there are a few exceptions (e.g., Carney, Henry, et al., 2013), the vast majority of research studies have reported that children with DS perform significantly worse on verbal STM tasks compared not only with typically developing children matched on mental age but also children with other forms of ID (e.g., Bower & Hayes, 1994; Edgin, Pennington, et al., 2010; Jarrold & Baddeley, 1997; Jarrold, Baddeley, &

Hewes, 1999; Marcell & Cohen, 1992; Marcell & Weeks, 1988; Varnhagen, Das, & Varnhagen, 1987; Wang & Bellugi, 1994).

One may ask whether the verbal STM deficit found in DS is due exclusively to their difficulties with language skills or whether it reflects a global (i.e., not modality specific) deficit in STM. Findings from research studies that have utilized nonverbal STM tasks with individuals with DS are mixed. For example, some studies have reported better per-formance on spatial span tasks by young children with DS relative to mental age-matched controls (e.g., Frenkel & Bourdin, 2009), while others have reported similar levels of performance (e.g., Hick et al., 2005; Jarrold & Baddeley, 1997; Visu-Petra, Benga, Tincas, & Miclea, 2007). In contrast, there is also evidence from the literature for nonverbal STM impairments relative to mental age matched controls in older chil-dren with DS using tasks such as picture recognition, spatial span, visual pattern memory, and imitation (Frenkel & Bourdin, 2009; Lanfranchi, Toffanin, Zilli, Panzeri, & Viancllo, 2014; Vicari et al., 2000). With regard to the syndromic-specificity of these findings, it has been reported that groups with DS outperform groups with WS on visual-spatial short-term memory tasks (while the opposite is true for verbal STM; Edgin, Pennington et al., 2010; Wang & Bellugi, 1994). Additionally, children with DS have been shown to demonstrate faster rates of improvement over time on visuospatial STM tasks when compared with children with specific language impairments (Hick et al., 2005).

In contrast to DS, youth with WS have been reported to perform simi-larly to mental age matched controls on verbal STM tasks such as digit span and word list recall (Carney, Henry, et al., 2013; Vicari, Brizzolara, Carlesimo, Pezzini, & Volterra, 1996). Furthermore, previous research has provided consistent evidence that verbal STM skills are stronger for individuals with WS than those with DS (Costanzo et al., 2013; Edgin, Pennington et al., 2010; Wang & Bellugi, 1994). With regard to visual short-term memory (i.e., memory for designs), Vicari, Bellucci, and Carlesimo (2003) reported similar performance to mental age matched typically developing controls. However, consistent with the larger WS cognitive-behavioral phenotype, children with WS have significant weaknesses on visuospatial STM tasks. In fact, typically developing children matched on mental age outperform children with WS on tasks such as spatial span, immediate recall on the Rey Complex Figure task, and location identification tasks (Carney, Henry et al., 2013; Costanzo, et al., 2013; Rhodes, Riby, Park, Fraser, & Campbell, 2010; Vicari et al., 2003, 1996).

Research examining the memory abilities of children with FXS is much more limited in comparison to research on WS and DS. Most of the studies reviewed in the following sections only include males with FXS, given that ID occurs significantly more often in males than females with the disorder and many studies compare youth with FXS to other youth with ID. Of the limited existing research, there is consistent evidence that males with FXS have significant impairments in both verbal and nonverbal STM in comparison to mental age matched peers (Johnson-Glenberg, 2008; Munir, Cornish, & Wilding, 2000b; Ornstein et al., 2008). For example, typically developing children remember significantly more words on verbal STM tasks and make fewer errors in comparison with boys with FXS (Johnson-Glenberg, 2008; Ornstein et al., 2008). Furthermore, when compared to mental age matched children, boys with FXS have been reported to have significant impairments on tasks of spatial memory, imitation, and picture recognition, suggesting impairments in spatial and visual STM as well (Johnson-Glenberg, 2008; Munir et al., 2000b; Ornstein et al., 2008).

5.1.2 Long-Term Memory

Although STM abilities vary by modality and disorder, LTM abilities are generally weak regardless of modality for DS, FXS, and WS. However, the data are very limited for FXS, and there are also only a few studies on WS. Not surprisingly, a large body of work has examined long-term memory abilities of adults and youth with DS, due to the high prevalence of early-onset comorbid Alzheimer's disease (Lott, 1982; Zigman et al., 2002). Prior to the onset of dementia, there is consistent support for impairment in both verbal and visual long-term memory (LTM) in adults with DS (e.g., Ellis, Woodley-Zanthos, & Dulaney, 1989; Vicari, Bellucci, & Carlesimo, 2005). Consistent with adult findings, children and adolescents with DS perform worse than both typically developing children and children with ID on verbal LTM tasks, such as supraspan word list learning recall measures (Carlesimo, Marotta, & Vicari, 1997; Pennington et al., 2003). Additionally, youth with DS perform significantly below their mental age on visual associative memory tasks and pattern recognition tasks (Pennington et al., 2003; Visu-Petra et al., 2007). Furthermore, youth with DS have also shown impaired spatial long-term memory, as demonstrated by significantly worse performance on maze location tasks and spatial location recall tasks (Pennington et al., 2003; Visu-Petra et al., 2007).

Although these studies provide insight into adolescent LTM skills, very few studies have examined long-term memory abilities in young children with DS. An exception is Roberts and Richmond (2015), who examined preschool age children on object location recall and deferred imitation tasks (Roberts & Richmond, 2015). Contrary to older children's memory performance, preschoolers with DS did not perform significantly worse than their mental age matched peers. Roberts and Richmond subsequently concluded that LTM abilities were not a specific cognitive deficit in early childhood. However, Milojevich and Lukowski (2016) conversely found that children with DS were significantly worse at recalling a sequence of information and argued long-term memory deficits did emerge in the preschool years for DS (Milojevich & Lukowski, 2016). The discrepancy between these findings may be due to the differences in method, specifically, the nature of the tasks and length of the delays. Consequently, more research is needed examining the memory abilities of young children with DS in order to provide a clearer understanding of the trajectory of long-term memory impairments in this group.

Research indicates that children with WS generally perform worse on LTM tasks compared with typically developing children. In particular, children with WS have been noted to perform significantly worse on word list delayed recall tasks compared to mental age matched controls (Vicari et al., 1996). In addition, Edgin, Pennington, et al (2010) found children with WS performed significantly worse than children with DS on a Word List Learning task. These results suggest that children with WS may have a dissociation between verbal STM (with is relatively commensurate with mental age) and verbal LTM (which appears below mental age expectations) skills. In addition to these verbal LTM deficits, children with WS perform worse than mental age matched controls on picture recognition tasks (Jarrold, Baddeley, & Phillips, 2007). Moreover, WS groups show impairment on visuospatial LTM tasks. For example, in comparison to mental age matched children, children with WS commit more errors on immediate and delayed trials of the Rey Figure Learning Test (Vicari et al., 1996). Furthermore, research has found spatial route learning abilities are weaker than mental age matched ID groups in children with WS (Farran, Blades, Boucher, & Tranter, 2010). However, when given verbal directions and descriptions of route landmarks, children with WS were able to learn as many of the route turns as the typically developing group (Farran et al., 2010). Additionally, on more complex routes, children with WS outperformed their mental age matched peers (Purser et al., 2015). Therefore, although spatial memory is a specific STM weakness for children with WS, spatial LTM abilities appear to be more variable depending on task demands and supports given.

Lastly, research examining long-term memory abilities of children with FXS is very limited. In one of the few studies examining verbal long-term memory, Johnson-Glenberg (2008) found that males with FXS performed significantly worse than mental age-matched children on a list learning delay trial. Additionally, Munir et al. (2000b) found that typically developing children outperformed males with FXS on a story-retelling task. However, on a spatial association delayed task, children with FXS were able to place toys back in their proper location with comparable accuracy as typically developing children (Johnson-Glenberg, 2008).

5.2 Executive Function

Executive functioning (EF) is an "umbrella" term that refers to a multifaceted cognitive construct thought to be crucial for future-oriented, goal-directed behaviors. It includes skills such as working memory, inhibition, set-shifting, cognitive flexibility, and planning (Costanzo et al., 2013; Diamond, 2013; Lezak, 1995; Stuss & Benson, 1986). These complex higher-level skills are characterized by protracted maturation in children and adolescents with typical development (for a review, see Best & Miller, 2010), which parallels the maturation of the neural structures, most notably the prefrontal cortex, thought to underlie them (for a review, see Giedd et al., 2009). We will focus our review on three subcomponents of EF, namely working memory, inhibition, and cognitive flexibility/shifting, as these have been identified as somewhat unique (but related) EF constructs in the seminal work of Miyake et al. (2000).

Given the cognitive complexity of EF tasks, it is not surprising that EF deficits are frequently observed in children, adolescents, and adults with ID. Understanding the nature of these deficits may provide important insights into the neuropsychological underpinnings of key aspects of ID, as impaired EF has been found to be related to adaptive functioning (Edgin, Pennington et al., 2010; Pennington et al., 2003) and a variety of academic problems in groups with (Belacchi et al., 2014) and without ID (Blair & Razza, 2007). Moreover, there is a suggestion in the literature that impaired EF can serve as an early sign of later cognitive decline in groups with ID, such as DS (Ball, Holland, Treppner, Watson, & Huppert, 2008). With this background, we will review what is known about the domains of working memory, inhibition, and cognitive flexibility based on findings from studies employing laboratory measures of EF. For studies that include measures of everyday EF impairments based on informant report question-naires, see the following papers for DS (Daunhauer et al., 2014; Lee et al., 2015), WS (Hocking, Reeve, & Porter, 2015), and FXS (Klusek, Martin, & Losh, 2014).

5.2.1 Working Memory (WM)

While different cognitive models of WM exist (e.g., Baddeley & Hitch, 1974; Cowan, 1995), most clinicians and researchers agree that there is a distinction between the demands associated with classic STM and WM tasks. Specifically, STM tasks require holding information in immediate memory for verbatim recall, while WM tasks require not only brief storage of infor-mation but also manipulation or additional processing of that information to complete some task. A classic distinction is between digit span forward, a verbal STM task, and digit span backward, a verbal WM task. The latter re-quires not only brief storage of the to-be-recalled digits but also manipula-tion of the order of those digits in active memory in order to provide the list in reverse order. Thus, in the simplest of terms, working memory tasks require more cognitive 'work' than simple short-term memory tasks that just require brief storage and recall.

The distinction between WM and STM is particularly relevant to DS, because unlike the STM literature where the modality of the stimuli to be recalled appears to impact findings (at least in some studies), most studies of WM in DS suggest impairments relative to mental age on both verbal and nonverbal WM tasks (e.g., Carney, Brown, & Henry, 2013; Costanzo et al., 2013; Lanfranchi, Baddeley, Gathercole, & Vianello, 2012; Lanfranchi, Cornoldi, & Vianello, 2004; Lanfranchi, Jerman, & Vianello, 2009; Lanfranchi, Jerman, Dal Pont, Alberti, & Vianello, 2010; Munir et al., 2000b; Vicari, Carlesimo, & Caltagirone, 1995; Visu-Petra et al., 2007).

In contrast, the WM literature for youth with WS is more variable. While consistent support exists for impaired visuospatial WM in WS (e.g., Costanzo et al., 2013; Menghini, Addona, Costanzo, & Vicari, 2010; Rhodes et al., 2010), verbal WM deficits are reported in some studies (e.g., Costanzo et al., 2013; Menghini et al., 2010), but not others (e.g., Carney, Brown, et al., 2013). Lastly, there is strong and consistent evidence that males with FXS have impaired WM. A review of the literature reveals that the majority of studies report global WM deficits, without specific mo-dality related effects; that is, deficits are noted on both verbal (Baker et al., 2011; Hooper et al., 2008; Lanfranchi, Cornoldi, Drigo, & Vianello, 2009; Ornstein et al., 2008) and nonverbal (Baker et al., 2011; Lanfranchi,

Cornoldi, et al., 2009; Ornstein et al., 2008) WM tasks. In sum, it appears that WM is a domain that is consistently impaired relative to mental age expectations across the three groups. While the findings are mixed for WS on verbal WM tasks, the general trend across the groups is for WM to be an area of significant impairment.

5.2.2 Inhibition

A critical function for human survival is one's ability to stop or modify his or her thoughts, feelings, or behaviors in response to his or her own internal or external environment (Diamond, 2013; Logan & Cowan, 1984), with failure to inhibit (i.e., disinhibition) being one of the most prominent features of psychopathology (Nigg, 2000). As Miyake et al. (2000) points out, inhibition is a broad term that may be used to refer to a variety of different processes, depending on one's discipline. That said, for our purposes, it refers to one's ability to ignore or censure distracting or irrelevant stimuli, and, instead focus one's attention and respond only to those stimuli that the individual deems relevant to the task at hand (also known as cognitive control; Brunamonti et al., 2011). For instance, in a standard go/no-go task, an individual might be asked respond to a specific stimulus (e.g., green light on the screen) while inhibiting responses to other stimuli.

Across the studies that have examined inhibition in individuals with DS, findings have been somewhat mixed, with the majority of studies reporting impairments (Borella, Carretti, & Lanfranchi, 2013; Brunamonti et al., 2011; Costanzo et al., 2013; Edgin, Mason, et al., 2010; Kopp, Krakow, & Johnson, 1983; Lanfranchi et al., 2010; Wilding, Cornish, & Munir, 2002) and a select few failing to find impairments relative to mental age matched comparison groups (Carney, Brown, et al., 2013; Pennington et al., 2003). Similar to other domains of EF, it has been suggested (Schuchardt, Gebhardt, & Maehler, 2010) that these conflicting results can be explained by differences across studies in either the samples chosen (i.e., typically developing vs. another group with ID) or tasks administered. For instance, with regard to the work of Pennington et al. (2003), it was suggested that failure to find group differences on their go/no-go task may have been more attributable to the young age of the control group and developmental level required for successful completion of the task than to the DS neuropsychological phenotype per se.

It is also evident that the inhibition tasks employed across studies have varied considerably, and, thus, in interpreting a study's findings, one must carefully consider the task administered. This is particularly important when one considers that inhibition is unlikely to be a unitary construct (see Nigg, 2000). As such, different tasks might tap into different aspects of inhibition, subsequently leading to discrepant findings. Moreover, the cognitive demands of different inhibition tasks vary, which results in some tasks being more cognitively taxing than others. In addition, performance for individuals with DS may vary as a function of the task's modality. A recent study by Costanzo et al. (2013) provides preliminary support for this suggestion, with the DS group exhibiting impairments on a Stroop (i.e., verbal) task but not on a simple go/no-go task (i.e., visual-motor). In sum, it appears that individuals with DS have impaired inhibition; however, whether the impairment spans across modalities (verbal and spatial) or is modality specific (i.e., verbal) remains unclear.

Lastly, with regard to inhibition impairments relative to other groups with ID, results have been mixed. For example, Brunamonti et al. (2011) reported that individuals with DS exhibited visual-motor inhibition deficits (on a stop signal task) not only relative to typically developing mental age matched peers but also relative to those with idiopathic ID. It has also been reported that in comparison to mental aged matched peers with WS, those with DS displayed more difficulties with inhibition on verbal tasks (Costanzo et al., 2013). In contrast, impairments on a task of verbal inhibition (i.e., Shape-School Stroop task) were not found relative to a group with WS in the work of Porter, Coltheart, and Langdon (2007). Finally, in comparison to FXS, youth with DS have been reported to perform better on visual spatial inhibition tasks (Cornish, Scerif, & Karmiloff-Smith, 2007; Wilding et al., 2002).

While there is some evidence that inhibition abilities are below mental age expectations for individuals with WS, findings are somewhat mixed. For example, some studies have reported inhibition impairments relative to mental age on both verbal and visual inhibition tasks (e.g., Menghini et al., 2010; Tager-Flusberg, Sullivan, & Boshart, 1997), while others have failed to do so (Costanzo et al., 2013). Despite these inconsistencies, it is noteworthy that in one of the first studies to examine inhibition in WS, Tager-Flusberg et al. (1997) reported that only 25% of their sample with WS was able to complete the Stroop and 17% was able to complete a motor inhibition task. These results suggest that inhibition may be particularly impaired in WS, given that such a small portion of the sample could complete the tasks. However, another possibility is that other cognitive demands made these tasks challenging for those with WS to understand. This is difficult to tease out, but something that should be considered in future research. Lastly, it should be noted that some research has suggested that the modality of the information to be inhibited impacts performance for WS. For example, Atkinson et al. (2003) reported that while those with WS were able to perform similarly to vocabulary matched controls on a task of verbal inhibition (Day-Night Stroop), their performance was lower and more impaired on inhibition tasks that were spatially demanding, consistent with the larger WS phenotype. Thus, it appears more research is needed in order to come to a conclusion about the nature of inhibition abilities in WS.

With regard to FXS, there is more known about inhibition than other executive function domains. While there is a suggestion that inhibition is impaired in males with FXS (e.g., Munir, Cornish, & Wilding, 2000a), the severity of inhibition impairments may not be adequately captured in research literature, largely due to floor effects reported in some studies. For example, in one of the more recent studies of inhibition in FXS, Hooper et al. (2008) found that males with FXS had greater difficulty completing inhibition tasks than their mental aged matched peers, with only 57% being able to complete the components of the Contingency Naming Task that tap inhibition. Thus, the results of this study suggested that while FXS is associated with inhibition deficits, the severity of these deficits may not be adequately captured by existing studies because some participants scores' may not be included in group means due to floor-level performance.

In spite of this potential limitation of existing research, most studies that have examined inhibition in individuals with (full mutation) FXS relative to either premutation participants or typically developing mental age matched peers have documented impairments (Hooper et al., 2008; Munir, et al., 2000a), even in very early development (Cornish et al., 2007; Scerif, Cornish, Wilding, Driver, & Karmiloff-Smith, 2004). Furthermore, as expected, inhibition deficits become even more pronounced in FXS as task demands increase (Munir et al., 2000a; Scerif et al., 2004). Finally, it appears that inhibition deficits occur across modalities in FXS (Hooper et al., 2008 (verbal); Scerif, Cornish, Wilding, Driver, & Karmiloff-Smith, 2007 (nonverbal); Sullivan et al., 2007 (verbal and nonverbal); Wilding et al., 2002 (nonverbal)). However, there are far fewer studies that have examined inhibition in the verbal domain in this group.

With regard to the syndromic-specificity of these findings, Cornish et al. (2007) found that despite the fact that individuals with FXS and WS both exhibit poor performance relative to mental age matched controls on tasks of inhibition, they do so for different reasons. Whereas individuals with FXS display problems with inhibition, those with WS have problems with disengaging. With regard to the extent of the inhibition deficit relative to other groups with ID, research suggests that those with FXS perform more poorly than those with DS on inhibition tasks (Wilding et al., 2002).

5.2.3 Cognitive Flexibility/Shifting

As outlined by Miyake et al. (2000), cognitive flexibility or shifting, has been conceptualized as the ability to modify one's thinking or attention in response to changes in his/her own internal or external environment. One common method for assessing this domain is card sorting. On card sorting tasks, individuals are asked to sort a series of cards based on different dimensions of the stimuli (e.g., color vs. shape). Compared to other domains of executive functioning, such as working memory, fewer studies have explored the domain of cognitive flexibility in DS, FXS, and WS. Nevertheless, based on the limited information available, there is evidence to suggest that all three groups have impaired performance on cognitive flexibility tasks relative to mental age, though there are less consistent reports for WS, which will be described further below.

Zelazo, Burack, Frye, and Benedetto (1996) were one of the first to document that in comparison to mental age matched controls, individuals with DS have greater difficulty shifting between conflicting rules and concepts using the widely-known Dimensional Change Card Sort task. Consistent with these early findings, several reports have emerged documenting difficulties with cognitive flexibility using nonverbal tasks (Costanzo et al., 2013; Lanfranchi et al., 2010) and verbal tasks (Carney, Brown et al., 2013; Costanzo et al., 2013). While most evidence points to shifting problems across modality, it should be noted that some studies have reported difficulties on verbal but not non-verbal shifting tasks (Carney, Brown, et al., 2013). With regard to cross-syndrome comparisons, when youth with DS were compared to those with WS on a verbal shifting task, greater impairments were noted in the DS group (Costanzo et al., 2013). Finally, as additional evidence that individuals with DS display a more global rather than modality specific shifting impairment, it has been demonstrated that relative to those with WS (Costanzo et al., 2013; Landry, Russo, Dawkins, Zelazo, & Burack, 2012), youth with DS displayed either similar to or worse performance on a visual spatial shifting task (a task that one would hypothesize would be more impaired in WS due to the prominent visuospatial processing impairments associated with the syndrome).

Across the few studies that have examined shifting in individuals with WS, findings have been largely mixed. For example, Rhodes et al. (2010) evaluated attention shifting in WS on the CANTAB intra-dimensional/extra-dimensional set shift task by comparing their performance to typically developing peers matched on chronological age or verbal abilities. Their results revealed that those with WS performed worse than both control groups, demonstrating more errors overall and reaching a lower stage on the task. Menghini et al. (2010) reported mixed findings — they reported that youth with WS performed more poorly than typically developing mental age matched peers on one verbal shifting task (Trail Making) and one visual shifting task (Forma Forma); however, they did not find impairments when verbal category shifting was evaluated. Similarly, Carney, Brown, et al. (2013) reported mixed findings — that is, impaired verbal shifting but unimpaired nonverbal shifting in WS. Lastly, Costanzo et al. (2013) noted no differences between WS and typically developing mental age matched participants on either verbal or nonverbal shifting tasks.

Lastly, deficits in cognitive flexibility are frequently documented in the literature on FXS, with more studies utilizing nonverbal shifting tasks and demonstrating deficits (Scerif et al., 2004; Wilding et al., 2002) than verbal shifting tasks (Hooper et al., 2008). However, similar to inhibition, our knowledge about the extent of these difficulties is limited by floor effects in some studies. For example, in a large scale study of EF, Hooper et al. (2008) found that only 26% of their male FXS sample was able to complete the shift/cognitive-flexibility components of the Contingency Naming Task. Thus, it is likely that shifting abilities are even more impaired than some studies may suggest, due to floor effects that may exclude some participants' scores from being included in group analyses. Lastly, with regard to cross syndrome comparisons, research suggests greater shifting impairments in males with FXS than DS (Wilding et al., 2002).

6. DISCUSSION

In the current chapter, we begin to address the question of what neuropsychology can teach us about ID by closely examining the commonalities (and differences) in memory and executive function skills in youth with three distinct genetic ID syndromes, namely DS, WS, and FXS. Findings from the existing research literature are summarized in Table 1. Specifically, we have categorized findings across studies of memory (i.e., short- and long-term memory) and executive function (i.e., working memory, inhibition, and cognitive flexibility/shift) for the three ID groups as being below

Table 1 Summary of Findings From Existing Literature on Memory and Executive Functions in Youth With DS, WS, and FXS

DOMAIN/Subdomain	ID Groups Relative to Mental Age Matched Typically Development (TD) Groups		
	DS	WS	FXS
Explicit Memory			
Short-Term Memory			
Verbal	<	~	<
Nonverbal	M	<	<
Long-Term Memory			
Verbal	<	M	<
Nonverbal	<	<	★
Executive Function			
Working Memory			
Verbal	<	M	<
Nonverbal	<	<	<
Inhibition			
Verbal	<	M	<
Nonverbal	M	<	<
Shift			
Verbal	<	M	<
Nonverbal	<	M	<

< ID group more impaired than TD group in most studies, operationalized as ≥70% of studies/tasks reviewed where ID < TD.
M Mixed Findings, operationalized as <70% of studies/tasks reviewed with a consistent pattern of findings.
~ Similar performance to TD, as operationalized as ≥70% of studies/tasks reviewed showing no statistically significant difference between TD and ID.
★ Not enough studies of youth to make accurate conclusion.

mental age expectations (<, ID group performed worse than TD group in at least 70% of studies/tasks reviewed across studies), similar to mental age expectations (~, at least ≥70% of studies/tasks reviewed across studies showed no statistically significant difference between TD and ID group), or mixed (M, less than 70% of studies/tasks reviewed across studies with consistent findings). The memory and executive function subdomains reviewed are further divided in the table by the modality of the tasks employed — that is, whether the task had primarily verbal or nonverbal demands. This subdivision was deemed necessary as executive function and memory tasks can never truly be 'pure' tasks of these cognitive domains, as they require participants to remember, maintain and manipulate, inhibit or shift between different types of stimuli that are either verbal or nonverbal. As a result, impairments in verbal and nonverbal abilities may impact performance on memory and executive function tasks. Thus, when evidence was available for memory or executive function impairments that crossed modalities (i.e., a group was impaired on both verbal and nonverbal tasks within that domain), we felt this provided more compelling support that a particular cognitive domain was impaired in that group.

So what does this table tell us? First, we will review the nature of EF and memory impairments by syndrome. If we look down the columns at the particular syndromes, we see that despite the fact that the literature is smallest for FXS, there appears to be the most consistent support for impairment (relative to mental age) across memory and executive function subdomains. The one exception to this is for nonverbal LTM where there was insufficient research to state whether the trend in the literature is for impairments relative to mental age or not. Similar to (though slightly less consistent than) the findings for FXS, there is large support for impairments in DS across memory and executive function systems. There were two exceptions to this; that is, there are mixed findings for nonverbal STM and nonverbal inhibition, with some studies reporting impairments relative to mental age and others failing to do so. Thus, in this case, it may be that impairments in verbal abilities unduly impact performance on STM and inhibition tasks, and thus, poor performance on these tasks may be related more to language impairments in DS than impairments in these cognitive subdomains, per se. In contrast to FXS and DS, the findings for WS were more variable, with mixed findings for verbal LTM, verbal WM, and verbal and nonverbal shifting. Moreover, unlike FXS and DS, the extant literature appears to suggest that verbal short-term memory capacities are not significantly below mental age expectations in WS.

In conceptualizing the pattern of findings for WS relative to FXS and DS, it is interesting to note that research suggests differences in IQ trajectories in these groups. While relative stability in IQ is reported in childhood and young adulthood in WS, the opposite is true for DS and FXS. Perhaps differences in the nature of their memory and executive function abilities could be a contributing factor to this key cognitive trajectory difference. We are not able to answer this question as of yet; however, this is certainly something that could investigated in future research using a longitudinal study design (i.e., do executive function or memory impairments predict changes or stability in IQ over time in these three groups).

Now we will turn to the focus of our chapter, that is identifying which neuropsychological domains are consistently impaired in DS, WS, and FXS, by looking across the rows in Table 1. While the trend in the literature is for all of these cognitive domains to be impacted by ID, the two with the most consistent impairment across disorders (and stimuli presentation modality) are long-term memory and working memory. First, we will explore the long-term memory findings. What do we know about the neural structures associated with long-term memory in these three groups? Neuroimaging studies have provided evidence that all three syndromes are associated with atypicalities in the hippocampus, a neural structure thought to be central to learning and long-term memory formation. While DS is associated with reduced hippocampal volume (after controlling for smaller total brain volume; Pinter, Brown et al., 2001), WS and FXS are associated with either enlarged hippocampi (FXS: Reiss et al., 1994; WS: Sampaio et al., 2010) or shape differences in the hippocampal formation (Meyer-Lindenberg et al., 2005). Of these disorders, DS is probably most widely recognized for hippocampal abnormalities, both early in development and later in development, particularly as this structure relates to the development of Alzheimer's disease. However, the consistency in memory deficits across these three ID groups suggests that hippocampal function may be central to our understanding of ID. This is not surprising, as research suggests that the hippocampus is a structure that is important for rapid, error driven learning of unique associations (for reviews see, Davis & Gaskell, 2009; McClelland, 1998). In its simplest form, ID is a disorder that is characterized by slower, less efficient learning. Thus, impaired hippocampal function could certainly play a role in this aspect of ID. Moreover, the hippocampus and related structures are thought to play a central role in spatial navigation and memory abilities (Maguire et al., 1998). These abilities are clearly important for 'wayfinding,' an important aspect of adaptive function that is crucial for independence and has been found to be impaired in DS (Davis, Merrill, Conners, & Roskos, 2014) and WS (Broadbent, Farran, & Tolmie, 2014).

Turning to WM, research suggests strong ties between this domain and intellectual abilities in the typical population (e.g., see Conway et al., 2003 for a review). Thus, it should not come as a surprise that this domain is fairly consistently impaired in these three ID groups. With regard to its neural correlates, research suggests that they are widespread, with prominent involvement of the frontal-parietal and frontal-striatal brain networks (Eriksson, Vogel, Lansner, Bergstrom, & Nyberg, 2015). Given the large network of regions that underlie WM functioning, one might expect that there would be fairly consistent evidence for impairment across these groups, as atypicalities in any aspect of the WM network are likely to result in impaired performance. In fact, research on the neuroanatomy of these ID syndromes has provided evidence for prominent frontal abnormalities being associated with DS and FXS (e.g., Bray et al., 2011; Lee et al., 2015), parietal abnormalities with WS (e.g., Boddaert et al., 2006), and striatal abnormalities with FXS (Hazlett et al., 2012).

By integrating findings from studies of the neuropsychology and neuroanatomy of genetic ID syndromes, we have identified hypothetical links in our causal model (see Fig. 1) between the levels of brain and cognition. However, limited research is available that directly tests relations between these constructs and brain physiology using functional neuroimaging in ID groups. Exceptions to this include two functional MRI studies of cognitive control in WS and females with FXS, which tied task performance to atypicalities in the frontal lobes and other brain regions (Levitin et al., 2003; Tamm, Menon, Johnston, Hessl, & Reiss, 2002). While these initial studies are a first step (and there are certainly other studies that have examined brain-cognition relations in other domains for ID groups; e.g., Losin, Rivera, O'Hare, Sowell, & Pinter, 2009 for story listening in DS), more research is needed that directly relates cognitive performance in these domains to neural functioning in ID groups. The challenge, of course, is completing neuroimaging studies with people, particularly children, with ID. Such a task is extremely difficult even when structural neuroimaging is involved and participants can sleep or watch a movie while completing scans. For example, in a study conducted by Lee et al. (2016), only 65% of their sample of children and young adults with DS could complete structural MRI scans. Thus, the challenges of completing functional MRI studies to examine brain-behavior relations are even greater. It is hoped that with the creation of new MRI imaging protocols that allow for correction of motion in the MRI scanner and new imaging modalities (like functional near infrared spectroscopy; fNIRS), more participants with ID will be able to complete functional imaging tasks that will help us tie cognitive abnormalities to brain atypicalities more directly.

Moving down the model outlined in Fig. 1, we turn to cognition-behavior relations — namely, associations between executive function and memory domains and both IQ and adaptive function. While there are many studies that have examined executive function and memory and have also included measures of IQ and adaptive function, surprisingly few have examined relations between the two. In one of these studies,

Pennington et al. (2003) reported that both long-term memory and executive function scores were related to intellectual functioning (mental age in this case) in youth with DS. In addition, they reported that long-term memory related to adaptive function in this group. Similarly, in a study examining short-term, long-term, and working memory, Edgin, Pennington, et al (2010) found that associative (long-term) memory was related to adaptive functioning in young people with DS, while working memory was related to adaptive behavior in WS. These findings suggest that the neuropsychological correlates of intellectual and adaptive functioning may vary by genetic syndrome (e.g., impaired adaptive functioning or IQ scores in one group may be more strongly tied to working memory difficulties than long-term memory difficulties). Lastly, we will briefly mention one other study that examined executive function -IQ relations. Osório et al. (2012) reported high correlations between working memory, inhibition, and IQ in their sample with WS (and interestingly, not in their control group). While the findings for inhibition were compelling, those for WM are more difficult to interpret because this study utilized the full version of the Wechsler scales as a measure of IQ, which includes a working memory composite. (This composite makes up ∼¼ of the test's content). Thus, it is difficult to determine if the high correlation between the WM tasks and IQ in the WS group in this study was due to similar measures being included in both the IQ and WM assessments or a true association between impaired working memory and intellectual functioning. Regardless, these studies among others, provide preliminary evidence for relations between executive functions, long-term memory, and behavioral measures of ID, suggesting that it may be beneficial for these domains of neuropsychological functioning to be the target of treatments in future studies aimed at ameliorating the impairments associated with ID.

In conclusion, research on the neuropsychology of ID has certainly revealed a great deal of valuable information about the cognitive profiles that characterize different ID syndromes. However, some limitations in the existing research literature still exist. First, there appear to be limitations in the ability of existing neuropsychological instruments to measure cognitive function in people with ID of varying levels of severity — that is, floor effects are problematic, particularly for tasks tapping executive function. Thus, more work on task development is needed in order to capture the range and severity of difficulties faced by many individuals with ID and to measure changes in functioning as a result of different forms of intervention. Second, studies of brain-behavior relations are limited and are an important next step in identifying the brain bases of neuropsychological impairments in these groups. Such research will be particularly important for basic scientists studying brain-gene relations either in human participants or animal models, as it will highlight what neural structures may play a central role in a particular genetic syndrome's behavioral phenotype. Third, additional research is needed examining the developmental unfolding of these particular cognitive deficits. This research will add to the growing literature on developmental trajectories across different cognitive domains in these groups (e.g., Cornish et al., 2007; Quintin et al., 2015; Steele, Scerif, Cornish, & Karmiloff-Smith, 2013) and hopefully provide insights into key points in development in which targeted interventions may be most effective. Fourth, more research is needed examining links between different neuropsychological domains and real world functioning. While this research base is growing, it will be helpful to continue to investigate these relations both cross-sectionally and longitudinally in order to look for similarities and differences across ID groups. This may help to highlight the neuropsychological deficits that may be most closely related to deficits in intellectual and adaptive functioning in each group and may provide important clues about specific targets of treatment (either educational or biomedical) that could be tailored to each syndrome with the long-term goal of improving cognitive outcomes and ultimately independence. Lastly, systematic treatment studies are needed to test the possible causal role long-term memory and working memory (along with other cognitive domains) play in the development of ID. If researchers are able to target and improve one or more of these domains and show secondary improvements in intellectual functioning or adaptive behavior, there would be more compelling support that these neuropsychological domains play a causal role in the development of ID. It is the opinion of these authors that this is an important next step in research on the neuropsychology of ID.

REFERENCES

Abbeduto, L., Murphy, M. M., Cawthon, S. W., Richmond, E. K., Weissman, M. D., Karadottir, S., & O'Brien, A. (2003). Receptive language skills of adolescents and young adults with Down syndrome or fragile X syndrome. *American Journal on Mental Retardation,* *108*(3), 149—160. http://dx.doi.org/10.1352/0895-8017(2003)108<0149: RLSOAA>2.0.CO;2.
American Psychiatric Association. (2013). *Diagnostic and statistical manual of mental disorders* (5th ed.) Washington, DC: Author.

Atkinson, J., Braddick, O., Anker, S., Curran, W., Andrew, R., Wattam-Bell, J., & Braddick, F. (2003). Neurobiological models of visuospatial cognition in children with Williams syndrome: measures of dorsal-stream and frontal function. *Developmental Neuropsychology, 23*(1–2), 139–172. http://dx.doi.org/10.1207/s15326942dn231&2_7.

Baddeley, A. D., & Hitch, G. (1974). Working memory. *The Psychology of Learning and Motivation, 8,* 47–89.

Bailey, D. J. (2004). Newborn screening for fragile X syndrome. *Mental Retardation and Developmental Disabilities Research Reviews, 10*(1), 3–10. http://dx.doi.org/10.1002/mrdd.20002.

Baker, S., Hooper, S., Skinner, M., Hatton, D., Schaaf, J., Ornstein, P., & Bailey, D. (2011). Working memory subsystems and task complexity in young boys with fragile X syndrome. *Journal of Intellectual Disability Research, 55*(1), 19–29.

Baldo, J. V., Katseff, S., & Dronkers, N. F. (2012). Brain regions underlying repetition and auditory-verbal short-term memory deficits in Aphasia: evidence from voxel-based lesion symptom mapping. *Aphasiology, 26*(3–4), 338–354.

Ball, S. L., Holland, A. J., Treppner, P., Watson, P. C., & Huppert, F. A. (2008). Executive dysfunction and its association with personality and behaviour changes in the development of Alzheimer's disease in adults with Down syndrome and mild to moderate learning disabilities. *British Journal of Clinical Psychology, 47,* 1–29. http://dx.doi.org/10.1348/014466507x230967.

Barnes, E., Roberts, J., Long, S. H., Martin, G. E., Berni, M. C., Mandulak, K. C., & Sideris, J. (2009). Phonological accuracy and intelligibility in connected speech of boys with fragile X syndrome or Down syndrome. *Journal of Speech, Language, and Hearing Research, 52*(4), 1048–1061. http://dx.doi.org/10.1044/1092-4388(2009/08-0001).

Baumgardner, T. L., Reiss, A. L., Freund, L. S., & Abrams, M. T. (1995). Specification of the neurobehavioral phenotype in males with fragile X syndrome. *Pediatrics, 95*(5), 744–752.

Belacchi, C., Passolunghi, M. C., Brentan, E., Dante, A., Persi, L., & Cornoldi, C. (2014). Approximate additions and working memory in individuals with Down syndrome. *Research in Developmental Disabilities, 35*(5), 1027–1035.

Bennetto, L., & Pennington, B. F. (2002). The neuropsychology of Fragile X syndrome. In R. J. Hagerman, & A. Cronister (Eds.), *Fragile X syndrome: Diagnosis, treatment, and research* (3rd ed., pp. 210–248). Baltimore, MD: Johns Hopkins University Press.

Berglund, E., Eriksson, M., & Johansson, I. (2001). Parental reports of spoken language skills in children with Down syndrome. *Journal of Speech, Language, And Hearing Research, 44*(1), 179–191. http://dx.doi.org/10.1044/1092-4388(2001/016).

Best, J. R., & Miller, P. H. (2010). A developmental perspective on executive function. *Child Development, 81*(6), 1641–1660. http://dx.doi.org/10.1111/j.1467-8624.2010.01499.x.

Bihrle, A. M., Bellugi, U., Delis, D., & Marks, S. (1989). Seeing either the forest or the trees: dissociation in visuospatial processing. *Brain and Cognition, 11*(1), 37–49.

Blair, C., & Razza, R. P. (2007). Relating effortful control, executive function, and false belief understanding to emerging math and literacy ability in kindergarten. *Child Development, 78,* 647–663. http://dx.doi.org/10.1111/j.1467-8624.2007.01019.x.

Boddaert, N., Mochel, F., Meresse, I., Seidenwurm, D., Cachia, A., Brunelle, F., ... Zilbovicius, M. (2006). Parieto-occipital grey matter abnormalities in children with Williams syndrome. *NeuroImage, 30*(3), 721–725. http://dx.doi.org/10.1016/j.neuroimage.2005.10.051.

Borella, E., Carretti, B., & Lanfranchi, S. (2013). Inhibitory mechanisms in Down syndrome: is there a specific or general deficit? *Research in Developmental Disabilities, 34*(1), 65–71.

Bower, A., & Hayes, A. (1994). *Short-term memory deficits and Down's syndrome: A comparative study* (Vol. 2).

Bray, S., Hirt, M., Jo, B., Hall, S. S., Lightbody, A. A., Walter, E., ... Reiss, A. L. (2011). Aberrant frontal lobe maturation in adolescents with fragile X syndrome is related to delayed cognitive maturation. *Biological Psychiatry, 70*(9), 852–858. http://dx.doi.org/10.1016/j.biopsych.2011.05.038.

Broadbent, H. J., Farran, E. K., & Tolmie, A. (2014). Egocentric and allocentric navigation strategies in Williams syndrome and typical development. *Developmental Science, 17*(6), 920–934. http://dx.doi.org/10.1111/desc.12176.

Brunamonti, E., Pani, P., Papazachariadis, O., Onorati, P., Albertini, G., & Ferraina, S. (2011). Cognitive control of movement in Down syndrome. *Research in Developmental Disabilities, 32*(5), 1792–1797.

Carlesimo, G. A., Marotta, L., & Vicari, S. (1997). Long-term memory in mental retardation: evidence for a specific impairment in subjects with Down's syndrome. *Neuropsychologia, 35*(1), 71–79.

Carney, D. P., Brown, J. H., & Henry, L. A. (2013). Executive function in Williams and down syndromes. *Research in Developmental Disabilities, 34*(1), 46–55. http://dx.doi.org/10.1016/j.ridd.2012.07.013.

Carney, D. J., Henry, L. A., Messer, D. J., Danielsson, H., Brown, J. H., & Rönnberg, J. (2013). Using developmental trajectories to examine verbal and visuospatial short-term memory development in children and adolescents with Williams and Down syndromes. *Research in Developmental Disabilities, 34*(10), 3421–3432.

Carr, J. (1970). Mental and motor development in young mongol children. *Journal of Mental Deficiency Research, 14*(3), 205–220.

Carr, J. (2012). Six weeks to 45 years: a longitudinal study of a population with Down syndrome. *Journal of Applied Research in Intellectual Disabilities, 25*(5), 414–422. http://dx.doi.org/10.1111/j.1468-3148.2011.00676.x.

Caselli, M. C., Monaco, L., Trasciani, M., & Vicari, S. (2008). Language in Italian children with Down syndrome and with specific language impairment. *Neuropsychology, 22*(1), 27–35. http://dx.doi.org/10.1037/0894-4105.22.1.27.

Chapman, R. S., Schwartz, S. E., & Bird, E. K. (1991). Language-skills of children and adolescents with Down-syndrome. 1. Comprehension. *Journal of Speech and Hearing Research, 34*(5), 1106–1120.

Chapman, R. S., Seung, H. K., Schwartz, S. E., & Kay-Raining Bird, E. (1998). Language skills of children and adolescents with Down syndrome: II. Production deficits. *Journal of Speech, Language, and Hearing Research, 41*(4), 861–873.

Coffee, B., Keith, K., Albizua, I., Malone, T., Mowrey, J., Sherman, S. L., & Warren, S. T. (2009). Incidence of fragile X syndrome by newborn screening for methylated FMR1 DNA. *American Journal of Human Genetics, 85*(4), 503–514. http://dx.doi.org/10.1016/j.ajhg.2009.09.007.

Conway, A. R., Kane, M. J., & Engle, R. W. (2003). Working memory capacity and its relation to general intelligence. *Trends in Cognitive Science, 7*(12), 547–552.

Cordeiro, L., Ballinger, E., Hagerman, R., & Hessl, D. (2011). Clinical assessment of DSM-IV anxiety disorders in fragile X syndrome: prevalence and characterization. *Journal of Neurodevelopmental Disorders, 3*(1), 57–67. http://dx.doi.org/10.1007/s11689-010-9067-y.

Cornish, K. M., Munir, F., & Cross, G. (1999). Spatial cognition in males with fragile-X syndrome: evidence for a neuropsychological phenotype. *Cortex, 35*(2), 263–271. http://dx.doi.org/10.1016/s0010-9452(08)70799-8.

Cornish, K., Scerif, G., & Karmiloff-Smith, A. (2007). Tracing syndrome-specific trajectories of attention across the lifespan. *Cortex, 43*(6), 672–685.

Costanzo, F., Varuzza, C., Menghini, D., Addona, F., Gianesini, T., & Vicari, S. (2013). Executive functions in intellectual disabilities: a comparison between Williams syndrome and Down syndrome. *Research in Developmental Disabilities, 34*(5), 1770–1780. http://dx.doi.org/10.1016/j.ridd.2013.01.024.

Cowan, N. (1995). *Attention and memory: An integrated framework.* Oxford [Oxfordshire]: Oxford University Press.

Daunhauer, L. A., Fidler, D. J., Hahn, L., Will, E., Lee, N. R., & Hepburn, S. (2014). Profiles of everyday executive functioning in young children with Down syndrome. *American Journal on Intellectual and Developmental Disabilities, 119*(4), 303–318. http://dx.doi.org/10.1352/1944-7558-119.4.303.

Davies, M., Howlin, P., & Udwin, O. (1997). Independence and adaptive behavior in adults with Williams syndrome. *American Journal of Medical Genetics, 70*(2), 188–195.

Davis, M. H., & Gaskell, M. G. (2009). A complementary systems account of word learning: neural and behavioural evidence. *Philosophical Transactions of the Royal Society B: Biological Sciences, 364,* 3773–3800.

Davis, M., Merrill, E. C., Conners, F. A., & Roskos, B. (2014). Patterns of differences in wayfinding performance and correlations among abilities between persons with and without Down syndrome and typically developing children. *Frontiers in Psychology, 5,* 1446. http://dx.doi.org/10.3389/fpsyg.2014.01446.

Diamond, A. (2013). Executive functions. *Annual Review of Psychology, 64,* 135.

DiGuiseppi, C., Hepburn, S., Davis, J. M., Fidler, D. J., Hartway, S., Lee, N. R., ... Robinson, C. (2010). Screening for autism spectrum disorders in children with Down syndrome: population prevalence and screening test characteristics. *Journal of Developmental and Behavioral Pediatrics, 31*(3), 181–191. http://dx.doi.org/10.1097/DBP.0b013e3181d5aa6d.

Dykens, E. M. (2007). Psychiatric and behavioral disorders in persons with Down syndrome. *Mental Retardation and Developmental Disabilities Research Reviews, 13*(3), 272–278. http://dx.doi.org/10.1002/mrdd.20159.

Dykens, E. M., Hodapp, R. M., & Evans, D. W. (1994). Profiles and development of adaptive behavior in children with Down syndrome. *American Journal on Mental Retardation, 98,* 580–587.

Dykens, E. M., Hodapp, R. M., & Evans, D. W. (2006). Profiles and development of adaptive behavior in children with Down syndrome. *Down Syndrome: Research & Practice, 9,* 45–50. http://dx.doi.org/10.3104/reprints.293.

Dykens, E., Leckman, J., Paul, R., & Watson, M. (1988). Cognitive, behavioral, and adaptive functioning in fragile X and non-fragile X retarded men. *Journal of Autism and Developmental Disorders, 18*(1), 41–52. http://dx.doi.org/10.1007/BF02211817.

Dykens, E. M., Shah, B., Davis, B., Baker, C., Fife, T., & Fitzpatrick, J. (2015). Psychiatric disorders in adolescents and young adults with Down syndrome and other intellectual disabilities. *Journal of Neurodevelopmental Disorders, 7*(1), 9. http://dx.doi.org/10.1186/s11689-015-9101-1.

Edgin, J. O., Mason, G. M., Allman, M. J., Capone, G. T., DeLeon, I., Maslen, C., & Nadel, L. (2010). Development and validation of the Arizona cognitive test battery for Down syndrome. *Journal of Neurodevelopmental Disorders, 2*(3), 149.

Edgin, J. O., Pennington, B. F., & Mervis, C. B. (2010). Neuropsychological components of intellectual disability: the contributions of immediate, working, and associative memory. *Journal of Intellectual Disability Research, 54*(5), 406–417. http://dx.doi.org/10.1111/j.1365-2788.2010.01278.x.

Eliez, S., Blasey, C. M., Freund, L. S., Hastie, T., & Reiss, A. L. (2001). Brain anatomy, gender and IQ in children and adolescents with fragile X syndrome. *Brain, 124,* 1610–1618.

Ellis, N. R., Woodley-Zanthos, P., & Dulaney, C. L. (1989). Memory for spatial location in children, adults, and mentally retarded persons. *American Journal on Mental Retardation, 93*(5), 521–526.

Epstein, C. J. (1989). Down syndrome. In C. R. Scriver, A. L. Beaudet, W. S. Sly, & P. Valle (Eds.), *The metabolic basis of inherited disease* (pp. 291–396). New York: McGraw.

Eriksson, J., Vogel, E. K., Lansner, A., Bergstrom, F., & Nyberg, L. (2015). Neurocognitive architecture of working memory. *Neuron, 88*(1), 33–46. http://dx.doi.org/10.1016/j.neuron.2015.09.020.

Farran, E., Blades, M., Boucher, J., & Tranter, L. (2010). How do individuals with Williams syndrome learn a route in a real-world environment? *Developmental Science*, 454–468.

Fidler, D. J., Most, D. E., Booth-LaForce, C., & Kelly, J. F. (2008). Emerging social strengths in young children with Down syndrome. *Infants and Young Children, 21*(3), 207–220.

Finestack, L. H., Richmond, E. K., & Abbeduto, L. (2009). Language development in individuals with fragile X syndrome. *Topics in Language Disorders, 29*, 133–148.

Finke, C., Braun, M., Ostendorf, F., Lehmann, T. N., Hoffmann, K. T., Kopp, U., & Ploner, C. J. (2008). The human hippocampal formation mediates short-term memory of colour-location associations. *Neuropsychologia, 46*, 614–623.

Fisch, G. S., Carpenter, N., Howard-Peebles, P. N., Holden, J. J., Tarleton, J., & Simensen, R. (2010). The course of cognitive-behavioral development in children with the FMR1 mutation, Williams-Beuren syndrome, and neurofibromatosis type 1: the effect of gender. *American Journal of Medical Genetics A, 152A*(6), 1498–1509. http://dx.doi.org/10.1002/ajmg.a.33412.

Fisch, G. S., Holden, J. J. K., Carpenter, N. J., Howard-Peebles, P. N., Maddalena, A., Pandya, A., & Nance, W. (1999). Age-related language characteristics of children and adolescents with fragile X syndrome. *American Journal of Medical Genetics, 83*(4), 253–256.

Fisch, G. S., Shapiro, L. R., Simensen, R., Schwartz, C. E., Fryns, J. P., Borghgraef, M., … Mavrou, A. (1992). Longitudinal changes in IQ among fragile X males: clinical evidence of more than one mutation? *American Journal of Medical Genetics, 43*(1–2), 28–34.

Frenkel, S., & Bourdin, B. (2009). Verbal, visual, and spatio-sequential short-term memory: assessment of the storage capacities of children and teenagers with Down's syndrome. *Journal of Intellectual Disability Research, 53*(2), 152–160.

Giedd, J. N., Lalonde, F. M., Celano, M. J., White, S. L., Wallace, G. L., Lee, N. R., & Lenroot, R. K. (2009). Anatomical brain magnetic resonance imaging of typically developing children and adolescents. *Journal of the American Academy of Child and Adolescent Psychiatry, 48*, 465–470. http://dx.doi.org/10.1097/CHI.0b013e31819f2715.

Grant, J., Valian, V., & Karmiloff-Smith, A. (2002). A study of relative clauses in Williams syndrome. *Journal of Child Language, 29*(2), 403–416.

Greer, M. K., Brown, F. R., Pai, G. S., Choudry, S. H., & Klein, A. J. (1997). Cognitive, adaptive, and behavioral characteristics of Williams syndrome. *American Journal of Medical Genetics, 74*(5), 521–525.

Hagerman, P. J. (2008). The fragile X prevalence paradox. *Journal of Medical Genetics, 45*(8), 498–499. http://dx.doi.org/10.1136/jmg.2008.059055.

Hahn, L. J., Fidler, D. J., & Hepburn, S. L. (2014). Adaptive behavior and problem behavior in young children with Williams syndrome. *American Journal on Intellectual and Developmental Disabilities, 119*(1), 49–63.

Hatton, D. D., Hooper, S. R., Bailey, D. B., Skinner, M. L., Sullivan, K. M., & Wheeler, A. (2002). Problem behavior in boys with fragile X syndrome. *American Journal of Medical Genetics, 108*(2), 105–116.

Hazlett, H. C., Poe, M. D., Lightbody, A. A., Styner, M., MacFall, J. R., Reiss, A. L., & Piven, J. (2012). Trajectories of early brain volume development in fragile X syndrome and autism. *Journal of the American Academy of Child and Adolescent Psychiatry, 51*(9), 921–933. http://dx.doi.org/10.1016/j.jaac.2012.07.003.

Hick, R. F., Botting, N., & Conti-Ramsden, G. (2005). Short-term memory and vocabulary development in children with Down syndrome and children with specific language impairment. *Developmental Medicine and Child Neurology, 47*(8), 532–538. http://dx.doi.org/10.1017/s0012162205001040.

Hocking, D. R., Reeve, J., & Porter, M. A. (2015). Characterising the profile of everyday executive functioning and relation to IQ in adults with Williams syndrome: is the brief adult version a valid rating scale? *PLoS One, 10*(9), 18. http://dx.doi.org/10.1371/journal.pone.0137628.

Hodapp, R. M., & Zigler, E. (1990). Applying the developmental perspective to individuals with Down syndrome. In D. M. Cicchetti, & Beeghly (Eds.), *Children with Down syndrome* (pp. 1–28). New York Cambridge University Press.

Hoeft, F., Walter, E., Lightbody, A. A., Hazlett, H. C., Chang, C., Piven, J., & Reiss, A. L. (2011). Neuroanatomical differences in toddler boys with fragile X syndrome and idiopathic autism. *Archives of General Psychiatry, 68*(3), 295–305. http://dx.doi.org/10.1001/archgenpsychiatry.2010.153.

Hooper, S. R., Hatton, D., Sideris, J., Sullivan, K., Hammer, J., Schaaf, J., … Bailey, D. P., Jr. (2008). Executive functions in young males with fragile X syndrome in comparison to mental age-matched controls: baseline findings from a longitudinal study. *Neuropsychology, 22*(1), 36–47. http://dx.doi.org/10.1037/0894-4105.22.1.36.

Jacola, L. M., Hickey, F., Howe, S. R., Esbensen, A., & Shear, P. K. (2014). Behavior and adaptive functioning in adolescents with Down syndrome: specifying targets for intervention. *Journal of Mental Health Research in Intellectual Disabilities, 7*, 287–305. http://dx.doi.org/10.1080/19315864.2014.920941.

Jarrold, C., & Baddeley, A. D. (1997). Short-term memory for verbal and visuospatial information in Down's syndrome. *Cognitive Neuropsychiatry, 2*(2), 101–122. http://dx.doi.org/10.1080/135468097396351.

Jarrold, C., Baddeley, A. D., & Hewes, A. K. (1999). Genetically dissociated components of working memory: evidence from Downs and Williams syndrome. *Neuropsychologia, 37*(6), 637–651.

Jarrold, C., Baddeley, A. D., & Hewes, A. K. (2000). Verbal short-term memory deficits in Down syndrome: a consequence of problems in rehearsal? *Journal of Child Psychology and Psychiatry and Allied Disciplines, 41*(2), 233–244. http://dx.doi.org/10.1111/1469-7610.00604.

Jarrold, C., Baddeley, A. D., & Phillips, C. E. (2002). Verbal short-term memory in Down syndrome: a problem of memory, audition, or speech? *Journal of Speech Language and Hearing Research, 45*(3), 531–544. http://dx.doi.org/10.1044/1092-4388(2002/042).

Jarrold, C., Baddeley, A. D., & Phillips, C. (2007). Long-term memory for verbal and visual information in Down syndrome and Williams syndrome: performance on the doors and people test. *Cortex, 43*(2), 233–247. http://dx.doi.org/10.1016/s0010-9452(08)70478-7.

Jarrold, C., Nadel, L., & Vicari, S. (2009). Memory and neuropsychology in Down syndrome. *Down Syndrome: Research & Practice, 12*(3), 196–201.

Jarvinen, A., Korenberg, J. R., & Bellugi, U. (2013). The social phenotype of Williams syndrome. *Current Opinion in Neurobiology, 23*(3), 414–422. http://dx.doi.org/10.1016/j.conb.2012.12.006.

Jernigan, T. L., & Bellugi, U. (1990). Anomalous brain morphology on magnetic resonance images in Williams syndrome and Down syndrome. *Archives of Neurology, 47,* 529–533.

Johnson-Glenberg, M. C. (2008). Fragile X syndrome: neural network models of sequencing and memory. *Cognitive Systems Research, 9*(4), 274–292. http://dx.doi.org/10.1016/j.cogsys.2008.02.002.

Kirchner, R. M., Martens, M. A., & Andridge, R. R. (2016). Adaptive behavior and development of infants and toddlers with Williams syndrome. *Frontiers in Psychology, 7.*

Klaiman, C., Quintin, E., Jo, N., Lightbody, A. A., Hazlett, H. C., Piven, J., ... Reiss, A. L. (2014). Longitudinal profiles of adaptive behavior in fragile X syndrome. *Pediatrics, 134,* 315–324.

Klein, B. P., & Mervis, C. B. (1999). Contrasting patterns of cognitive abilities of 9-and 10-year-olds with Williams syndrome or Down syndrome. *Developmental Neuropsychology, 16*(2), 177–196. http://dx.doi.org/10.1207/s15326942dn1602_3.

Klusek, J., Martin, G. E., & Losh, M. (2014). Consistency between research and clinical diagnoses of autism among boys and girls with fragile X syndrome. *Journal of Intellectual Disability Research, 58,* 940–952. http://dx.doi.org/10.1111/jir.12121.

Kogan, C. S., Boutet, I., Cornish, K., Graham, G. E., Berry-Kravis, E., Drouin, A., & Milgram, N. W. (2009). A comparative neuropsychological test battery differentiates cognitive signatures of Fragile X and Down syndrome. *Journal of Intellectual Disability Research, 53,* 125–142. http://dx.doi.org/10.1111/j.1365-2788.2008.01135.x.

Konkel, A., & Cohen, N. J. (2009). Relational memory and the hippocampus: representations and methods. *Frontiers in Neuroscience, 3*(2), 166–174.

Kopp, C. B., Krakow, J. B., & Johnson, K. L. (1983). Strategy production by young Down syndrome children. *American Journal of Mental Deficiency, 88.*

Landry, O., Russo, N., Dawkins, T., Zelazo, P. D., & Burack, J. A. (2012). The impact of verbal and nonverbal development on executive function in Down syndrome and Williams syndrome. *Journal on Developmental Disabilities, 18*(2).

Lanfranchi, S., Baddeley, A., Gathercole, S., & Vianello, R. (2012). Working memory in Down syndrome: is there a dual task deficit? *Journal of Intellectual Disability Research, 56*(2), 157–166.

Lanfranchi, S., Cornoldi, C., Drigo, S., & Vianello, R. (2009). Working memory in individuals with fragile X syndrome. *Child Neuropsychology, 15*(2), 105–119.

Lanfranchi, S., Cornoldi, C., & Vianello, R. (2004). Verbal and visuospatial working memory deficits in children with Down syndrome. *American Journal on Mental Retardation, 109*(6), 456–466.

Lanfranchi, S., Jerman, O., Dal Pont, E., Alberti, A., & Vianello, R. (2010). Executive function in adolescents with down syndrome. *Journal of Intellectual Disability Research, 54,* 308–319. http://dx.doi.org/10.1111/j.1365-2788.2010.01262.x.

Lanfranchi, S., Jerman, O., & Vianello, R. (2009). Working memory and cognitive skills in individuals with Down syndrome. *Child Neuropsychology, 15*(4), 397–416.

Lanfranchi, S., Toffanin, E., Zilli, S., Panzeri, B., & Vianello, R. (2014). Memory coding in individuals with Down syndrome. *Child Neuropsychology, 20*(6), 700–712.

Laws, G., & Bishop, D. V. M. (2003). A comparison of language abilities in adolescents with Down syndrome and children with specific language impairment. *Journal of Speech Language and Hearing Research, 46*(6), 1324–1339. http://dx.doi.org/10.1044/1092-4388(2003/103).

Lee, N. R., Adeyemi, E. I., Lin, A., Clasen, L. S., Lalonde, F. M., Condon, E., ... Giedd, J. N. (2016). Dissociations in cortical morphometry in youth with Down syndrome: evidence for reduced surface area but increased thickness. *Cerebral Cortex, 26,* 2982–2990. http://dx.doi.org/10.1093/cercor/bhv107.

Lee, N. R., Anand, P., Will, E., Adeyemi, E. I., Clasen, L. S., Blumenthal, J. D., ... Edgin, J. O. (2015). Everyday executive functions in Down syndrome from early childhood to young adulthood: evidence for both unique and shared characteristics compared to youth with sex chromosome trisomy (XXX and XXY). *Frontiers in Behavioral Neuroscience, 9.* http://dx.doi.org/10.3389/fnbh.2015.00254.

Lee, N. R., Pennington, B. F., & Keenan, J. (2010). Verbal short-term memory deficits in Down syndrome: phonological, semantic, or both? *Journal of Neurodevelopmental Disorders, 2,* 9—25. http://dx.doi.org/10.1007/s11689-009-9029-4. Epub 2009 Sep 10.

Levitin, D. J., Menon, V., Schmitt, J. E., Eliez, S., White, C. D., Glover, G. H., ... Reiss, A. L. (2003). Neural correlates of auditory perception in Williams syndrome: an fMRI study. *NeuroImage, 18*(1), 74—82.

Leyfer, O. T., Woodruff-Borden, J., Klein-Tasman, B. P., Fricke, J. S., & Mervis, C. B. (2006). Prevalence of psychiatric disorders in 4 to 16-year-olds with Williams syndrome. *American Journal of Medical Genetics Part B: Neuropsychiatric Genetics, 141B,* 615—622. http://dx.doi.org/10.1002/ajmg.b.30344.

Lezak, M. (1995). *Neuropsychological testing.* Oxford: University Press.

Lincoln, A. J., Searcy, Y. M., Jones, W., & Lord, C. (2007). Social interaction behaviors discriminate young children with autism and Williams syndrome. *Journal of the American Academy of Child and Adolescent Psychiatry, 46*(3), 323—331. http://dx.doi.org/10.1097/chi.0b013e31802b9522.

Logan, G. D., & Cowan, W. B. (1984). On the ability to inhibit thought and action: a theory of an act of control. *Psychological Review, 91*(3), 295.

Losin, E. A. R., Rivera, S. M., O'Hare, E. D., Sowell, E. R., & Pinter, J. D. (2009). Abnormal fMRI activation pattern during story listening in individuals with down syndrome. *American Journal on Intellectual and Developmental Disabilities, 114*(5), 369—380. http://dx.doi.org/10.1352/1944-7558-114.5.369.

Lott, I. T. (1982). Down's syndrome, aging, and Alzheimer's disease: a clinical review. *Annals of the New York Academy of Sciences, 396,* 15—27.

Mackenzie, S., & Hulme, C. (1987). Memory span development in Down's syndrome, severely subnormal and normal subjects. *Cognitive Neuropsychology, 4*(3), 303—319.

Maguire, E. A., Burgess, N., Donnett, J. G., Frackowiak, R. S., Frith, C. D., & O'Keefe, J. (1998). Knowing where and getting there: a human navigation network. *Science, 280*(5365), 921—924.

Marcell, M. M., & Cohen, S. (1992). Hearing abilities of Down syndrome and other mentally handicapped adolescents. *Research in Developmental Disabilities, 13*(6), 533—551.

Marcell, M. M., & Weeks, S. L. (1988). Short-term memory difficulties and Down's syndrome. *Journal of Intellectual Disability Research, 32*(2), 153—162.

Martens, M. A., Wilson, S. J., & Reutens, D. C. (2008). Research Review: Williams syndrome: a critical review of the cognitive, behavioral, and neuroanatomical phenotype. *Journal of Child Psychology and Psychiatry, 49*(6), 576—608. http://dx.doi.org/10.1111/j.1469-7610.2008.01887.x.

Martin, G. E., Klusek, J., Estigarribia, B., & Roberts, J. E. (2009). Language characteristics of individuals with down syndrome. *Topics in Language Disorders, 29*(2), 112—132.

McClelland, J. L. (1998). Complementary learning systems in the brain. A connectionist approach to explicit and implicit cognition and memory. *Annals of the New York Academy of Sciences, 843,* 153—169.

McDade, M. L., & Adler, S. (1980). Down syndrome and short-term memory impairment: a storage or retrieval deficit? *American Journal of Mental Deficiency, 84*(6), 561—567.

Meguid, N. A., Fahim, C., Sami, R., Nashaat, N. H., Yoon, U., Anwar, M., ... Evans, A. C. (2012). Cognition and lobar morphology in full mutation boys with fragile X syndrome. *Brain and Cognition, 78*(1), 74—84. http://dx.doi.org/10.1016/j.bandc.2011.09.005.

Menghini, D., Addona, F., Costanzo, F., & Vicari, S. (2010). Executive functions in individuals with Williams syndrome. *Journal of Intellectual Disability Research, 54*(5), 418—432.

Mervis, C. B. (2009). Language and literacy development of children with Williams syndrome. *Topics in Language Disorders, 29*(2), 149—169.

Mervis, C. B., & John, A. E. (2010). Cognitive and behavioral characteristics of children with Williams syndrome: implications for intervention approaches. *American Journal of Medical Genetics Part C-Seminars in Medical Genetics, 154C*(2), 229—248. http://dx.doi.org/10.1002/ajmg.c.30263.

Mervis, C. B., & John, A. E. (2008). Vocabulary abilities of children with Williams syndrome: strengths, weaknesses, and relation to visuospatial construction ability. *J Speech Lang Hear Res, 51*(4), 967—982. http://dx.doi.org/10.1044/1092-4388(2008/071).

Mervis, C. B., & Klein-Tasman, B. P. (2000). Williams syndrome: cognition, personality, and adaptive behavior. *Mental Retardation and Developmental Disabilities Research Reviews, 6*(2), 148—158.

Meyer-Lindenberg, A., Mervis, C. B., Sarpal, D., Koch, P., Steele, S., Kohn, P., ... Berman, K. F. (2005). Functional, structural, and metabolic abnormalities of the hippocampal formation in Williams syndrome. *Journal of Clinical Investigation, 115*(7), 1888—1895. http://dx.doi.org/10.1172/JCI24892.

Milojevich, H., & Lukowski, A. (2016). Recall memory in children with Down syndrome and typically developing peers matched on developmental age. *Journal of Intellectual Disability Research, 60*(1), 89—100. http://dx.doi.org/10.1111/jir.12242.

Miyake, A., Friedman, N. P., Emerson, M. J., Witzki, A. H., Howerter, A., & Wager, T. D. (2000). The unity and diversity of executive functions and their contributions to complex "frontal lobe" tasks: a latent variable analysis. *Cognitive Psychology, 41*(1), 49—100.

Morton, J., & Frith, U. (1995). *Causal Modelling: A structural approach to developmental psychopathology, Manual of Developmental Psychopathology*. Oxford: John Wiley & Sons.

Mostofsky, S. H., Mazzocco, M. M., Aakalu, G., Warsofsky, I. S., Denckla, M. B., & Reiss, A. L. (1998). Decreased cerebellar posterior vermis size in fragile X syndrome: correlation with neurocognitive performance. *Neurology, 50*(1), 121—130.

Munir, F., Cornish, K. M., & Wilding, J. (2000a). A neuropsychological profile of attention deficits in young males with fragile X syndrome. *Neuropsychologia, 38*(9), 1261—1270.

Munir, F., Cornish, K. M., & Wilding, J. (2000b). Nature of the working memory deficit in Fragile-X syndrome. *Brain and Cognition, 44*(3), 387—401. http://dx.doi.org/10.1006/brcg.1999.1200.

Nigg, J. T. (2000). On inhibition/disinhibition in developmental psychopathology: views from cognitive and personality psychology and a working inhibition taxonomy. *Psychological Bulletin, 126*(2), 220.

Næss, K. B., Lervåg, A., Lyster, S. H., & Hulme, C. (2015). Longitudinal relationships between language and verbal short-term memory skills in children with Down syndrome. *Journal of Experimental Child Psychology*, 13543—13555.

Ornstein, P. A., Schaaf, J. M., Hooper, S. R., Hatton, D. D., Mirrett, P., & Bailey, D. B. (2008). Memory skills of boys with fragile X syndrome. *American Journal on Mental Retardation, 113*(6), 453—465. http://dx.doi.org/10.1352/2008.113:453-465.

Osório, A., Cruz, R., Sampaio, A., Garayzábal, E., Martínez-Regueiro, R., Gonçalves, Ó. F., ... Fernández-Prieto, M. (2012). How executive functions are related to intelligence in Williams syndrome. *Research in Developmental Disabilities, 33*(4), 1169—1175.

Parker, S. E., Mai, C. T., Canfield, M. A., Rickard, R., Wang, Y., Meyer, R. E., ... National Birth Defects Prevention Network. (2010). Updated national birth prevalence estimates for selected birth defects in the United States, 2004—2006. *Birth Defects Research Part A: Clinical and Molecular Teratology, 88*(12), 1008—1016. http://dx.doi.org/10.1002/bdra.20735.

Pennington, B. F. (1999). Toward an integrated understanding of dyslexia: genetic, neurological, and cognitive mechanisms. *Developmental Psychopathology, 11*, 629—654.

Pennington, B. F. (2006). From single to multiple deficit models of developmental disorders. *Cognition, 101*, 385—413.

Pennington, B. F., Moon, J., Edgin, J., Stedron, J., & Nadel, L. (2003). The neuropsychology of Down syndrome: evidence for hippocampal dysfunction. *Child Development, 74*(1), 75—93. http://dx.doi.org/10.1111/1467-8624.00522.

Peoples, R., Franke, Y., Wang, Y. K., Perez-Jurado, L., Paperna, T., Cisco, M., & Francke, U. (2000). A physical map, including a BAC/PAC clone contig, of the Williams-Beuren syndrome—deletion region at 7q11.23. *The American Journal of Human Genetics, 66*(1), 47—68. http://dx.doi.org/10.1086/302722.

Piekema, C., Kessels, R. P., Mars, R. B., Petersson, K. M., & Fernández, G. (2006). The right hippocampus participates in short-term memory maintenance of object—location associations. *NeuroImage, 33*(1), 374—382. http://dx.doi.org/10.1016/j.neuroimage.2006.06.035.

Pinter, J. D., Brown, W. E., Eliez, S., Schmitt, J. E., Capone, G. T., & Reiss, A. L. (2001). Amygdala and hippocampal volumes in children with Down syndrome: a high-resolution MRI study. *Neurology, 56*(7), 972—974.

Pinter, J. D., Eliez, S., Schmitt, J. E., Capone, G. T., & Reiss, A. L. (2001). Neuroanatomy of Down's syndrome: a high-resolution MRI study. *American Journal of Psychiatry, 158*(10), 1659—1665.

Porter, M. A., & Coltheart, M. (2006). Global and local processing in Williams syndrome, autism, and Down syndrome: perception, attention, and construction. *Developmental Neuropsychology, 30*(3), 771—789. http://dx.doi.org/10.1207/s15326942dn3003_1.

Porter, M. A., Coltheart, M., & Langdon, R. (2007). The neuropsychological basis of hypersociability in Williams and Down syndrome. *Neuropsychologia, 45*(12), 2839—2849.

Price, J., Roberts, J., Vandergrift, N., & Martin, G. (2007). Language comprehension in boys with fragile X syndrome and boys with Down syndrome. *Journal of Intellectual Disability Research, 51*(4), 318—326. http://dx.doi.org/10.1111/j.1365-2788.2006.00881.x.

Purser, H. R., Farran, E. K., Courbois, Y., Lemahieu, A., Sockeel, P., Mellier, D., & Blades, M. (2015). The development of route learning in Down syndrome, Williams syndrome and typical development: investigations with virtual environments. *Developmental Science, 18*(4), 599—613. http://dx.doi.org/10.1111/desc.12236.

Quintin, E. M., Jo, B., Hall, S. S., Bruno, J. L., Chromik, L. C., Raman, M. M., ... Reiss, A. L. (2015). The cognitive developmental profile associated with fragile X syndrome: a longitudinal investigation of cognitive strengths and weaknesses through childhood and adolescence. *Developmental Psychopathology,* 1—13. http://dx.doi.org/10.1017/S0954579415001200.

Raz, N., Torres, I. J., Briggs, S. D., Spencer, W. D., Thornton, A. E., Loken, W. J., ... Acker, J. D. (1995). Selective neuroanatomical abnormalities in Downs-syndrome and their cognitive correlates — evidence from MRI morphometry. *Neurology, 45*(2), 356—366.

Reilly, J., Losh, M., Bellugi, U., & Wulfeck, B. (2004). Frog, where are you?" Narratives in children with specific language impairment, early focal brain injury, and Williams syndrome. *Brain and Language, 88*(2), 229—247. http://dx.doi.org/10.1016/S0093-934X(03)00101-9.

Reiss, A. L., Aylward, E., Freund, L. S., Joshi, P. K., & Bryan, R. N. (1991). Neuroanatomy of fragile X syndrome: the posterior fossa. *Annals of Neurology, 29*(1), 26—32. http://dx.doi.org/10.1002/ana.410290107.

Reiss, A. L., Eckert, M. A., Rose, F. E., Karchemskiy, A., Kesler, S., Chang, M., ... Galaburda, A. (2004). An experiment of nature: brain anatomy parallels cognition and behavior in Williams syndrome. *The Journal of Neuroscience, 24*(21), 5009—5015. http://dx.doi.org/10.1523/JNEUROSCI.5272-03.2004.

Reiss, A. L., Lee, J., & Freund, L. (1994). Neuroanatomy of fragile X syndrome: the temporal lobe. *Neurology, 44*(7), 1317—1324.

Rhodes, S. M., Riby, D. M., Park, J., Fraser, E., & Campbell, L. E. (2010). Executive neuropsychological functioning in individuals with Williams syndrome. *Neuropsychologia, 48*(5), 1216—1226. http://dx.doi.org/10.1016/j.neuropsychologia.2009.12.021.

Roberts, J., Long, S. H., Malkin, C., Barnes, E., Skinner, M., Hennon, E. A., & Anderson, K. (2005). A comparison of phonological skills of boys with fragile X syndrome and Down syndrome. *Journal of Speech, Language, and Hearing Research, 48*(5), 980—995. http://dx.doi.org/10.1044/1092-4388(2005/067).

Roberts, J., Martin, G. E., Moskowitz, L., Harris, A. A., Foreman, J., & Nelson, L. (2007). Discourse skills of boys with fragile X syndrome in comparison to boys with Down syndrome. *Journal of Speech, Language, and Hearing Research, 50*(2), 475—492. http://dx.doi.org/10.1044/1092-4388(2007/033).

Roberts, J., Price, J., Barnes, E., Nelson, L., Burchinal, M., Hennon, E. A., ... Hooper, S. R. (2007). Receptive vocabulary, expressive vocabulary, and speech production of boys with fragile X syndrome in comparison to boys with Down syndrome. *American Journal on Mental Retardation, 112*(3), 177—193. http://dx.doi.org/10.1352/0895-8017(2007) 112[177:RVEVAS]2.0.CO;2.

Roberts, L. V., & Richmond, J. L. (2015). Preschoolers with Down syndrome do not yet show the learning and memory impairments seen in adults with Down syndrome. *Developmental Science, 18*(3), 404—419.

Sampaio, A., Sousa, N., Fernandez, M., Vasconcelos, C., Shenton, M. E., & Goncalves, O. F. (2010). Williams syndrome and memory: a neuroanatomic and cognitive approach. *Journal of Autism and Developmental Disorders, 40*(7), 870—877. http://dx.doi.org/10.1007/ s10803-010-0940-z.

Scerif, G., Cornish, K., Wilding, J., Driver, J., & Karmiloff-Smith, A. (2004). Visual search in typically developing toddlers and toddlers with Fragile X or Williams syndrome. *Developmental Science, 7*(1), 116—130.

Scerif, G., Cornish, K., Wilding, J., Driver, J., & Karmiloff-Smith, A. (2007). Delineation of early attentional control difficulties in fragile X syndrome: focus on neurocomputational changes. *Neuropsychologia, 45*(8), 1889—1898.

Schalock, R., Borthwick-Duffy, S., Bradley, V., Buntinx, W., Coulter, D., Craig, E., ... Yeager, M. H. (2010). *Intellectual disability: definition, classification, and systems of supports* (11th ed.). Washington, DC: American Association on Intellectual and Developmental Disabilities.

Schalock, R. L., Luckasson, R. A., & Shogren, K. A. (2007). The renaming of mental retardation: understanding the change to the term intellectual disability. *Intellectual and Developmental Disabilities, 45*, 116—124.

Schuchardt, K., Gebhardt, M., & Mäehler, C. (2010). Working memory functions in children with different degrees of intellectual disability. *Journal of Intellectual Disability Research, 54*(4), 346—353.

Sherman, S. L. (2002). Epidemiology. In R. J. Hagerman, & P. J. Hagerman (Eds.), *Fragile X syndrome: Diagnosis, treatment and research* (3rd ed.). Baltimore, MD: The Johns Hopkins University Press.

Squire, L. R., Stark, C. E., & Clark, R. E. (2004). The medial temporal lobe. *Annual Review of Neuroscience, 27*, 279—306. http://dx.doi.org/10.1146/annurev.neuro.27.070203.144130.

Steele, A., Scerif, G., Cornish, K., & Karmiloff-Smith, A. (2013). Learning to read in Williams syndrome and Down syndrome: syndrome-specific precursors and developmental trajectories. *Journal of Child Psychology and Psychiatry, 54*(7), 754—762. http://dx.doi.org/ 10.1111/jcpp.12070.

Stromme, P., Bjornstad, P. G., & Ramstad, K. (2002). Prevalence estimation of Williams syndrome. *Journal of Child Neurology, 17*(4), 269—271.

Stuss, D. T., & Benson, D. F. (1986). *The frontal lobes*. Raven Pr.

Sudhalter, V., Scarborough, H. S., & Cohen, I. L. (1991). Syntactic delay and pragmatic deviance in the language of fragile X males. *American Journal of Medical Genetics, 38*(2—3), 493—497.

Sullivan, K., Hatton, D. D., Hammer, J., Sideris, J., Hooper, S., Ornstein, P. A., & Bailey, D. B. (2007). Sustained attention and response inhibition in boys with fragile X syndrome: measures of continuous performance. *American Journal of Medical Genetics Part B-Neuropsychiatric Genetics, 144B*(4), 517—532. http://dx.doi.org/10.1002/ajmg.b.30504.

Tager-Flusberg, H., Sullivan, K., & Boshart, J. (1997). Executive functions and performance on false belief tasks. *Developmental Neuropsychology, 13*(4), 487—493.

Tamm, L., Menon, V., Johnston, C. K., Hessl, D. R., & Reiss, A. L. (2002). fMRI study of cognitive interference processing in females with fragile X syndrome. *Journal of Cognitive Neuroscience, 14*(2), 160—171. http://dx.doi.org/10.1162/089892902317236812.

Thompson, P. M., Lee, A. D., Dutton, R. A., Geaga, J. A., Hayashi, K. M., Eckert, M. A., ... Reiss, A. L. (2005). Abnormal cortical complexity and thickness profiles mapped in Williams syndrome. *The Journal of Neuroscience, 25*(16), 4146—4158. http://dx.doi.org/10.1523/JNEUROSCI.0165-05.2005.

Turk, J. (1998). Fragile X syndrome and attentional deficits. *Journal of Applied Research in Intellectual Disabilities, 11*, 175—191.

Varnhagen, C. K., Das, J. P., & Varnhagen, S. (1987). Auditory and visual memory span: cognitive processing by TMR individuals with Down syndrome or other etiologies. *American Journal of Mental Deficiency, 91*(4), 398—405.

Vicari, S. (2004). Memory development and intellectual disabilities. *Acta Paediatrica Supplement, 93*(445), 60—63. discussion 63—64.

Vicari, S., Bellucci, S., & Carlesimo, G. A. (2000). Implicit and explicit memory: a functional dissociation in persons with Down syndrome. *Neuropsychologia, 38*(3), 240—251. http://dx.doi.org/10.1016/s0028-3932(99)00081-0.

Vicari, S., Bellucci, S., & Carlesimo, G. A. (2003). Visual and spatial working memory dissociation: evidence from Williams syndrome. *Developmental Medicine and Child Neurology, 45*(4), 269—273.

Vicari, S., Bellucci, S., & Carlesimo, G. A. (2005). Visual and spatial long-term memory: differential pattern of impairments in Williams and Down syndromes. *Developmental Medicine and Child Neurology, 47*(5), 305—311.

Vicari, S., Brizzolara, D., Carlesimo, G. A., Pezzini, G., & Volterra, V. (1996). Memory abilities in children with Williams syndrome. *Cortex, 32*(3), 503—514.

Vicari, S., Carlesimo, A., & Caltagirone, C. (1995). Short-term memory in persons with intellectual disabilities and Down's syndrome. *Journal of Intellectual Disability Research, 39*(6), 532—537.

Visu-Petra, L., Benga, O., Tincas, I., & Miclea, M. (2007). Visual-spatial processing in children and adolescents with Down's syndrome: a computerized assessment of memory skills. *Journal of Intellectual Disability Research, 51*(12), 942—952. http://dx.doi.org/10.1111/j.1365-2788.2007.01002.x.

Wang, P., & Bellugi, U. (1994). Evidence from two genetic syndromes for a dissociation between verbal and visual-spatial short-term memory. *Journal of Clinical and Experimental Neuropsychology, 16*(2), 317—322.

Warner, G., Moss, J., Smith, P., & Howlin, P. (2014). Autism characteristics and behavioural disturbances in ~ 500 children with Down's syndrome in England and Wales. *Autism Research, 7*(4), 433—441. http://dx.doi.org/10.1002/aur.1371.

Wildgruber, D., Kischka, U., Ackermann, H., Klose, U., & Grodd, W. (1999). Dynamic pattern of brain activation during sequencing of word strings evaluated by fMRI. *Cognitive Brain Research, 7*(3), 285—294.

Wilding, J., Cornish, K., & Munir, F. (2002). Further delineation of the executive deficit in males with fragile-X syndrome. *Neuropsychologia, 40*(8), 1343—1349. http://dx.doi.org/10.1016/s0028-3932(01)00212-3.

Yang, Y., Conners, F. A., & Merrill, E. C. (2014). Visuo-spatial ability in individuals with Down syndrome: is it really a strength? *Research in Developmental Disabilities, 35*(7), 1473—1500. http://dx.doi.org/10.1016/j.ridd.2014.03.002.

Zelazo, P. D., Burack, J. A., Benedetto, E., & Frye, D. (1996). Theory of mind and rule use in individuals with Down's syndrome: a test of the uniqueness and specificity claims. *Journal of Child Psychology and Psychiatry, 37*(4), 479—484.

Zigman, W. B., Schupf, N., Urv, T., Zigman, A., & Silverman, W. (2002). Incidence and temporal patterns of adaptive behavior change in adults with mental retardation. *American Journal on Mental Retardation, 107*(3), 161—174. http://dx.doi.org/10.1352/0895-8017(2002)107<0161:IATPOA>2.0.CO;2.

CHAPTER TWO

Characterizing Emergent Anxiety Through the Lens of Fragile X

B.L. Tonnsen*[,1], J.E. Roberts[§]
*Purdue University, West Lafayette, IN, United States
[§]University of South Carolina, Columbia, SC, United States
[1]Corresponding author: E-mail: btonnsen@purdue.edu

Contents

International Review of Research in Developmental Disabilities, Volume 51
ISSN 2211-6095
http://dx.doi.org/10.1016/bs.irrdd.2016.07.003

© 2016 Elsevier Inc.
All rights reserved.

Abstract

Fragile X syndrome (FXS) is a single-gene disorder highly associated with anxiety, with over 75% of males meeting clinical diagnostic criteria for at least one anxiety disorder. Due to the known genetic mechanisms of FXS, examining emergent anxiety through the lens of FXS offers unique insight into the complex intersection of genetics, development, and environment. This work may inform both syndrome-specific patterns of risk, as well as general models of anxiety relevant to non-FXS populations. In this review, we synthesize the emergent literature on prodromal anxiety in young children with FXS with goals to (1) establish a working model for anxiety emergence in infants and toddlers with FXS and (2) identify current limitations and next steps needed to develop translational, phenotypically calibrated treatments. We present evidence that further investigating specific prodromal features of anxiety emergence in infants and toddlers with FXS may pave the way to identifying malleable markers of risk and resilience, which may be targeted to optimize child and family outcomes.

Anxiety disorders are among the most commonly reported forms of child psychopathology, affecting approximately 32% of adolescents (Merikangas et al., 2010). Given the high public health costs and individual impact associated with anxiety, increased efforts have been devoted to characterizing early precursors and contributors to anxiety emergence, with the intention of potentially preventing symptoms before they emerge.

One underutilized approach to characterizing the natural landscape of prodromal anxiety in early childhood is to examine its emergence in neurogenetic syndromes associated with elevated anxiety risk. Whereas community-based studies of anxiety emergence require large cohorts to ensure adequately powered subsamples of children with anxiety, prospectively following children with "high-risk" neurogenetic status provides an efficient, high-powered model for examining emergent changes over time. Fragile X syndrome is a single-gene disorder highly associated with anxiety, with up to 86% of males meeting DSM-IV criteria for at least one anxiety disorder (Cordeiro, Ballinger, Hagerman, & Hessl, 2011; Crawford, Acuña, & Sherman, 2001; Harris et al., 2008). Because FXS can be diagnosed at or before birth, examining emergent anxiety through the lens of FXS offers unique insight into the complex intersection of genetics, development, and environment, informing both syndrome-specific patterns of risk, as well as general models of anxiety relevant to non-FXS populations.

In this review, we synthesize the emergent literature on prodromal anxiety in young children with FXS with goals to (1) establish a working model for anxiety emergence in infants and toddlers with FXS and (2) identify current limitations and next steps needed to the translation of this work to targeted, effective, and phenotypically sensitive treatment. We propose that identifying malleable, early emerging risk factors for anxiety in FXS may pave the way for more targeted and effective treatments, reducing anxiety-associated impairments in this high-risk population.

1. ANXIETY IN FRAGILE X SYNDROME

Fragile X syndrome is a single-gene disorder that affects approximately 1:3700–8900 males (Crawford et al., 2001; Hagerman & Hagerman, 2002; Hunter et al., 2014) and is the leading heritable form of intellectual disability. FXS is caused by a CGG triplet repeat mutation that results in methylation of the *FMR1* gene and subsequent absence of fragile X mental retardation protein (FMRP) necessary for synaptic plasticity (Fernández, Rajan, & Bagni, 2013). The behavioral phenotype is most severe in males and includes intellectual disability, anxiety, and autism symptoms, heightened emotional and physiological reactivity, sensory issues, social avoidance and withdrawal, and hyperactivity (Bailey, Raspa, Olmsted, & Holiday, 2008; Cordeiro et al., 2011; Tonnsen, Grefer, Hatton, & Roberts, 2014; Tonnsen, Shinkareva, Deal, Hatton, & Roberts, 2013).

Anxiety is one of the most common co-occurring conditions in FXS, with up to 86% of males meeting DSM-IV criteria for at least one anxiety disorder (Cordeiro et al., 2011) and 70% seeking treatment. Symptoms of anxiety in FXS vary across individuals but may manifest through fear, avoidance and withdrawal, reduced eye contact, arguing, and staring (Cohen et al., 1988; Hall, DeBernardis, & Reiss, 2006; Roberts, Weisenfeld, Hatton, Heath, & Kaufmann, 2006; Sullivan, Hooper, & Hatton, 2007; Wolff, Gardner, Paccia, & Lappen, 1989). In a pivotal study characterizing anxiety disorders in children and adults with FXS using DSM-IV clinical interviews, the most common anxiety disorders in FXS were identified as social phobia (58%), specific phobia (60%), selective mutism (25%), generalized anxiety disorder (24%), and obsessive compulsive disorder (24%) (Cordeiro et al., 2011).

In addition to the direct effects of anxiety on individual well-being, co-occurring anxiety has been described as a catalyst for increased problem behaviors common to FXS. For example, caregiver-reported aggression is more severe among individuals with FXS who have histories of anxiety, relative to those without previous anxiety diagnoses (Wheeler, Raspa, Bishop, & Bailey, 2015). Similarly, anxiety is associated with greater restrictive interests, compulsive behaviors, and ritualistic sameness among 6-to 10-year-old children with FXS (Oakes et al., 2016). Indeed, it has been suggested that repetitive behaviors may serve to reduce anxiety in disorders such as autism spectrum disorder and FXS (Leekam, Prior, & Uljarevic, 2011; Oakes et al., 2016) and therefore may be considered a secondary consequence of anxiety symptoms. In addition to these correlational studies, problem behaviors have been shown to increase in frequency during experimental social stress tasks in children with FXS (Hall et al., 2006), suggesting anxiety-provoking situations may intensify maladaptive behaviors common to the FXS phenotype. Together, these correlational and experimental studies speak to the intensity and pervasiveness of anxiety in FXS, as well as the potential downstream effects of anxiety on broader quality of life.

2. CANDIDATE MARKERS FOR EMERGENT ANXIETY IN FRAGILE X SYNDROME

Patterns of atypical negative affect, withdrawal, arousal, and attention in FXS are consistent with Barlow et al. (Barlow, 1988, 2000; Barlow, Chorpita, & Turovsky, 1996; Hoffman & Barlow, 2002) commonly endorsed etiological theory of anxiety disorders. According to Barlow's theory, anxiety is an integrated cognitive-affective construct that plays a vital role in the human defensive motivational system. The "anxious apprehension" process involves complex, cyclical interactions among environmental cues, negative affect, attention, arousal modulation, hypervigilance, and dysfunctional behavior (Barlow, 2000). Negative affect, attention, and arousal construct a positive feedback loop, with negative affect leading to shifts in attention that increase arousal, further contributing to negative affect. In addition to biased thoughts and behaviors that may emerge from this feedback loop, anxious apprehension gives rise to coping mechanisms such as avoidance and worry, which function to reduce negative affect.

Although moderate anxiety may reflect adaptive capacity to adapt to stress and plan for the future (Barlow, 1988), anxiety becomes maladaptive when chronic (Barlow, 2000). That is, avoidance and worrying become habitual and uncontrollable, reflecting a "perpetual readiness to confront danger" (Barlow, 2000). These behavioral and cognitive patterns of anxiety are also reflected in physiological hyperarousal and more specific failure to modulate sympathetic nervous system activity (Thayer, Friedman, & Borkovec, 1996). Although the cognitive component of this model may present differently in children with intellectual disabilities, FXS is associated with atypical expression of many components of Barlow's model, including components of negative affect, behavioral withdrawal, arousal, and attentional control. Here, we briefly review existing FXS studies relevant to each of these constructs, as well as the broader contextual factors relevant to FXS, describing both parallel and distinct patterns from those established in non-FXS populations.

2.1 Temperamental Negative Affect

Early temperament is one of the most powerful predictors of problem behaviors in typically developing (e.g., Calkins, Blandon, Williford, & Keane, 2007; Caspi & Silva, 1995; Lemery, Essex, & Smider, 2002) and clinical (e.g., Hutman et al., 2010; Whiteside-Mansell, Bradley, Casey, Fussell, & Conners-Burrow, 2009; Zwaigenbaum et al., 2005) populations. Temperament is a biologically grounded series of emotional, attentional, and regulatory processes or traits that influence how an individual responds to his or her environment (Goldsmith et al., 1987; Goldsmith & Lemery, 2000; Rothbart & Derryberry, 1981). Temperament contains both reactive and self-regulatory dimensions that influence behavioral and physiological excitability and arousal modulation (Rothbart, Ahadi, & Evans, 2000; Rothbart and Derryberry, 1981). Although temperament is considered the basis of behavioral regulation during infancy and early childhood, temperament becomes the foundation of more complex personality development during middle and late childhood (Rothbart & Ahadi, 1994; Shiner, 1998).

Three empirically supported domains of temperament include extraversion, negative affectivity (neuroticism), and effortful control (Rothbart, Bates, & Damon, 1998). Although considerable research has been devoted to understanding relationships among early temperament traits and childhood and adult outcomes (e.g., Feldman, 2010; Pitzer, Jennen-Steinmetz, Esser, Schmidt, & Laucht, 2011; Schmidt, Miskovic, Boyle, & Saigal, 2008), traits associated with negative affect have received particular attention in their capacity to predict later problem behaviors (e.g., Grant, Bagnell, Chambers, & Stewart, 2009; Leve, Kim, & Pears, 2005). Negative affect includes subconstructs of sadness, anger, discomfort, low soothability, fear, and approach (Putnam, Rothbart, & Garstein, 2008). Although negative affect can constitute an appropriate response to environmental demands, dysregulated over- or underexpression of negative affect is associated with externalizing and internalizing disorders, respectively (Chaplin & Cole, 2005).

A number of studies have prospectively associated components of infant negative affectivity, particularly fear and low soothability, with later anxiety outcomes. Gartstein et al. (2010) found that both initial levels of infant fear at 4 months as well as increases in infant fearfulness across the first year of life predicted anxiety symptoms in typically developing toddlers. Mount, Crockenberg, Barrig Jo, and Wagar (2010) demonstrated that behavioral inhibition, which they measured by compiling measures of fear and shyness, significantly relates to concurrent anxious and withdrawn problem behaviors in 2.5-year-old typically developing children. Using a large, nationally representative sample, Grant et al. (2009) found that fussiness and unadaptability at ages 2—3 years prospectively predicted anxiety in later childhood, although effects diminished after age 10 years.

Whereas fear and low soothability are closely associated with anxiety outcomes, other negative affect components are less closely associated with anxiety specifically. For example, uncontrollability that results in sadness in childhood may predispose children to approach future difficulties with sadness, thus increasing vulnerability for depression (Blumberg & Izard, 1985). Elevated anger is strongly correlated with externalizing problems in preschool and school-age children (e.g., Cole, Zahnwaxler, & Smith, 1994; Eisenberg et al., 2001; Zeman, Shipman, & Suveg, 2002), and longitudinal studies endorse elevated anger as a risk factor for later problem behaviors (e.g., Bates, Dodge, Pettit, & Ridge, 1998; Eisenberg et al., 1997). Thus although negative affect predicts problematic outcomes in general, fear and soothability are the negative affect subcomponents most relevant to anxiety-specific risk.

2.1.1 Negative Affect in Fragile X Syndrome

Several studies have examined temperamental profiles of children with FXS, although no single temperament profile has been established. Parent reports of temperament in young boys with FXS generally report stable, atypical elevations in activity, as well as lower levels of intensity, approachability, adaptability, and persistence (Hatton, Bailey, Hargett-Beck, Skinner, & Clark, 1999). Compared to children with developmental delay, young children with FXS have been rated by parents as exhibiting higher avoidance behavior, lower withdrawal behavior, and higher positive mood, although groups did not differ in attention, difficulty with change, irritability, somatic complaints, or anxiety and depression (Kau, Reider, Payne, Meyer, & Freund, 2000). Relative to males with autism, males with FXS are rated as less distractible, more rhythmic, and more intense (Bailey, Hatton, Mesibov, Ament, & Skinner, 2000). In this study, children with autism were also described as requiring a higher threshold for response than controls. Thus at a group level, individuals with FXS exhibit different parent-reported temperament profiles than typically developing children and those with ASD, with some components overexpressed (e.g., avoidance, activity level) and other components underexpressed (intensity, adaptability, persistence, distractability), depending on the reference group. Importantly, children with FXS also exhibit variability in temperament profiles across individuals, laying the foundation for individual differences in later personality and behavioral features.

To this end, several studies have examined temperament in FXS in relation to behavioral profiles. For example, Shanahan, Roberts, Hatton, Reznick, and Goldsmith (2008) compared parent-reported measures of temperament to experimentally elicited frustration behaviors in 3-year-old boys with FXS (n = 25) and a large group of same-age typically developing boys (n = 64). Parents rated children with FXS as exhibiting lower levels of sadness and anger than controls. During an experimental arm restraint paradigm designed to elicit frustration, groups did not differ in levels of total struggle, facial anger, or distress vocalizations. However, children with FXS showed less facial sadness by the end of the frustration task, whereas the non-FXS showed increased facial sadness. Parent-reported sadness was negatively correlated with autistic symptoms within the FXS groups, although no relationship emerged between autism and parent-reported anger. Despite the authors' expectation that elevated problem behaviors in FXS would be reflected by higher reactivity during early childhood, the FXS group showed lower negative reactivity than controls.

Together, these studies indicate that children with FXS show lower levels of adaptability (Bailey et al., 2000; Hatton et al., 1999; Roberts, Weisenfeld, et al., 2006), sadness (Shanahan et al., 2008), and anger (Shanahan et al., 2008), as well as higher levels of avoidance (Kau et al., 2000) and withdrawal (Bailey et al., 2000) compared to controls. Patterns of temperament appear to be stable between ages three and six in FXS (Shanahan et al., 2008). Thus although some components of negative affect, such as sadness and anger, are not generally elevated in FXS, children with FXS exhibit stable, elevated patterns of avoidance and withdrawal from an early age, which may predispose them to anxiety disorders in later childhood. A next step of this work, which we have begun to address in our prospective studies of anxiety emergence in FXS included in this review (Tonnsen, Cornish, Wheeler, & Roberts, 2014; Tonnsen, Malone, Hatton, & Roberts, 2013; Tonnsen, Shinkareva, et al., 2013), is to determine whether variability of negative affect among children with FXS may index anxiety risk in this population. In other words, given the variability observed across constructs (e.g., elevated withdrawal, reduced anger) and individuals with FXS, can specific negative affect profiles index later anxiety risk within FXS?

2.2 Behavioral Inhibition and Withdrawal

Behavioral inhibition is described as a tendency to respond to novel situations with restraint, shy, or timid responses (Hirshfeld et al., 1992; Kagan, Reznick, Clarke, Snidman, & Garcia-Coll, 1984; Kagan, Reznick, & Snidman, 1988). Although increases in inhibited, shy responses are typical during certain developmental periods, such as the onset of "stranger fear" in infancy, extreme inhibition is associated with greater risk for internalizing symptoms in later development (Hirshfeld et al., 1992), with behaviorally inhibited children exhibiting greater than seven times risk for social anxiety disorder relative to uninhibited peers (Clauss & Blackford, 2012). Behavioral inhibition is well-studied in non-FXS populations, with emergent findings in FXS suggesting atypical profiles that may index early emergent anxiety risk in this population.

One of the most well-studied presentations of behavioral inhibition is stranger fear, defined as the tendency to become inhibited when presented with a novel social partner. Stranger fear typically emerges by 6 months of age, then exhibits two periods of increased intensity, the first from 6 to 12 months of age and the second as children approach the preschool age period (Brooker et al., 2013; Gartstein et al., 2010). Although "typical" stranger fear patterns vary across individuals, approximately 76% of children exhibit relatively low levels of fear at 6 months that increase steadily over time (Brooker et al., 2013). This developmental enhancement of the stranger response is considered adaptive, both reflecting the enhanced selectivity of the infants' attachment to trusted social partners, as well as limiting potential safety issues associated with infants' environmental curiosity (Brooker et al., 2013).

Whereas some developmental changes in behavioral inhibition are adaptive and typical, extreme stranger fear has been linked to maladaptive outcomes such as social anxiety (Biederman et al., 1993, 2001; Clauss & Blackford, 2012; Hirshfeld et al., 1992; Rapee, 2014), presenting an atypical extreme of an otherwise normative process. Although sharp increases in behavioral inhibition during infancy are associated with anxiety outcomes (Gartstein et al., 2010), several studies suggest that children with stable, high levels of inhibition are at greatest risk for anxiety outcomes, moreso than children whose behavioral inhibition fluctuates over time (Brooker et al., 2013; Chronis-Tuscano et al., 2009; Hirshfeld et al., 1992). For example, Brooker et al. (2013) identified a minority of children whom exhibited high rates of fear at 6 months that remained stable (12%; "chronic high fear") or decreased (12%) from 6 to 36 months, relative to typical patterns of low fear that increased with time. Chronic high fear was associated with the greatest behavioral inhibition and parasympathetic dysregulation at 36 months. In a prospective study of children followed from infancy through adolescence, stable parent-reported behavioral inhibition from ages 14 months to 7 years was associated with over 3.5 times higher odds for a lifetime diagnosis of social anxiety disorder by the teenage years (Chronis-Tuscano et al., 2009). Thus across various aged cohorts, elevations in behavioral inhibition, particularly when persistent over time, are associated with the greatest risk for later socially anxious behaviors. Chronically high levels of fear are also highly heritable (Brooker et al., 2013), suggesting some children predisposed to social anxiety may exhibit identifiable risk factors early in development.

2.2.1 Behavioral Inhibition in Fragile X Syndrome

A number of studies in FXS have examined facets of behavioral inhibition, most typically measured through responses to novel situations, and suggest abnormal approach behaviors that may both correlate with and precede anxiety symptoms. During experimental social situations, children with FXS exhibit a number of atypical behavioral features including abnormal eye contact, facial expression, vocal quality, and behavioral movements. For example, children with FXS display less approaching eye contact, behavioral movements, and facial expressions relevant to non-FXS controls upon meeting a novel examiner (Roberts et al., 2007; Roberts, Clarke, et al., 2009), although behaviors tend to improve as familiarity increases (Hall, Lightbody, Huffman, Lazzeroni, & Reiss, 2009; Roberts et al., 2007). Compared to their unaffected siblings, children with FXS also exhibit greater gaze aversion, behavioral distress, atypical vocal qualities, and task avoidance during a social challenge tasks (Hall et al., 2009; Hessl, Glaser, Dyer-Friedman, & Reiss, 2006). Among individuals with FXS, increased inhibition (Hessl et al., 2001) and autistic behaviors (Hatton et al., 2006) have been associated with reduced levels of FMRP, suggesting inhibited behaviors may be directly linked to the degree of gene dysfunction. Importantly, reduced social gaze appears to be more atypical in FXS than in individuals with other developmental disabilities, suggesting relatively specific impairments in FXS (Cohen et al., 1988; Hall et al., 2015; Murphy, Abbeduto, Schroeder, & Serlin, 2007). These behaviors also appear to emerge quite early, with abnormal increases in facial fear reported in 12- to 58-month-old children with FXS during stranger approach paradigms (Tonnsen, Shinkareva, et al., 2013). Thus, behavioral approach in FXS appears to represent a pervasive and early emerging component of the phenotype, although few studies have addressed when and how abnormal approach emerges in early childhood (Tonnsen, Shinkareva, et al., 2013; Tonnsen et al., under review) or the predictive utility of behavioral approach in identifying children most at risk for anxiety in later development.

When considering behavioral approach features in FXS, it is also important to consider additional comorbidities such as autism. Autism features are highly prevalent in FXS, with 25–60% of children with FXS meeting autism diagnostic criteria and up to 90% displaying elevated autism symptoms (Farzin et al., 2006; Kaufmann et al., 2004; Rogers, Wehner, Hagerman, & Wehner, 2001). Several studies have suggested that comorbid autism symptoms may impact atypical behavioral approach patterns in FXS. For example, whereas children with FXS and low levels of autism symptoms generally "warm up" during the context of an assessment, those with high levels of autism symptoms maintain low approach behaviors across sustained social interactions (Roberts et al., 2007). These experimental findings are consistent with reports that children with FXS and high autism symptoms receive elevated parent-reported ratings on items tapping social avoidance and withdrawal (Budimirovic et al., 2006) and exhibit particular challenges with peer relationships and adaptive socialization (Budimirovic et al., 2006; Hernandez et al., 2009). However, within FXS, abnormal social gaze persists in the absence of high autism symptoms and does not appear to be driven by comorbid diagnoses (Cohen, Vietze, Sudhalter, Jenkins, & Brown, 1991; Hall et al., 2015). Thus, it is possible that comorbid autism features compound social difficulties already core to the FXS phenotype, although high rates of autism features alone do not explain the atypical approach behaviors observed in FXS.

2.3 Autonomic Functioning

Both anxiety and behavioral inhibition are associated with abnormal autonomic activity across sympathetic and parasympathetic domains. Whereas the sympathetic system increases arousal in response to environmental demands, parasympathetic activity enables the system to recover. In relation to anxiety, Friedman (2007, p. 186) describes dysfunction in these systems as a "sticky accelerator" (sympathetic) versus a "bad brake" (parasympathetic). Indeed, abnormal autonomic activity across both systems has been associated with anxiety and presents atypically in FXS.

The predominant models for explaining associations between autonomic functioning and anxiety have evolved in recent years. Initial work described autonomic dysfunction in anxiety as difficulty maintaining physiological homeostasis due to overactive sympathetic functioning (Cannon, 1939). Indeed, higher sympathetic reactivity is associated with a number of physiological responses, including elevated heart rate, reduced heart rate variability, pupillary dilation, and increased norepinephrine (Kagan et al., 1988). These physiological changes may manifest physically through symptoms commonly associated with panic (e.g., sweating, heart palpitations, shaking), as well as through cognitive processes such as worry (Friedman & Thayer, 1998; Thayer et al., 1996). However, studies specifically linking anxiety disorders to sympathetic functioning have produced mixed results. In a number of studies, children who are more behaviorally inhibited exhibit faster heart rate during laboratory tasks (Garcia-Coll, Kagan, & Reznick, 1984; Kagan et al., 1984). Other studies report no association between sympathetic factors and either behavioral inhibition (Asendorpf & Meier, 1993; Calkins & Fox, 1992) or social anxiety (Mauss, Wilhelm, & Gross, 2003). In models of anxiety emergence in young children, it has been suggested that although behavioral inhibition and heart rate are not universally correlated, faster heart rate may predict the stability of behavioral inhibition over time (Marshall & Stevenson-Hinde, 1998). Thus although hyperarousal is theoretically and empirically associated with anxiety, the association is often complex and likely varies across situational and developmental factors.

Increased sympathetic functioning has also received empirical attention due to long-term psychosocial and health risks associated with chronic hyperarousal. This phenomenon is often described as increased allostatic load (Mcewen & Stellar, 1993), or "wear and tear" resulting from chronic use or nonuse of physiological systems associated with acute adaptation to environmental challenges (McEwen, 1998). Specifically, repeated activation of the integrated systems involved in stress response, including cardiovascular, metabolic, immune, and neurological systems, results in compromised capacity to adaptively respond to acute challenges (McEwen, 1998). Negative health outcomes associated with allostatic load include hypertension, obesity, inflammatory and autoimmune disorders, immunosuppression, diabetes, potential for stroke, and death of nerve cells (see McEwen, 1998, for review). For example, constant elevated levels of glucocorticoids may compromise long-term functions such as learning and memory to permit acute stress response through hippocampal damage (Kirschbaum, Wolf, May, Wippich, & Hellhammer, 1996; Mcewen & Sapolsky, 1995). Thus, maintaining high levels of arousal associated with chronic anxiety may pose both acute and long-term risks, which may be particularly debilitating to children during key periods of early development (Duke, 2008).

In contrast to initial anxiety-arousal models that nearly exclusively focused on sympathetic functioning, more recent frameworks emphasize parasympathetic functioning as critical to conceptualizing and measuring anxiety-related arousal. For example, Friedman (2007) popularized the theory that anxiety emerges through compromised autonomic flexibility and neurovisceral integration. Whereas initial models focused on sympathetic overreactivity, Friedman's model, which builds on previous work by Porges (1995a), hinges on poorer response inhibition as a mechanism for anxiety. Indeed, failure to inhibit fear and defensiveness is central to clinical models and a criterion for anxiety, as in the case of chronic worry in generalized anxiety (Thayer & Friedman, 2002). Thus Friedman's model proposes that the association between anxiety and autonomic functioning manifests through individuals' difficulty in flexibly modulating autonomic responses, rather than purely sympathetic overreactivity.

Parasympathetic functioning is regulated by the vagus (cranial nerve X), which influences autonomic functioning through the heart's sinoatrial node (see Porges, 1995a, for review). High vagal tone operates on this node as a "brake," inhibiting or slowing heart rate. When vagal tone relaxes and lowers, this break is lifted, reducing inhibition and permitting acceleration of heart rate. Modulating the vagal brake is important to both mobilizing physiological resources during states of acute stress and promoting restoration in the absence of threat. Notably, both cardiac and facial muscles are regulated by fibers that originate from the same nucleus within the vagus. Thus, vagal health affects both effective modulation of heart activity, as well as more complex behaviors such as facial expression and vocalizations. Because the vagus facilitates communication between the brain and a wide number of visceral processes implicated in neurodevelopmental disorders such as autism (e.g., digestion, metabolic functioning, cardiovascular activity, temperature regulation), polyvagal theory has received increased attention as an explanatory framework for the neurobiology of social approach symptoms in neurodevelopmental disorders (Bal et al., 2010; Klusek, Roberts, & Losh, 2015; Quintana, Guastella, Outhred, Hickie, & Kemp, 2012).

Vagal tone is commonly estimated using respiratory sinus arrhythmia (RSA) (Porges, 1995a, 1995b, 2004), an index of cardiac activity associated with respiration. Modulating RSA during periods of stress is generally viewed as an adaptive mechanism to support the body's recovery from increased heart rate. A number of studies have quantified individual differences in RSA in relation to behavioral inhibition and anxiety. In young children, higher RSA is often associated with greater concurrent behavioral reactivity during stressful events (Calkins & Fox, 1992; Fox, 1989; Hastings et al., 2008; Stifter & Fox, 1990), with some studies suggesting positive consequences of high RSA later in development (Fox, 1989; Porges, Doussard Roosevelt, Lourdes Portales, & Suess, 1994). For example, infants with higher vagal tone at 5 months are more likely to react to a mild stressor yet also display stronger self-regulation skills, as measured by social references and vocalizations (Fox, 1989). These same infants exhibit greater social approach and are less likely to remain near their mothers during novel situations at age 14 months, although other prospective studies have failed to predict behavioral inhibition from infant RSA (Calkins & Fox, 1992). Given these associations, it has proposed that higher vagal tone in early infancy contributes to the developmental maturation of cortical inhibitory circuits and greater ability to modulate reactivity effectively (Fox, 1989; Porges, 1976). Indeed, a number of studies report associations between poorer RSA modulation and pediatric anxiety disorders (Henje Blom, Olsson, Serlachius, Ericson, & Ingvar, 2010; Monk et al., 2001; Sharma, Balhara, Sagar, Deepak, & Mehta, 2011). Thus, higher RSA in infancy may set the tone for greater behavioral and physiological regulation in later life, reducing risk for clinical anxiety.

2.3.1 Autonomic Functioning in Fragile X Syndrome

Abnormal autonomic functioning is well documented in FXS and has been the subject of recent review (Klusek et al., 2015). In general, children and adults with FXS exhibit hyperarousal, as reflected in faster heart rate (Hall et al., 2009; Heilman, Harden, Zageris, Berry-Kravis, & Porges, 2011; Klusek, Martin, & Losh, 2013; Roberts, Boccia, Bailey, Hatton, & Skinner, 2001; Roberts, Tonnsen, Robinson, & Shinkareva, 2012; Tonnsen, Shinkareva, et al., 2013) and lower vagal tone (Hall et al., 2009; Heilman et al., 2011; Roberts et al., 2001; Roberts, Boccia, Hatton, Skinner, & Sideris, 2006; Roberts et al.,2012; Tonnsen, Shinkareva, et al., 2013).

Although patterns are relatively consistent in children and adults, emerging evidence suggests that patterns of heart activity in infants with FXS may undergo age-related shifts, with relative hypoarousal in younger participants that changes to hyperarousal in early toddlerhood (Roberts et al., 2012). Thus autonomic functioning in FXS may not present linearly across development, particularly in young children.

Most findings suggest that hyperarousal in FXS is a chronic state, rather than task-dependent, across both cognitive tasks (Boccia & Roberts, 2000; Heilman et al., 2011) and social stressors (Hall et al., 2009; Klusek et al., 2013; Tonnsen, Shinkareva, et al., 2013). Similarly, vagal responses in FXS are similar to non-FXS samples during social stress tasks (Hall et al., 2009; Klusek et al., 2013; Tonnsen, Shinkareva, et al., 2013). However, vagal tone suppression during cognitive stressors does appear to vary in FXS, with males with FXS displaying less vagal suppression (Boccia & Roberts, 2000; Roberts et al., 2001; Roberts, Boccia, et al., 2006), and in one instance increased vagal tone (Heilman et al., 2011), during cognitive challenges than non-FXS peers. Paired with evidence of chronic hyperarousal in FXS, these findings have led to the hypothesis that social stressors exert similar influence on arousal in FXS as in non-FXS groups, although "baseline" arousal is higher in FXS.

2.4 Attention

In addition to autonomic functioning, other components of self-regulation, such as attention, have been implicated in anxiety emergence. Indeed, Barlow's model describes attention as a core cognitive component in the etiology of anxiety. A number of theories have been proposed to explain this association, particularly as related to attention toward threat. For example, Williams et al. (1988) proposed that individuals high in anxiety exhibit increased sensitivity to threat-related stimuli during early stages of stimuli processing. Others have proposed that anxiety is related to poor modulation of attention to threat during later stages of stimulus processing. In support of this theory, individuals high in anxiety exhibit difficulty disengaging from threatening stimuli, as opposed to exhibiting increased likelihood to initially detect the threatening stimuli (Fox, Russo, Bowles, & Dutton, 2007; Fox, Russo, & Dutton, 2002). More recent comprehensive meta-analytic findings support evidence from both perspectives, with greater anxiety associated with threat perception across preattentive, attentional, and postattentive phases across 172 studies (Bar-Haim, Lamy, Pergamin, Bakermans-Kranenburg, & van IJzendoorn, 2007). In addition, attention to threat changes as a function of treatment, suggesting attentional biases are malleable and may offer a promising indicator of treatment efficacy (Lundh & Öst, 2001; Mathews, Mogg, Kentish, & Eysenck, 1995; Mattia, Heimberg, & Hope, 1993). Thus although the specific mechanisms for threat-related attentional biases in anxiety are likely complex and multifaceted, attention to threat is a consistent correlate of anxiety and may offer a useful marker for targeted treatment.

2.4.1 Attention in Fragile X Syndrome

Although cognitive paradigms traditionally used to study attention to threat have not been applied in FXS, atypical social attention is commonly reported across behavioral and neurophysiological studies. Relative to developmentally matched controls, adolescents and adults with FXS exhibit reduced social gaze, as measured by time spent looking toward a face during naturalistic social interactions (Hall et al., 2015). At the neural level, individuals with FXS also display reduced habituation to face and eye gaze stimuli, with particularly reduced habituation among females with lower levels of FMRP (Bruno, Garrett, Quintin, Mazaika, & Reiss, 2014). Higher anxiety symptoms in preschoolers with FXS are also predicted by increasing approach-related temperament across infancy and toddlerhood, potentially suggesting anxiety in FXS relates to difficulties modulating environmental engagement (Tonnsen, Malone, et al., 2013).

Although these studies loosely suggest vulnerability for atypical threat-related attention in FXS, additional work is needed to establish whether attentional biases and responses in FXS parallel those in the non-FXS literature. Indeed, it has been suggested that targeting attention to threat to reduce or prevent anxiety may be more efficacious in children than traditional cognitive behavioral treatments, in part due to children's limited ability to discuss cognitions with therapists (Fox & Pine, 2012). Thus examining attention to threat in FXS may facilitate stronger conceptualization of anxiety symptoms, as well as provide new windows for anxiety measurement that is not contingent on self-expressed symptoms.

Neuroimaging studies, particularly those related to the amygdala, have provided evidence of atypical processing of social and threat-related stimuli in FXS at the neural level. Structure and function of the amygdala have received particular attention due to the amygdala's role in fear response, emotional regulation, and threat appraisal. Amygdala size is generally reduced in young children FXS (Hazlett et al., 2009, 2012; Hoeft et al., 2011), potentially indicating delayed development of emotional regulation and fear processing networks in the brain that are particularly evident during early childhood. The amygdala and anterior cingulate have also been described as less interactive in FXS network connectivity studies (Bruno et al., 2016). In addition, a number of studies have also demonstrated hypo-activity of the amygdala response in FXS. For example, attenuated amygdala responses have been observed toward fearful faces using during both func-tional MRI (Kim et al., 2012) and emotion-potentiated startle tasks (Ballin-ger, Cordeiro, Chavez, Hagerman, & Hessl, 2014), with similar findings observed in males with the *FMR*1 premutation (Hessl et al., 2007, 2011). Adolescents with FXS have also exhibited increased amygdala sensitization to direct gaze, deviating from typical patterns of desensitization (Watson, Hoeft, Garrett, Hall, & Reiss, 2008). These studies have led to the sugges-tion that amygdala hyporeactivity may contribute to the anxious phenotypic features in FXS (Ballinger et al., 2014).

Further supporting the relevance of the amygdala in anxiety expression in FXS, several studies have linked amygdala structure and function to specific dose—response characteristics of *FMR*1 mutations. FMRP, the pri-mary protein depleted in FXS, is highly expressed in the amygdala and is responsible for maintaining healthy synaptic functioning. Activation ratio, the proportion of cells unaffected by FXS, is positively associated with fear-related activation of the amygdala and anterior cingulate in FXS (Kim et al., 2012). Among *FMR*1 premutation carriers, elevated mRNA and reduced FMRP are associated with amygdala hypoactivation, with FMRP accounting for greater variance in multiple regression models (Hessl et al., 2011). Nonlinear, inverse associations between amygdala volume and CGG repeat length have been suggested in individuals with lower repeats (CGG$\geq$55 and <85) only, with no associations between amygdala volume and repeat length in those with high premutation repeat lengths ($\geq$85) (Selmeczy et al., 2011). Together, these studies support numerous biological mechanisms linking amygdala-related behavioral responses to *FMR*1 gene function.

At a more basic level, FXS is also associated with pervasive attention ori-enting difficulties that may contribute to anxiety emergence by restricting social experiences of affected individuals. A number of studies have reported atypical attention orienting in individuals with FXS across the lifespan, with longer latencies to disengage attention from visual stimuli reported among infants (Roberts, Hatton, Long, Anello, & Colombo, 2011; Tonnsen et al., under review), school-aged individuals (Lasker, Mazzocco, & Zee, 2007), and young adults (Lasker et al., 2007). Indeed, flexible orienting of attention is a core component of self-regulation and, when impaired, compromises an individual's ability to effectively interact with his or her environment. In typical development, the capacity to disengage attention emerges and improves across ages 2—6 months (Frick, Colombo, & Saxon, 1999) and continues to develop until preadolescence or later (Wainwright & Bryson, 2002). As early as 7 months of age, attentional disengagement intersects with threat appraisal, with typically developing infants demonstrating reduced disengagement from threatening faces versus other face and nonface stimuli (Peltola, Leppänen, Palokangas, & Hietanen, 2008). Given deficits in orienting and other attentional processes emerge in infancy in FXS, it has been suggested that attention impairments in early childhood "constrain" later developmental trajectories (Cornish, Cole, Longhi, Karmiloff-Smith, & Scerif, 2012), increasing risk for maladaptive outcomes such as anxiety (Tonnsen, Shinkareva, et al., 2013) and autism (Roberts et al., 2011). However, the explicit association between attention disengagement and anxiety has not been evaluated in developmental studies of young children with FXS.

2.5 Maternal and Familial Factors

The family environment provides a rich, multidirectional context for child development, including the emergence of behavioral problems such as anxiety. A number of studies have associated maternal anxiety with behavioral inhibition and anxiety in children (Aktar, Majdandžić, de Vente, & Bögels, 2013; Brooker et al., 2013; Hirshfeld et al., 1992; Hudson & Dodd, 2012). Indeed, children of parents with anxiety are over two times more likely to also develop anxiety, relative to children of nonanxious parents (McClure, Brennan, Hammen, & Le Brocque, 2001), with one study reporting 33% of children of anxious parents exhibiting anxiety compared to 9% of children of nonanxious parents (Beidel & Turner, 1997). Similarly, 35% of first-degree relatives of children with anxiety disorders also exhibit anxiety disorders, compared to 16% of relatives of children with no history of psychopathology (Last, Hersen, Kazdin, Orvaschel, & Perrin, 1991). These complex associations are best characterized through a multidimensional, interactive lens of biological and environmental factors.

It is widely accepted that anxiety disorders tend to aggregate in families. Twin studies suggest the majority of familial anxiety risk is genetic rather than environmental, with heritability estimates ranging from 30% to 80% across different anxiety disorders (Bolton et al., 2006; Hettema, Neale, & Kendler, 2001). Similarly, the heritability of behavioral inhibition in toddlers is quite high, with estimates ranging from 30% to 70% across various behavioral inhibition tasks and measures (Dilalla, Kagan, & Reznick, 1994; Robinson, Kagan, Reznick, & Corley, 1992). Although these estimates reflect strong genetic contributions to anxiety risk, much of the variance remains unexplained by genetics, thus considering individual environment remains critical to conceptualizing risk. Features of the family environment are also consistently linked to anxiety and behavioral inhibition in young children, with the majority of studies focused on qualities of mother—child interactions and social bonds. In particular, higher parental control—the parent-initiated pressures for children to respond in specific ways—is strongly associated with child anxiety (Van der Bruggen, Stams, & Bögels, 2008). Whereas general parenting strategies are more loosely related to anxiety, parental control is estimated to account for up to 18% of child anxiety variance in meta-analyses (McLeod, Weisz, & Wood, 2007), supporting parental control as a potential moderator of risk trajectories within the family system. Although a number of other parenting behaviors, such as maternal warmth and positivity, have been associated with child anxiety (Hudson & Rapee, 2001; Moore, Whaley, & Sigman, 2004), these types of behaviors, when aggregated across studies, only account for approximately 4% of variance in child anxiety symptoms (McLeod et al., 2007). Thus within the context of parenting, aspects of control appear to be the strongest candidate for interventions targeting child anxiety emergence.

In addition to parenting behaviors directed toward the child, inadvertent modeling of anxious behaviors has also been posited as a mechanism for transmission of anxiety symptoms across generations (Fisak & Grills-Taquechel, 2007). For example, parents may display anxious behaviors or discuss anxiety around children, increasing likelihood that children will display similar tendencies through observational learning. A number of studies lend support to this framework (De Rosnay, Cooper, Tsigaras, & Murray, 2006; Gerull & Rapee, 2002; Muris, Steerneman, Merckelbach, & Meesters, 1996). For example, as early as toddlerhood, children respond with greater fear and avoidance to unpleasant stimuli (e.g., rubber snake and spider) when the stimuli are paired with images of their mothers exhibiting negative facial expression, relative to when the facial expression is neutral (Gerull & Rapee, 2002). Similarly, when mothers are trained to interact with a stranger in either a socially anxious or neutral manner, 12- to 14-month-oldinfants model their mothers' behaviors in their own interaction with the stranger, with children of anxious-acting mothers responding with greater fear and avoidance (De Rosnay et al., 2006).

Thus as early as infancy, children appear sensitive to the anxious reactions of their parents and may begin to model these behaviors, potentially intensifying their own symptom profiles over time.

2.5.1 Maternal and Familial Factors in Fragile X Syndrome

Families affected by fragile X syndrome exhibit a number of vulnerabilities that are particularly relevant to anxiety emergence in young children. Mothers of children with FXS are often carriers of the *FMR1* premutation, which is characterized by an expansion of 55–200 CGG repeats on the promotor region of the *FMR1* gene. Whereas FXS results from reduced production of mRNA that results in reduced or absent FMRP, the premutation is associated with increased levels of mRNA, which toxically affects cells. It was previously assumed that premutation "carriers" were unaffected by *FMR1* mutations, although it is now well established that a subset exhibit increased risk for a variety of health outcomes, including premature ovarian insufficiency (Allingham-Hawkins et al., 1999), fragile X-associated tremor/ataxia syndrome (FXTAS) (Hagerman et al., 2004; Jacquemont & Hagerman, 2004), and subtle deficits in executive function (Cornish et al., 2008; Kraan et al., 2013) and mathematic reasoning (Lachiewicz, Dawson, Spiridigliozzi, & McConkie-Rosell, 2006).

Importantly, a number of studies converge in reporting high levels of mood and anxiety disorders among women with the *FMR1* premutation (Boyle & Kaufmann, 2010; Kenna et al., 2013; Roberts, Bailey, et al., 2009; Roberts, Tonnsen, McCary, Long, & Bailey, n.d.), warranting further attention as to potential associations between maternal and child anxiety in families affected by *FMR1* mutations. This increase in premutation-associated internalizing symptoms appears to emerge early in development. For example, in a preliminary report of 5- to 23-year-old children, 71% of premutation carriers meeting criteria for at least one anxiety disorder relative to 23% of controls and 10% rates reported in the general population (Cordeiro, Abucayan, Hagerman, Tassone, & Hessl, 2015). Consistent with these findings, studies of premutation carrier mothers suggest the onset of mood and anxiety disorders often precedes the birth of a child with FXS (Roberts, Bailey, et al., 2009). Thus, risk for anxiety in premutation carriers emerges prior to adulthood and independent of environmental triggers related to parenting a child with a disability.

In addition to physical and mental health risks, a subset of premutation carriers report reductions in various quality of life indicators. Although the majority of premutation carriers report positive adaptation to challenges associated with FXS, over half report clinically significant symptoms in at least one domain of risk, most commonly related to high stress (Bailey, Sideris, et al., 2008). Elevated parenting stress is one of the most robust risks in families affected by FMR1 mutation, with 30–50% of mothers of children with FXS self-reporting clinical levels of impairment (Bailey, Sideris, et al., 2008; Wheeler, Hatton, Reichardt, & Bailey, 2007). Premutation carriers in particular may be at particular risk for stress, given multigenerational effects that FMR1 mutations project onto the family system. For example, a premutation carrier mother may be caretaking for a child with FXS, supporting aging parents with FXTAS, experiencing hormonal changes associated with premature ovarian insufficiency, and experiencing elevated baseline symptoms of anxiety and depression. Although the independent effects of many of these constructs have not been examined in relation to parent–child interactions, emerging work related to parenting stress supports the notion that maternal factors directly relate to child behaviors within the family system. Indeed, parenting stress is also associated with greater problem behaviors, particularly those related to social relatedness and self-regulation, among families affected by neurodevelopmental disorders (Davis & Carter, 2008; Wheeler et al., 2007). Within FXS, parenting stress has been directly associated with features of mother–child interactions, with higher levels of stress predicting fewer parent–child interactions in experimental studies (Wheeler et al., 2007). Thus elevated stress may further tax a vulnerable system, increasing risk for maladaptive outcomes.

3. CONSTRUCTING A MODEL OF PRODROMAL ANXIETY IN FRAGILE X SYNDROME

Building on previous literature in both non-FXS and FXS samples, we have begun to build a model of prodromal anxiety emergence in young children with FXS. Characterizing the emergence of anxiety in young children with FXS offers two primary benefits. First, it is possible that if anxiety is a trigger for debilitating symptoms such as aggression and repetitive behaviors, preventing anxiety in FXS may not only enhance the child's engagement in his or her learning environment, but also reduce downstream impairments that limit daily functioning. Second, given the known genetic pathway of FXS, characterizing early multifaceted contributors of anxiety emergence may inform models of anxiety emergence in cases with

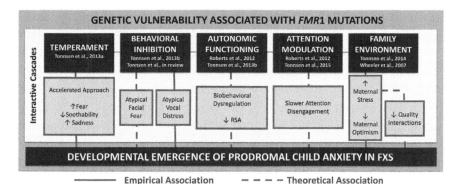

Figure 1 Potential anxiety moderators and current supporting evidence in infants and toddlers with fragile X syndrome.

and without neurogenetic conditions, informing broader public health efforts to develop more effective targeted interventions aimed to curb risk trajectories.

To this end, we recently produced a series of studies examining multifaceted predictors of anxiety in young males with FXS. In contrast to previous studies that examined correlational features associated with anxiety in cross-sectional samples of older children, this work has focused on predicting risk factors for anxiety symptoms as they emerge in infants and toddlers. Examining longitudinal patterns of risk is consistent with modern conceptualization of neurodevelopmental disorders as phenotypes that emerge through complex, multifaceted developmental interactions, rather than as static end products of linear, modular deficits (Cornish, Scerif, & Karmiloff-Smith, 2007; Karmiloff-Smith, 1998, 2009). Thus, we have examined longitudinal emergence of anxiety features in FXS by integrating multiple methods, including parent reported temperament, familial risk factors, and biobehavioral associations. Fig. 1 depicts key components of this work, contextualized in relevant early childhood studies from FXS literature. Here, we review and synthesize this emerging literature, focusing on convergent findings and next steps for research.

3.1 Parent-Reported Temperament

As a first step to characterizing early risk factors for anxiety in FXS, we examined whether early patterns of parent-reported negative affect differentially predicted anxiety, rather than autism features, in young children with FXS (Tonnsen, Malone, et al., 2013). The focus of this work was two-fold. First, we sought to establish whether early negative affect predicted anxiety features in FXS, paralleling previous studies in nonneurogenetic syndrome populations, potentially informing early risk factors and treatment targets for reducing symptomatology. Second, we sought to examine the specificity of this association given previous reports that negative affect is also related to emergent autism in "high-risk" infants (Bryson et al., 2007; Garon et al., 2009; Zwaigenbaum et al., 2005). For example, Garon et al. (2009) found that infants later diagnosed with autism showed low behavioral approach, low positive affect, high negative affect, and low control over behavior and attention, paralleling reports of increased negative affect in infants who later exhibit anxiety (Grant et al., 2009; Leve et al., 2005). Given this overlap in predictive associations and the high occurrence of autism features in FXS (Bailey, Raspa, et al., 2008), establishing the specificity of negative affect to anxiety within FXS was an important first step to modeling pathways of prodromal anxiety risk.

To examine patterns and specificity of negative affect and anxiety associations in FXS, we examined longitudinal patterns of parent-reported negative affect in 25 young males with FXS assessed between ages 8 and 71 months. Using linear mixed effects models, we examined the association between four components of negative affect—fear, anger, sadness, and soothability—and later anxiety and autism features. We measured negative affect using the Rothbart Temperament Scales, a series of parent-reported temperament measures that can be continuously used across infancy and childhood (Putnam et al., 2008) and have been validated in FXS (Roberts, Tonnsen, Robinson, McQuillin, & Hatton, 2014). We measured anxiety symptoms using the DSM-Anxiety subscale of the Child Behavior Checklist 1.5—5 (CBCL; Achenbach, 1991), which includes 10 items consistent with DSM-IV anxiety disorder criteria (Achenbach, Dumenci, & Rescorla, 2003). Autism symptoms were rated by examiners using the Childhood Autism Rating Scale (CARS; Schopler, Reichler, & Renner, 1998). Both the CBCL and CARS were completed after the child's final temperament assessment when the child was between 35 and 72 months old. Thus, we were able to prospectively examine whether early negative affect predicted later anxiety and autism symptoms during the preschool period.

Our results indicated that mean levels of higher fear, lower soothability, and greater sadness predicted anxiety, not autism, in young children with FXS. Additionally, we found that increasing levels of approach over time related to anxiety outcomes. These findings are generally consistent with temperament studies from non-FXS samples suggesting higher negative affect predicts later anxiety outcomes. However, increasing levels of approach behaviors also related to higher anxiety, which initially seemed counterintuitive given atypical patterns of poor approach and high withdrawal characteristic of FXS (Hall et al., 2009; Hessl et al., 2006; Roberts et al., 2007; Roberts, Clarke, et al., 2009). Indeed, the approach subscale of Rothbart's temperament questionnaires measures excitement and anticipation toward pleasurable activities, whereas the fear subscale measures startle, distress, or inhibition in the face of novelty. As such, the fear subscale better taps specific responses to novelty versus pleasure, more closely mapping onto "approach" as commonly described in FXS.

The association between anticipated pleasure and anxiety in FXS provided novel information about syndrome-specific vulnerabilities to anxiety emergence. A coherent interpretation may be that anxiety emergence in FXS is characterized not only by high fear, but also by increased difficulty modulating environmental engagement over time. This work informs prodromal anxiety emergence in FXS by demonstrating both shared patterns of risk (increased fear, lower soothability) and syndrome-specific patterns of risk (increased approach), warranting further study of the specific components of approach that may predict anxiety in FXS and be targeted to prevent anxiety emergence. In addition, this study validated negative affect as a specific marker of anxiety outcomes rather than a more generalized predictor of problem behaviors such as autism in young children with FXS.

3.2 Biobehavioral Characteristics of Approach in Fragile X Syndrome

Building on our findings that elevated negative affect and increased engagement prospectively predicted anxiety in FXS, we next examined biobehavioral predictors of social fear in young children in FXS (Tonnsen, Shinkareva, et al., 2013; Tonnsen et al., under review). Using a classic stranger approach paradigm, this work aimed to tease apart the specific behavioral and physiological responses characteristic of social novelty responses in FXS. In our first stranger approach study, we compared both behavioral indices of fear (facial fear, distress vocalizations, escape behaviors) and physiological arousal during stranger approach in a cross-sectional sample of children with FXS (Tonnsen, Shinkareva, et al., 2013). To contextualize these patterns in early development, we next examined prospective patterns of fear response as related to both anxiety and autism outcomes (Tonnsen et al., under review), paralleling our previous prospective study of parent-reported temperament in FXS (Tonnsen, Malone, et al., 2013).

Together, these studies aimed to inform the specific biobehavioral patterns of experimentally elicited approach in FXS, as well as the developmental emergence and outcomes associated with these patterns.

3.2.1 Cross-Sectional Fear Responses

Results from our cross-sectional study of 12- to 58-month-old children suggested unique age-related patterns of behavioral and physiological fear response in FXS (n = 21) compared to controls (n = 19) (Tonnsen, Shinkareva, et al., 2013). Although the FXS group exhibited similar mean levels of behavioral fear to low-risk controls, facial fear increased with age in FXS relative to age-related decreases in the control group. In addition to displaying different age-related patterns of facial fear, the FXS group generally displayed lower RSA, reflecting poorer readiness to confront task demands. Thus stranger response was characterized by both abnormal facial fear and poorer physiological adaptation, suggesting early emerging abnormalities that intensify with age.

Importantly, we also observed abnormal associations between behavior and heart activity across FXS and control groups. Whereas faster heart rate was exclusively associated with escape behavior in controls, the association between behavior and physiology varied across ages in FXS. Higher distress vocalizations corresponded to faster heart rate in younger participants (<29 months) versus slower heart rate and higher RSA in older participants (>51 and 47 months, respectively). This pattern suggests children with FXS may exhibit age-related shifts in physiological signature of behavioral fear, exhibiting hyperaroused responses in toddlerhood that may gradually become blunted across development. These "shifts" in arousal across early childhood are consistent with our previous work demonstrating age-related changes in heart activity associated with later autism outcomes in FXS (Roberts et al., 2012), in which infant hypoarousal and toddler hyperarousal were each associated with examiner-rated autism symptoms in later development. These studies support the notion that dysregulated autonomic functioning in young children with FXS may produce downstream developmental consequences, particularly as related to behavioral problems. The subtle developmental differences across age groups also speak to the importance of carefully examining age effects and developmental change, rather than assuming constructs are stable across time. Indeed, it appears that neurobiological changes during infancy and toddlerhood may represent pivotal windows of developmental changes that, with further study, may harness clues to the most effective targets and methods for intervention.

3.2.2 Longitudinal Fear Trajectories

Given the cross-sectional age-related differences we observed in our initial study of stranger fear, we next examined longitudinal trajectories of stranger responses in an expanded cohort of children with FXS (n = 46) and controls (n = 33) aged 10–60 months (Tonnsen et al., under review). Similar to our previous study of parent-reported temperament (Tonnsen, Malone, et al., 2013), we examined associations between behavioral fear and anxiety, withdrawal, and autism symptoms using the CBCL and CARS. Results indicated that both FXS and control groups exhibited stable distress vocalizations across development and increased escape behaviors. However, the FXS group also exhibited lower, increasing facial fear compared to decreased facial fear in control participants, paralleling our cross-sectional findings (Tonnsen, Shinkareva, et al., 2013). Thus, similar to our previous study, abnormal approach in FXS was primarily restricted to facial fear, which intensified with age.

We next examined associations between fear trajectories and later anxiety, withdrawal and autism symptoms to determine whether longitudinal approach patterns across infancy and toddlerhood may inform later behavior problems in preschool. Higher autism symptoms were associated with lower overall escape behaviors, whereas higher withdrawal was associated with stable (versus decreasing) levels of distress vocalization over time. The differential associations between fear and both autism and withdrawal outcomes supports our previous findings that components of negative affect differentially predict anxiety versus autism outcomes in FXS (Tonnsen, Malone, et al., 2013). However, this work also highlights the complexity of associations among anxiety, withdrawal, autism, and arousal in FXS; although autism and withdrawal features are associated with differential patterns of social fear, both outcomes are predicted by aspects of early approach behaviors. This work warrants additional study of the potential overlapping and distinct features that predict anxiety, withdrawal, and autism symptoms in FXS, as well as the nuanced facets of approach relevant to each outcome, both to inform early intervention efforts as well as the broader etiological pathways associated with both comorbidities.

3.3 Parent–Child Associations

Given well-established associations between the developmental environment and child anxiety risk, we also sought to explore potential associations between child anxiety emergence and parental risk and resilience. This work is particularly relevant to FXS given the increased vulnerabilities for anxiety and mood disorders (Boyle & Kaufmann, 2010; Kenna et al., 2013; Roberts, Bailey, et al., 2009; Roberts et al., n.d.) and parenting stress (Bailey, Sideris, et al., 2008) associated with the *FMR1* premutation, as well as the likelihood that child problem behaviors may compound or intensify maternal vulnerabilities. Thus, we built on our initial study of negative affect emergence in FXS (Tonnsen, Malone, et al., 2013) to examine associations between child prodromal anxiety and maternal factors, such as parenting stress, mental health, and optimism. Given known associations between genetic markers and maternal well-being in the FMR1 premutation (Roberts, Bailey, et al., 2009; Seltzer, Barker, & Greenberg, 2012), we also examined biomarkers of risk relevant to the *FMR1* premutation, including CGG repeat length, activation ratio, and mRNA.

Throughout this study, our primary aims were to determine whether and how maternal factors relate to child anxiety, child trajectories of negative affect, and longitudinal anxiety—temperament associations. Although we acknowledge that maternal and child factors likely bidirectly influence each other over time, maternal data were drawn from the child's initial assessment, consistent with our focus on associations between maternal risk factors and subsequent child development. The broader goal of this work was to strengthen conceptualization of the broader family factors related to anxiety emergence in high-risk children with FXS, laying the foundation for more effective, targeted, and family-sensitive treatment.

Our results indicated a number of maternal factors were associated with child negative affect and anxiety. In addition to direct associations between higher child anxiety symptoms and both parenting stress and depression, higher mean levels of negative affect across development were associated with greater parenting stress and decreased optimism. Importantly, higher parenting stress was associated with lower activation ratio, the number of cells affected by the *FMR1* premutation, suggesting parenting stress may be sustained, in part, by a stable genetic vulnerability in premutation mothers. Together, these findings suggest that maternal mental health and stress is not only related to child anxiety outcomes in FXS but is also associated with earlier emergent anxiety vulnerabilities in this population, as well as with factors present in the broader family system. Because negative affect is closely associated with anxiety outcomes in FXS, these data suggest that intervening on parenting stress early in development may temper developmental cascades that precede child anxiety outcomes. Given the correlational nature of these findings, the data also underscore the possibility that early detection and treatment of childhood anxiety may reduce maternal risks and impairment, particularly in mothers who exhibit genetic vulnerabilities for stress, as identified in the present study, as well as mood and anxiety disorders (Roberts, Bailey, et al., 2009). Indeed, the genetically mediated vulnerabilities of both children and mothers further support attention toward the syndrome-specific vulnerabilities that affect families across the *FMR1* spectrum of involvement.

4. CONCLUDING THOUGHTS

Anxiety disorders are the most commonly diagnosed pediatric psychiatric disorder (Merikangas et al., 2010); thus identifying precursors and predictors of anxiety constitutes a public health concern. Examining anxiety through the lens of FXS, a single-gene disorder with well-identified biological and phenotypic features, may improve conceptualization of anxiety emergence by identifying patterns of risk in a more homogeneous, higher-risk subgroup than the general population. This work benefits individuals with FXS affected by anxiety by identifying syndrome-specific patterns that may be targeted through behavioral or pharmacological treatment. However, this work also exerts a broader impact by providing a rich, multifaceted context for teasing apart the complex associations between biology, environment, and development that contribute to anxiety risk, potentially improving diagnostic and treatment practices for millions of affected children. Here we reflect on next steps that may pave the way for this translational line of work.

4.1 Focus on Resilience

Previous research and our proposed model also highlight the complexities of anxiety emergence, which likely occurs through multidirectional interactions across multiple units of analyses. Indeed, despite well-established connections between behavioral inhibition and anxiety, the early progression of anxiety is in no way deterministic. Rather, a number of infants who are behaviorally inhibited do not, in fact, go on to develop anxiety disorders. In addressing this issue in relation to behavioral inhibition, Degnan and Fox (2007) emphasize that factors such as attention, parenting, and contextual changes are best framed as moderators capable of promoting resilience. Using this framework, we propose considering "predictors" of anxiety in FXS instead as potential moderators of genetically induced risk. By identifying the strongest moderators of early developmental trajectories in FXS, we can better understand which components of the model are most malleable and suitable for intervention.

4.2 Continue Extending Anxiety Studies to Young Children With Fragile X Syndrome

Together, previous studies from our group and others suggest anxiety is highly common in FXS and may be detectable early in development. As depicted in Fig. 1, a number of studies have begun to characterize prodromal features associated with anxiety in infants and toddlers with FXS, although this work is very much in its infancy. Indeed, few studies have explicitly examined longitudinal precursors of anxiety symptoms in FXS (Tonnsen, Cornish, et al., 2014; Tonnsen, Malone, et al., 2013), despite well-characterized temperamental and approach features evident in older children. Thus, a critical need remains for additional prospective research across a number of domains, particularly autonomic and attentional functioning, to explicitly examine the generalizability of previously established anxiety risk factors to FXS.

4.3 Integrate Sensitive Biobehavioral Markers of Change

At a methodological level, data across multiple studies of FXS and non-FXS samples suggest that experimental measures, administered longitudinally over time, provide highly sensitive markers of change that are particularly relevant to psychopathology risk (Roberts et al., 2011; Tonnsen, Cornish, et al., 2014; Tonnsen, Grefer, et al., 2014; Tonnsen, Malone, et al., 2013). Given challenges associated with identifying suitable and sensitive treatment markers in young children with intellectual disabilities (Berry-Kravis et al., 2013), these studies suggest that experimental tasks may be integrated to better clarify developmental changes over time. For example, further validating standardized experimental batteries and concurrently measured biomarkers appropriate for very young children with FXS, such as stranger approach and social response tasks, may provide opportunities for more fine-grained analyses of developmental changes that are masked by standardized, parent-report measures. In our previous studies integrating both parent-reported and experimental measures of attention in FXS, experimental measures more sensitively detected and indexed developmental changes over time, whereas parent-report measures exhibited greater stability and stagnation (Tonnsen, Grefer, et al., 2014). Thus whenever possible, mapping development across multiple units of analysis will likely produce the greatest sensitivity to developmental variables malleable to change, informing both etiological risk models and treatment efficacy studies.

4.4 Prioritize Longitudinal Studies of Risk and Resilience

Continuing to expand the breadth and depth of longitudinal studies is also critical to continued maturation of our anxiety conceptualization in FXS. Although the benefits of longitudinal surveillance in FXS are broadly endorsed (Cornish et al., 2012; Roberts et al., 2012; Tonnsen, Grefer, et al., 2014; Tonnsen, Malone, et al., 2013), the complex developmental sequences relevant to anxiety emergence necessitate further developmental study of risk precursors most relevant to the disorder. For example, given evidence that stable, high trajectories of behavioral inhibition are most closely linked to anxiety risk in non-FXS samples (Brooker et al., 2013; Chronis-Tuscano et al., 2009; Hirshfeld et al., 1992), future work is needed to determine whether individual stability of developmental trajectories provides unique information about anxiety emergence in FXS, relative to current focus on group-level changes over time. Indeed, a number of our previous studies detected differences in anxiety- and attention-related behaviors that were detected at the level of individual slope trajectories only (Tonnsen, Cornish, et al., 2014; Tonnsen, Grefer, et al., 2014; Tonnsen, Malone, et al., 2013). Further zooming in on the temporal characteristics of individual trajectories, such as to distinguish between children who exhibit fluctuating versus stable behavioral inhibition over time, may require new analytic approaches and frameworks, particularly given the small samples inherent to experimental syndromic research. However, these techniques are likely to greatly expand the specificity of identified moderators, promoting more seamless translational efforts and more effective interventions.

4.5 Validate Through Treatment and Prevention

Given the intense, multifaceted system of risks associated with anxiety emergence in FXS, additional studies are warranted to experimentally examine associations between various parts of the anxiety emergence system. Treatment studies may be designed to experimentally manipulate candidate moderators of anxiety risk in young children, directly promoting beneficial change while also providing evidence for broader anxiety emergence models. For example, given associations between high maternal control and child anxiety, parent—child interaction therapies focused on reduced parental control (Eyberg, 1988) may enhance child resilience against anxiety emergence if adapted appropriately to FXS. An exciting new direction for anxiety treatment is the notion that anxiety could be prevented by identifying behaviorally inhibited children in infancy and toddlerhood, then intervening before anxiety symptoms emerge (LaFreniere & Capuano, 1997; Rapee, Kennedy, Ingram, Edwards, & Sweeney, 2005). This approach has shown promise in large-scale community studies (LaFreniere & Capuano, 1997; Rapee et al., 2005) and may also be relevant in FXS given increased behavioral inhibition is detectable in early development and associated with anxiety outcomes. Evaluating efficacy of these treatment protocols in FXS may not only benefit the child, but may also provide guidance on which portions of the anxiety emergence model are most malleable to intervention-mediated change.

5. CONCLUSION

In summary, our synthesis of anxiety emergence in FXS supports that impairments associated with anxiety may be malleable, arising through complex interactions across multiple genetic, behavioral, and environmental moderators. Importantly, evidence from non-FXS samples suggest these risk factors are modifiable, and potentially preventable, warranting hope towards developing effective prevention mechanisms well-calibrated to the FXS phenotype. However, a number of important empirical steps must be addressed to facilitate this translational work, including expanded multidimensional, longitudinal studies of anxiety emergence in young children with FXS. Given the well-established literature base on anxiety emergence in non-FXS samples and emergent work suggesting parallel processes in FXS, the time is ripe to empirically examine these complex, multisystemic pathways. This work is likely to benefit both the FXS community as well as the broader field of anxiety research by identifying malleable markers of risk and resilience that may be modified to promote optimal child and family outcomes.

ACKNOWLEDGMENTS

Funding was provided by the National Institutes of Health (F31MH095318 PI Tonnsen; R01MH090194 PI Roberts).

REFERENCES

Achenbach, T. (1991). *Manual for the child behavior checklist/4—18 and 1991 profile.* Burlington: University of Vermont Department of Psychiatry.
Achenbach, T., Dumenci, L., & Rescorla, L. (2003). DSM-oriented and empirically based approaches to constructing scales from the same item pools. *Journal of Clinical Child and Adolescent Psychology,* 37—41. http://dx.doi.org/10.1207/S15374424JCCP3203. November 2013.

Aktar, E., Majdandžić, M., de Vente, W., & Bögels, S. M. (2013). Parental social anxiety disorder prospectively predicts toddlers' fear/avoidance in a social referencing paradigm. *Journal of Child Psychology and Psychiatry, and Allied Disciplines.* http://dx.doi.org/10.1111/jcpp.12121.

Allingham-Hawkins, D. J., Babul-Hirji, R., Chitayat, D., Holden, J. J., Yang, K. T., Lee, C., ... Vieri, F. (1999). Fragile X premutation is a significant risk factor for premature ovarian failure: the International Collaborative POF in fragile X study—preliminary data. *American Journal of Medical Genetics, 83*(4), 322—325. Retrieved from http://www.pubmedcentral.nih.gov/articlerender.fcgi?artid=3728646&tool=pmcentrez&rendertype=abstract.

Asendorpf, J. B., & Meier, G. H. (1993). Personality effects on children's speech in everyday life: sociability-mediated exposure and shyness-mediated reactivity to social situations. *Journal of Personality and Social Psychology, 64*(6), 1072—1083. http://dx.doi.org/10.1037/0022-3514.64.6.1072.

Bailey, D. B., Hatton, D. D., Mesibov, G., Ament, N., & Skinner, M. (2000). Early development, temperament, and functional impairment in autism and fragile X syndrome. *Journal of Autism and Developmental Disorders, 30*(1), 49—59. Retrieved from http://www.ncbi.nlm.nih.gov/pubmed/10819120.

Bailey, D. B., Jr., Raspa, M., Olmsted, M., & Holiday, D. B. (2008). Co-occurring conditions associated with FMR1 gene variations: findings from a national parent survey. *American Journal of Medical Genetics. Part A, 146A*(16), 2060—2069. http://dx.doi.org/10.1002/ajmg.a.32439.

Bailey, D. B., Sideris, J., Roberts, J., & Hatton, D. (2008). Child and genetic variables associated with maternal adaptation to fragile X syndrome: a multidimensional analysis. *American Journal of Medical Genetics. Part A, 146A*(6), 720—729. http://dx.doi.org/10.1002/ajmg.a.32240.

Bal, E., Harden, E., Lamb, D., Van Hecke, A. V., Denver, J. W., & Porges, S. W. (2010). Emotion recognition in children with autism spectrum disorders: relations to eye gaze and autonomic state. *Journal of Autism and Developmental Disorders, 40*(3), 358—370. Retrieved from http://www.ncbi.nlm.nih.gov/pubmed/19885725.

Ballinger, E. C., Cordeiro, L., Chavez, A. D., Hagerman, R. J., & Hessl, D. (2014). Emotion potentiated startle in fragile X syndrome. *Journal of Autism and Developmental Disorders, 44*(10), 2536—2546. http://dx.doi.org/10.1007/s10803-014-2125-7.

Bar-Haim, Y., Lamy, D., Pergamin, L., Bakermans-Kranenburg, M. J., & van IJzendoorn, M. H. (2007). Threat-related attentional bias in anxious and nonanxious individuals: a meta-analytic study. *Psychological Bulletin, 133*(1), 1—24. http://dx.doi.org/10.1037/0033-2909.133.1.1.

Barlow, D. H. (1988). *Anxiety and its disorders: The nature and treatment of anxiety and panic.* New York: Guilford Press.

Barlow, D. H. (2000). Unraveling the mysteries of anxiety and its disorders from the perspective of emotion theory. *The American Psychologist, 55*(11), 1247—1263.

Barlow, D. H., Chorpita, B. F., & Turovsky, J. (1996). Fear, panic, anxiety, and disorders of emotion. *Nebraska Symposium on Motivation, 43*, 251—328.

Bates, J. E., Dodge, K. A., Pettit, G. S., & Ridge, B. (1998). Interaction of temperamental resistance to control and restrictive parenting in the development of externalizing behavior. *Developmental Psychology, 34*(5), 982—995.

Beidel, D. C., & Turner, S. M. (1997). At risk for anxiety: I. Psychopathology in the offspring of anxious parents. *Journal of the American Academy of Child and Adolescent Psychiatry, 36*(7), 918—924. http://dx.doi.org/10.1097/00004583-199707000-00013.

Berry-Kravis, E., Hessl, D., Abbeduto, L., Reiss, A. L., Beckel-Mitchener, A., Urv, T. K., & Outcome Measures Working Groups. (2013). Outcome measures for clinical trials in fragile X syndrome. *Journal of Developmental & Behavioral Pediatrics, 34*(7), 508—522. http://dx.doi.org/10.1097/DBP.0b013e31829d1f20.

Biederman, J., Hirshfeld-Becker, D. R., Rosenbaum, J. F., Hérot, C., Friedman, D., Snidman, N., ... Faraone, S. V. (2001). Further evidence of association between behavioral inhibition and social anxiety in children. *The American Journal of Psychiatry, 158*(10), 1673—1679. Retrieved from http://www.ncbi.nlm.nih.gov/pubmed/11579001.

Biederman, J., Rosenbaum, J. F., Bolduc-Murphy, E. A., Faraone, S. V., Chaloff, J., Hirshfeld, D. R., & Kagan, J. (1993). A 3-year follow-up of children with and without behavioral inhibition. *Journal of the American Academy of Child and Adolescent Psychiatry, 32*(4), 814—821. http://dx.doi.org/10.1097/00004583-199307000-00016.

Blumberg, S. H., & Izard, C. E. (1985). Affective and cognitive characteristics of depression in 10- and 11-year-old children. *Journal of Personality and Social Psychology, 49*(1), 194—202.

Boccia, M. L., & Roberts, J. E. (2000). Behavior and autonomic nervous system function assessed via heart period measures: the case of hyperarousal in boys with fragile X syndrome. *Behavior Research Methods, Instruments, & Computers: A Journal of the Psychonomic Society, Inc., 32*(1), 5—10.

Bolton, D., Eley, T. C., O'Connor, T. G., Perrin, S., Rabe-Hesketh, S., Rijsdijk, F., & Smith, P. (2006). Prevalence and genetic and environmental influences on anxiety disorders in 6-year-old twins. *Psychological Medicine, 36*(3), 335—344. http://dx.doi.org/10.1017/S0033291705006537.

Boyle, L., & Kaufmann, W. E. (2010). The behavioral phenotype of FMR1 mutations. *American Journal of Medical Genetics Part C Seminars In Medical Genetics, 154C*(4), 469—476. Retrieved from http://www.ncbi.nlm.nih.gov/pubmed/20981777.

Brooker, R. J., Buss, K. A., Lemery-Chalfant, K., Aksan, N., Davidson, R. J., & Goldsmith, H. H. (2013). The development of stranger fear in infancy and toddlerhood: normative development, individual differences, antecedents, and outcomes. *Developmental Science, 16*(6), 864—878. http://dx.doi.org/10.1111/desc.12058.

Bruno, J. L., Garrett, A. S., Quintin, E. M., Mazaika, P. K., & Reiss, A. L. (2014). Aberrant face and gaze habituation in fragile X syndrome. *American Journal of Psychiatry, 171*(10), 1099—1106. http://dx.doi.org/10.1176/appi.ajp.2014.13111464.

Bruno, J. L., Hosseini, S. M. H., Saggar, M., Quintin, E.-M., Raman, M. M., & Reiss, A. L. (2016). Altered brain network segregation in fragile X syndrome revealed by structural connectomics. *Cerebral Cortex*, bhw055. http://dx.doi.org/10.1093/cercor/bhw055.

Bryson, S. E., Zwaigenbaum, L., Brian, J., Roberts, W., Szatmari, P., Rombough, V., & McDermott, C. (2007). A prospective case series of high-risk infants who developed autism. *Journal of Autism and Developmental Disorders, 37*(1), 12—24. http://dx.doi.org/10.1007/s10803-006-0328-2.

Budimirovic, D. B., Bukelis, I., Cox, C., Gray, R. M., Tierney, E., & Kaufmann, W. E. (2006). Autism spectrum disorder in fragile X syndrome: differential contribution of adaptive socialization and social withdrawal. *American Journal of Medical Genetics. Part A, 140A*, 1814—1826.

Calkins, S. D., Blandon, A. Y., Williford, A. P., & Keane, S. P. (2007). Biological, behavioral, and relational levels of resilience in the context of risk for early childhood behavior problems. *Development and Psychopathology, 19*(3), 675—700. http://dx.doi.org/10.1017/S095457940700034X. pii:S095457940700034X.

Calkins, S. D., & Fox, N. A. (1992). The relations among infant temperament, security of attachment, and behavioral inhibition at twenty-four months. *Child Development, 63*(6), 1456—1472. http://dx.doi.org/10.2307/1131568.

Cannon, W. B. (1939). *The wisdom of the body*. New York: W.W. Norton.

Caspi, A., & Silva, P. A. (1995). Temperamental qualities at age three predict personality traits in young adulthood: longitudinal evidence from a birth cohort. *Child Development, 66*(2), 486—498.

Chaplin, T. M., & Cole, P. M. (2005). The role of emotionl regulation in the development of psychopathology. In B. L. Hankin, & J. R. Z. Abela (Eds.), *Development of psychopathology: A vulnerability-stress perspective* (pp. 49–74). Thousand Oaks, CA: Sage.

Chronis-Tuscano, A., Degnan, K. A., Pine, D. S., Perez-Edgar, K., Henderson, H. A., Diaz, Y., ... Fox, N. A. (2009). Stable early maternal report of behavioral inhibition predicts lifetime social anxiety disorder in adolescence. *Journal of the American Academy of Child and Adolescent Psychiatry, 48*(9), 928–935. http://dx.doi.org/10.1097/CHI.0b013e3181ae09df.

Clauss, J. A., & Blackford, J. U. (2012). Behavioral inhibition and risk for developing social anxiety disorder: a meta-analytic study. *Journal of the American Academy of Child and Adolescent Psychiatry, 51*(10), 1066–1075. http://dx.doi.org/10.1016/j.jaac.2012.08.002.

Cohen, I. L., Fisch, G. S., Sudhalter, V., Wolf-Schein, E. G., Hanson, D., Hagerman, R., ... Brown, W. T. (1988). Social gaze, social avoidance, and repetitive behavior in fragile X males: a controlled study. *American Journal of Mental Retardation, 92*(5), 436–446.

Cohen, I. L., Vietze, P. M., Sudhalter, V., Jenkins, E. C., & Brown, W. T. (1991). Effects of age and communication level on eye contact in fragile X males and non-fragile X autistic males. *American Journal of Medical Genetics, 38*(2–3), 498–502. http://dx.doi.org/10.1002/ajmg.1320380271.

Cole, P. M., Zahnwaxler, C., & Smith, K. D. (1994). Expressive control during a disappointment — variations related to preschoolers behavior problems. *Developmental Psychology, 30*(6), 835–846.

Cordeiro, L., Abucayan, F., Hagerman, R., Tassone, F., & Hessl, D. (2015). Anxiety disorders in fragile X premutation carriers: preliminary characterization of probands and non-probands. *Intractable & Rare Diseases Research, 4*(3), 123–130. http://dx.doi.org/10.5582/irdr.2015.01029.

Cordeiro, L., Ballinger, E., Hagerman, R., & Hessl, D. (2011). Clinical assessment of DSM-IV anxiety disorders in fragile X syndrome: prevalence and characterization. *Journal of Neurodevelopmental Disorders, 3*(1), 57–67. http://dx.doi.org/10.1007/s11689-010-9067-y.

Cornish, K. M., Cole, V., Longhi, E., Karmiloff-Smith, A., & Scerif, G. (2012). Does attention constrain developmental trajectories in fragile X syndrome? A 3-year prospective longitudinal study. *American Journal on Intellectual and Developmental Disabilities, 117*(2), 103–120. http://dx.doi.org/10.1352/1944-7558-117.2.103.

Cornish, K. M., Li, L., Kogan, C. S., Jacquemont, S., Turk, J., Dalton, A., ... Hagerman, P. J. (2008). Age-dependent cognitive changes in carriers of the fragile X syndrome. *Cortex; A Journal Devoted to the Study of the Nervous System and Behavior, 44*(6), 628–636. http://dx.doi.org/10.1016/j.cortex.2006.11.002.

Cornish, K. M., Scerif, G., & Karmiloff-Smith, A. (2007). Tracing syndrome-specific trajectories of attention across the lifespan. *Cortex; A Journal Devoted to the Study of the Nervous System and Behavior, 43*, 672–685.

Crawford, D. C., Acuña, J. M., & Sherman, S. L. (2001). FMR1 and the fragile X syndrome: human genome epidemiology review. *Genetics in Medicine Official Journal of the American College of Medical Genetics, 3*(5), 359–371. Retrieved from http://www.ncbi.nlm.nih.gov/pubmed/11545690.

Davis, N. O., & Carter, A. S. (2008). Parenting stress in mothers and fathers of toddlers with autism spectrum disorders: associations with child characteristics. *Journal of Autism and Developmental Disorders, 38*(7), 1278–1291. http://dx.doi.org/10.1007/s10803-007-0512-z.

De Rosnay, M., Cooper, P. J., Tsigaras, N., & Murray, L. (2006). Transmission of social anxiety from mother to infant: an experimental study using a social referencing paradigm. *Behaviour Research and Therapy, 44*(8), 1165–1175. http://dx.doi.org/10.1016/j.brat.2005.09.003.

Degnan, K. A., & Fox, N. A. (2007). Behavioral inhibition and anxiety disorders: multiple levels of a resilience process. *Development and Psychopathology, 19*(3), 729—746. http://dx.doi.org/10.1017/S0954579407000363.

Dilalla, L. F., Kagan, J., & Reznick, J. S. (1994). Genetic etiology of behavioral inhibition among 2-year-old children. *Infant Behavior and Development, 17*(4), 405—412. http://dx.doi.org/10.1016/0163-6383(94)90032-9.

Duke, B. J. (2008). Pathogenic effects of central nervous system hyperarousal. *Medical Hypotheses, 71*(2), 212—217. http://dx.doi.org/10.1016/j.mehy.2008.03.037. pii:S0306-9877(08)00147-3.

Eisenberg, N., Cumberland, A., Spinrad, T. L., Fabes, R. A., Shepard, S. A., Reiser, M., ... Guthrie, I. K. (2001). The relations of regulation and emotionality to children's externalizing and internalizing problem behavior. *Child Development, 72*(4), 1112—1134.

Eisenberg, N., Fabes, R. A., Shepard, S. A., Murphy, B. C., Guthrie, I. K., Jones, S., ... Maszk, P. (1997). Contemporaneous and longitudinal prediction of children's social functioning from regulation and emotionality. *Child Development, 68*(4), 642—664.

Eyberg, S. (1988). Parent-child interaction therapy: integration of traditional and behavioral concerns. *Child & Family Behavior Therapy, 10*(1), 33—46.

Farzin, F., Perry, H., Hessl, D., Loesch, D., Cohen, J., Bacalman, S., ... Hagerman, R. (2006). Autism spectrum disorders and attention-deficit/hyperactivity disorder in boys with the fragile X premutation. *Journal of Developmental and Behavioral Pediatrics, 27*(2 Suppl.), S137—S144. http://dx.doi.org/10.1097/00004703-200604002-00012.

Feldman, R. (2010). The relational basis of adolescent adjustment: trajectories of mother-child interactive behaviors from infancy to adolescence shape adolescents' adaptation. *Attachment & Human Development, 12*(1—2), 173—192. http://dx.doi.org/10.1080/14616730903282472. pii:919622480.

Fernández, E., Rajan, N., & Bagni, C. (October 2013). The FMRP regulon: from targets to disease convergence. *Frontiers in Neuroscience, 7*, 191. http://dx.doi.org/10.3389/fnins.2013.00191.

Fisak, B., & Grills-Taquechel, A. E. (2007). Parental modeling, reinforcement, and information transfer: risk factors in the development of child anxiety? *Clinical Child and Family Psychology Review, 10*(3), 213—231. http://dx.doi.org/10.1007/s10567-007-0020-x.

Fox, N. A. (1989). Psychophysiological correlates of emotional reactivity during the first year of life. *Developmental Psychology, 25*(3), 364—372. http://dx.doi.org/10.1037/0012-1649.25.3.364.

Fox, N. A., & Pine, D. S. (2012). Temperament and the emergence of anxiety disorders. *Journal of the American Academy of Child and Adolescent Psychiatry, 51*(2), 125—128. http://dx.doi.org/10.1016/j.jaac.2011.10.006.

Fox, E., Russo, R., Bowles, R., & Dutton, K. (2007). Do threatening stimuli draw or hold visual attention in subclinical anxiety? *Journal of Experimental Psychology. General, 130*(4), 681—700. Europe PMC Funders Group.

Fox, E., Russo, R., & Dutton, K. (2002). Attentional bias for threat: evidence for delayed disengagement from emotional faces. *Cognition & Emotion, 16*, 355—379. http://dx.doi.org/10.1080/02699930143000527. October.

Frick, J. E., Colombo, J., & Saxon, T. F. (1999). Individual and developmental differences in disengagement of fixation in early infancy. *Child Development, 70*(3), 537—548. Retrieved from http://www.ncbi.nlm.nih.gov/pubmed/10368908.

Friedman, B. H. (2007). An autonomic flexibility-neurovisceral integration model of anxiety and cardiac vagal tone. *Biological Psychology, 74*(2), 185—199. http://dx.doi.org/10.1016/j.biopsycho.2005.08.009.

Friedman, B. H., & Thayer, J. F. (1998). Autonomic balance revisited: panic anxiety and heart rate variability. *Journal of Psychosomatic Research, 44*(1), 133—151. http://dx.doi.org/10.1016/S0022-3999(97)00202-X.

Garcia-Coll, C., Kagan, J., & Reznick, J. S. (1984). Behavioral inhibition in young children. *Child Development, 55*(3), 1005—1019. http://dx.doi.org/10.2307/1130152.

Garon, N., Bryson, S. E., Zwaigenbaum, L., Smith, I. M., Brian, J., Roberts, W., & Szatmari, P. (2009). Temperament and its relationship to autistic symptoms in a high-risk infant sib cohort. *Journal of Abnormal Child Psychology, 37*(1), 59—78. http://dx.doi.org/10.1007/s10802-008-9258-0.

Gartstein, M. A., Bridgett, D. J., Rothbart, M. K., Robertson, C., Iddins, E., Ramsay, K., & Schlect, S. (2010). A latent growth examination of fear development in infancy: contributions of maternal depression and the risk for toddler anxiety. *Developmental Psychology, 46*(3), 651—668. http://dx.doi.org/10.1037/a0018898.

Gerull, F. C., & Rapee, R. M. (2002). Mother knows best: effects of maternal modelling on the acquisition of fear and avoidance behaviour in toddlers. *Behaviour Research and Therapy, 40*(3), 279—287. Retrieved from http://www.ncbi.nlm.nih.gov/pubmed/11863238.

Goldsmith, H. H., Buss, A. H., Plomin, R., Rothbart, M. K., Thomas, A., Chess, S., ... McCall, R. B. (1987). Roundtable: what is temperament? Four approaches. *Child Development, 58*(2), 505—529.

Goldsmith, H. H., & Lemery, K. S. (2000). Linking temperamental fearfulness and anxiety symptoms: a behavior-genetic perspective. *Biological Psychiatry, 48*(12), 1199—1209. pii:S0006322300010039.

Grant, V. V., Bagnell, A. L., Chambers, C. T., & Stewart, S. H. (2009). Early temperament prospectively predicts anxiety in later childhood. *Canadian Journal of Psychiatry, 54*(5), 320—330.

Hagerman, R. J., & Hagerman, P. J. (2002). The fragile X premutation: into the phenotypic fold. *Current Opinion in Genetics & Development, 12*(3), 278—283. Retrieved from http://linkinghub.elsevier.com/retrieve/pii/S0959437X0200299X.

Hagerman, R. J., Leavitt, B. R., Farzin, F., Jacquemont, S., Greco, C. M., Brunberg, J. A., ... Hagerman, P. J. (2004). Fragile-X-associated tremor/ataxia syndrome (FXTAS) in females with the FMR1 premutation. *American Journal of Human Genetics, 74*(5), 1051—1056. http://dx.doi.org/10.1086/420700.

Hall, S. S., DeBernardis, M., & Reiss, A. (2006). Social escape behaviors in children with fragile X syndrome. *Journal of Autism and Developmental Disorders, 36*(7), 935—947. http://dx.doi.org/10.1007/s10803-006-0132-z.

Hall, S. S., Frank, M. C., Pusiol, G. T., Farzin, F., Lightbody, A. A., & Reiss, A. L. (2015). Quantifying naturalistic social gaze in fragile X syndrome using a novel eye tracking paradigm. *American Journal of Medical Genetics, Part B: Neuropsychiatric Genetics, 168*(7), 564—572. http://dx.doi.org/10.1002/ajmg.b.32331.

Hall, S. S., Lightbody, A. A., Huffman, L. C., Lazzeroni, L. C., & Reiss, A. L. (2009). Physiological correlates of social avoidance behavior in children and adolescents with fragile x syndrome. *Journal of the American Academy of Child and Adolescent Psychiatry, 48*(3), 320—329. Retrieved from http://www.ncbi.nlm.nih.gov/pubmed/19182690.

Harris, S. W., Hessl, D., Goodlin-Jones, B., Ferranti, J., Bacalman, S., Barbato, I., ... Hagerman, R. J. (2008). Autism profiles of males with fragile X syndrome. *American Journal of Mental Retardtion, 113*(6), 427—438.

Hastings, P. D., Nuselovici, J. N., Utendale, W. T., Coutya, J., McShane, K. E., & Sullivan, C. (2008). Applying the polyvagal theory to children's emotion regulation: social context, socialization, and adjustment. *Biological Psychology, 79*(3), 299—306. http://dx.doi.org/10.1016/j.biopsycho.2008.07.005.

Hatton, D. D., Bailey, D. B., Hargett-Beck, M. Q., Skinner, M., & Clark, R. D. (1999). Behavioral style of young boys with fragile X syndrome. *Developmental Medicine and Child Neurology, 41*(9), 625—632. Retrieved from http://www.ncbi.nlm.nih.gov/pubmed/10503921.

Hatton, D. D., Sideris, J., Skinner, M., Mankowski, J., Bailey, D. B., Roberts, J. E., & Mirrett, P. (2006). Autistic behavior in children with fragile X syndrome: prevalence, stability, and the impact of FMRP. *American Journal of Medical Genetics Part A, 140A*(17), 1804—1813. Retrieved from http://onlinelibrary.wiley.com/doi/10.1002/ajmg.a.31286/full.

Hazlett, H. C., Poe, M. D., Lightbody, A. A., Gerig, G., Macfall, J. R., Ross, A. K., ... Piven, J. (2009). Teasing apart the heterogeneity of autism: same behavior, different brains in toddlers with fragile X syndrome and autism. *Journal of Neurodevelopmental Disorders, 1*(1), 81—90. http://dx.doi.org/10.1007/s11689-009-9009-8.

Hazlett, H. C., Poe, M. D., Lightbody, A. A., Styner, M., MacFall, J. R., Reiss, A. L., & Piven, J. (2012). Trajectories of early brain volume development in fragile X syndrome and autism. *Journal of the American Academy of Child and Adolescent Psychiatry, 51*(9), 921—933. http://dx.doi.org/10.1016/j.jaac.2012.07.003.

Heilman, K. J., Harden, E. R., Zageris, D. M., Berry-Kravis, E., & Porges, S. W. (2011). Autonomic regulation in fragile X syndrome. *Developmental Psychobiology, 53*(8), 785—795. http://dx.doi.org/10.1002/dev.20551.

Henje Blom, E., Olsson, E. M., Serlachius, E., Ericson, M., & Ingvar, M. (2010). Heart rate variability (HRV) in adolescent females with anxiety disorders and major depressive disorder. *Acta Paediatrica, International Journal of Paediatrics, 99*(4), 604—611. http://dx.doi.org/10.1111/j.1651-2227.2009.01657.x.

Hernandez, R. N., Feinberg, R. L., Vaurio, R., Passanante, N. M., Thompson, R. E., & Kaufmann, W. E. (2009). Autism spectrum disorder in fragile X syndrome: a longitudinal evaluation. *American Journal of Medical Genetics. Part A, 149A*(6), 1125—1137. http://dx.doi.org/10.1002/ajmg.a.32848.

Hessl, D., Dyer-Friedman, J., Glaser, B., Wisbeck, J., Barajas, R. G., Taylor, A., & Reiss, A. L. (2001). The influence of environmental and genetic factors on behavior problems and autistic symptoms in boys and girls with fragile X syndrome. *Pediatrics, 108*(5), E88. pii:108/5/e88.

Hessl, D., Glaser, B., Dyer-Friedman, J., & Reiss, A. L. (2006). Social behavior and cortisol reactivity in children with fragile X syndrome. *Journal of Child Psychology and Psychiatry, and Allied Disciplines, 47*(6), 602—610. http://dx.doi.org/10.1111/j.1469-7610.2005.01556.x.

Hessl, D., Rivera, S., Koldewyn, K., Cordeiro, L., Adams, J., Tassone, F., ... Hagerman, R. J. (2007). Amygdala dysfunction in men with the fragile X premutation. *Brain: A Journal of Neurology, 130*(Pt 2), 404—416. http://dx.doi.org/10.1093/brain/awl338.

Hessl, D., Wang, J. M., Schneider, A., Koldewyn, K., Le, L., Iwahashi, C., ... Rivera, S. M. (2011). Decreased fragile X mental retardation protein expression underlies amygdala dysfunction in carriers of the fragile X premutation. *Biological Psychiatry, 70*(9), 859—865. http://dx.doi.org/10.1016/j.biopsych.2011.05.033.

Hettema, J. M., Neale, M. C., & Kendler, K. S. (2001). A review and meta-analysis of the genetic epidemiology of anxiety disorders. *American Journal of Psychiatry.* http://dx.doi.org/10.1176/appi.ajp.158.10.1568.

Hirshfeld, D. R., Rosenbaum, J. F., Biederman, J., Bolduc, E. A., Faraone, S. V., Snidman, N., ... Kagan, J. (1992). Stable behavioral inhibition and its association with anxiety disorder. *Journal of the American Academy of Child and Adolescent Psychiatry, 31*(1), 103—111. http://dx.doi.org/10.1097/00004583-199201000-00016.

Hoeft, F., Walter, E., Lightbody, A. A., Hazlett, H. C., Chang, C., Piven, J., & Reiss, A. L. (2011). Neuroanatomical differences in toddler boys with fragile X syndrome and idiopathic autism. *Archives of General Psychiatry, 68*(3), 295–305. http://dx.doi.org/10.1001/archgenpsychiatry.2010.153.

Hoffman, S. G., & Barlow, D. H. (2002). Social phobia (social anxiety disorder). In *Anxiety and its disorders: The nature and treatment of anxiety and panic* (2nd ed.). New York: Guilford Press.

Hudson, J. L., & Dodd, H. F. (2012). Informing early intervention: preschool predictors of anxiety disorders in middle childhood. *PLoS One, 7*(8), e42359. http://dx.doi.org/10.1371/journal.pone.0042359.

Hudson, J. L., & Rapee, R. M. (2001). Parent-child interactions and anxiety disorders: an observational study. *Behaviour Research and Therapy, 39*(12), 1411–1427. http://dx.doi.org/10.1016/S0005-7967(00)00107-8.

Hunter, J., Rivero-Arias, O., Angelov, A., Kim, E., Fotheringham, I., & Leal, J. (2014). Epidemiology of fragile X syndrome: a systematic review and meta-analysis. *American Journal of Medical Genetics. Part A, 164A*(7), 1648–1658. http://dx.doi.org/10.1002/ajmg.a.36511.

Hutman, T., Rozga, A., DeLaurentis, A. D., Barnwell, J. M., Sugar, C. A., & Sigman, M. (2010). Response to distress in infants at risk for autism: a prospective longitudinal study. *Journal of Child Psychology and Psychiatry, and Allied Disciplines, 51*(9), 1010–1020. http://dx.doi.org/10.1111/j.1469-7610.2010.02270.x. pii:JCPP2270.

Jacquemont, S., & Hagerman, R. (2004). Penetrance of the fragile X–associated tremor/ataxia syndrome in a premutation carrier population. *JAMA: The Journal of American Medical Association, 291*(4). Retrieved from http://jama.ama-assn.org/content/291/4/460.short.

Kagan, J., Reznick, S., Clarke, C., Snidman, N., & Garcia-Coll, C. (1984). Behavioral inhibition to the unfamiliar. *Child Development, 55*, 2212–2225.

Kagan, J., Reznick, J. S., & Snidman, N. (1988). Biological bases of childhood shyness. *Science, 240*(4849), 167–171. http://dx.doi.org/10.1126/science.3353713.

Karmiloff-Smith, A. (1998). Development itself is the key to understanding developmental disorders. *Trends in Cognitive Sciences, 2*(10), 389–398. http://dx.doi.org/10.1016/S1364-6613(98)01230-3.

Karmiloff-Smith, A. (2009). Nativism versus neuroconstructivism: rethinking the study of developmental disorders. *Developmental Psychology, 45*(1), 56–63. http://dx.doi.org/10.1037/a0014506.

Kaufmann, W. E., Cortell, R., Kau, A. S. M., Bukelis, I., Tierney, E., Gray, R. M., ... Stanard, P. (2004). Autism spectrum disorder in fragile X syndrome: communication, social interaction, and specific behaviors. *American Journal of Medical Genetics Part A, 129A*(3), 225–234. Retrieved from http://www.ncbi.nlm.nih.gov/pubmed/15326621.

Kau, A. S., Reider, E. E., Payne, L., Meyer, W. A., & Freund, L. (2000). Early behavior signs of psychiatric phenotypes in fragile X syndrome. *American Journal of Mental Retardation, 105*(4), 286–299. http://dx.doi.org/10.1352/0895-8017(2000)105<0286:EBSOPP>2.0.CO;2.

Kenna, H. A., Tartter, M., Hall, S. S., Lightbody, A. A., Nguyen, Q., de Los Angeles, C. P., ... Rasgon, N. L. (2013). High rates of comorbid depressive and anxiety disorders among women with premutation of the FMR1 gene. *American Journal of Medical Genetics. Part B, Neuropsychiatric Genetics: The Official Publication of the International Society of Psychiatric Genetics, 162B*(8), 872–878. http://dx.doi.org/10.1002/ajmg.b.32196.

Kim, S.-Y., Burris, J., Bassal, F., Koldewyn, K., Chattarji, S., Tassone, F., ... Rivera, S. M. (2012). Fear-specific amygdala function in children and adolescents on the fragile X spectrum: a dosage response of the FMR1 gene. *Cerebral Cortex (New York, N.Y.: 1991), (Adolphs 2010)*, 1–14. http://dx.doi.org/10.1093/cercor/bhs341.

Kirschbaum, C., Wolf, O. T., May, M., Wippich, W., & Hellhammer, D. H. (1996). Stress-and treatment-induced elevations of cortisol levels associated with impaired declarative memory in healthy adults. *Life Sciences, 58*(17), 1475—1483. pii:002432059600118X.

Klusek, J., Martin, G. E. G., & Losh, M. (2013). Physiological arousal in autism and fragile X syndrome: group comparisons and links with pragmatic language. *American Journal of Intellectual and Developmental Disablities, 118*(6), 475—495. http://dx.doi.org/10.1352/1944.7558-118.6.475.Physiological.

Klusek, J., Roberts, J. R., & Losh, M. (2015). Cardiac autonomic regulation in autism and fragile X syndrome: a review. *Psychological Bulletin, 141.*

Kraan, C. M., Hocking, D. R., Georgiou-Karistianis, N., Metcalfe, S. A., Archibald, A. D., Fielding, J., ... Cornish, K. M. (2013). Impaired response inhibition is associated with self-reported symptoms of depression, anxiety, and ADHD in female FMR1 premutation carriers. *American Journal of Medical Genetics. Part B, Neuropsychiatric Genetics: The Official Publication of the International Society of Psychiatric Genetics.* http://dx.doi.org/10.1002/ajmg.b.32203.

Lachiewicz, A., Dawson, D., Spiridigliozzi, G., & McConkie-Rosell, A. (2006). Arithmetic difficulties in females with the fragile X premutation. *American Journal of Medical Genetics. Part A, 140,* 665—672. http://dx.doi.org/10.1002/ajmg.a.

LaFreniere, P., & Capuano, F. (1997). Preventive intervention as means of clarifying direction of effects in socialization: anxious-withdrawn preschoolers case. *Development and Psychopathology, 9,* 551—564. Retrieved from http://journals.cambridge.org/production/action/cjoGetFulltext?fulltextid=43482.

Lasker, A. G., Mazzocco, M. M., & Zee, D. S. (2007). Ocular motor indicators of executive dysfunction in fragile X and Turner syndromes. *Brain and Cognition, 63*(3), 203—220. http://dx.doi.org/10.1016/j.bandc.2006.08.002.

Last, C. G., Hersen, M., Kazdin, A., Orvaschel, H., & Perrin, S. (1991). Anxiety disorders in children and their families. *Archives of General Psychiatry, 48*(10), 928—934. http://dx.doi.org/10.1001/archpsyc.1991.01810340060008.

Leekam, S. R., Prior, M. R., & Uljarevic, M. (2011). Restricted and repetitive behaviors in autism spectrum disorders: a review of research in the last decade. *Psychological Bulletin, 137*(4), 562—593. http://dx.doi.org/10.1037/a0023341.

Lemery, K. S., Essex, M. J., & Smider, N. A. (2002). Revealing the relation between temperament and behavior problem symptoms by eliminating measurement confounding: expert ratings and factor analyses. *Child Development, 73*(3), 867—882.

Leve, L. D., Kim, H. K., & Pears, K. C. (2005). Childhood temperament and family environment as predictors of internalizing and externalizing trajectories from ages 5 to 17. *Journal of Abnormal Child Psychology, 33*(5), 505—520. http://dx.doi.org/10.1007/s10802-005-6734-7.

Lundh, L., & Öst, L. (2001). Attentional bias, self-consciousness and perfectionism in social phobia before and after cognitive-behavior therapy. *Cognitive Behaviour Therapy, 30*(1), 4—16. http://dx.doi.org/10.1080/02845710117841.

Marshall, P. J., & Stevenson-Hinde, J. (1998). Behavioral inhibition, heart period, and respiratory sinus arrhythmia in young children. *Developmental Psychobiology, 33*(3), 283—292. http://dx.doi.org/10.1111/1467-8624.00058.

Mathews, A., Mogg, K., Kentish, J., & Eysenck, M. (1995). Effect of psychological treatment on cognitive bias in generalized anxiety disorder. *Behaviour Research and Therapy, 33*(3), 293—303. http://dx.doi.org/10.1016/0005-7967(94)E0022-B.

Mattia, J. I., Heimberg, R. G., & Hope, D. A. (1993). The revised stroop color-naming task in social phobics. *Behaviour Research and Therapy, 31*(3), 305—313. http://dx.doi.org/10.1016/0005-7967(93)90029-T.

Mauss, I. B., Wilhelm, F. H., & Gross, J. J. (2003). Autonomic recovery and habituation in social anxiety. *Psychophysiology, 40*(4), 648—653. http://dx.doi.org/10.1111/1469-8986.00066.

McClure, E. B., Brennan, P. A., Hammen, C., & Le Brocque, R. M. (2001). Parental anxiety disorders, child anxiety disorders, and the perceived parent—child relationship in an Australian high-risk sample. *Journal of Abnormal Child Psychology, 29*(1), 1—10. http://dx.doi.org/10.1023/A:1005260311313.

McEwen, B. S. (1998). Stress, adaptation, and disease — allostasis and allostatic load. *Neuroimmunomodulation, 840,* 33—44.

Mcewen, B. S., & Sapolsky, R. M. (1995). Stress and cognitive function. *Current Opinion in Neurobiology, 5*(2), 205—216.

Mcewen, B. S., & Stellar, E. (1993). Stress and the individual — mechanisms leading to disease. *Archives of Internal Medicine, 153*(18), 2093—2101.

McLeod, B. D., Weisz, J. R., & Wood, J. J. (2007). Examining the association between parenting and childhood depression: a meta-analysis. *Clinical Psychology Review, 27*(8), 986—1003. http://dx.doi.org/10.1016/j.cpr.2007.03.001.

Merikangas, K. R., He, J.-P., Burstein, M., Swanson, S. A., Avenevoli, S., Cui, L., … Swendsen, J. (2010). Lifetime prevalence of mental disorders in US adolescents: results from the National Comorbidity Survey Replication — Adolescent Supplement (NCS-A). *Journal of the American Academy of Child and Adolescent Psychiatry, 49*(10), 980—989. http://dx.doi.org/10.1016/j.jaac.2010.05.017.

Monk, C., Kovelenko, P., Ellman, L. M., Sloan, R. P., Bagiella, E., Gorman, J. M., & Pine, D. S. (2001). Enhanced stress reactivity in paediatric anxiety disorders: implications for future cardiovascular health. *International Journal of Neuropsychopharmacology, 4*(2), 199—206. http://dx.doi.org/10.1017/S146114570100236X.

Moore, P. S., Whaley, S. E., & Sigman, M. (2004). Interactions between mothers and children: impacts of maternal and child anxiety. *Journal of Abnormal Psychology, 113*(3), 471—476. http://dx.doi.org/10.1037/0021-843X.113.3.471.

Mount, K. S., Crockenberg, S. C., Barrig Jo, P. S., & Wagar, J. L. (2010). Maternal and child correlates of anxiety in 21/2-year-old children. *Infant Behavior and Development, 33*(4), 567—578. http://dx.doi.org/10.1016/j.infbeh.2010.07.008.

Muris, P., Steerneman, P., Merckelbach, H., & Meesters, C. (1996). The role of parental fearfulness and modeling in children's fear. *Behaviour Research and Therapy, 34*(3), 265—268. http://dx.doi.org/10.1016/0005-7967(95)00067-4.

Murphy, M. M., Abbeduto, L., Schroeder, S., & Serlin, R. (2007). Contribution of social and information-processing factors to eye-gaze avoidance in fragile X syndrome. *American Journal of Mental Retardation: AJMR, 112*(5), 349—360. http://dx.doi.org/10.1352/0895-8017(2007)112[0349:COSAIF]2.0.CO;2.

Oakes, A., Thurman, A. J., McDuffie, A., Bullard, L. M., Hagerman, R. J., & Abbeduto, L. (2016). Characterising repetitive behaviours in young boys with fragile X syndrome. *Journal of Intellectual Disability Research, 50,* 54—67. http://dx.doi.org/10.1111/jir.12234.

Peltola, M. J., Leppänen, J. M., Palokangas, T., & Hietanen, J. K. (2008). Fearful faces modulate looking duration and attention disengagement in 7-month-old infants. *Developmental Science, 11*(1), 60—68. http://dx.doi.org/10.1111/j.1467-7687.2007.00659.x.

Pitzer, M., Jennen-Steinmetz, C., Esser, G., Schmidt, M. H., & Laucht, M. (2011). Prediction of preadolescent depressive symptoms from child temperament, maternal distress, and gender: results of a prospective, longitudinal study. *Journal of Developmental and Behavioral Pediatrics, 32*(1), 18—26. http://dx.doi.org/10.1097/DBP.0b013e3181f4a474.

Porges, S. W. (1976). Peripheral and neurochemical parallels of psychopathology: a psychophysiological model relating autonomic imbalance to hyperactivity, psychopathy, and autism. *Advances in Child Development and Behavior, 11,* 35—65. Retrieved from http://www.ncbi.nlm.nih.gov/pubmed/11648.

Porges, S. W. (1995a). Cardiac vagal tone: a physiological index of stress. *Neuroscience and Biobehavioral Reviews, 19*(2), 225—233. http://dx.doi.org/10.1016/0149-7634(94)00066-A.

Porges, S. W. (1995b). Orienting in a defensive world: mammalian modifications of our evolutionary heritage. A polyvagal theory. *Psychophysiology, 32,* 301—318. Retrieved from http://onlinelibrary.wiley.com/doi/10.1111/j.1469-8986.1995. tb01213.x/full.

Porges, S. W. (2004). The vagus: a mediator of behavioral and physiologic features associated with autism. In M. L. Bauman, & T. L. Kemper (Eds.), *The neurobiology of autism* (pp. 65—78). Baltimore, MD: JHU Press.

Porges, S. W., Doussard Roosevelt, J. A., Lourdes Portales, A., & Suess, P. E. (1994). Cardiac vagal tone: stability and relation to difficultness in infants and 3-year-olds. *Developmental Psychobiology, 27*(5), 289—300. http://dx.doi.org/10.1002/dev.420270504.

Putnam, S. P., Rothbart, M. K., & Garstein, M. A. (2008). Homotypic and heterotypic continuity of fine-grained temperament during infancy, toddlerhood, and early childhood. *Infant and Child Development, 17,* 387—405.

Quintana, D. S., Guastella, A. J., Outhred, T., Hickie, I. B., & Kemp, A. H. (2012). Heart rate variability is associated with emotion recognition: direct evidence for a relationship between the autonomic nervous system and social cognition. *International Journal of Psychophysiology, 86*(2), 168—172. http://dx.doi.org/10.1016/j.ijpsycho.2012.08.012.

Rapee, R. M. (2014). Preschool environment and temperament as predictors of social and nonsocial anxiety disorders in middle adolescence. *Journal of the American Academy of Child and Adolescent Psychiatry, 53*(3), 320—328. http://dx.doi.org/10.1016/j.jaac.2013.11.014.

Rapee, R. M., Kennedy, S., Ingram, M., Edwards, S., & Sweeney, L. (2005). Prevention and early intervention of anxiety disorders in inhibited preschool children. *Journal of Consulting and Clinical Psychology, 73*(3), 488—497. http://dx.doi.org/10.1037/0022-006X.73.3.488.

Roberts, J. E., Bailey, D. B., Mankowski, J., Ford, A., Sideris, J., Weisenfeld, L. A., ... Golden, R. N. (2009). Mood and anxiety disorders in females with the FMR1 premutation. *American Journal of Medical Genetics. Part B, Neuropsychiatric Genetics: The Official Publication of the International Society of Psychiatric Genetics, 150B*(1), 130—139. http://dx.doi.org/10.1002/ajmg.b.30786.

Roberts, J. E., Boccia, M. L., Bailey, D. B., Hatton, D. D., & Skinner, M. (2001). Cardiovascular indices of physiological arousal in boys with fragile X syndrome. *Developmental Psychobiology, 39*(2), 107—123. Retrieved from http://www.ncbi.nlm.nih.gov/pubmed/11568881.

Roberts, J. E., Boccia, M. L., Hatton, D. D., Skinner, M. L., & Sideris, J. (2006). Temperament and vagal tone in boys with fragile X syndrome. *Journal of Developmental and Behavioral Pediatrics: JDBP, 27*(3), 193—201.

Roberts, J. E., Clarke, M. A., Alcorn, K., Carter, J. C., Long, A. C. J., & Kaufmann, W. E. (2007). Social approach and autistic behavior in children with fragile X syndrome. *Journal of Autism and Developmental Disorders, 1*(4), 1748—1760. Retrieved from http://www.ncbi.nlm.nih.gov/pubmed/17180715.

Roberts, J. E., Clarke, M. A., Alcorn, K., Carter, J. C., Long, A. C. J., & Kaufmann, W. E. (2009). Autistic behavior in boys with fragile X syndrome: social approach and HPA-axis dysfunction. *Journal of Neurodevelopmental Disorders, 1*(4), 283—291. http://dx.doi.org/10.1007/s11689-009-9028-5.

Roberts, J. E., Hatton, D. D., Long, A. C. J., Anello, V., & Colombo, J. (2011). Visual attention and autistic behavior in infants with fragile X syndrome. *Journal of Autism and Developmental Disorders, 42*(6), 937—946. http://dx.doi.org/10.1007/s10803-011-1316-8.

Roberts, J. E., Tonnsen, B. L., McCary, L. M., Long, A. C. J., & Bailey, D. B. (n.d.). *Longitudinal mood and anxiety disorders in women with the FMR1 premutation.*

Roberts, J. E., Tonnsen, B. L., Robinson, M., McQuillin, S. D., & Hatton, D. D. (2014). Temperament factor structure in fragile X syndrome: the children's behavior questionnaire. *Research in Developmental Disabilities, 35*(2), 563–571. http://dx.doi.org/10.1016/j.ridd.2013.11.024.

Roberts, J. E., Tonnsen, B. L., Robinson, A., & Shinkareva, S. V. (2012). Heart activity and autistic behavior in infants and toddlers with fragile X syndrome. *American Journal on Intellectual and Developmental Disabilities, 117*(2), 90–102. http://dx.doi.org/10.1352/1944-7558-117.2.90.

Roberts, J. E., Weisenfeld, L. A. H., Hatton, D. D., Heath, M., & Kaufmann, W. E. (2006). Social approach and autistic behavior in children with fragile X syndrome. *Journal of Autism and Developmental Disorders, 37*(9), 1748–1760. http://dx.doi.org/10.1007/s10803-006-0305-9.

Robinson, J. L., Kagan, J., Reznick, J. S., & Corley, R. (1992). The heritability of inhibited and uninhibited behavior: a twin study. *Developmental Psychology, 28*(6), 1030–1037. http://dx.doi.org/10.1037//0012-1649.28.6.1030.

Rogers, S. J., Wehner, D. E., Hagerman, R., & Wehner, E. (2001). The behavioral phenotype in fragile X: symptoms of autism in very young children with fragile X syndrome, idiopathic autism, and other developmental disorders. *Journal of Developmental and Behavioral Pediatrics, 22*(6), 410–417. Retrieved from http://scholar.google.com/scholar?hl=en&btnG=Search&q=intitle:The+behavioral+phenotype+in+fragile+X:+Smyptoms+of+autism+in+very+young+children+with+fragile+X+syndrome,+idiopatic+autism,+and+other+developmental+disorders#0.

Rothbart, M., & Ahadi, S. A. (1994). Temperament and the development of personality. *Journal of Abnormal Psychology, 103*(1), 55–66. http://dx.doi.org/10.1037/0021-843X.103.1.55.

Rothbart, M. K., Ahadi, S. A., & Evans, D. E. (2000). Temperament and personality: origins and outcomes. *Journal of Personality and Social Psychology, 78*(1), 122–135. http://dx.doi.org/10.1037/0022-3514.78.1.122.

Rothbart, M. K., Bates, J. E., & Damon, W. (1998). Temperament. In N. Eisenberg (Ed.), *Handbook of child psychology* (5th ed., pp. 105–176). New York: Wiley.

Rothbart, M. K., & Derryberry, D. (1981). Development of individual differences in temperament. In M. E. Lamb, & A. L. Brown (Eds.), *Advances in developmental psychology* (Vol. 1, pp. 37–86). Hillsdale, NJ: Erlbaum. SRC - G.

Schmidt, L. A., Miskovic, V., Boyle, M. H., & Saigal, S. (2008). Shyness and timidity in young adults who were born at extremely low birth weight. *Pediatrics, 122*(1), e181–e187. http://dx.doi.org/10.1542/peds.2007-3747. pii:122/1/e181.

Schopler, E., Reichler, R., & Renner, B. (1998). *The childhood autism rating scale.* Los Angeles: Western Psychological Services.

Selmeczy, D., Koldewyn, K., Wang, J. M., Lee, A., Harvey, D., Hessl, D. R., … Rivera, S. M. (2011). Investigation of amygdala volume in men with the fragile X premutation. *Brain Imaging and Behavior, 5*(4), 285–294. http://dx.doi.org/10.1007/s11682-011-9132-5.

Seltzer, M., Barker, E., & Greenberg, J. (2012). Differential sensitivity to life stress in FMR1 premutation carrier mothers of children with fragile X syndrome. *Health Psychology, 31*(5), 612–622. http://dx.doi.org/10.1037/a0026528.Differential.

Shanahan, M., Roberts, J. E., Hatton, D., Reznick, J., & Goldsmith, H. (2008). Early temperament and negative reactivity in boys with fragile X syndrome. *Journal of Intellectual Disability Research: JIDR, 52*(10), 842–854. Retrieved from http://www.ncbi.nlm.nih.gov/pubmed/18498331.

Sharma, R. K., Balhara, Y. P. S., Sagar, R., Deepak, K. K., & Mehta, M. (2011). Heart rate variability study of childhood anxiety disorders. *Journal of Cardiovascular Disease Research, 2*(2), 115–122. http://dx.doi.org/10.4103/0975-3583.83040.

Shiner, R. L. (1998). How shall we speak of children's personalities in middle Childhood? A preliminary taxonomy. *Psychological Bulletin, 124*(3), 308—332.

Stifter, C. A., & Fox, N. A. (1990). Infant reactivity: physiological correlates of newborn and 5-month temperament. *Developmental Psychology, 26*(4), 582—588. http://dx.doi.org/10.1037/0012-1649.26.4.582.

Sullivan, K., Hooper, S., & Hatton, D. (2007). Behavioural equivalents of anxiety in children with fragile X syndrome: parent and teacher report. *Journal of Intellectual Disability Research, 51*(1), 54—65. http://dx.doi.org/10.1111/j.1365-2788.2006.00899.x.

Thayer, J. F., & Friedman, B. H. (2002). Stop that! Inhibition, sensitization, and their neurovisceral concomitants. *Scandinavian Journal of Psychology, 43*(2), 123—130. http://dx.doi.org/10.1111/1467-9450.00277.

Thayer, J. F., Friedman, B. H., & Borkovec, T. D. (1996). Automatic characteristics of generalized anxiety disorder and worry. *Biological Psychiatry, 39*(95), 255—266.

Tonnsen, B. L., (2015). Behavioral and heart-defined attention in infants at high genetic risk for autism. (Unpublished doctoral dissertation). University of South Carolina, Columbia, SC.

Tonnsen, B. L., Cornish, K. M., Wheeler, A. C., & Roberts, J. E. (2014). Maternal predictors of anxiety risk in young males with fragile X. *American Journal of Medical Genetics. Part B, Neuropsychiatric Genetics: The Official Publication of the International Society of Psychiatric Genetics.* http://dx.doi.org/10.1002/ajmg.b.32244.

Tonnsen, B. L., Grefer, M. L., Hatton, D. D., & Roberts, J. E. (2014). Developmental trajectories of attentional control in preschool males with fragile X syndrome. *Research in Developmental Disabilities, 36C*, 62—71. http://dx.doi.org/10.1016/j.ridd.2014.09.015.

Tonnsen, B. L., Malone, P. S., Hatton, D. D., & Roberts, J. E. (2013). Early negative affect predicts anxiety, not autism, in preschool boys with fragile X syndrome. *Journal of Abnormal Child Psychology, 41*(2), 267—280. http://dx.doi.org/10.1007/s10802-012-9671-2.

Tonnsen, B. L., Shinkareva, S. V., Deal, S. C., Hatton, D. D., & Roberts, J. E. (2013). Biobehavioral indicators of social fear in young children with fragile X syndrome. *American Journal on Intellectual and Developmental Disabilities, 118*(6), 447—459. http://dx.doi.org/10.1352/1944-7558-118.6.447.

Tonnsen, B. L., Scherr, J., Reisinger, D., & Roberts, J. E., (under review). Behaivoral markers of emergent anxiety and autism in infants with fragile X syndrome.

Van der Bruggen, C. O., Stams, G. J., & Bögels, S. M. (2008). Research review: the relation between child and parent anxiety and parental control: a meta-analytic review. *Journal of Child Psychology and Psychiatry, and Allied Disciplines, 49*(12), 1257—1269. http://dx.doi.org/10.1111/j.1469-7610.2008.01898.x.

Wainwright, A., & Bryson, S. E. (2002). The development of exogenous orienting: mechanisms of control. *Journal of Experimental Child Psychology, 82*(2), 141—155. Retrieved from http://www.ncbi.nlm.nih.gov/pubmed/12083793.

Watson, C., Hoeft, F., Garrett, A. S., Hall, S. S., & Reiss, A. L. (2008). Aberrant brain activation during gaze processing in boys with fragile X syndrome. *Archives of General Psychiatry, 65*(11), 1315—1323. http://dx.doi.org/10.1001/archpsyc.65.11.1315.

Wheeler, A., Hatton, D., Reichardt, A., & Bailey, D. (2007). Correlates of maternal behaviours in mothers of children with fragile X syndrome. *Journal of Intellectual Disability Research: JIDR, 51*(Pt 6), 447—462. http://dx.doi.org/10.1111/j.1365-2788.2006.00896.x.

Wheeler, A. C., Raspa, M., Bishop, E., & Bailey, D. B. (2015). Aggression in fragile X syndrome. *Journal of Intellectual Disability Research, 60*. http://dx.doi.org/10.1111/jir.12238.

Whiteside-Mansell, L., Bradley, R. H., Casey, P. H., Fussell, J. J., & Conners-Burrow, N. A. (2009). Triple risk: do difficult temperament and family conflict increase the likelihood of behavioral maladjustment in children born low birth weight and preterm? *Journal of Pediatric Psychology, 34*(4), 396—405. http://dx.doi.org/10.1093/jpepsy/jsn089.

Williams, J. M. G., Watts, F. N., MacLeod, C., & Matthews, A. (1988). *Cognitive psychology and emotional disorders.* Chichester, England: Wiley.

Wolff, P. H., Gardner, J., Paccia, J., & Lappen, J. (1989). The greeting behavior of fragile X males. *American Journal on Mental Retardation, 93.* Children's Hospital, Boston, MA 02115. SRC - Pubmed ID2—2522786 FG - 0.

Zeman, J., Shipman, K., & Suveg, C. (2002). Anger and sadness regulation: predictions to internalizing and externalizing symptoms in children. *Journal of Clinical Child and Adolescent Psychology: The Official Journal for the Society of Clinical Child and Adolescent Psychology, American Psychological Association, Division 53, 31*(3), 393—398. http://dx.doi.org/10.1207/S15374424JCCP3103_11.

Zwaigenbaum, L., Bryson, S., Rogers, T., Roberts, W., Brian, J., & Szatmari, P. (2005). Behavioral manifestations of autism in the first year of life. *International Journal of Developmental Neuroscience, 23*(2—3), 143—152. Retrieved from http://www.ncbi.nlm.nih.gov/pubmed/15749241.

CHAPTER THREE

Assessment and Treatment of Executive Function Impairments in Autism Spectrum Disorder: An Update

G.L. Wallace*,1, B.E. Yerys§,¶, C. Peng*, E. Dlugi*, L.G. Anthony‖,#, L. Kenworthy‖,#

*George Washington University, Washington, DC, United States
§Children's Hospital of Philadelphia, Philadelphia, PA, United States
‖Children's National Health System, Washington, DC, United States
#George Washington University School of Medicine, Washington, DC, United States
¶University of Pennsylvania, Philadelphia, PA, United States
1Corresponding author: E-mail: gwallac1@gwu.edu

Contents

International Review of Research in Developmental Disabilities, Volume 51
ISSN 2211-6095
http://dx.doi.org/10.1016/bs.irrdd.2016.07.004

© 2016 Elsevier Inc.
All rights reserved.

Abstract

Empirical evidence for executive function (EF) impairments in autism spectrum disorder (ASD) was first established more than 30 years ago. In the interim, a large literature has emerged that supports a profile of relatively intact and impaired (e.g., flexibility) EF subdomains in ASD. We pick up where our last review (Kenworthy, Yerys, Anthony, & Wallace, 2008; *Neuropsychology Review*) left off by examining both laboratory-based and ecologically valid EF assessment findings in ASD, how the presence of comorbid attention deficit hyperactivity disorder (ADHD) symptoms and/or diagnosis affects EF in ASD, and a newly emerging evidence base for intervention studies targeting EF impairments in ASD. The evidence to date suggests that laboratory-based EF findings remain more mixed than those based on ecologically valid assessment of EF (which more consistently reveal EF deficits in ASD), nevertheless, the latter requires more study. Findings also suggest that subgrouping ASD based on ADHD symptomatology might clarify heretofore mixed findings, particularly in terms of inhibitory control deficits. Finally, EF is proving to be a viable treatment target in ASD, although much more work is needed in this area.

Executive function (EF) is often described as an "umbrella" term because it encapsulates several goal-directed and self-regulatory cognitive skills such as inhibitory control, working memory, flexibility, and planning. These cognitive skills all serve to regulate behavior and aid in attaining goals. Early cognitive theories of autism spectrum disorder (ASD) sought to explain the core features of the disorder, particularly the social–communication deficits (e.g., the "theory of mind" account of ASD; Baron-Cohen, Leslie, Frith, 1985). However, social-cognitive theories, for example, did not explain the repetitive behaviors and restricted interests characteristic of ASD. Therefore, the EF theory of ASD was invoked to explain these nonsocial features of the disorder. Indeed, the "frontal lobe analogy," wherein behavioral patterns (e.g., perseveration) of individuals with frontal lobe pathology were considered akin to behaviors characteristic of ASD, such as inflexibility/insistence on sameness, was first invoked by Damasio and Maurer (1978). This represents one of the first conceptual linkages of EF and ASD; however, Rumsey (1985) initiated investigating this connection empirically by using the Wisconsin Card Sorting Test to document EF difficulties in ASD. Work in this area has continued unabated and has produced a large literature and several reviews over the last two decades (Hill, 2004; Kenworthy et al., 2008; Pennington & Ozonoff, 1996). Our own previous review on this topic (Kenworthy et al., 2008) focused on the state of the science of EF profiles in ASD utilizing both laboratory-based and ecologically valid assessment approaches. Here, we update the literature in these areas, particularly focusing on the rapidly growing assessment of ecologically valid EF in ASD. Since our last review of the literature on EF in ASD (Kenworthy et al., 2008), there have been several developments that warrant revisiting the state of the science beyond cataloging the robustness of previously documented EF deficits. One major change has been an update to the diagnostic criteria for ASD. Although the *Diagnostic and Statistical Manual of Mental Disorders* (DSM)-IV (American Psychiatric Association, 1994) subdivided the autism spectrum into several diagnoses based primarily upon developmental language level and/or sub/threshold symptom presentation, DSM-5 (American Psychiatric Association, 2013) reconstitutes the spectrum under one rubric, ASD, with qualifiers utilized to dissect the spectrum into subgroups (e.g., with or without intellectual disability [ID]). And likely most relevant to this review, DSM-5 speaks, for the first time, to issues of EF impairments in ASD and allows for the comorbid diagnosis of ASD and attention deficit/hyperactivity disorder (ADHD). Finally, there is now a burgeoning literature on novel treatments targeting EF in ASD that was nearly nonexistent at the time of our 2008 review. Given this direct acknowledgement of the importance of EF in the presentation and assessment/diagnosis of ASD, the open question of the effects of comorbid ADHD symptomatology/diagnosis on EF in ASD, as well as the emergence of EF interventions for ASD groups, this paper seeks to update our review of the literature since we last conducted a survey (Kenworthy et al., 2008).

1. FINDINGS FROM LABORATORY-BASED ASSESSMENT OF EXECUTIVE FUNCTION IN AUTISM SPECTRUM DISORDER

Because previous studies predominantly utilized laboratory-based assessment of EF, prior reviews of EF in ASD focused on performance on these types of tasks (Hill, 2004; Pennington & Ozonoff, 1996). Remarkably, examining the literature since 2008 reveals that the findings, when taken as a whole, remain essentially unchanged from prior reports of the state of the science from other investigators (Hill, 2004; Pennington & Ozonoff, 1996) and our own prior review (Kenworthy, Yerys, Anthony, & Wallace, 2008). Therefore, the summary here will be brief. Results remain mixed in many areas; however, more robust ASD-related deficits continue to be found in flexibility/shifting (Brunsdon et al., 2015; McLean, Harrison, Zimak, Joseph, & Morrow, 2014; Yasuda et al., 2014) and to a lesser extent in planning (Brunsdon et al., 2015), corroborating prior reviews of the literature. In contrast, inhibitory control and working memory are more often found to be intact in ASD when taken as a whole (Matsuura et al., 2014; Wilson et al., 2014); however, individual studies do provide exceptions (e.g., Geurts & Vissers, 2012). Subgrouping based on comorbid ADHD symptomatology might clarify prior findings in this area (for further discussion, see the section below entitled "Does the presence of ADHD symptoms correlate with Executive Function performance for individuals with ASD?"). Because there has been a relative explosion of work examining ecologically valid assessment of EF in ASD since our last review, we will provide a more thorough treatment of these findings below.

2. FINDINGS FROM ECOLOGICALLY VALID ASSESSMENT OF EXECUTIVE FUNCTION IN AUTISM SPECTRUM DISORDER

The variability in assessment approach to EF is strongly influenced by the complexity of the EF construct. Theoretically, EF is considered a central, domain-general, cognitive process; thus, modality of assessment (e.g., verbal vs. visuospatial tasks) and its concomitant task demands can complicate interpretation of results. Additionally, contextual variables can affect EF performance. In other words, the highly structured nature of clinical and laboratory settings might lend themselves to optimal performance on tasks of EF, whereas "real-world" environments do not naturally scaffold performance and therefore could elicit EF deficits that might not be apparent in the clinic/lab. These potential confounds to traditional laboratory-based assessment of EF have provided the avenue to pursue more ecologically valid approaches to EF assessment in ASD (although it is important to note that these approaches are not immune to these same issues at times).

The research to date has been conducted predominantly with a couple of instruments. The Behavior Rating Inventory of Executive Function (BRIEF), a standardized rating scale that assesses the frequency of problems related to EF, particularly the school-age version (5–18 years) of this instrument (Gioia, Isquith, Guy, & Kenworthy, 2000), has been the most commonly used ecologically valid measure to assess EF in ASD in studies published between 2009 and 2016 (see Table 1). This is likely because, as a rating scale (whether parent, teacher, or self reports), the BRIEF is relatively easy to administer. The various age-based versions of the BRIEF have also proven to be highly sensitive to EF impairments in ASD, as deficits are revealed not only among school-age children (Blijd-Hoogewys, Bezemer, van Geert, 2014; Granader et al., 2014; Hovik et al., 2014; Kalbfleisch & Loughan, 2012; Leung, Vogan, Powell, Anagnostou, & Taylor, 2016; McLean et al., 2014; Panerai, Tasca, Ferri, D'Arrigo, & Elia, 2014; Rosenthal et al., 2013), but also among preschoolers (McLean et al., 2014; Smithson et al., 2013) and adults (Wallace et al., 2016) alike.

Table 1 Review of Real-World Executive Function in ASD (2009–2016)

References	Groups/Ages (Years)	Matching Criteria	Executive Function Task	Impairment? (TD/Others)[a]
White et al. (2009)	ASD (n = 45): (mean 9.58) TD (n = 27): (mean 9.88)	Age, sex, verbal, and performance IQ	BADS-C:	
			Cards task	Y
			Water task	N
			Zoo map	Y (number of rule breaks)
			Key search	Y
			Six parts test	Y
			MHSCT-C	Y
Bramham et al. (2009)	ASD (n = 45) (mean 32.76) ADHD (n = 53) (mean 31.04) TD (n = 31) (mean 32.81)	Age, sex	BADS:	
			Zoo map (version 1 and version 2)	Y/Y
Cederlund, Hagberg, and Gillberg (2010)	ASD males (n = 76) (mean 21.8)	N/A[b]	Key search	Y/Y
			DEX	Y[b]
Kalbfleisch and Loughan (2012)	ASD (n = 19) (mean 12.5) TD (n = 25) (mean 11.9)	Age, IQ	BRIEF:	
			GEC	Y
			BRI	Y
			MI	Y
			Inhibit	Y
			Shift	Y
			Initiate	Y
			Working memory	Y
			Planning and organization	Y
			Monitor	Y
Smithson et al. (2013)	ASD (n = 39) (mean 4.38) TD (n = 39) (mean 4.40)	Age, sex	BRIEF-P:	
			GEC	Y
			Inhibitory Self-Control Index	Y
			Flexibility Index	Y

(Continued)

Table 1 Review of Real-World Executive Function in ASD (2009–2016)—cont'd

References	Groups/Ages (Years)	Matching Criteria	Executive Function Task	Impairment? (TD/Others)[a]
			Emergent Metacognition Index	Y
			Inhibit	Y
			Shift	Y
			Emotional control	Y
			Working memory	Y
			Plan/organize	Y
Rosenthal et al. (2013)	ASD (n = 185) (range 5–18)	IQ, sex, autism symptom severity	BRIEF:	
			Inhibit	Y
			Shift	Y
			Emotional control	Y
			Initiate	Y
			Working memory	Y
			Plan/organize	Y
			Organization of materials	Y
			Self-monitor	Y
Salcedo-Marin et al. (2013)	ASD males (n = 23) (mean 10.57) ADHD combined type males (n = 62) (mean 11.24) ADHD inattentive type males (n = 18) (mean 11.94)	Age, IQ	BADS—zoo map	Y/Y (total number of errors in version 1)
McLean et al. (2014)	ASD (n = 168) (mean 9.4) Unaffected siblings (n = 114) (mean 9.0)	N/A[c]	BRIEF:	
			BRI	Y/Y
			MI	Y/Y
			BRIEF-P:	
			Inhibitory Self-	Y/Y

Study	Groups	Matching	Measure	Result
			Control Index	Y/Y
			Flexibility Index	
			Emergent Metacognition Index	Y/Y
Granader et al. (2014)	ASD (n = 411) (mean 10.7) TD (n = 467) (mean 10.2)	Age, sex	BRIEF:	
			GEC	Y
			BRI	Y
			MI	Y
			Inhibit	Y
			Shift	Y
			Emotional control	Y
			Initiate	Y
			Working memory	Y
			Plan/organize	Y
			Organization of materials	Y
			Self-monitor	Y
Hovik et al. (2014)	ASD (n = 34) (mean 11.9) TD (n = 50) (mean 11.6) TS (n = 19): (mean 11.8) ADHD-C (n = 33) (mean 11.6) ADHD-I (n = 43) (mean 11.6)	Age	BRIEF:	
			GEC	Y/N/N/N
			BRI	Y/N/N/N
			MI	Y/N/N/N
			Inhibit	Y/N/N/N
			Shift	Y/N/Y/Y
			Emotional control	Y/N/N/N
			Initiate	Y/N/N/N
			Working memory	Y/N/N/N
			Plan/organize	Y/N/N/N
			Organization of materials	Y/N/N/N
			Monitor	Y/N/N/N

(Continued)

Table 1 Review of Real-World Executive Function in ASD (2009–2016)—cont'd

References	Groups/Ages (Years)	Matching Criteria	Executive Function Task	Impairment? (TD/Others)[a]
Panerai et al. (2014)	Total ASD ($n = 27$ with and without comorbid ID) (mean 9.82)	Age, sex, nonverbal IQ	BRIEF:	
			GEC	Y
			MI	N[d]
	Total non-ASD ($n = 34$ TD and non-ASD ID) (mean 11.32)		BRI	Y
Blijd-Hoogewys et al. (2014)	ASD ($n = 127$) (mean 11.23)	N/A[c]	BRIEF:	
			Inhibit	Y
			Shift	Y
			Emotional control	Y
			Initiate	Y
			Working memory	Y
			Plan/organize	Y
			Organization of materials	Y
			Monitor	Y
Leung et al. (2016)	ASD ($n = 70$) (mean 11.23) TD ($n = 71$) (mean 11.69)	Age, sex	BRIEF:	
			BRI	Y
			MI	Y
Parsons and Carlew (2016)	ASD ($n = 8$) (mean 22.88)	IQ, sex	Virtual classroom bimodal Stroop task without distractors	N
	TD ($n = 10$) (mean 18.8)		Virtual classroom bimodal Stroop task with distractors	Y
Wallace et al. (2016)	ASD ($n = 35$) (mean 21.55)	N/A[c]	BRIEF-A:	
			BRI	Y

MI	Y
Inhibit	Y
Shift	Y
Emotional control	Y
Self-monitor	Y
Initiate	Y
Working memory	Y
Plan/organize	Y
Task monitor	Y
Organization of materials	Y

ADHD, attention deficit hyperactivity disorder; *ADHD-C*, attention deficit hyperactivity disorder—combined subtype; *ADHD-I*, attention deficit hyperactivity disorder—inattentive subtype; *ASD*, autism spectrum disorder; *BADS-C*, behavioral assessment of the dysexecutive syndrome—children; *BRI*, behavior rating index; *BRIEF-A*, behavior rating inventory of executive functioning—adult version; *BRIEF-P*, behavior rating inventory of executive function—preschool version; *DBD*, disruptive behavior disorder; *DEX*, dysexecutive questionnaire; *DS*, down syndrome; *DSM*, diagnostic statistical manual; *EF*, executive functioning; *FSIQ*, full-scale intelligence quotient; *GEC*, global executive composite; *HFA*, high functioning autism; *MHSCT-C*, modified hayling sentence completion task for children; *MCI*, metacognition index; *PDDNOS*, pervasive developmental disorder not otherwise specified; *TD*, typically developing; N/A, not applicable.

[a]"Y/Y", "Y/Y/Y", and "Y/Y/Y/Y" denotes whether the ASD group is impaired (Y = yes) or not (N = no) relative to the next group listed under the "groups/ages" column.

[b]This study did not assess impairment statistically against a control group or norms, but instead compared scores visually against previously completed studies of control groups (ASD scores much lower) and other clinical groups (ASD scores comparable to those reported for traumatic brain injury and schizophrenia).

[c]These studies compared performance in the ASD group against the standardization sample norms using one-sample *t*-tests.

[d]If the sample was limited to ASD without ID compared to ASD with ID, the Metacognition Index score would be significantly impaired in the ASD group.

Moreover, it appears that flexibility/shifting is the peak or one of the peak EF deficit areas in ASD (paralleling findings from lab-based studies) across childhood, adolescence, and adulthood based on ratings from the BRIEF (Granader et al., 2014; Wallace et al., 2016). Nevertheless, more work is needed to examine the convergent and divergent validity of the BRIEF, particularly with performance-based ecologically valid EF tools (e.g., the Behavioral Assessment of Executive Dysfunction-Children's version; Emslie, Wilson, Burden, Nimmo-Smith, & Wilson, 2003). The Behavioral Assessment of Executive Dysfunction (both the adult and children's versions, which consist of a battery of tasks that require one to engage in familiar activities such as searching for lost keys and thus tap multiple EF constructs including shifting/flexibility, inhibition, planning, etc.) is the most commonly utilized performance-based measure of ecologically valid EF assessment in ASD. Similar to the BRIEF, the most recent studies using these instruments converge in revealing EF deficits in ASD (Bramham et al., 2009; Salcedo-Marin, Moreno-Granados, Ruiz-Veguilla, & Ferrin, 2013; White, Burgess, & Hill, 2009). Small correlations between performance on laboratory-based EF assessment tools and parent ratings of EF (e.g., the BRIEF; Mackinlay, Charman, & Karmiloff-Smith, 2006) underline their separable and complementary contributions to the broader understanding of structured one-on-one performance-based EF deficits found in the clinic or lab setting and real-world, everyday EF impairments often observed by caregivers. This becomes a particularly important issue when evaluating the utility of these instruments in intervention studies, whether cognitive-behavioral or pharmacological.

2.1 Developmental Differences in EF in ASD

Although knowledge of the EF profile in ASD has continued to greatly expand, only in recent years have investigators begun to examine possible developmental differences in EF, particularly using ecologically valid assessment, in ASD. In the context of typical development, it is now well established that EF is composed of a dynamically emerging set of cognitive skills with varying trajectories depending upon the domain in question (e.g., later maturing working memory and planning capacities; De Luca et al., 2003). Similarly, studies of the BRIEF in typical development have shown age-related declines in problematic EF-related behaviors during childhood and adolescence (Huizinga & Smidts, 2011). In contrast, these types of investigations, particularly examining real-world EF, in ASD are rather limited. Two relatively large studies have been completed to date that demonstrate contradictory findings. One study found discrepancies in age-related differences in parent ratings on the BRIEF (particularly for working memory and initiation) in ASD (scores diverged and implicated greater deficits with increasing age in ASD) compared to expectations derived from the BRIEF standardization sample (Rosenthal et al., 2013), whereas another study found limited evidence for discrepancies in age relations among children with ASD (Van den Bergh, Scheeran, Begeer, Koot, & Geurts, 2014). However, these questions of developmental effects on EF are not limited to childhood and adolescence. How might EF change with increasing age in ASD during adulthood? This is only beginning to be explored with evidence to date suggesting comparable age relations with EF in ASD and typical aging (Geurts & Vissers, 2012). Ultimately, there is a glaring need to examine developmental changes in EF among children, adolescents, and adults utilizing powerful longitudinal designs to provide more definitive answers as to the (a)typicality of EF trajectories in ASD.

2.2 Association Between EF in ASD and Outcome

Outcomes in ASD, including levels of employment and independent living, are particularly poor when compared to not only the general population, but also individuals with ID and other neurodevelopmental disorders (Howlin, Moss, Savage, & Rutter, 2013; Roux et al., 2013). There is growing evidence for links between outcome-based measures or those that affect outcome (e.g., adaptive functioning, quality of life, comorbid psychopathology) and ecologically valid EF in ASD. It is important to understand potential links between these outcome-related measures and EF given that if associations exist, alternate routes to improving adaptive functioning, for example, might be obtained via interventions targeting EF. Thus far, there is growing evidence that real-world EF is associated with important outcome measures in ASD. One recent study demonstrates significant cross-sectional associations and longitudinal predictive power between ecologically valid EF, utilizing the BRIEF, and adaptive functioning using the Vineland Adaptive Behavior Scales (Pugliese et al., 2015). In one of the few studies of adults with ASD on this topic, Wallace et al. (2016) also found significant cross-sectional correlations between ecologically valid EF, utilizing the adult version of the BRIEF, and adaptive functioning, based on the Adaptive Behavior Assessment System. Studies have also demonstrated significant correlations between impairments in behavior regulation, as measured by the BRIEF, and autism symptomatology (Kenworthy et al., 2009). Finally, EF has also been linked to other forms of psychopathology (aside from ADHD, which is discussed below). For example, at least one study of adults with ASD has shown significant correlations between deficits in metacognition (based on the adult version of the

BRIEF) and depression symptomatology on the one hand and between impairments in behavior regulation and anxiety symptomatology on the other hand (Wallace et al., 2016). Similarly, flexibility deficits (based on ratings from the BRIEF) were also associated with anxiety and depression symptoms in children with ASD (Lawson et al., 2015). In summary, there is mounting evidence for links between real-world EF and various outcome-related metrics in ASD. This only serves to underscore the important role that EF difficulties might play in the everyday lives of people with ASD.

2.3 Impact of ID on EF in ASD

One possible advantage of some ecologically valid EF assessments, such as the BRIEF and other behavioral ratings, over many laboratory-based EF tasks is their potential utility for individuals with co-occurring ASD and ID. Many traditional laboratory-based EF tasks include additional non-EF-related cognitive/language demands, which might exacerbate deficits among individuals with ID and cloud interpretations of what is driving observed difficulties. Nevertheless, very little work to date has examined the unique and shared aspects of the real-world EF profile among individuals with ASD with and without ID. One exception is work by Panerai et al. (2014). They demonstrate, for example, that based on BRIEF ratings, although behavioral regulation impairments (e.g., inflexibility) are shared between individuals with ASD with and without ID (as compared to IQ-matched control groups), as compared to typically developing controls, metacognitive impairments are not. In contrast, they found that metacognitive impairments are limited to ASD without ID. There is clearly a dearth of studies examining real-world EF among people with both ASD and ID. Utilization of these ecologically valid assessment tools might corroborate findings from the Panerai et al. (2014) study and therefore help to guide interventionists in isolating areas in need of improvement and developing intervention strategies unique to people with co-occurring ASD and ID.

2.4 Dynamic Assessment of Executive Function in Autism Spectrum Disorder

Finally, Parsons and Carlew (2016) have recently provided an excellent example of harnessing modern technology to allow for more dynamic assessment that provides hybrids of traditional lab-based EF assessment contextualized within the real world. They utilized virtual reality to adapt a Stroop-like classroom-based task with extra demands incorporated and found that including distractors with the task (which can reflect the sometimes chaotic nature of real-world settings) elicits deficits in ASD, unlike a comparable task without distractors. The marrying of ecological validity with both decades of research on traditional neuropsychological assessment and technological innovation allows for harnessing strengths of all of the above approaches.

2.5 Future Directions

Despite the largely consistent documentation of EF impairments in ASD using the BRIEF, and similarly, among other (mostly) performance-based, ecologically valid EF measures, the specificity of these deficits in ASD remains a largely open question. The vast majority of studies have examined group differences between ASD and typically developing (i.e., nonclinical) groups. However, the findings to date provide relatively minimal and mixed evidence as to the specificity of these deficits for ASD as opposed to other groups with EF deficits (e.g., ADHD, Tourette's syndrome; Hovik et al., 2014). Thus, one area to be pursued in future work is continued investigation of ecologically valid EF both within and across clinical groups. This has both theoretical and clinical implications. Theoretically, there has long been a debate about the power of the Executive Function Theory to account for deficits in ASD, with one prominent criticism being its lack of specificity (Happé & Frith, 1996). However, prior studies of at least one ecologically valid EF measure, the BRIEF, have provided compelling evidence for discrepant profiles of EF across groups of neurodevelopmental disorders (Gioia, Isquith, Kenworthy, & Barton, 2002). Clinically, whether or not EF deficits are specific to ASD could impact treatment approach and development. Where ASD deficits are unique, further ASD-specific treatment might be needed and where there are shared EF deficits, borrowing from other existing therapies (adapted for other unique aspects of the ASD cognitive/behavioral phenotype) is likely warranted to avoid "reinventing the wheel" (see the section below on "Executive Function Interventions for People with ASD").

Additionally, as indicated above, more work is needed on real-world EF during adulthood, particularly middle and older adulthood. There is a well-established literature in typical aging wherein both lab-based and ecologically valid EF measures reveal age-related declines in performance during older adulthood (Crawford, Bryan, Luszcz, Obonsawin, & Stewart, 2000). Whether or not the EF trajectory is atypical in ASD, it is important to assess individual strengths and difficulties in EF for adults with ASD to provide appropriate accommodations and/or interventions to maximize their employment participation and independent living. Similarly, although challenging, more work is needed to assess ecologically valid EF, including performance-based measures, among individuals with both ASD and ID. Finally, further development of ecologically valid assessment tools is also crucial to continued progress in this area. Novel assessment tools might serve to improve the arsenal of approaches clinicians have to assess real-world EF demands and more precisely identify areas of need for people with ASD.

3. DOES THE PRESENCE OF ADHD SYMPTOMS CORRELATE WITH EF PERFORMANCE FOR INDIVIDUALS WITH ASD?

Individuals with ASD have demonstrated both impaired and typical performance on lab-based EF measures (for reviews see Barendse et al., 2013; Geurts, Verté, Oosterlaan, Roeyers, & Sergeant, 2004; Hill, 2004; Kenworthy et al., 2008; Kercood, Grskovic, Banda, & Begeske, 2014; Poljac & Bekkering, 2012; Russo et al., 2007). Even before the release of the DSM-5 and the ability to diagnose both ASD and ADHD in the same individual, scientists questioned whether comorbid ADHD symptoms contributed to the inconsistent EF findings in ASD (Corbett, Constantine, Hendren, Rocke, & Ozonoff, 2009; Geurts, van den Bergh, & Ruzzano, 2014; Sinzig, Bruning, Morsch, & Lehmkuhl, 2008; Sinzig, Morsch, Bruning, Schmidt, & Lehmkuhl, 2008; Yerys et al., 2009). This argument is intuitive, because EF impairments are cardinal to ADHD (Castellanos & Tannock, 2002; Doyle et al., 2005; Willcutt, Doyle, Nigg, Faraone, & Pennington, 2005). The standard of care for diagnosing ADHD is the use of diagnostic interviews, parent and teacher questionnaires documenting symptoms and impairment, and classroom observations when possible (DuPaul et al., 2016). However, many studies examining EF performance in individuals with ASD have not measured ADHD symptoms with this level of precision or accounted for ADHD symptoms in their analyses. Thus, it is possible that some studies reporting differences in EF may have recruited samples with greater ADHD symptoms. Prior research in ADHD has shown that the most commonly affected EF process in the ADHD population is inhibition, but working memory and planning are also implicated (Castellanos & Tannock, 2002; Doyle et al., 2005; Geurts et al., 2004; Pennington & Ozonoff, 1996; Willcutt et al., 2005). In the following paragraphs we will review the current state of EF in ASD when taking into account ADHD symptoms either through a dimensional assessment (e.g., ADHD-IV Rating Scale or Connors Parent Rating Scale—Revised) or categorically with co-occurring ASD and ADHD clinical diagnoses (ASD + ADHD). Each paragraph will focus on an EF process, as well as ecologically valid EF assessments.

3.1 Inhibition

Inhibition is the most commonly assessed EF process when concerned about ASD + ADHD. As shown in Table 2, there are eight studies of lab-based EF measures in ASD that explicitly measure ADHD as a dimension or a category. All studies measured response inhibition with some form of a continuous performance task that required withholding a motor response. Four of the eight studies show either a clear correlation between poor task performance and greater ADHD symptoms in the ASD group (Corbett et al., 2009; Yerys, Kenworthy, Jankowski, Strang, & Wallace, 2013), or significant (or trending) differences for greater impairment in ASD + ADHD group relative to an ASD group (Adamo et al., 2013; Bühler, Bachmann, Goyert, Heinzel-Gutenbrunner, & Kamp-Becker, 2011). One study demonstrated that the relationship between poorer response inhibition performance and greater ADHD symptoms was independent from ASD symptoms (Yerys et al., 2013). Also, one study did not find differences among ASD + ADHD, ADHD, ASD, and control groups in standard metrics of accuracy or mean response time (RT), but the ASD + ADHD group demonstrated greater intrasubject RT variability compared to all other groups; the intrasubject RT variability measure is hypothesized to reflect lapses in attention (Adamo et al., 2013). Of the studies showing no group differences three were relatively underpowered to detect group differences in an analysis of variance (sample sizes < 25 per group for all groups) (Lundervold et al., 2012; Sinzig, Bruning, et al., 2008; Yerys et al., 2009); however, one of these studies reported medium effect sizes (Yerys et al., 2009). One study was adequately powered and found no differences between the ASD + ADHD group relative to the ASD alone and ADHD alone groups, or to standardized norms from the Tests of Variables of Attention (Nydén et al., 2010). One study also measured cognitive inhibition through the Delis—Kaplan Executive Function System's Inhibition task, which is a variation of the Stroop task (Corbett et al., 2009). The Stroop task requires responding to a target (the text color of a written word) while ignoring irrelevant information (reading the word which names a color). The ASD group performed significantly worse than controls and an ADHD group, and both diagnosis and ADHD symptoms predicted performance on this Inhibition

Table 2 Summary of All Executive Function Investigations Targeting Comorbid ASD + ADHD in Which an ASD + ADHD Group was Compared to at Least an ASD and/or Control Group

References	Groups (n)/Ages (Years)	Matching Criteria	Executive Function Measures	Executive Function Domains	Impairments?[a]	Effect Sizes[a]
Sinzig, Bruning, et al. (2008)	TYP (n = 30): 12.8 ASD (n = 20): 14.5 ADHD (n = 30): 12.9 ASD + ADHD (n = 21): 10.7	Sex ratio, IQ	TAP: go/no-go TAP: divided attention	Inhibition Working memory	TYP = ASD = ADHD = ASD + ADHD ASD > ASD + ADHD (trend on false alarms)	Not reported
Corbett et al. (2009)	TYP (n = 18): 9.56 ADHD (n = 18): 9.40 ASD (n = 18): 9.44	Age, sex ratio	IVACPT-VRCQ IVACPT-ARCQ D-KEFS inhibition (Stroop) SSP SWM between errors SWM strategy ID/ED-shift DK T-switch CCTT2 SOC min moves SOC initial thinking SOC subthinking DK letter DK category	Inhibition Inhibition Inhibition Working memory Working memory Working memory Flexibility Flexibility Flexibility Planning Planning Planning Generativity Generativity	TYP > ASD[b] ASD > ADHD[b] TYP > ASD[b] TYP > ADHD[b] TYP = ADHD > ASD TYP > ASD TYP > ADHD TYP > ASD ADHD > ASD TYP > ASD ADHD > ASD TYP = ASD = ADHD ADHD > ASD TYP > ASD TYP = ASD = ADHD TYP = ASD = ADHD TYP = ASD = ADHD TYP = ASD = ADHD TYP = ASD = ADHD TYP = ASD = ADHD	$\eta^2 = 0.33$ $\eta^2 = 0.21$ $\eta^2 = 0.29$ $\eta^2 = 0.16$ $\eta^2 = 0.14$ $\eta^2 = 0.15$ $\eta^2 = 0.01$ $\eta^2 = 0.34$ $\eta^2 = 0.14$
Gomarus et al. (2009)	TYP (n = 15): 10.15 ADHD (n = 15): 9.82 PDDNOS (n = 15): 10.25 PDD/HD: (n = 15): 10.13	Age, VIQ, sex ratio	Visual selective Memory search task	Working memory	TYP = ADHD = ASD = ASD + ADHD	Not reported

Study	Sample	Matched variables	Measures	EF domain	Results	Effect size
Yerys et al. (2009)	TYP ($n = 21$): 10.3 ASD ($n = 28$): 9.7 ASD + ADHD ($n = 21$): 9.7	Age, SES, IQ, sex ratio	Digit span SWM-CANTAB Walk, don't walk BRIEF-inhibit BRIEF-shift BRIEF-BRI BRIEF-MCI	Working memory Working memory Inhibition Inhibition (real world) Flexibility (real world) Multiple EF (real world) Multiple EF (real world)	TYP > ASD + ADHD ASD = ASD + ADHD TYP = ASD + ADHD ASD = ASD + ADHD TYP = ASD + ADHD ASD = ASD + ADHD TYP < ASD < ASD + ADHD TYP < ASD < ASD + ADHD TYP < ASD < ASD + ADHD TYP < ASD < ASD + ADHD	$d = 1.01$ $d = 0.59$ $d = 0.65$ $d = 0.42$ $d = 0.53$ $d = 0.42$ $d = 2.34/0.99$ $d = 2.67/0.72$ $d = 3.40/1.04$ $d = 4.97/1.76$
Nydén et al. (2010)	ASD ($n = 55$): 32.02 ADHD ($n = 73$): 33.18 ASD + ADHD ($n = 33$): 32.37	Age, sex ratio	Digit span TOL TOVA: commission, omission, and RT	Working memory Planning Inhibition	ASD = ADHD = ASD + ADHD ASD = ADHD = ASD + ADHD ASD = ADHD = ASD + ADHD	Not reported
Bühler et al. (2011)	ASD ($n = 86$): 10.75 ADHD ($n = 84$): 9.58 ASD + ADHD ($n = 52$): 10.08	None	TAP: go/no-go	Inhibition	ASD > ADHD ASD > ASD + ADHD (trend)	$r = 0.35$ $r = -0.22$
Yerys et al. (2011)	TYP ($n = 18$): 11.07 ASD ($n = 28$): 10.89	Age, FSIQ, sex ratio, SES, race	CTT	Working memory	TYP > ASD (unrelated to ADHD symptoms)	$d = 1.03$
Lundervold et al. (2012)	TYP ($n = 134$): 9.7 ADHD ($n = 38$): 10.0 ASD ($n = 9$): 10.3 ADHD + ASD ($n = 11$):10.6	None	CPT index	Inhibition	TYP = ASD = ADHD = ASD + ADHD	Not reported
Adamo et al. (2013)	TYP ($n = 36$): 10 ADHD ($n = 46$): 10 ASD ($n = 46$): 10	Age, IQ, SES	Go/no-go (mean RT, accuracy, SD-RT) Go/no-go (RT-ISV);	Inhibition	TYP = ADHD = ASD TYP = ASD > ADHD = ASD + ADHD	Not reported

(Continued)

Table 2 Summary of All Executive Function Investigations Targeting Comorbid ASD + ADHD in Which an ASD + ADHD Group was Compared to at Least an ASD and/or Control Group—cont'd

References	Groups (n)/Ages (Years)	Matching Criteria	Executive Function Measures	Executive Function Domains	Impairments?[a]	Effect Sizes[a]
Andersen et al. (2013)	ASD (n = 22): 11.9; ADHD (n = 79): 11.6; TYP (n = 50): 11.6; ASD + ADHD (n = 16): 12.2	Age, VIQ	LNS	Working memory	TYP > ASD = ADHD > ASD + ADHD	$\eta^2 = 0.171$
Yerys et al. (2013)	TYP (n = 23): 10.62; ASD (n = 21): 10.22	Age, IQ, sex ratio	Emotional go/no-go	Inhibition	TYP > ASD[b]	$\eta^2 = 0.13$

ADHD, attention deficit/hyperactivity disorder; *ANT*, amsterdam neuropsychological tasks; *ASD*, autism spectrum disorders; *CCTT2*, children's color trails test—second edition; *CPT*, continuous performance test; *CTT*, consonant trigrams test; *DK T-Switch*, D-KEFS category switching; *FSIQ*, full-scale intelligence quotient; *HVLT-R*, hopkins verbal learning test – revised; *ID/ED-CANTAB*, intradimensional/extradimensional shift test—CANTAB; *IQ*, intelligence quotient; *IVACPT-ARCQ*, integrated visual and auditory continuous performance task—auditory response control quotient; *IVACPT-VRCQ*, integrated visual and auditory continuous performance task—visual response control quotient; *LNS*, letter–number sequencing test; *MCI*, metacognition index; *MCST*, modified card sorting test; *PDD/HD*, symptoms of both *PDD-NOS* and ADHD; *PDDNOS*, pervasive developmental disorder not otherwise specified; *RCFT*, rey complex figure test; *RT-ISV*, response time intrasubject variability; *SART- random*, sustained attention to response task – random condition; *SD-RT*, standard deviation of response time; *SES*, socioeconomic status; *SOC*, stockings of Cambridge; *SSP*, spatial span; *SWM-CANTAB*, spatial working memory CANTAB; *TAP*, test battery for attention performance; *TOL*, Tower of London; *TOVA*, Tests of Variables of Attention; *TYP*, typically developing children or neurotypical adults; *VIQ*, Verbal IQ.
[a]This column refers to whether there is an impairment reported with a particular focus on an ASD group where ADHD symptoms are measured or when ASD and ASD + ADHD groups are defined. Impairments are always noted with a ">" between groups, regardless of whether a higher or lower score is considered better. For example, TYP > ASD may be noted for a CPT even if the TYP group made *fewer* false alarms.
[b]There was a significant regression/correlation of ADHD symptoms EF performance in children with ASD.

task. Unfortunately, the study does not break out the ASD and ASD + ADHD subgroups to demonstrate that the group difference for the ASD group was driven by the ASD + ADHD subgroup. Taken together, the findings suggest that ADHD symptoms may relate to impaired performance on inhibition tasks in ASD. Thus, the inconsistent findings of inhibitory control impairments in the broader ASD literature may result from failing to take into account this crucial "third" variable (i.e., ADHD symptoms/comorbid ADHD diagnosis).

3.2 Working Memory

Working memory is also assessed in multiple studies examining EF in ASD + ADHD populations. There is a great deal of diversity in how working memory is assessed. The most common approach is to use span tasks that require individuals to store a sequence of numbers, letters, or spatial locations (Andersen, Hovik, Skogli, Egeland, & Oie, 2013; Corbett et al., 2009; Nydén et al., 2010; Yerys et al., 2009). Other methods include maintenance of prior responding while engaged in a visual search task (Gomarus, Wijers, Minderaa, & Althaus, 2009; Yerys et al., 2009), and divided attention tasks (Sinzig, Bruning, et al., 2008; Yerys, Wallace, Jankowski, Bollich, & Kenworthy, 2011). There are three studies of verbal span tasks and two reported that the ASD + ADHD group demonstrated impaired working memory performance (Andersen et al., 2013; Yerys et al., 2009), although it is notable that one of these studies only reported a difference between ASD + ADHD and typically developing controls. There was a medium effect size group difference between the ASD + ADHD and ASD groups on a digit span task (Yerys et al., 2009). This is important as the third study showing no differences compared ASD, ADHD, and ASD + ADHD samples (Nydén et al., 2010). One study used a traditional spatial span task and found no relationship between ADHD symptoms and the ASD group's impaired performance (Corbett et al., 2009). Two studies examined spatial working memory through the Cambridge Neuropsychological Test Automated Battery (CANTAB) (Corbett et al., 2009; Yerys et al., 2009), but neither demonstrated a greater impairment with a dimensional measure of ADHD symptoms or categorical separation into an ASD + ADHD group. Both of these studies had modest samples, and this may have limited their ability to detect a relationship or to identify a group difference. To wit Yerys et al. (2009) reported medium-to-large effect sizes associated with the nonsignificant differences between the ASD + ADHD group and both control and ASD alone groups. Two studies assessed verbal working memory through divided attention tasks but one study found a weak effect (Sinzig, Bruning, et al., 2008), and the other explicitly ruled out a relationship between poor performance and comorbid ADHD symptoms (Yerys et al., 2011). Taken together, the findings to date suggest that the presence of ADHD symptoms in ASD is not strongly related to verbal or spatial working memory performance. However, it is important to note that only one study had a particularly large sample (Nydén et al., 2010), and therefore research with well-powered samples is needed to understand the relationship between ADHD symptoms and working memory function among individuals with ASD.

3.3 Planning and Generativity

Planning and generativity are two constructs under the umbrella of EF, but are typically assessed with complex tasks that recruit multiple EF processes. To date only two studies have examined planning while considering the influence of ADHD symptoms. On the Tower of London, an ASD + ADHD group performed similarly to ASD alone and ADHD alone groups (Nydén et al., 2010). On the CANTAB's Stockings of Cambridge task the ASD and typically developing control groups performed similarly, and ADHD symptoms did not correlate with performance for the ASD group (Corbett et al., 2009). Generativity was assessed with Letter and Category Fluency tasks from the DKEFS, and similar to the planning tasks no group differences were found between the ASD group and ADHD or typically developing control groups (Corbett et al., 2009). Furthermore, ADHD symptoms did not correlate with performance on either Fluency task. Taking these two studies together suggests that the presence of ADHD symptoms in ASD is not strongly related to performance on planning or generativity tasks.

3.4 Flexibility

Flexibility—also referred to as shifting or task switching—is an area of impairment most commonly associated with ASD (Hill, 2004; Kenworthy et al., 2008; Pennington & Ozonoff, 1996); however, it remains a possibility that this EF process may be influenced by ADHD symptoms as there is some evidence suggesting it is affected in ADHD as well (Willcutt et al., 2005). To date, there is only one study examining flexibility while accounting for ADHD symptoms, and this study reported no impairment in the ASD sample for two of three measures (Corbett et al., 2009), with impairment reported only for a modified Stroop task—Task Switching from the DKEFS—that requires children to switch among three conditions: reading words, naming the color of ink, and inhibition (Stroop condition). Furthermore, ADHD symptoms were not reported as correlating with DKEFS Task Switch performance. This preliminary study suggests that the presence of ADHD symptoms is not strongly related to performance on flexibility tasks; however, the body of research is very limited; thus, more work is needed before definitive conclusions can be drawn.

3.5 Ecologically Valid Measures of Executive Function

To date only one study has examined EF in an ASD + ADHD group using an ecologically valid measure (Yerys et al., 2009). The BRIEF's two indices and the Inhibit and Shift scales were examined in controls, ASD, and ASD + ADHD groups. The two specific scales (i.e., Inhibit and Shift) were selected because they represent profile peaks for ADHD and ASD, respectively (Gioia et al., 2002). The ASD + ADHD group was rated by parents as experiencing significantly greater impairments across the Behavior Regulation and Metacognition indices and the two scales compared to the ASD and control groups. This preliminary study suggests that the presence of ADHD symptoms is strongly related to EF in real-world settings; however, as suggested above, additional research is needed here as well before definitive conclusions can be drawn.

3.6 Summary and Future Directions

To summarize this nascent area of research, evidence thus far suggests that Inhibition is the EF process most likely to be affected by the presence of co-morbid ADHD symptoms in ASD. The remaining EF processes—Working Memory, Planning, Generativity, and Flexibility—have relatively few and/ or underpowered studies that show little relationship between task performance and ADHD symptoms. However, the one ecologically valid study suggests there may be a large relationship between the presence of comorbid ADHD symptoms and EF in the real world. Therefore, future directions to explore include replication and extension of existing studies with larger samples that combine both dimensional and gold standard categorical measures of ADHD (e.g., structured interviews) to improve ADHD diagnostics in ASD. Another future direction is to focus on the dynamic developmental trajectory of EF processes as the trajectory may differ for children with ASD + ADHD relative to ASD alone. Finally, there should be a greater emphasis on increasing our knowledge about ASD + ADHD in adults and in individuals with both ASD and ID. These samples are underrepresented in the current literature.

4. EXECUTIVE FUNCTION INTERVENTIONS FOR PEOPLE WITH AUTISM SPECTRUM DISORDER

Originating with Fisher and Happé's seminal trial in 2005, there is a small but growing literature on interventions targeting EF in children with ASD (see Table 3). EF treatments include a number of different treatment modalities, including cognitive behavior therapy (CBT), computer training, medicines, and biofeedback. EF treatment in many of these modalities shows promise for people with ASD, but there is a notable lack of methodological rigor in most studies. Only five randomized controlled trials (RCT) are summarized below, and of those, two (one CBT and one biofeedback intervention) showed gains in EF abilities as a result.

4.1 Cognitive Behavior Therapy

Several social skills CBT interventions with an EF training component have been evaluated in uncontrolled single group studies and reveal improvement on parent reported EF behaviors (Stichter et al., 2010; Stichter, O'Connor, Herzog, Lierheimer, & McGhee, 2012) and EF/problem solving task performance (Bauminger, 2007; Stichter et al., 2010). One of these interventions is called Social Skills Training (Bauminger, 2007). It emphasizes ecological validity and was implemented over 7 months in school-based small group sessions and individual meetings. Students learned and practiced a variety of skills, including reading emotions, having conversations, and cooperating with others, including the EF components of planning and compromising. A second CBT intervention is Stichter and colleagues' Social Competence Intervention (Stichter et al., 2010, 2012), which addresses recognition of facial expression, sharing ideas with others, taking turns in conversations, recognizing emotions, and the EF component of problem solving. The intervention was delivered in a clinic setting and included instruction, modeling, and practice of skills, with a strong emphasis on a "scaffolded approach by which the concepts and skills learned in previous units were incorporated into latter units" (p.1071; Stichter et al., 2010). This intervention was initially developed for adolescents (Stichter et al., 2010) and then adapted for elementary school age children (Stichter et al., 2012) with ASD. In a third CBT intervention, Solomon et al. employed a wait list control methodology to evaluate the Social Adjustment Enhancement Curriculum, which addressed facial expression recognition, theory of mind, and executive functions, "with a special emphasis on individual and group problem solving"

Table 3 Review of EF Intervention Studies in ASD

References	Diagnostic Groups/Mean Age/Mean IQ	Intervention Type/Name/ Duration	Study Methodology	EF Domains Targeted	EF Outcome Measures	Key EF Outcomes	Effect Size If Reported
Bauminger (2007)	ASD (n = 26) 8–9 years Average IQ	CBT Social skills training 50 lessons	Single group, pre- and posttreatment assessment	Global (including cognitive flexibility)	D-KEFS sorting subtest number of sorts	Improvement	$\eta^2 = 0.14$
					D-KEFS sorting subtest strategies generated	Improvement	$\eta^2 = 0.16$
					D-KEFS sorting subtest strategies recognized	Improvement	$\eta^2 = 0.16$
Fisher and Happé (2005)	ASD (n = 21) social communication disorder (n = 6) 10 years	CBT Theory of mind (ToM) and EF 4–10 sessions	RCT G1 = ToM (n = 10) G2 = EF (n = 10) G3 = No intervention (n = 7)	Flexibility	Modified Wisconsin Card Sort Task Trails task	ToM group only: improved on Card Sort perseverative errors No evidence of any improvement by any group on Trails	
Kenworthy et al. (2014)	ASD (n = 67) 9 years Average IQ	CBT Unstuck and on target and social skills 27 lessons	RCT G1 = unstuck (n = 47) G2 = social skills (n = 20)	Flexibility Planning Organization	BRIEF-T Shift Scale	Unstuck > Social Skill	Cohen's d = −0.89
					BRIEF-T Plan/Org Scale	Unstuck > Social Skill	Cohen's d = −0.57
					BRIEF-P Shift Scale	Unstuck > Social Skill	Cohen's d = −0.66
					BRIEF-P Plan/Org Scale	Unstuck > Social Skill	Cohen's d = −0.45
					Wechsler Block Design	Unstuck > Social Skill	Cohen's d = 0.65
					Executive Function Challenge Task Flexibility	Unstuck > Social Skill	Cohen's d = −0.72
					Executive Function Challenge Task Plan	Unstuck > Social Skill	Cohen's d = −0.27

(Continued)

Table 3 Review of EF Intervention Studies in ASD—cont'd

References	Diagnostic Groups/Mean Age/Mean IQ	Intervention Type/Name/Duration	Study Methodology	EF Domains Targeted	EF Outcome Measures	Key EF Outcomes	Effect Size If Reported
Solomon et al. (2004)	ASD (n = 18) Younger group = 8, older group = 10 Younger group = high average IQ Older group = low average IQ	CBT Social adjustment enhancement curriculum 20 sessions	Wait list control (n = 9) Intervention group (n = 9)	Problem solving	Test of problem solving (TOPS)	Improvement: Younger intervention group	
Stichter et al. (2010)	ASD (n = 27) 12 years Average IQ	CBT Social competence intervention 20 sessions	Single group, pre- and posttreatment assessment	Global Behavior regulation Metacognition Problem solving	BRIEF global executive composite BRIEF Behavior Regulation Index BRIEF Metacognition Index TOPS-3 making inferences TOPS-3 problem solving	Improvement Improvement Improvement Improvement Improvement	
Stichter et al. (2012)	ASD (n = 20) 8 years Average IQ	CBT Social competence intervention 20 sessions	Single group, pre- and posttreatment assessment	Global Behavior regulation Metacognition Problem solving	BRIEF global executive composite BRIEF Behavior Regulation Index BRIEF Metacognition Index TOPS-3 total	Improvement Improvement Improvement No improvement	Cohen's d = 0.35 Cohen's d = 0.23 Cohen's d = 0.42 Cohen's d = 0.15

Study	Population	Intervention	Design	EF domain	Outcome measure	Results	Effect size
de Vries et al. (2015)	ASD ($n = 121$) 8–12 years Average IQ	Computer training Braingame Brian 25 sessions	RCT G1 = working memory training ($n = 40$) G2 = cognitive flexibility training ($n = 37$) G3 = mock training ($n = 38$)	Working memory Flexibility Inhibition Sustained attention	Corsi block tapping task N-back BRIEF Working Memory Scale Gender-emotion switching task Number-gnome switch task Sustained attention response task Stop task	Trend: Greater improvement in Working Memory Group No intervention-specific improvements No intervention-specific improvements No intervention-specific improvements No intervention-specific improvements No intervention-specific improvements No intervention-specific improvements	$\eta^2 = 0.06$ $\eta^2 = 0.01–0.03$ $\eta^2 = 0.02$ $\eta^2 = 0.02–0.03$ $\eta^2 = 0.01–0.03$ $\eta^2 = 0.03$ $\eta^2 = 0.03$
Hilton et al. (2014)	ASD ($n = 7$) 9 years Average IQ	Computer training Exergame-Makoto Arena 30 sessions	Single group, pre- and posttreatment assessment	Metacognition Working memory Global	BRIEF Metacognition Index BRIEF Working Memory Scale All other BRIEF scales	Improvement Improvement No improvement	Cohen's $d = -1.01$ Cohen's $d = -0.53$ Cohen's $d = -0.04$ to -0.36
Kouijzer et al. (2013)	ASD ($n = 38$) 14/15 years Average IQ	EEG biofeedback Seven 3-min intervals of visual biofeedback on	RCT G1: EEG biofeedback G2: skin	Cognitive flexibility Inhibition Planning Working memory	Trail making test (part C time, part B time) Stroop part (C time,	EEG-biofeedback group only: Improvement No intervention-	$\eta^2 = 0.731$

(Continued)

Table 3 Review of EF Intervention Studies in ASD—cont'd

References	Diagnostic Groups/Mean Age/Mean IQ	Intervention Type/Name/ Duration	Study Methodology	EF Domains Targeted	EF Outcome Measures	Key EF Outcomes	Effect Size If Reported
		EEG or SC 40 sessions	conductance biofeedback		part B time) Tower of London (total correct) WISC–III NL Digit Span subtest	specific improvements No intervention-specific improvements No intervention-specific improvements	
Handen et al. (2011)	ASD (n = 34) 11 years Average IQ	Medication Donepezil 10 weeks; final dose: 10 mg/day	RCT G1: donepezil (n = 18) G2: placebo (n = 16)	Global	D-KEFS: card sorting D-KEFS: verbal fluency D-KEFS: 20 questions TMT time VF switching DFT switching CWI inhibition/ switch EF rating scale: cognitive plans EF rating scale: time management EF rating scale: self-regulation	No intervention-specific improvements No intervention-specific improvements No intervention-specific improvements No intervention-specific improvements No intervention-specific improvements No intervention-specific improvements No intervention-specific improvements No intervention-specific improvements	

Study	Sample	Intervention	Design	Measure	Outcome	Effect size
Joshi et al. (2016)	ASD (n = 18) 28 years Average IQ	Medication Memantine 12 weeks; maximum dose: 20 mg	Single group, pre- and posttreatment assessment	Global	No intervention-specific improvements	
					No intervention-specific improvements	
				BRIEF-adult self-report: GEC	Improvement	Cohen's $d = -0.67$
				BRIEF-adult self-report: BRI	Improvement	Cohen's $d = -0.59$
				BRIEF-adult self-report: MCI	Improvement	Cohen's $d = -0.55$
				CANTAB: SWM between errors	No improvement	Cohen's $d = -0.33$
				CANTAB: IDED total errors	Improvement	Cohen's $d = -0.02$
				CANTAB: SOC problems solved in min. moves		Cohen's $d = 0.52$

ASD, autism spectrum disorder; *BRI*, behavioral regulation index (from BRIEF); *BRIEF*, behavior rating inventory of executive function (from BRIEF); *BRIEF-P*, behavior rating inventory of executive function—parent; *BRIEF-T*, behavior rating inventory of executive function—teacher; *CBT*, cognitive behavioral therapy; *CANTAB*, Cambridge neuropsychological test automated battery; *CWI*, color–word interference; *DFT*, Design Fluency Test; *D-KEFS*, delis–kaplan executive function system; *EEG*, electroencephalography; *EF*, executive function; *GEC*, global executive composite (from BRIEF); *IDED*, intra–extra dimensional set shift (from CANTAB); *MCI*, metacognition index (from BRIEF); *IQ*, intelligence quotient; *NL*, Netherlands; *RCT*, randomized controlled trial; *SC*, skin conductance; *SOC*, stockings of Cambridge (from CANTAB); *SWM*, spatial working memory (from CANTAB); *TMT*, trail making test; *ToM*, theory of mind; *TOPS*, test of problem solving; *VF*, verbal fluency; *WISC-III*, Wechsler Intelligence Scales for Children–III.

(p. 652, Solomon, Goodlin-Jones, & Anders, 2004). This clinic-based group/individual intervention includes more lessons focused on specific EF skills than the two interventions described above. For example, there are lessons on identifying relevant information, prioritizing problems, and another lesson on flexibility in generating alternative solutions to problems. The intervention and waitlist control groups were divided into younger (8—10 years) and older (10—12 years) age groups and the younger intervention group showed significant gains on a problem solving task following intervention, in contrast to the younger waitlist control group, whose mean performance dropped on this measure. Each of these studies is limited by the lack of pre-/post-intervention treatment-blind assessments of EF outcome. Although they indicate initial promise for CBT approaches to enhance social awareness and EF in ASD, more rigorous further testing of these interventions is needed.

We are aware of only two RCTs of CBT EF interventions in ASD. Fisher and Happé (2005) contrasted two brief clinic-based trainings, targeting EF and theory of mind skills training, respectively. They found that both contributed to improvements in theory of mind, whereas only the theory of mind intervention improved EF, as indicated by reduced perseverative errors on a carding sorting task. They concluded that longer-term school- or home-based interventions that assess real-world behaviors were warranted. The second RCT compared the Unstuck and On Target curriculum (UOT; Cannon, Kenworthy, Alexander, Werner, & Anthony, 2011) to an equal intensity social skills curriculum (Baker, 2003). UOT focuses directly on the EF skills of flexibility, organization, and planning in a small group format that teaches what flexibility, planning, and organization are, why they are useful, and how to be more flexible, planful, and organized through the use of self-regulatory scripts. The advantages of flexibility in social interactions are also addressed. School-based small group sessions introduce and practice skills using games, vignettes/movies, consistent visuals, and extensive modeling. Parents were provided with a manual, homework, and two trainings describing how to model and support the use of flexibility and planning scripts at home. The Social Skills intervention followed the same teaching format to introduce social-communication skills lessons from Baker's curriculum (Baker, 2003). Participants in both interventions improved, but significantly greater improvements resulted from UOT than the social skills intervention on treatment-blind EF measures of flexibility, planning, organization, and problem solving in a variety of modalities, including blinded performance-based tasks, parent/teacher report, and blinded observed classroom behavior (Kenworthy et al., 2014). UOT and social skills interventions had equivalent impacts on social skills.

4.2 Computer-Based Interventions

Two trials of computer-based interventions to improve EF reveal mixed results. A small, uncontrolled single group study of a computer game that requires physical activity found gains in parent reported working memory and metacognitive control (Hilton et al., 2014). On the other hand, a large rigorous RCT of three conditions of Braingame Brian, working memory-training, flexibility-training, and mock-training (Prins et al., 2013), revealed no significant intervention specific improvements on a range of working memory, cognitive flexibility, and attention measures. A trend toward improvement in performance on a near-transfer (i.e., task resembles training activity) working memory task following the working memory training was reported in a second publication on the same intervention trial (de Vries et al., 2015).

4.3 Medication

Two medication trials targeting EF in people with ASD demonstrate a similar pattern, with significant improvement reported only in the less methodologically rigorous study. A small, uncontrolled single group study of memantine, an Alzheimer's disease medication acting on the glutamatergic system, found improvements in self-reported EF and performance on a planning task (Joshi et al., 2016). A larger RCT comparing placebo and Donepezil, a centrally acting reversible acetylcholinesterase inhibitor, also used to improve cognition and behavior of people with Alzheimer's disease, found no intervention-related improvements (Handen, Johnson, McAuliffe-Bellin, Murray, & Hardan, 2011).

4.4 Biofeedback/Transcranial Magnetic Stimulation

An RCT comparing electroencephalogram (EEG)-biofeedback to skin conductance biofeedback found that 54% of participants significantly reduced delta and/or theta power during EEG-biofeedback sessions, and these "EEG-regulators" showed significant gains on a cognitive flexibility performance task compared to those who learned to regulate skin conductance response, although no gains were reported on planning, inhibition or working memory tasks (Kouijzer, van Schie, Gerrits, Buitelaar, & de Moor, 2013). Two waitlist-controlled studies of response to repetitive transcranial magnetic stimulation (rTMS) applied over the dorso-lateral prefrontal cortex found reported improvements in EF (Sokhadze, El-Baz, Sears, Opris, & Casanova, 2014; Sokhadze, El-Baz, Tasman, et al., 2014). One of these studies followed rTMS with EEG-biofeedback (Sokhadze, El-Baz, Tasman, et al., 2014). These investigations are not listed in Table 3 because they assessed behavioral response to treatment with an oddball task that is generally understood as a measure of sustained attention, rather than a component of EF.

4.5 Summary

In summary, the increasing number of interventions using EF outcome measures reflects an exciting new interest in treatments that target specific, well-characterized EF deficits with specific measures of outcome. This contrasts with the multiply determined behavioral targets (e.g. irritability) that have dominated in the past. Another key component of these treatments is the emphasis on ecological validity, which is implicitly recognized in many studies by the use of real-world measures of EF outcomes and is directly invoked in a subset of the studies reviewed here. De Vries et al. (2015) address the challenge of generalization in their use of near and far transfer outcome measures and Kenworthy et al. (2014) use blinded classroom observations as a tool for measuring transfer of skills to real-world settings. Consistent with Dingfelder and Mandell's (2011) directive that we must "link intervention development and the settings in which we hope interventions ultimately will be used" (p. 607), two interventions reviewed here occur in the school setting. Finally, the CBT approaches consistently demonstrate a blurring of EF and social skills, such that most interventions target some component of both skill sets, and several studies found that purported treatments for EF or social understanding improved skills in the other area (Fisher & Happé, 2005; Kenworthy et al., 2014). This is consistent with evidence that EF abilities may be precursors to Theory of Mind abilities (Flynn, 2007), or in any case are correlated with them (Pellicano, 2007; Perner & Lang, 1999).

4.6 Future Directions

An important area for future research to tackle is individual differences/ subgrouping. Despite DSM-5 clumping previous "subtypes" of ASD utilized in DSM-IV, there is a larger move toward an individualized medicine approach. Profiles of intact and impaired EF could serve to inform intervention approach more broadly regardless of DSM diagnosis (e.g., ASD, ADHD). EF phenotype-specific interventions and outcome measures that target flexibility, for example, could be tested in *all* children with flexibility problems, which would include the majority of children with ASD (Granader et al., 2014) and also sizable proportions of children with other developmental and psychiatric disorders, such as ADHD and anxiety. Targeting interventions to specific EF profiles not only expands potential recipients of the treatment beyond diagnostic borders, it also encourages researchers to investigate the broader range of treatments, which have been developed for a range of different diagnoses.

Furthermore, it is important that EF intervention studies evaluate the full range of co-occurring conditions and ability levels in study participants. The presence or absence of depression, impulsivity, anxiety, and social cognitive differences in participants with ASD might interact with EF and therefore impact the chosen intervention and the outcome.

There are also obvious gaps in the types of people studied in this literature to date. Females of all IQ levels must be studied in adequate numbers for treatment response to be evaluated for each gender. We do not know if females respond differently than males in different treatment paradigms. We also need all treatment studies to explore contributions of cultural beliefs, family income, insurance benefits, and minority status to treatment outcome.

From a methodological perspective, it will be important to confirm many of the results reported here with better controlled trials with: random assignment to multiple active treatment conditions of equal intensity and treatment blind outcome data collection (Dawson & Burner, 2011; Kasari & Lawton, 2010). It is also notable among the CBT trials that investigators are studying interventions they themselves have created. In order for this promising area to fully develop it will be essential that initial positive findings from RCTs, such as that reported above for the UOT Intervention and the EEG biofeedback trials, are followed by effectiveness trials run by new investigators that measure the impact of these interventions compared to other promising techniques.

Finally, investigations of EF intervention in ASD must also use diverse laboratory- and real world-based outcome measures to comprehensively assess the change in EF. As has been previously shown (Mackinlay et al., 2006), there are relatively weak correlations between performance on laboratory-based EF assessment tools and parent ratings of EF (e.g., the BRIEF). This highlights their complementary contributions to the broader understanding of EF deficits. New and creative tools for evaluating ecologically valid EF skills in the laboratory that include social demands, such as the Executive Function Challenge Task (Kenworthy et al., 2014), are also needed.

5. CONCLUSIONS

The current review of EF in ASD based on extant studies published since the time of our last review (Kenworthy et al., 2008) reveals mixed evidence for laboratory-based EF deficits, which corroborates the broader (and older) literature (Hill, 2004; Pennington & Ozonoff, 1996). Nevertheless, flexibility/set-shifting is the EF domain most frequently implicated as impaired in ASD using lab-based assessment. In contrast, findings are much more consistent and robust for EF deficits in ASD when utilizing ecologically valid assessment, whether utilizing ratings scales or performance-based measures. Additionally, with the advent of DSM-V, ADHD can now be diagnosed alongside ASD, which has profound implications, given that both disorders share EF deficits, although the profiles of EF impairment are distinct. The small group of studies completed to date suggests that previously mixed findings for inhibitory control deficits in ASD might be explained, at least in part, by co-occurring ADHD symptomatology. Finally, perhaps the most impactful development since the completion of our last review is the development of interventions targeting EF in ASD. This emerging literature represents an excellent start toward the fulfillment of the promise that prior EF characterization and natural history studies have provided.

Although great progress has been made in the last several years, expansion of this work should continue and novel future directions should be pursued. As highlighted above, further development of ecologically valid assessment tools is needed, particularly those that harness the power of modern technology. Utilization of longitudinal designs to assess the (a)typicality of developmental trajectories of real-world EF in ASD should be examined not only in children and adolescents, but also during adult aging. Indeed, adulthood is thus far a relatively neglected window of development in understanding EF in ASD. As such, more work on understanding the impact of co-occurring ADHD symptoms during adulthood in ASD as well as EF intervention development during this period could prove fruitful. It is also important to point out that the vast majority of the research reported here was conducted with participants without ID, indicating a need for new assessment tools and interventions that address EF in those with ASD and

ID. Similarly, there is a strong need to raise the bar in terms of both methodological rigor (e.g., for intervention studies: blinded pre- and post-treatment assessment of EF and replication of effects across research groups) and inclusiveness (e.g., females with ASD as well as minorities and traditionally underserved groups who also carry the ASD diagnosis) in all research, particularly intervention-based work. The hope is that by addressing these and other outstanding issues, this work will help push forward the broader goal of improving quality of life and life satisfaction for people with ASD of all ages and from all backgrounds.

REFERENCES

Adamo, N., Huo, L., Adelsberg, S., Petkova, E., Castellanos, F. X., & Di Martino, A. (2013). Response time intra-subject variability: commonalities between children with autism spectrum disorders and children with ADHD. *European Child & Adolescent Psychiatry, 23*(2), 69–79. http://dx.doi.org/10.1007/s00787-013-0428-4.

American Psychiatric Association. (1994). *Diagnostic and statistical manual of mental disorders* (4th ed.). Washington, DC: Author.

American Psychiatric Association. (2013). *Diagnostic and statistical manual of mental disorders* (5th ed.). Washington, DC: Author.

Andersen, P. N., Hovik, K. T., Skogli, E. W., Egeland, J., & Oie, M. (2013). Symptoms of ADHD in children with high-functioning autism are related to impaired verbal working memory and verbal delayed recall. *PLoS One, 8*(5), e64842. http://dx.doi.org/10.1371/journal.pone.0064842.

Baker, J. (2003). *Social skills training for children and adolescents with Asperger syndrome and social-communications problems* (1st ed.). Autism Asperger Publishing Co.

Barendse, E. M., Hendriks, M. P., Jansen, J. F., Backes, W. H., Hofman, P. A., Thoonen, G., … Aldenkamp, A. P. (2013). Working memory deficits in high-functioning adolescents with autism spectrum disorders: neuropsychological and neuro-imaging correlates. *Journal of Neurodevelopmental Disorders, 5*(1), 14. http://dx.doi.org/10.1186/1866-1955-5-14.

Baron-Cohen, S., Leslie, A. M., & Frith, U. (1985). Does the autistic child have a 'theory of mind'? *Cognition, 21,* 37–46.

Bauminger, N. (2007). Brief report: group social-multimodal intervention for HFASD. *Journal of Autism and Developmental Disorders, 37,* 1605–1615.

Blijd-Hoogewys, E. M., Bezemer, M. L., & van Geert, P. L. (2014). Executive functioning in children with ASD: an analysis of the BRIEF. *Journal of Autism and Developmental Disorders, 44,* 3089–3100.

Bramham, J., Ambery, F., Young, S., Morris, R., Russell, A., Xenitidis, K., … Murphy, D. (2009). Executive functioning differences between adults with attention deficit hyperactivity disorder and autistic spectrum disorder in initiation, planning and strategy formation. *Autism, 13*(3), 245–264.

Brunsdon, V. E. A., Colvert, E., Ames, C., Garnett, T., Gillan, N., Hallett, V., … Happé, F. (2015). Exploring the cognitive features in children with autism spectrum disorder, their co-twins, and typically developing children within a population-based sample. *Journal of Child Psychology and Psychiatry, 56*(8), 893–902.

Bühler, E., Bachmann, C., Goyert, H., Heinzel-Gutenbrunner, M., & Kamp-Becker, I. (2011). Differential diagnosis of autism spectrum disorder and attention deficit hyperactivity disorder by means of inhibitory control and "theory of mind. *Journal of Autism and*

Developmental Disorders, 41(12), 1718—1726. http://dx.doi.org/10.1007/s10803-011-1205-1.

Cannon, L., Kenworthy, L., Alexander, K., Werner, M., & Anthony, L. (2011). In *Unstuck and on target!: An executive function curriculum to improve flexibility for children with autism spectrum disorders* (Research ed.). Baltimore, MD: Brookes.

Castellanos, F. X., & Tannock, R. (2002). Neuroscience of attention-deficit/hyperactivity disorder: the search for endophenotypes. *Nature Reviews Neuroscience, 3*(8), 617—628. http://dx.doi.org/10.1038/nrn896.

Cederlund, M., Hagberg, B., & Gillberg, C. (2010). Asperger syndrome in adolescent and young adult males. interview, self- and parent assessment of social, emotional, and cognitive problems. *Research in Developmental Disabilities, 31*, 287—298.

Corbett, B. A., Constantine, L. J., Hendren, R., Rocke, D., & Ozonoff, S. (2009). Examining executive functioning in children with autism spectrum disorder, attention deficit hyperactivity disorder and typical development. *Psychiatry Research, 166*(2—3), 210—222. http://dx.doi.org/10.1016/j.psychres.2008.02.005.

Crawford, J. R., Bryan, J., Luszcz, M. A., Obonsawin, M. C., & Stewart, L. (2000). The executive decline hypothesis of cognitive aging: do executive deficits qualify as differential deficits and do they mediate age-related memory decline? *Aging, Neuropsychology, and Cognition: A Journal on Normal and Dysfunctional Development, 7*, 9—31.

Damasio, A. R., & Maurer, R. G. (1978). A neurological model for childhood autism. *Archives of Neurology, 35*, 777—786.

Dawson, G., & Burner, K. (2011). Behavioral interventions in children and adolescents with autism spectrum disorder: a review of recent findings. *Current Opinion in Pediatrics, 23*(6), 616—620.

De Luca, C. R., Wood, S. J., Anderson, V., Buchanan, J. A., Proffitt, T. M., Mahony, K., & Pantelis, C. (2003). Normative data from the CANTAB. I: development of executive function over the lifespan. *Journal of Clinical and Experimental Neuropsychology, 25*(2), 242—254.

Dingfelder, H. E., & Mandell, D. S. (2011). Bridging the research-to practice gap in autism intervention: an application of diffusion of innovation theory. *Journal of Autism and Developmental Disorders, 41*(5), 597—609.

Doyle, A. E., Faraone, S. V., Seidman, L. J., Willcutt, E. G., Nigg, J. T., Waldman, I. D., ... Biederman, J. (2005). Are endophenotypes based on measures of executive functions useful for molecular genetic studies of ADHD? *Journal of Child Psychology and Psychiatry, 46*(7), 774—803. http://dx.doi.org/10.1111/j.1469-7610.2005.01476.x.

DuPaul, G. J., Reid, R., Anastopoulos, A. D., Lambert, M. C., Watkins, M. W., & Power, T. J. (2016). Parent and teacher ratings of attention-deficit/hyperactivity disorder symptoms: factor structure and normative data. *Psychological Assessment, 28*(2), 214—225. http://dx.doi.org/10.1037/pas0000166.

Emslie, H., Wilson, F. C., Burden, V., Nimmo-Smith, I., & Wilson, B. A. (2003). *Behavioural assessment of the dysexecutive syndrome in children (BADS-C)*. London, U.K: Harcourt Assessment.

Fisher, N., & Happé, F. (2005). A training study of theory of mind and executive function in children with autistic spectrum disorders. *Journal of Autism and Developmental Disorders, 35*(6), 757—771.

Flynn, E. (2007). The role of inhibitory control in false belief understanding. *Infant and Child Development, 16*(1), 53—69.

Geurts, H. M., van den Bergh, S. F. W. M., & Ruzzano, L. (2014). Prepotent Response inhibition and interference control in autism spectrum disorders: two meta-analyses. *Autism Research, 7*(4), 407—420. http://dx.doi.org/10.1002/aur.1369.

Geurts, H. M., Verté, S., Oosterlaan, J., Roeyers, H., & Sergeant, J. A. (2004). How specific are executive functioning deficits in attention deficit hyperactivity disorder and autism? *Journal of Child Psychology and Psychiatry, 45*(4), 836–854. http://dx.doi.org/10.1111/j.1469-7610.2004.00276.x.

Geurts, H. M., & Vissers, M. E. (2012). Elderly with autism: executive functions and memory. *Journal of Autism and Developmental Disorders, 42*, 665–675.

Gioia, G. A., Isquith, P. K., Guy, S., & Kenworthy, L. (2000). *BRIEF: Behavior rating inventory of executive function*. Odessa, FL: Psychological Assessment Resources.

Gioia, G. A., Isquith, P. K., Kenworthy, L., & Barton, R. M. (2002). Profiles of everyday executive function in acquired and developmental disorders. *Child Neuropsychology, 8*(2), 121–137.

Gomarus, H., Wijers, A., Minderaa, R., & Althaus, M. (2009). ERP correlates of selective attention and working memory capacities in children with ADHD and/or PDD-NOS. *Clinical Neurophysiology, 120*(1), 60–72. http://dx.doi.org/10.1016/j.clinph.2008.10.018.

Granader, Y., Wallace, G. L., Hardy, K. K., Yerys, B. E., Lawson, R. A., Rosenthal, M., ... Kenworthy, L. (2014). Characterizing the factor structure of parent reported executive function in autism spectrum disorders: the impact of cognitive inflexibility. *Journal of Autism and Developmental Disorders, 44*, 3056–3062.

Handen, B. L., Johnson, C. R., McAuliffe-Bellin, S., Murray, P. J., & Hardan, A. Y. (2011). Safety and efficacy of Donepezil in children and adolescents with autism: neuropsychological measures. *Journal of Child and Adolescent Pscyhopharmacology, 21*(1), 43–50.

Happé, F., & Frith, U. (1996). The neuropsychology of autism. *Brain, 119*(Pt 4), 1377–1400.

Hill, E. L. (2004). Evaluating the theory of executive dysfunction in autism. *Developmental Review, 24*(2), 189–233.

Hilton, C. L., Cumpata, K., Klohr, C., Gaetka, S., Artner, A., Johnson, H., & Dobbs, S. (2014). Effects on exergaming on executive function and other motor skills in children with autism spectrum disorder: a pilot study. *American Journal of Occupational Therapy, 68*(1), 57–65.

Hovik, K. T., Egeland, J., Isquith, P. K., Gioia, G., Skogli, E. W., Andersen, P. N., & Øie, M. (2014). Distinct patterns of everyday executive function problems distinguish children with Tourette syndrome from children with ADHD or autism spectrum disorders. *Journal of Attention Disorders*, 1–13.

Howlin, P., Moss, P., Savage, S., & Rutter, M. (2013). Social outcomes in mid- to later adulthood among individuals diagnosed with autism and average nonverbal IQ as children. *Journal of the American Academy of Child and Adolescent Psychiatry, 52*(6), 572–581. http://dx.doi.org/10.1016/j.jaac.2013.02.017.

Huizinga, M., & Smidts, D. P. (2011). Age-related changes in executive function: a normative study with the Dutch version of the behavior rating inventory of executive function (brief). *Child Neuropsychology, 17*(1), 51–66. http://dx.doi.org/10.1080/09297049.2010.509715.

Joshi, G., Wozniak, J., Faraone, S. V., Fried, R., Chan, J., Furtak, S., ... Biederman, J. (2016). A prospective open-label trial of Memantine hydrochloride for the treatment of social deficits in intellectually capable adults with autism spectrum disorder. *Journal of Clinical Psychopharmacology, 36*, 262–271.

Kalbfleisch, M. L., & Loughan, A. R. (2012). Impact of IQ discrepancy on executive function in high-functioning autism: insight into twice exceptionality. *Journal of Autism and Developmental Disorders, 42*, 390–400.

Kasari, C., & Lawton, K. (2010). New directions in behavioral treatment of autism spectrum disorders. *Current Opinion in Neurology, 23*, 137–143.

Kenworthy, L., Anthony, L. G., Naiman, D. Q., Cannon, L., Wills, M. C., Luong-Tran, C., ... Wallace, G. L. (2014). Randomized controlled effectiveness trial of executive function intervention for children on the autism spectrum. *Journal of Child Psychology and Psychiatry, 55*(4), 374—383.

Kenworthy, L., Yerys, B. E., Anthony, L. G., & Wallace, G. L. (2008). Understanding executive control in autism spectrum disorders in the lab and in the real world. *Neuropsychology Review, 18*(4), 320—338. http://dx.doi.org/10.1007/s11065-008-9077-7.

Kenworthy, L. E., Black, D. O., Harrison, B., della Rosa, A., & Wallace, G. L. (2009). Are executive control functions related to autism symptoms in high functioning children? *Child Neuropsychology, 15*, 425—440. http://dx.doi.org/10.1080/09297040802646983.

Kercood, S., Grskovic, J. A., Banda, D., & Begeske, J. (2014). Working memory and autism: a review of literature. *Research in Autism Spectrum Disorders, 8*(10), 1316—1332. http://dx.doi.org/10.1016/j.rasd.2014.06.011.

Kouijzer, M. E. J., van Schie, H. T., Gerrits, B. J. L., Buitelaar, J. K., & de Moor, J. M. H. (2013). Is EEG-biofeedback an effective treatment in autism spectrum disorder? A randomized controlled trial. *Applied Psychophysiology and Biofeedback, 38*, 17—28.

Lawson, R. A., Papadakis, A. A., Higginson, C. I., Barnett, J. E., Wills, M. C., Strang, J. F., ... Kenworthy, L. (2015). Everyday executive function impairments predict comorbid psychopathology in autism spectrum and attention deficit hyperactivity disorders. *Neuropsychology, 29*(3), 445—453.

Leung, R. C., Vogan, V. M., Powell, T. L., Anagnostou, E., & Taylor, M. J. (2016). The role of executive functions in social impairment in autism spectrum disorder. *Child Neuropsychology, 22*(3), 336—344.

Lundervold, A. J., Stickert, M., Hysing, M., Sørensen, L., Gillberg, C., & Posserud, M.-B. (2012). Attention deficits in children with combined autism and ADHD: a CPT study. *Journal of Attention Disorders.* http://dx.doi.org/10.1177/1087054712453168.

Mackinlay, R., Charman, T., & Karmiloff-Smith, A. (2006). High functioning children with autism spectrum disorder: a novel test of multitasking. *Brain and Cognition, 61*, 14—24.

Matsuura, N., Ishitobi, M., Arai, S., Kawamura, K., Asano, M., Inohara, K., Narimoto, T., Wada, Y., Hiratani, M., & Kosaka, H. (2014). Distinguishing between autism spectrum disorder and attention deficit hyperactivity disorder by using behavioral checklists, cognitive assessments, and neuropsychological test battery. *Asian Journal of Psychiatry, 12*, 50—57. http://dx.doi.org/10.1016/j.ajp.2014.06.011.

McLean, R. L., Harrison, A. J., Zimak, E., Joseph, R. M., & Morrow, E. M. (2014). Executive function in probands with autism with average IQ and their unaffected first degree relatives. *Journal of the American Academy of Child and Adolescent Psychiatry, 53*(9), 1001—1009.

Nydén, A., Niklasson, L., Stahlberg, O., Anckarsater, H., Wentz, E., Rastam, M., & Gillberg, C. (2010). Adults with autism spectrum disorders and ADHD neuropsychological aspects. *Research in Developmental Disabilities, 31*(6), 1659—1668. http://dx.doi.org/10.1016/j.ridd.2010.04.010.

Panerai, S., Tasca, D., Ferri, R., D'Arrigo, V. G., & Elia, M. (2014). Executive functions and adaptive behaviour in autism spectrum disorders with and without intellectual disability. *Psychiatry Journal*, 1—11.

Parsons, T. D., & Carlew, A. R. (2016). Bimodal virtual reality stroop for assessing distractor inhibition in autism spectrum disorders. *Journal of Autism and Developmental Disorders, 46*, 1255—1267.

Pellicano, E. (2007). Links between theory of mind and executive function in young children with autism: clues to developmental primacy. *Developmental Psychology, 43*(4), 974—990.

Pennington, B. F., & Ozonoff, S. (1996). Executive functions and developmental psychopathology. *Journal of Child Psychology and Psychiatry, 37*(1), 51—87.

Perner, J., & Lang, B. (1999). Development of theory of mind and executive control. *Trends in Cognitive Sciences, 3*(9), 337–344.

Poljac, E., & Bekkering, H. (2012). A review of intentional and cognitive control in autism. *Frontiers in Psychology, 3*, 436. http://dx.doi.org/10.3389/fpsyg.2012.00436.

Prins, P. J., Brink, E. T., Dovis, S., Ponsioen, A., Geurts, H. M., de Vries, M., & van der Oord, S. (2013). "Braingame Brian": toward an executive function training program with game elements for children with ADHD and cognitive control problems. *Games for Health Journal, 2*(1), 44–49.

Pugliese, C. E., Anthony, L., Strang, J. F., Dudley, K., Wallace, G. L., & Kenworthy, L. (2015). Increasing adaptive behavior skill deficits from childhood to adolescence in autism spectrum disorder: role of executive function. *Journal of Autism and Developmental Disorders, 45*, 1579–1587. http://dx.doi.org/10.1007/s10803-014-2309-1.

Rosenthal, M., Wallace, G. L., Lawson, R., Wills, M. C., Dixon, E., Yerys, B. E., & Kenworthy, L. (2013). Impairments in real-world executive function increase from childhood to adolescence in autism spectrum disorders. *Neuropsychology, 27*(1), 13–18.

Roux, A. M., Shattuck, P. T., Cooper, B. P., Anderson, K. A., Wagner, M., & Narendorf, S. C. (2013). Postsecondary employment experiences among young adults with an autism spectrum disorder. *Journal of the American Academy of Child and Adolescent Psychiatry, 52*(9), 931–939. http://dx.doi.org/10.1016/j.jaac.2013.05.019.

Rumsey, J. M. (1985). Conceptual problem-solving in highly verbal, nonretarded autistic men. *Journal of Autism and Developmental Disorders, 15*, 23–36.

Russo, N., Flanagan, T., Iarocci, G., Berringer, D., Zelazo, P. D., & Burack, J. A. (2007). Deconstructing executive deficits among persons with autism: implications for cognitive neuroscience. *Brain and Cognition, 65*(1), 77–86. http://dx.doi.org/10.1016/j.bandc.2006.04.007.

Salcedo-Marin, M. D., Moreno-Granados, J. M., Ruiz-Veguilla, M., & Ferrin, M. (2013). Evaluation of planning dysfunction in attention deficit hyperactivity disorder and autistic spectrum disorders using the zoo map task. *Child Psychiatry and Human Development, 44*, 166–185.

Sinzig, J., Bruning, N., Morsch, D., & Lehmkuhl, G. (2008). Attention profiles in autistic children with and without comorbid hyperactivity and attention problems. *Acta Neuropsychiatrica, 20*(4), 207–215. http://dx.doi.org/10.1111/j.1601-5215.2008.00292.x.

Sinzig, J., Morsch, D., Bruning, N., Schmidt, M. H., & Lehmkuhl, G. (2008). Inhibition, flexibility, working memory and planning in autism spectrum disorders with and without comorbid ADHD-symptoms. *Child and Adolescent Psychiatry and Mental Health, 2*(1), 4. http://dx.doi.org/10.1186/1753-2000-2-4.

Smithson, P. E., Kenworthy, L., Wills, M. C., Jarrett, M., Atmore, K., & Yerys, B. E. (2013). Real world executive control impairments in preschoolers with autism spectrum disorder. *Journal of Autism and Developmental Disorders, 43*(8), 1967–1975.

Sokhadze, E. M., El-Baz, A. S., Sears, L. L., Opris, I., & Casanova, M. F. (2014). rTMS neuromodulation improves electrocortical functional measures of information processing and behavioral responses in autism. *Frontiers in Systems Neuroscience, 134*(8), 1–15.

Sokhadze, E. M., El-Baz, A. S., Tasman, A., Sears, L. L., Wang, Y., Lamina, E. V., & Casanova, M. F. (2014). Neuromodulation integrating rTMS and neurofeedback for the treatment of autism spectrum disorder: an exploratory study. *Applications of Psychophysiological Biofeedback, 39*(3–4), 237–257.

Solomon, M., Goodlin-Jones, B. L., & Anders, T. F. (2004). A social adjustment enhancement intervention for high functioning autism, Asperger's syndrome, and pervasive developmental disorder NOS. *Journal of Autism and Developmental Disorders, 34*, 649–668.

Stichter, J. P., Herzog, M. J., Visovsky, K., Schmidt, C., Randolph, J., Schultz, T., & Gage, N. (2010). Social competence intervention for youth with Asperger syndrome and high-functioning autism: an initial investigation. *Journal of Autism and Developmental Disorders, 40,* 1067—1079.

Stichter, J. P., O'Connor, K. V., Herzog, M. J., Lierheimer, K., & McGhee, S. D. (2012). Social competence intervention for elementary students with Aspergers syndrome and high functioning autism. *Journal of Autism and Developmental Disorders, 42,* 354—366.

Van den Bergh, S. F., Scheeran, A. M., Begeer, S., Koot, H. M., & Geurts, H. M. (2014). Age related differences of executive functioning problems in everyday life of children and adolescents in the autism spectrum. *Journal of Autism and Developmental Disorders, 44,* 1959—1971.

de Vries, M., Prins, P. J. M., Schmand, B. A., & Geurts, H. M. (2015). Working memory and cognitive flexibility-training for children with an autism spectrum disorder: a randomized controlled trial. *Journal of Child Psychology and Psychiatry, 56*(5), 566—576.

Wallace, G. L., Kenworthy, L., Pugliese, C. E., Popal, H. S., White, E. I., Brodsky, E., & Martin, A. (2016). Real-world executive functions in adults with autism spectrum disorder: profiles of impairment and associations with adaptive functioning and co-morbid anxiety and depression. *Journal of Autism and Developmental Disorders, 46,* 1071—1083.

White, S. J., Burgess, P. W., & Hill, E. L. (2009). Impairments on "open-ended" executive function tests in autism. *Autism Research, 2,* 138—147.

Willcutt, E. G., Doyle, A. E., Nigg, J. T., Faraone, S. V., & Pennington, B. F. (2005). Validity of the executive function theory of attention-deficit/hyperactivity disorder: a meta-analytic review. *Biological Psychiatry, 57*(11), 1336—1346. http://dx.doi.org/ 10.1016/j.biopsych.2005.02.006.

Wilson, C. E., Happé, F., Wheelwright, S. J., Ecker, C., Lombardo, M. V., Johnston, P., Daly, E., Murphy, C. M., Spain, D., Lai, M. C., Chakrabarti, B., Sauter, D. A., AIMS Consortium, M. R. C., Baron-Cohen, S., & Murphy, D. G. (2014). The neuropsychology of male adults with high-functioning autism or Asperger syndrome. *Autism Research, 7,* 568—581.

Yasuda, Y., Hashimoto, R., Ohi, K., Yamamori, H., Fujimoto, M., Umeda-Yano, S., … Takeda, M. (2014). Cognitive inflexibility in Japanese adolescents and adults with autism spectrum disorders. *World Journal of Psychiatry, 4*(2), 42—48. http:// dx.doi.org/10.5498/wjp.v4.i2.42.

Yerys, B. E., Kenworthy, L., Jankowski, K. F., Strang, J., & Wallace, G. L. (2013). Separate components of emotional go/no-go performance relate to autism versus attention symptoms in children with autism. *Neuropsychology, 27*(5), 537—545.

Yerys, B. E., Wallace, G. L., Jankowski, K. F., Bollich, A., & Kenworthy, L. (2011). Impaired Consonant Trigrams Test (CTT) performance relates to everyday working memory difficulties in children with autism spectrum disorders. *Child Neuropsychology, 17*(4), 391—399. http://dx.doi.org/10.1080/09297049.2010.547462.

Yerys, B. E., Wallace, G. L., Sokoloff, J. L., Shook, D. A., James, J. D., & Kenworthy, L. (2009). Attention deficit/hyperactivity disorder symptoms moderate cognition and behavior in children with autism spectrum disorders. *Autism Research, 2*(6), 322—333. http://dx.doi.org/10.1002/aur.103.

CHAPTER FOUR

Joint Attention and Early Social Developmental Cascades in Neurogenetic Disorders

L.J. Hahn
University of Illinois, Champaign, IL, United States
E-mail: ljhahn@illinois.edu

Contents

Abstract

This review examines what is known about joint attention and early social development in three neurogenetic syndromes: Down syndrome, Williams syndrome, and fragile X syndrome. In addition, the potential cascading effects of joint attention on subsequent social development, especially social interaction and social cognition, are proposed. The potential issues and complexities associated with conducting prospective, longitudinal studies of infant social development in neurogenetic disorders are discussed.

The presentation of phenotypic outcomes in neurogenetic disorders has received significant research attention in the last several decades. Behavioral phenotypes are the measureable behavioral outcomes observed in individuals with neurogenetic disorders (Dykens, 1995; O'Brien, 1992). According

International Review of Research in Developmental Disabilities, Volume 51
ISSN 2211-6095
http://dx.doi.org/10.1016/bs.irrdd.2016.08.002

© 2016 Elsevier Inc.
All rights reserved.

to Dykens (1995, p. 523), a behavioral phenotype is conceptualized as "the heightened probability or likelihood that people with a given syndrome will exhibit certain behavioral or developmental sequelae relative to those without the syndrome". Therefore, within a specific neurogenetic disorder, there are behaviors that are more probable, but these behaviors may not emerge for all individuals with that disorder (Dykens, 1995; Hodapp, 2004; Hodapp & Desjardin, 2002). In addition, while certain behaviors may be associated with a specific syndrome, they may not be completely unique to that syndrome (e.g., sociability in Down syndrome and Williams syndrome; Dilts, Morris, & Leonard, 1990). As the field has advanced, more nuanced investigations have been conducted that provide deeper insight into and understanding of the behavioral phenotype associated with syndromes such as Down syndrome, Williams syndrome, and fragile X syndrome, as well as the potential implications of these behavioral phenotypes for other aspects of development and on subsequent development.

One domain that has been of great interest to researchers who study neurogenetic disorders is social development, particularly aspects of social cognition. Social cognition is the ability to think and reason about the social world (Tager-Flusberg, Skwerer, & Joseph, 2006; Trevarthen & Aitken, 2001). Like other domains of development, social development starts in the very first days of life. Interestingly, only a limited amount of research has been conducted on early social development in neurogenetic disorders, despite recognition from the field of the importance of examining the early developmental profiles associated with neurogenetic disorders, or "starting states" (Karmiloff-Smith, 1998; Karmiloff-Smith & Thomas, 2003). A greater understanding of early social development and social starting states in neurogenetic disorders can shed light on how social phenotypic profiles emerge and develop over time. To conceptualize how such behavioral profiles may emerge over time, Fidler, Lunkenheimer, and Hahn (2011) proposed the notion of using dynamic systems theory and developmental cascades.

Dynamic systems theory provides a useful framework for conceptualizing how development occurs over time (Granic, 2005; Thelen & Smith, 2006, pp. 258–312). According to this approach, developmental outcomes can be understood as a product of a process called self-organization. Self-organization is the emergence and consolidation of new forms (e.g., behaviors) that comes from interactions between simpler forms (Lewis, 1997, 2000). Within the context of self-organization, emergence is defined as the ongoing process of the "coming-into-existence" of new forms or properties within a system (Lewis, 2000). The process of self-organization can involve the interaction of genes, brain, behavior, and environment (Howe & Lewis, 2005). This framework aligns with the neuroconstructivist approach that has been used to conceptualize development in neurogenetic disorders as a dynamic, ongoing process of atypical brain development resulting in different developmental patterns and pathways (Karmiloff-Smith, 1998, 2006; Karmiloff-Smith & Thomas, 2003). Based on these perspectives, development occurs when a new form or behavior emerges, and in turn it may cause change in other areas or systems either directly or indirectly (Karmiloff-Smith & Thomas, 2003; Lewis, 1997).

One way to conceptualize these direct and indirect effects that occur in human development is through the analogy of developmental cascades. Developmental cascades are the process by which early functioning in a domain influence, or have a cumulative effect, on the development of other domains of functioning over time (Masten & Cicchetti, 2010). Thus a self-organization framework may help researchers understand how emerging behavioral phenotypes shape development, and have cascading effects on development in multiple domains throughout the life course in neurogenetic disorders (Fidler et al., 2011).

1. EARLY SOCIAL DEVELOPMENT

The first signs of social interest and understanding develop during infancy. This is also known as intersubjectivity, which is conceptualized as the intuitive recognition and understanding of the impulses and desires of another's mind (Trevarthen & Aitken, 2001). Intersubjectivity can be divided into primary intersubjectivity and secondary intersubjectivity. Primary intersubjectivity occurs when infants consolidate the skills of maintaining mutually regulated, dynamic interactions and show an active and responsive appreciation for the communications of their social partners, usually their caregivers (Trevarthen, 1979, pp. 321–347). Thus primary intersubjectivity provides infants with the ability to participate in mutually regulated, dynamic interactions. This in turn supports the ability to incorporate objects and events outside the social interaction into the dynamic interaction, which leads to secondary intersubjectivity. Secondary intersubjectivity occurs when infants show dynamic awareness for both people and objects or person-person-object awareness (Trevarthen, 1998; Trevarthen & Hubley, 1978). Together, the development of primary and secondary intersubjectivity provides infants and young children with the necessary foundational skills to function in the social world (Meltzoff & Moore, 1994, 1998; Trevarthen & Aitken, 2001). There are many skills associated with both primary and secondary intersubjectivity that are important for social development; however, one skill associated with secondary intersubjectivity that seems to be particularly critical for social development is joint attention.

1.1 Joint Attention

Joint attention is a uniquely human skill (Tomasello, Carpenter, & Hobson, 2005) that involves shared attention between an infant and social partner around an object or event of interest (Mundy et al., 2003; Wetherby & Prizant, 2003). Because of the dynamic nature of joint attention, researchers have found it helpful to define instances of joint attention as either initiating or responding (Bruinsma, Koegel, & Koegel, 2004; Mundy & Newell, 2007). Initiating joint attention involves the infant seeking the attention of a social partner to start the interaction, while responding to joint attention involves responding to a social partner in order to maintain the interaction. In the field of intellectual and developmental disabilities, there has been a great interest in the role that joint attention plays in impacting social development.

Joint engagement is another term that is used to describe periods of joint attention between an infant and a social partner (Adamson, Bakeman, & Deckner, 2004; Adamson & Chance, 1998; Bakeman & Adamson, 1984). Joint engagement adds additional complexity to the study of joint attention by differentiating the emergence of joint attention, referred to as supported joint engagement, and the consolidation of the skills needed to actively use joint attention in interactions with social partners, referred to as coordinated joint engagement (Adamson & Chance, 1998). Specifically, supported joint engagement occurs when an infant and a social partner are engaged with the same object, but the social partner is scaffolding the interaction and the infant is not actively and reciprocally responding to the social partner (Adamson et al., 2004; Bakeman & Adamson, 1984), while coordinated joint engagement is when the infant is actively engaged with the object and the social partner in a dynamic and reciprocal interaction (Adamson et al., 2004; Bakeman & Adamson, 1984). Therefore, during supported joint engagement, the ability to share attention with a social partner is just emerging for the infant and needs support in order for this skill to fully develop into the active, reciprocal process that is characteristic of joint attention. Regardless of the term, both joint attention and joint engagement involve a consolidation of the other skills associated with intersubjectivity (i.e., using eye gaze and affect to share interest with a social partner in a dynamic interaction), making joint attention a critical skill for infants because its emergence and development indicate a shift in the way infants interact with the world, especially the social world (Hubley & Trevarthen, 1979; Meltzoff & Moore, 1994, 1998; Trevarthen & Hubley, 1978). Furthermore, joint attention continues to influence social interactions throughout the life course (Brazelton, Koslowski, & Main, 1974, p. 264; Stern, 1974; Tronick, 1982).

In order to share attention and communicate interest to social partners, infants use a combination of eye contact, vocalizations, facial expressions, and gestures (Bates, Benigni, Bretherton, Camaioni, & Volterra, 1979). Most of the time these behaviors are combined to provide most information to the social partner, and they can be used either to initiate an interaction with a social partner or respond to a social partner. For example, an infant may use eye gaze and a vocalization to indicate that they see a toy their caregiver is showing them (i.e., responding to joint attention). Or, an infant may look to her caregiver, vocalize to get the caregiver's attention, and then with her eyes direct the caregiver to a toy while smiling and vocalizing (i.e., initiating joint attention). The infant will then look back to the caregiver to see whether they see the toy too. However, if there are many toys in the room it may not be clear to the caregiver to what the infant is interested in. The addition of a gesture, especially a pointing gesture, will help to clarify this.

Pointing can have two broad functions: to direct attention (i.e., a protodeclarative point), and to control or manipulate the behavior of others (i.e., a protoimperative point; Bates et al., 1979; Bates, Camaioni, & Volterra, 1975). Protodeclaratives usually take the form of a point, or an approximation of a point (i.e., hand or several fingers extended), and can be either proximal (close to the infant) or distal (far away from the infant). For example, an infant may notice leaves moving in a tree and think the movement is interesting leading the infant to point up at the leaves to share her excitement with her caregiver, as if to say, "Hey! Do you see these things moving above us?" An infant may also use a point as a protoimperative to tell the caregiver that she wants more milk by pointing to the milk carton on the counter. Pointing falls within the category of deictic gestures, which are used to direct attention or reference an object or event. Other deictic gestures include reaching, pushing, giving, and showing. All of these gestures can be used to share interests and attention with a social partner. To initiate an interaction an infant may give a caregiver a ball in order to start a back and forth play routine, or they may show them an object they found in the sandbox that is unfamiliar to the infant. Or if a caregiver notices their infant with a ball, the caregiver may say, "Oh! Do you have a ball?" leading the infant to look at the caregiver and show the ball.

Collectively, joint attention becomes integrated into other skill sets in order to support the development of the more complex social understanding that is needed for functioning in everyday life (i.e., social interaction, communication, learning, etc.) throughout the life course in a variety of contexts (e.g., school, work, home) and in many different social situations (e.g., making friends, dating, interviewing for a job, etc.). For example, we use joint attention skills to coordinate our attention to the topic our teacher is discussing in class (Mundy & Sigman, 2006), or to share in the excitement of a friend receiving a good grade (Tomasello, 1995). Both of these examples also depend on social cognition, which is supported by the development of joint attention. Specifically, through the development of joint attention, young children begin to attribute emotions, desires, and intentions to the actions people produce (Trevarthen & Aitken, 2001). This in turn leads to the understanding that people are intentional beings who have their own thoughts and minds (Meltzoff & Moore, 1998; Tager-Flusberg, 2005). Therefore, the behavior of others can be interpreted in terms of mental states (Tager-Flusberg, 2005). This, in turn, leads to the development of theory of mind or the ability to understand, or to theorize about, what another person is thinking and take their perspective—a key component of social cognition (Tager-Flusberg & Skwerer, 2007, pp. 87—116; Zinck, 2008).

Taken together, then, joint attention is hypothesized to have a cascading influence (see Fidler et al., 2011; Karmiloff-Smith, 2011), on subsequent social interactions and social cognition (Bukowski, Newcomb, & Hartup, 1998; Carpendale & Lewis, 2006; Mundy & Newell, 2007). Successfully achieving joint attention can promote development in these domains, while frequent and repeated disruptions in achieving joint attention can lead to adverse effects in these domains (Murphy & Abbeduto, 2005).

2. EARLY SOCIAL DEVELOPMENT IN NEUROGENETIC DISORDERS

Considering the importance of joint attention on development, the question that arises is, what happens when these skills do not develop in the manner that is expected? Specifically, how does this influence the trajectory of development and what are the implications of typical or atypical joint attention on subsequent development? It is speculated here that disruptions in joint attention can lead to not initiating as many interactions with a social partner and not always responding in a manner that helps to sustain the interaction, which results in fewer opportunities to participate in a social exchange and gain information about social interactions. The cumulative effect of these limited social experiences over time will result in a lack of the social knowledge needed to respond and participate appropriately in social situations throughout the life course. Thus, it is important to conduct nuanced examinations of joint attention to understand the starting state of these skills, followed by examinations of how they develop and change over time. This will allow for unique insight into the cascading effects of joint attention related to the social phenotype of a specific neurogenetic disorder. Additionally, this type of prospective characterization of behavioral phenotypes has the potential to provide meaningful implications for the timing and targets of early interventions.

Three neurogenetic disorders that are particularly relevant for examining early social developmental cascades are Down syndrome (DS), Williams syndrome (WS), and fragile X syndrome (FXS). For all three neurogenetic disorders there is a critical need to examine the emergence of joint attention. The social phenotypes of these three neurogenetic disorders suggest that while there may be areas of overlap, there are also syndrome-specific patterns of social development. In addition, these three syndromes can be viewed on a continuum from developmentally appropriate competence in social skills (DS) to dysregulated social behavior (WS) to impaired social skills (FXS). In the following sections, I provide information on what is known about joint attention and early social development in these three syndrome groups and identify areas where more research is needed to inform future intervention and treatment work.

2.1 Down Syndrome

DS is the most common and recognizable neurogenetic disorder associated with intellectual disability (incidence rate of 1 in 691 live births; Parker et al., 2010). A relative strength in social functioning is a hallmark feature of children, adolescents, and adults with DS (Fidler, Barrett, & Most, 2005; Fidler, Most, Booth-laforce, & Kelly, 2008; Gilmore, Campbell, & Cuskelly, 2003; Rosner, Hodapp, Fidler, Sagun, & Dykens, 2004). These social strengths appear to emerge in infancy as evidenced by the majority of infants with DS achieving the developmental milestones associated with primary intersubjectivity (Fidler, 2006). However, there are noticeable differences in the achievement of these milestones as compared to the typical trajectory. For example, mutual gaze in infants with DS is slow to emerge, but then persists at a high level into the middle of the first year at a time when typically developing infants begin to shift their focus from people to the world around them (Berger & Cunningham, 1981; Carvajal & Iglesias, 2000; Slonims & Mcconachie, 2006).

Despite strengths in social functioning, children with DS are at elevated risk for autism spectrum disorder with 7—18% meeting diagnostic criteria (Diguiseppi et al., 2010; Kent et al., 1999; Lowenthal, Paula, Schwartzman, Brunoni, & Mercadante, 2007). Nonetheless, some have argued that social strengths serve as a protective factor for many individuals with DS; others have argued that children with DS tend to overuse there social skills to compensate or to distract others when presented with a challenge (Fidler, 2006; Freeman & Kasari, 2002; Pitcairn & Wishart, 1994; Ruskin, Kasari, Mundy, & Sigman, 1994). Thus a critical question related to social development in DS that needs to be examined is, what is the impact of early social competencies on development?

2.1.1 Joint Attention in Down Syndrome

Studies of young children with DS indicate mental age-appropriate levels of initiating joint attention (Fidler, Philofsky, Hepburn, & Rogers, 2005; Mundy, Kasari, Sigman, & Ruskin, 1995; Mundy, Sigman, Kasari, & Yirmiya, 1988) and total joint attention (Kasari, Freeman, Mundy, & Sigman, 1995; Kasari, Mundy, Yirmiya, & Sigman, 1990). All of these studies have used the Early Social Communication Scale (Mundy et al., 2003; Seibert, Hogan, & Mundy, 1982) to examine joint attention and other related early social skills (i.e., social interaction behaviors and requesting), which has a standardized administration and scoring procedure. Similar to the results related to joint attention, behaviors related to social interaction (e.g., turn taking) appear to be used with relative ease with studies reporting either more social interaction behaviors used by children with DS (Mundy et al., 1988) or commensurate levels as compared to mental age-matched peers (Mundy et al., 1995). Specifically, toddlers with DS demonstrate evidence of increased nonverbal social acts including gesturing, pointing, smiling, turn taking, and play acts than typical peers (Franco & Wishart, 1995; Kasari, Mundy, et al., 1990; Mundy et al., 1995, 1988).

Interestingly, despite appropriate use of joint attention and social inter-action behaviors, fewer social referencing shifts have been reported in children with DS (Kasari et al., 1995). One possible explanation for this is difficulties with shifting attention. However, if this were the case then dif-ficulties with joint attention would also be observed in DS. The other pos-sibility is that there is a preference for social over nonsocial stimuli (Kasari et al., 1995). In an earlier study, Kasari, Sigman, Mundy, and Yirmiya (1990) noted that children with DS look more to their social partner's face, which would suggest a preference for social stimuli. However, children with DS also looked away from the social interaction more than mental age-matched typically developing children. In addition, this longer looking time to a social partner's face in children with DS was negatively related to joint attention, such that those who shared shorter looks with their social partner used more joint attention behaviors (i.e., pointing, showing, etc.). Taken together, perhaps there is a combination of both difficulties shifting attention and a preference for social stimuli in DS. Specifically, for those with great difficulties with shifting attention, they are less able to shift their attention away from a social partner—the preferred stimuli. This preference for social stimuli may also be present in the use of requesting behaviors.

In contrast to these studies indicating strengths in joint attention, there are several studies that suggest initiating joint attention may be particularly difficult for infants with DS between 12 and 26 months (Legerstee & Fisher, 2008; Legerstee & Weintraub, 1997). In these studies, infants with DS were more likely to passively share attention to objects, rather than actively initiate an interaction by pointing to objects leading to fewer instances of initiating joint attention (Legerstee & Fisher, 2008; Legerstee & Weintraub, 1997). There are several potential reasons for these different findings. Frist, Legerstee et al. (Legerstee & Fisher, 2008; Legerstee & Weintraub, 1997) coded joint attention during naturalistic play observations with the infant's mother. Thus, unlike the studies using the Early Social Communication Scales, there is no standard administration or scoring. In addition, the Early Social Communication Scales provide opportunities for joint attention and other social behaviors that may not always occur during a 20- to 30-min interaction. There are also differences in the chronological age ranges of these studies. Studies noting mental age-appropriate joint attention in young children with DS have been conducted with children anywhere be-tween 12 and 55 months. However, the two studies reporting difficulties with joint attention have used a more narrow age range (12—26 months). Because these studies are cross-sectional with a large age range, it is difficult to discern when joint attention emerges and perhaps these differences indicate that joint attention is emerging during the second year in DS (i.e., after 12 months). Nonetheless, it has been suggested that the joint attention presentation in DS involves a unique combination of social strengths and cognitive weaknesses (i.e., shifting attention, instrumental thinking; Fidler, Philofsky et al., 2005; Moore, Oates, Hobson, & Goodwin, 2002; Ruskin et al., 1994).

2.1.2 Proposed Early Social Developmental Cascade in Down Syndrome

It could be speculated that the strengths observed in joint attention and related behaviors in DS should support the development of social cognition. However, there is evidence that social cognition in children with DS may be compromised and that joint attention may not serve the same supporting role in overall development as it does in typically developing children (Cebula, Moore, & Wishart, 2010; Cebula & Wishart, 2008; Wishart, 2007). The most studied aspect of social cognition in DS is theory of mind. Collectively, these studies suggest difficulties with most standard theory of mind tasks (e.g., appearance reality, false belief, and representational change tasks; Yirmiya, Solomonica-Levi, Shulman, & Pilowsky, 1996; Zelazo, Burack, Benedetto, & Frye, 1996).

To examine the influence of joint attention on early theory of mind performance, Hahn, Fidler, Hepburn, and Rogers (2013) examined the performance of children with DS on a failed intentions task (i.e., the behavioral reenactment procedure; Meltzoff, 1995), and how this performance related to joint attention and affect sharing. Results indicated that the ability to view a social partner's actions as intentional is not an area of particular strength or weakness in children with DS. Additionally, although high rates of both joint attention and affect sharing were observed in this study, they did not appear to be supporting the development of the understanding of intentionality in the manner that would be expected. Specifically, neither joint attention nor affect sharing were significant predictors of children's ability to accurately interpret their social partner's failed intentional action. Also, higher levels of affect sharing in children with DS did predict more imitations of the social partner's failed intentional action, which suggests that high affect sharing may be a barrier to the understanding of intentionality. Together, these findings indicate that intersubjective skills may influence the development of more complex social cognitive skills via two pathways. First, children with DS who experience deficits in joint attention (Cebula & Wishart, 2008; Legerstee & Weintraub, 1997) may miss the intentional information needed to interpret the intentions of others. Second, high affect sharing, or an overuse of social skills, in children with DS may interfere with joint attention (Fidler, Philofsky, et al., 2005; Kasari et al., 1995; Mundy et al., 1988; Sigman & Ruskin, 1999), which in turn may negatively impact the development of more complex social cognitive skills, such as the understanding of intentionality, in the manner that is expected based on the typical trajectory (Cebula & Wishart, 2008; Wishart, 2007). Collectively, the early phenotypic characteristics of children with DS may have a cascading effect on the understanding of intentionality, which may continue to influence the development of subsequent social cognitive skills and social interactions (i.e., ability to understand the perspectives of others; Fidler et al., 2011).

In sum, there are many questions and avenues for future research on social phenotype associated with DS. Specifically, there is a need to examine the emergence and trajectory of early social development starting from infancy. These studies will allow for a better understanding of whether these skills, especially joint attention, are intact, delayed, or different from the typical trajectory. This will also support the examination of how these early social skills may have a cascading effect on social interactions for individuals with DS.

2.2 Williams Syndrome

WS is one of the most widely researched neurogenetic disorders (Bellugi, Lichtenberger, Jones, Lai, & St George, 2000), with an incidence rate of 1 in 7500 (Strømme, Bjørnstad, & Ramstad, 2002). There is a distinct social profile associated within WS that emerges in infancy (for a review see Järvinen, Korenberg, & Bellugi, 2013; Järvinen-Pasley et al., 2008; Thurman & Fisher, 2015), characterized by an overly friendly, highly sociable (termed hypersociability; Gosch & Pankau, 1997), highly approachable, highly gregarious, and people-oriented personality style (Mervis & Klein-Tasman, 2000). Children with WS are described as good social partners who are very friendly, highly empathic, and able to tune into other people's mental states because they seem to have special sensitivity to the emotional states of others (Dykens & Rosner, 1999; Gosch & Pankau, 1997; Hodapp & Desjardin, 2002; Jones et al., 2001; Plesa-Skwerer, Faja, Schofield, Verbalis, & Tager-Flusberg, 2006). A combination of relative strengths in interpersonal skills and the distinct social profile associated with WS drives individuals with WS to socially engage with others (Hodapp & Desjardin, 2002; Jones et al., 2001; Mervis & Klein-Tasman, 2000).

Indications of the distinct social phenotype associated with WS are apparent from infancy. This includes increased frequency of smiling behavior, increased frequency of attending to the faces of others (Järvinen-Pasley et al., 2008), a strong interest in people (Tager-Flusberg et al., 2006), and a preference for social stimuli over nonsocial stimuli (Järvinen-Pasley et al., 2008). Also, infants and toddlers with WS spend more time looking at their mother and at strangers than typically developing infants and toddlers of the same chronological or developmental age (Mervis et al., 2003). However, despite these strengths, it seems that children with WS have poorer than expected joint attention. In addition, it is possible that there are two related, but different processes influencing social development in WS: social-perceptual skills (i.e., skills related to the affective system that involve making judgments based on the perceptual, social, and emotional information available during a social interaction) and social-cognitive skills (i.e., the higher order thinking abilities that make up the traditional conceptualization of theory of mind; Hepburn, Fidler, Hahn, & Philofsky, 2011; Tager-Flusberg, 2005; Tager-Flusberg & Sullivan, 2000).

2.2.1 Joint Attention in Williams Syndrome

Young children with WS appear to have difficulties with joint attention in comparison to both mental age- and chronological age-matched peers (Laing et al., 2002; Mervis & Bertrand, 1993, 1997; Mervis et al., 2003). Specifically, fewer instances of initiating joint attention and initiating requests, including protodeclarative and protoimperative pointing, have been reported in comparison to mental age-matched, typically developing peers (Laing et al., 2002). Considering the strong social drive and orientation of infants and young children with WS, it would not be surprising if they showed mental age appropriate, or even strengths, in joint attention. However, it has been noted that during a triadic social interaction (i.e., between the infant, a social partner, and a toy) children with WS quickly turn this interaction into a dyadic interaction (i.e., a face-to-face interaction with the social partner that does not include the toy), especially when a novel person is present (Doyle, Bellugi, Korenberg, & Graham, 2004). There are two possible explanations for this shift in the interaction. First, this may be related to poor joint attention skills (Laing et al., 2002; Mervis & Bertrand, 1993, 1997; Mervis et al., 2003). On the other hand, this pattern may also be related to an overall preference for dyadic interaction (Järvinen-Pasley et al., 2008). This preference for dyadic interactions, or dyadic strength (Laing et al., 2002), may reduce the opportunity for children with WS to engage in joint attention and, in turn, lead to delays in this skill. Specifically, there appears to be a split in abilities in young children with WS, such that initiating joint attention skills are delayed, while responding to joint attention develops similar to the typical trajectory (Hepburn et al., 2011). This split in joint attention abilities could disrupt, and influence, subsequent social development (Hepburn et al., 2011).

2.2.2 Proposed Early Social Developmental Cascade in Williams Syndrome

Given their high levels of empathy, emotional responsivity, and attunement to others, it would be plausible to speculate that children with WS might show relative sparing or even strength in social cognition. However, research on social cognition in WS indicates a combination of strengths and weaknesses in this population that likely stem from difficulties with joint attention (Gagliardi et al., 2003; Plesa-Skwerer et al., 2006; Riby & Back, 2010; Tager-Flusberg, Boshart, & Baron-Cohen, 1998; Tager-Flusberg et al., 2006; Tager-Flusberg & Skwerer, 2007, pp. 87—116). These studies combined with the research on the social profile associated with WS, lead to the hypothesis that there are two processes that underlie the development of social cognition, especially theory of mind: social-perceptual skills and social-cognitive skills (Tager-Flusberg, 2005; Tager-Flusberg & Sullivan, 2000). This split in social cognitive abilities may emerge from early difficulties with joint attention.

In order to make the types of social judgments associated with theory of mind, individuals use skills that are supported by joint attention. That is, instead of sharing attention about an object or event with a social partner they need to consider the mind of that individual based on the linguistic and emotional information provided as the third variable in social interaction. The difficulties reported in joint attention may make it challenging for individuals with WS to obtain this type of information, especially when there is little or conflicting emotional information (e.g., your friend says, "I'm fine," but they are showing facial indicators of sadness). When clear emotional cues are present it is possible that individuals with WS are more successful at understanding their social partner's perspective due to their strong interest in the emotions of others (Dykens & Rosner, 1999; Gosch & Pankau, 1997; Hodapp & Desjardin, 2002; Jones et al., 2001; Plesa-Skwerer et al., 2006). This could explain why stronger social-perceptual skills and weaker social-cognitive skills are reported in WS (Tager-Flusberg & Sullivan, 2000). It is also likely that this dissociation is also observed in early social cognitive skills prior to the development of theory of mind (Fidler, Hepburn, Most, Philofsky, & Rogers, 2007; Laing et al., 2002).

In order to explore the emergence of this dissociation in 2- to 5-year-olds with WS, Hepburn et al. (2011) used the Early Social Communication Scale (Mundy et al., 2003; Seibert et al., 1982) and the Autism Diagnostic Observation Schedule (Lord et al., 2012). Examples of social-perceptual skills in this study included directing facial expressions, shared enjoyment, and smiling, while social-cognitive skills included initiating and responding to joint attention and integrating eye gaze. Results indicated that young children with WS demonstrated intact social-perceptual skills and emerging deficits in social-cognitive skills (Hepburn et al., 2011). The conceptualization of social-cognitive skills in this study included both initiating and responding to joint attention, therefore, it is possible that early difficulties in joint attention, especially initiating joint attention, lead to subsequent weaknesses in the social-cognitive skills associated with theory of mind. What is still unclear from this study is how these two processes are manifesting in infancy (i.e., prior to 2 years), and how they are developing over time, which may help to clarify the social phenotype associated with WS. Taken together, despite the social strengths in WS, difficulties with joint attention may help to clarify why they struggle with some areas of social development, especially those related to social cognition (e.g., social reciprocity, making and maintaining friendships) throughout the life course (Jawaid et al., 2012; Riby, Bruce, & Jawaid, 2012; van der Fluit, Gaffrey, Klein-Tasman, 2012). These areas of strength and weakness in social development continue to provide interesting research avenues within this population, and opportunities to explore the nuances and complexity of these skills on other domains of development.

2.3 Fragile X Syndrome

FXS is the most common inherited form of intellectual disability with an incidence rate of 1 in 4000 males and 1 in 6000 females (CDC, 2011; Hagerman, 2007). FXS is also the most common single-gene cause of autism spectrum disorders with 30—74% of individuals with FXS meeting diagnostic criteria (Auerbach, Osterweil, & Bear, 2011; Bailey, Raspa, Olmsted, & Holiday, 2008; Clifford et al., 2007; Darnell et al., 2011; Hall, Lightbody, Hirt, Rezvani, & Reiss, 2010; Harris et al., 2008). Individuals with FXS show impairments in social interactions across the life span (Bailey, Hatton, & Skinner, 1998; Cohen et al., 1988; Murphy, Abbeduto, Schroeder, &

Serlin, 2007; Wolff, Gardner, Paccia, & Lappen, 1989). Specifically starting in early childhood, individuals with FXS tend to show social withdrawal and anxiety during social interactions, especially those with strangers or in new settings (Bailey, Mesibov, et al., 1998; Cohen et al., 1988; Hall, Lightbody, Huffman, Lazzeroni, & Reiss, 2009; Hessl, Glaser, Dyer-Friedman, & Reiss, 2006; Roberts, Clarke, et al., 2009; Roberts, Weisenfeld, Hatton, Heath, & Kaufmann, 2007). Thus, it can be hypothesized that these early impairments in social interaction in FXS may stem from even earlier atypical development of joint attention and joint attention-related behaviors that has a cascading effect on social development throughout the life course.

2.3.1 Joint Attention in Fragile X Syndrome

Research on joint attention in FXS is still in the preliminary stages. However, while there is initial evidence that some aspects of joint attention appear to be mental age appropriate in FXS (Hahn, Brady, Fleming, & Warren, in press; Marschik et al., 2014; Roberts, Mirrett, Anderson, Burchinal, & Neebe, 2002), there is also evidence that disruptions in gesture use exist (Flenthrope & Brady, 2010; Roberts et al., 2002). While more research is needed, the available research on joint attention and joint attention-related behaviors provides insight into early social development in FXS.

Based on a retrospective video analysis, there is evidence that 9- and 12-month-old infants with FXS direct attention to themselves during social interactions (e.g., getting attention, seeking comfort) and respond to utterances directed toward them (Marschik et al., 2014). Similarly, observational studies of young children with FXS suggest that joint attention and joint engagement are commensurate with developmental level (Hahn et al., in press; Roberts et al., 2002). Also during social interactions, it seems that young children with FXS are particularly skilled at using eye gaze shifts for the purpose of sharing interests, making requests, and commenting (Roberts et al., 2002), despite the extant research on children, adolescents, and adults with FXS that reports impairments in eye gaze, especially for social purposes (Cohen et al., 1988; Hall et al., 2015; Hessl et al., 2006; Murphy et al., 2007; Wolff et al., 1989). Thus, it is possible that difficulties with eye gaze have not yet emerged as a phenotypic behavior in very young children with FXS (Marschik et al., 2014; Wolff et al., 1989) and may actually be a key behavior that supports joint attention in early development.

However, eye gaze alone is not enough to support the increasing complexity of social interactions, which is where the addition of gestures are needed—an area of impairment in FXS. Specifically, several studies reported limited gesture use during social interactions in both infants and young children with FXS (Flenthrope & Brady, 2010; Marschik et al., 2014; Roberts et al., 2002). Examinations of the types of gestures used by young children with FXS indicate they use less complex gestures, such as contact gestures, with more ease and frequency than advanced gestures, such as conventional and distal gestures (i.e., gestures where there is no contact between the child and the referent, such as pointing to something that is at a distance; Flenthrope & Brady, 2010; Roberts et al., 2002). Although contact gestures can support joint attention, the support they provide is limited to objects and events that the child can touch, and, therefore, do not support bringing in objects and events from outside the interaction (i.e., such as directing attention to a picture on the wall). Also, early impairments in gesture use may be a contributing factor for why no infants in Marschik et al. (2014) study were observed using requesting actions, requesting information, making choices (e.g., between objects), or imitating their social partners. All of these early social interactions may include a gestural component to clarify an infant's intent, such as reaching to request a toy or pointing to make a choice. Thus, this limited gesture use may disrupt the development of joint attention. Coupled with impairments in expressive language (Abbeduto, McDuffie, Brady, & Kover, 2011) and subsequent difficulties with eye gaze, impairments in gestures use may result in very little support for interacting with others subsequent in development.

2.3.2 Proposed Early Social Developmental Cascade in Fragile X Syndrome

Gestures serve as a way to initiate an interaction, share interest, and imitate a social partner. Without the support of gestures, joint attention may not develop in the manner that is expected, and together this may lead to difficulties interpreting information during a social interaction that is usually acquired by using theory of mind. The ability to understand the minds of others involves the accumulation of information from multiple proximal factors (i.e., gestures, facial expressions, vocalizations, context, etc.). Thus, one hypothetical link as to why impairments in theory of mind have been reported in adolescents and adults with FXS (Cornish et al., 2005; Garner, Callias, & Turk, 1999; Grant, Apperly, & Oliver, 2007; Mazzocco, Pennington, & Hagerman, 1994) is a cascading effect of limited gesture use that disrupts the development of joint attention. Specifically, using gestures during a social interaction allows social partners to share thoughts that may not be easily represented by speech alone (e.g., to show how big a spider was that scared the social partner telling the story; Goldin-Meadow & McNeill, 1999). Also, using gestures to support a social interaction is particularly important when an individual does not have the words to share their thoughts clearly to a social partner, like individuals with FXS (Goldin-Meadow, 1999). In addition, difficulties interpreting mental state information by individuals with FXS may lead them to not know how to appropriately respond in social situations. That is, they do not know how to interpret the mental state information provided by their social partner and, in turn, do not always provide a socially appropriate response. This may contribute to social avoidance and anxiety that is observed in FXS.

While more research is needed on joint attention, and early social developmental more broadly, there is initial evidence of unique profile of early social development in FXS. This leads to a preliminary hypothesis that the impairments in social development observed in older children, adolescents, and adults with FXS are the result of a cascading effect of early impairments in gesture use. However, more research is needed to examine this hypothesis. To date, there have been no investigations of less complex social cognitive skills like understanding desires and intentions, or studies linking early social skills to subsequent social cognitive skills. Also, future studies examining the emergence of joint attention in FXS, prospectively from infancy, have the potential to identify the starting state of joint attention and explore if gesture impairments in FXS disrupt the development of joint attention and subsequent social development, providing insight into the social phenotype associated with FXS.

3. CONCLUSIONS AND FUTURE DIRECTIONS

Although advances have been made in characterizing the social phenotypes associated with DS, WS, and FXS, there are still many aspects of social development that are unclear, especially in regards to how the social phenotype is emerging in infancy—what the starting state is—and the cascading effects on subsequent development. For all three neurogenetic disorders there is a need to examine the emergence of joint attention. Based on the available evidence it seems that similar to the typical trajectory, joint attention is a critical and foundational skill that has a cascading influence on social development. In addition to examining joint attention there are several important questions for future research that are unique to each disorder. Specifically in DS, while there is initial evidence that social strengths can have both positive and negative effects on development, there is a need for more nuanced investigations of social skills. These studies should seek to help clarify the divide within different social skills and the interaction of these skills with other contexts and developmental domains. For example, why is pointing used effectively in social sharing contexts, but not in requesting contexts? In WS, the suggestion that there is a dissociation in social-perceptual and social-cognitive skills warrants further investigation in the area of social cognition, as well as, how this dissociation impacts other domains of development, such as language. Also, examination of this dissociation has yet to be explicitly examined in infancy. Finally in FXS, there is a need for more research on joint attention and other related skills, especially gesture use, in order to elucidate the development of these skills and their connection to subsequent social development. This will help in clarifying available research suggesting a mixed profile of strengths and weaknesses in joint attention despite many researchers hypothesizing deficits in this skill set. Thus, there are many potential research avenues to explore.

However, the future of research on early social development in infants and young children with neurogenetic disorders will need to overcome primary challenges in recruiting these infants, continuing to refine techniques for examining development, and the rise of comorbid conditions, such as autism spectrum disorders. Although this work is challenging, it is feasible, especially as the field continues to work to identify better solutions to these challenges.

The most obvious issue associated with characterizing development in infancy is the need to identify infants with neurogenetic disorders within the first few months of life in order to examine starting states. While it is common for an infant with DS to be diagnosed prenatally or at birth (Bull, 2011), early identification is more difficult for other neurogenetic disorders, like WS and FXS, that are not commonly tested for at birth. Unfortunately, it is still common for WS to not be diagnosed until between 5 and 10 years, unless heart problems are present—which can instigate genetic testing—and then a diagnosis may occur between 12 and 16 months (Carrasco, Castillo, Aravena, Rothhammer, & Aboitiz, 2005; Ferrero et al., 2007). The average age of diagnosis for males with FXS is 35–37 and 41 months for females (Bailey et al., 2009); however, there has been a recent increase in infant studies associated with FXS. This is due in part to increased awareness and understanding of FXS, which leads families who already have a family member with FXS to test their newborns. At the same time, this increase in studies is also due to the tenacity and connectedness of the researchers. Specifically, researchers have fostered strong relationships with the families of children with FXS from prior research studies and are now assessing their infant siblings, cousins, and other family members. In addition, these researchers are connected with one another and are developing ways to refer or "share" participants. Thus, the feasibility of recruiting infants with FXS is becoming more attainable, by collaborating with those who have been successful, participating in the FXS community, fostering rapport with the families, and being tenacious in recruitment efforts. This list applies to all families with infants, and can serve to foster in more studies of infants with neurogenetic disorders. This will allow for a better understanding of early development and how behavioral phenotypes are emerging.

At the same time, it is important to be respectful of the families who have infants with neurogenetic disorders and take caution not to intrude. Thus, it is imperative to find the appropriate way to approach families about research opportunities for their infants. As more networks, registries, and parent groups are formed, more avenues are available for working relationships to be established with these groups. It is promising that many parents of children with neurogenetic disorders appear to reach a stage where they want more information about their child, leading them to want to participate in research opportunities. This leads to a need for researchers to consider our responsibilities in disseminating knowledge gained from our research in family-friendly ways, and to pursue translational research opportunities with clinicians.

Other issues with identifying potential participants in early infancy have to do with measurement and study design. Even with recruitment becoming more feasible, it may not be viable to conduct a prospective longitudinal study for five or more years, which would be needed to examine the potential cascading effects of joint attention on social development. However, there are statistical models that can help to overcome these issues. First, when a longitudinal study is not feasible, one approach that can be used is the cross-sectional developmental trajectory (Thomas et al., 2009). This approach was developed to examine research questions intended to determine if an atypical group shows a pattern of development different from the typical developmental pattern (Thomas et al., 2009). Also, this approach is ideal for studying the developmental trajectory of low incidence disorders because it uses a cross-sectional design instead of a longitudinal design, which is useful for small sample studies prior to longitudinal designs, albeit not as rigorous as a longitudinal design (Thomas et al., 2009). In this approach, the group of interest is compared to a chronological age-matched and developmental age-matched group of typically developing peers. Then the trajectories can be plotted together to examine if the trajectory of the group of interest resembles either of the comparison trajectories (Thomas et al., 2009). This type of trajectory method is particularly useful when there is a wide age range in the atypical group, which is an especially important feature for studying low incidence disorders. Finally, this approach can be particularly helpful as a starting point when it is not yet clear if a skill is simply delayed due to the presence of intellectual disability or if a skill has a different development pattern.

Still a necessary follow-up to a cross-sectional developmental trajectory, or any cross-sectional design, is a longitudinal study. By using multilevel modeling/longitudinal data analysis, it is possible to examine longitudinal trajectories even when all participants do not have the same number of data points (Singer & Willett, 2003). This approach allows for as much data to be used as possible to estimate the trajectory. One particularly useful longitudinal data analysis approach for studying development in neurogenetic disorders is a descriptive analysis of change over time (Singer & Willett, 2003), which can be used to examine individual change over time.

A final important factor to consider when examining early social development in neurogenetic disorders is the presence of comorbid autism spectrum disorder. In FXS, the prevalence rate of autism spectrum disorders is 30—74% (for a review see McCary & Roberts, 2013) and in DS the prevalence rate is 7—18% (for a review see Diguiseppi et al., 2010; Reilly, 2009). While no prevalence studies have been conducted in WS, it has been suggested that 10% meet diagnostic criteria for autism spectrum disorder (Lincoln, Searcy, Jones, & Lord, 2007). Deficits in joint attention, theory of mind, and language, especially social communication, are hallmark features of autism spectrum disorder (American Pscyhological Association, 2013; Bruinsma et al., 2004). Therefore, the presence of autism spectrum disorder will also have a cascading effect on early social development in neurogenetic disorders. For example, higher levels of autism spectrum disorder symptomatology have been consistently related to more impaired functioning in FXS (Bailey, Hatton, Skinner, & Mesibov, 2001; Hahn, Brady, Warren, & Fleming, 2015; Roberts, Mankowski, et al., 2009), and this pattern has also been observed in early social development (Flenthrope & Brady, 2010; Hahn et al., in press). Similarly, a study examining the presence of autism spectrum disorder in DS indicates that potential early indicators include impairments in social and communication skills (Hepburn, Philofsky, Fidler, & Rogers, 2008). Thus in addition to general within-syndrome variability in early social development, it is also possible that there are subphenotypes of children with comorbid autism spectrum disorder who will have a slightly different trajectory of development or show a greater level of impairment in these skills.

Studying development, especially in low incidence disorders, is always accompanied by challenges. Despite these challenges, continuing to examine early social development starting in infancy has the potential to have a tremendous influences on our understanding of the development of individuals with these neurogenetic disorders. While there have been numerous calls for translational research to promote positive development and well-being in neurogenetic syndromes, it is also important to ensure that we have identified appropriate targets and supports for intervention. Considering the importance of early intervention for promoting positive development, continuing to characterize the infant phenotype associated with a given disorder should provide insight into the optimal targets and supports. Specifically, if deficits in joint attention are identified in infants with neurogenetic disorders, then early interventions can be developed, or current interventions can be modified, to support positive development (Jones, Carr, & Feeley, 2006; Kasari, Freeman, & Paparella, 2006; Martins & Harris, 2006; Rocha, Schreibman, & Stahmer, 2007). At the same time, if areas of strength are identified, it is possible that these skills could be used as leverage points and serve as a bridge to support the development of more complex skills. Therefore, it is necessary to continue to use innovative methodologies to gain deeper understanding of early social development in neurogenetic disorders, especially the potential cascading effects of gene-brain-behavior pathways, to inform intervention and treatment work.

ACKNOWLEDGMENTS

Preparation for this article was supported by the National Institute of Mental Health Loan Repayment Grant #L40 MH108014. The author thanks Marie Moore Channell for her helpful feedback on earlier versions of this article. The author also extends her gratitude to Deborah Fidler for her guidance and support with this article.

REFERENCES

Abbeduto, L., McDuffie, A., Brady, N., & Kover, S. T. (2011). Language development in fragile X syndrome: syndrome-specific features, within-syndrome variation, and contributing factors. In J. A. Burack, R. M. Hodapp, G. Iarocci, & E. Zigler (Eds.), *The Oxford handbook of intellectual disability and development* (pp. 1—20). Oxford University Press. http://dx.doi.org/10.1093/oxfordhb/9780195305012.013.0014.

Adamson, L. B., Bakeman, R., & Deckner, D. F. (2004). The development of symbol-infused joint engagement. *Child Development, 75*(4), 1171—1187. http://dx.doi.org/10.1111/j.1467-8624.2004.00732.x.

Adamson, L. B., & Chance, S. (1998). Coordinating attention to people, objects, and language. In A. M. Wetherby, S. F. Warren, & J. Reichle (Eds.), *Transitions in prelinguistic communication* (7th ed., pp. 15—37). Baltimore, MD: Paul H. Brookes Publishing Co.

American Pscyhological Association. (2013). Neurodevelopmental disorders. In *Diagnostic and statistical manual of mental disorders*. American Psychiatric Association. http://dx.doi.org/10.1176/appi.books.9780890425596.dsm01.

Auerbach, B. D., Osterweil, E. K., & Bear, M. F. (2011). Mutations causing syndromic autism define an axis of synaptic pathophysiology. *Nature, 480*(7375), 63—68.

Bailey, D. B., Jr., Hatton, D., & Skinner, M. (1998). Early developmental trajectories of males with fragile X syndrome. *American Journal on Mental Retardation, 103*(1), 29—39. http://dx.doi.org/10.1352/0895-8017(1998)103<0029:EDTOMW>2.0.CO;2.

Bailey, D. B., Jr., Hatton, D., Skinner, M., & Mesibov, G. (2001). Autistic behavior, FMR1 protein, and developmental trajectories in young males with fragile X syndrome. *Journal of Autism and Developmental Disorders, 31*(2), 165—174. http://dx.doi.org/10.1023/A:1010747131386.

Bailey, D. B., Jr., Mesibov, G. B., Hatton, D. D., Clark, R., Roberts, J. E., & Mayhew, L. (1998). Autistic behavior in young boys with fragile X syndrome. *Journal of Autism and Developmental Disorders, 28*(6), 499. http://dx.doi.org/10.1023/A:1026048027397.

Bailey, D. B., Raspa, M., Bishop, E., Holiday, D., Bailey, D. B., Jr., Raspa, M., ... Holiday, D. (2009). No change in the age of diagnosis for fragile X syndrome: findings from a national parent survey. *Pediatrics, 124*(2), 527—533. http://dx.doi.org/10.1542/peds.2008-2992.

Bailey, D. B., Raspa, M., Olmsted, M., & Holiday, D. B. (2008). Co-occurring conditions associated with FMR1 gene variations: findings from a national parent survey. *American Journal of Medical Genetics. Part A, 146A*(16), 2060—2069. http://dx.doi.org/10.1002/ajmg.a.32439.

Bakeman, R., & Adamson, L. B. (1984). Coordinating attention to people and objects in mother-infant and peer-infant interaction. *Child Development, 55*(4), 1278—1289.

Bates, E., Benigni, L., Bretherton, I., Camaioni, L., & Volterra, V. (1979). *The emergence of symbols: Cognition and communication in infancy*. New York, NY: Academic Press.

Bates, E., Camaioni, L., & Volterra, V. (1975). The acquisition of performatives prior to speech. *Merrill-Palmer Quarterly, 21*(1), 205—224.

Bellugi, U., Lichtenberger, L., Jones, W., Lai, Z., & St George, M. (2000). The neurocognitive profile of Williams syndrome: a complex pattern of strengths and weaknesses. *Journal of Cognitive Neuroscience, 12*(Suppl. 1), 7—29.

Berger, J., & Cunningham, C. (1981). The development of eye contact between mothers and normal versus Down's syndrome infants. *Developmental Psychology, 17*(5), 678. http://dx.doi.org/10.1037/0012-1649.17.5.678.

Brazelton, T. B., Koslowski, B., & Main, M. (1974). *The origins of reciprocity: The early mother-infant interaction. The effect of the infant on its caregiver*. Oxford: Wiley-Interscience. xxiv, 264.

Bruinsma, Y., Koegel, R. L., & Koegel, L. K. (2004). Joint attention and children with autism: a review of the literature. *Mental Retardation and Developmental Disabilities Research Reviews, 10*(3), 169—175. http://dx.doi.org/10.1002/mrdd.20036.

Bukowski, W. M., Newcomb, A. F., & Hartup, W. W. (1998). *The company they keep: Friendships in childhood and adolescence.* Cambridge University Press.

Bull, M. J. (2011). Health supervision for children with Down syndrome. *Pediatrics, 128*(2), 393−406.

Carpendale, J., & Lewis, C. (2006). *How children develop social understanding.* Blackwell Publishing.

Carrasco, X., Castillo, S., Aravena, T., Rothhammer, P., & Aboitiz, F. (2005). Williams syndrome: pediatric, neurologic, and cognitive development. *Pediatric Neurology, 32*(3), 166−172.

Carvajal, F., & Iglesias, J. (2000). Looking behavior and smiling in Down syndrome infants. *Journal of Nonverbal Behavior, 24*(3), 225−236. http://dx.doi.org/10.1023/A:1006693121491.

Cebula, K. R., Moore, D. G., & Wishart, J. G. (2010). Social cognition in children with Down's syndrome: challenges to research and theory building. *Journal of Intellectual Disability Research, 54*(2), 113−134. http://dx.doi.org/10.1111/j.1365-2788.2009.01215.x.

Cebula, K. R., & Wishart, J. G. (2008). Social cognition in children with Down syndrome. *International Review of Research in Mental, 35,* 43−86. http://dx.doi.org/10.1016/S0074-7750(07)35002-7.

Center for Disease Control (CDC). (2011). *FMR1 and the fragile X syndrome.* Retrieved January 31, 2013 from http://www.cdc.gov/ncbddd/actearly/pdf/parents_pdfs/fragile_x.pdf.

Clifford, S., Dissanayake, C., Bui, Q. M., Huggins, R., Taylor, A. K., & Loesch, D. Z. (2007). Autism spectrum phenotype in males and females with fragile X full mutation and premutation. *Journal of Autism and Developmental Disorders, 37*(4), 738−747. http://dx.doi.org/10.1007/s10803-006-0205-z.

Cohen, I., Fisch, G., Sudhalter, V., Wolf-Scein, E. G., Hanson, D., Hagerman, R., ... Brown, W. T. (1988). Social gaze, social avoidance, and repetitive behaviors in fragile X males: a controlled study. *American Journal on Mental Retardation, 92*(5), 436−446.

Cornish, K., Burack, J. A., Rahman, A., Munir, F., Russo, N., & Grant, C. (2005). Theory of mind deficits in children with fragile X syndrome. *Journal of Intellectual Disability Research, 49*(5), 372−378. http://dx.doi.org/10.1111/j.1365-2788.2005.00678.x.

Darnell, J. C., Van Driesche, S. J., Zhang, C., Hung, K. Y. S., Mele, A., Fraser, C. E., ... Darnell, R. B. (2011). FMRP stalls ribosomal translocation on mRNAs linked to synaptic function and autism. *Cell, 146*(2), 247−261. http://dx.doi.org/10.1016/j.cell.2011.06.013.

Diguiseppi, C., Hepburn, S. L., Davis, J. M., Fidler, D. J., Hartway, S., Lee, R., ... Robinson, C. (2010). Screening for autism spectrum disorders in children with Down syndrome. *Jounral of Developmental & Behavioral Pediatrics, 31*(3), 181−191.

Dilts, C. V., Morris, C. A., & Leonard, C. O. (1990). Hypothesis for development of a behavioral phenotype in Williams syndrome. *American Journal of Medical Genetics, 37*(S6), 126−131. http://dx.doi.org/10.1002/ajmg.1320370622.

Doyle, T. F., Bellugi, U., Korenberg, J. R., & Graham, J. (2004). "Everybody in the world is my friend" hypersociability in young children with Williams syndrome. *American Journal of Medical Genetics. Part A, 124A*(3), 263−273. http://dx.doi.org/10.1002/ajmg.a.20416.

Dykens, E. M. (1995). Measuring behavioral phenotypes: provocations from the "new genetics". *American Journal on Mental Retardation, 99*(5), 522−532.

Dykens, E. M., & Rosner, B. A. (1999). Refining behavioral phenotypes: personality-motivation in Williams and Prader−Willi syndromes. *American Journal on Mental Retardation, 104*(2), 158−169. http://dx.doi.org/10.1352/0895-8017(1999)104<0158:RBPPIW>2.0.CO;2.

Ferrero, G. B., Biamino, E., Sorasio, L., Banaudi, E., Peruzzi, L., Forzano, S., … Silengo, M. C. (2007). Presenting phenotype and clinical evaluation in a cohort of 22 Williams—Beuren syndrome patients. *European Journal of Medical Genetics, 50*(5), 327—337.

Fidler, D. J. (2006). The emergence of a syndrome-specific personality profile in young children with Down syndrome. *Down's Syndrome, Research and Practice, 10*(2), 53—60. http:// dx.doi.org/10.3104/reprints.305.

Fidler, D. J., Barrett, K. C., & Most, D. E. (2005). Age-related differences in smiling and personality in Down syndrome. *Journal of Developmental and Physical Disabilities, 17*(3), 263—280. http://dx.doi.org/10.1007/s10882-005-4384-x.

Fidler, D. J., Hepburn, S. L., Most, D. E., Philofsky, A., & Rogers, S. J. (2007). Emotional responsivity in young children with Williams syndrome. *American Journal of Mental Retardation, 112*(3), 194—206. http://dx.doi.org/10.1352/0895-8017(2007)112[194: ERIYCW]2.0.CO;2.

Fidler, D. J., Lunkenheimer, E., & Hahn, L. J. (2011). Emerging behavioral phenotypes and dynamic systems theory. *International Review of Research on Developmental Disabilities, 40*, 17—42.

Fidler, D. J., Most, D. E., Booth-laforce, C., & Kelly, J. F. (2008). Emerging social strengths in young children with Down syndrome. *Infants & Young Children, 21*(3), 207—220. http://dx.doi.org/10.1097/01.IYC.0000324550.39446.1f.

Fidler, D. J., Philofsky, A., Hepburn, S. L., & Rogers, S. J. (2005). Nonverbal requesting and problem-solving by toddlers with Down syndrome. *American Journal of Mental Retardation, 110*(4), 312—322. http://dx.doi.org/10.1352/0895-8017(2005)110[312: NRAPBT]2.0.CO;2.

Flenthrope, J. L., & Brady, N. C. (2010). Relationships between early gestures and later language in children with fragile X syndrome. *American Journal of Speech-Language Pathology, 19*(2), 135—142. http://dx.doi.org/10.1044/1058-0360(2009/09-0018).

van der Fluit, F., Gaffrey, M. S., & Klein-Tasman, B. P. (2012). Social cognition in Williams syndrome: relations between performance on the social attribution task and cognitive and behavioral characteristics. *Frontiers in Psychology, 3*(June), 1—11. http://dx.doi.org/ 10.3389/fpsyg.2012.00197.

Franco, F., & Wishart, J. G. (1995). Use of pointing and other gestures by young children with Down syndrome. *American Journal on Mental Retardation, 100*(2), 160—182.

Freeman, S. F. N., & Kasari, C. (2002). Characteristics and qualities of the play dates of children with Down syndrome: emerging or true friendships? *American Journal of Mental Retardation, 107*(1), 16—31.

Gagliardi, C., Frigerio, E., Burt, D. M., Cazzaniga, I., Perrett, D. I., & Borgatti, R. (2003). Facial expression recognition in Williams syndrome. *Neuropsychologia, 41*(6), 733—738.

Garner, C., Callias, M., & Turk, J. (1999). Executive function and theory of mind performance of boys with fragile-X syndrome. *Journal of Intellectual Disability Research, 43*(Pt 6), 466—474. http://dx.doi.org/10.1046/j.1365-2788.1999.00207.x.

Gilmore, L., Campbell, J., & Cuskelly, M. (2003). Developmental expectations, personality stereotypes, and attitudes towards inclusive education: community and teacher views of Down syndrome. *International Journal of Disability, Development and Education, 50*(1), 65—76. http://dx.doi.org/10.1080/1034912032000053340.

Goldin-Meadow, S. (1999). The role of gesture in communication and thinking. *Trends in Cognitive Sciences, 3*(11), 419—429. http://dx.doi.org/10.1016/S1364-6613(99)01397-2.

Goldin-Meadow, S., & McNeill, D. (1999). The role of gesture and mimetic representation in making language the province of speech. In M. C. Corballis, & S. Lea (Eds.), *The descent of mind* (pp. 155—172). Oxford University Press.

Gosch, A., & Pankau, R. (1997). Personality characteristics and behavior problems in individuals of different ages with Williams syndrome. *Developmental Medicine and Child Neurology, 39*(8), 527—533.

Granic, I. (2005). Timing is everything: developmental psychopathology from a dynamic systems perspective. *Developmental Review, 25*(3—4), 386—407. http://dx.doi.org/10.1016/j.dr.2005.10.005.

Grant, C. M., Apperly, I., & Oliver, C. (2007). Is theory of mind understanding impaired in males with fragile X syndrome? *Journal of Abnormal Child Psychology, 35*(1), 17—28. http://dx.doi.org/10.1007/s10802-006-9077-0.

Hagerman, R. J. (2007). Etiology, diagnosis, and development in fragile X syndrome. In J. E. Roberts, R. S. Chapman, & S. F. Warren (Eds.), *Speech and language development and intervention in Down syndrome and fragile X syndrome* (pp. 27—42). Baltimore, MD: Brookes.

Hahn, L. J., Brady, N. C., Fleming, K. K., & Warren, S. F. Joint engagement in young children with fragile X syndrome. *Journal of Speech, Language and Hearing Research* (in press). http://dx.doi.org/10.1044/2016_JSLHR-L-15-0005

Hahn, L. J., Brady, N. C., Warren, S. F., & Fleming, K. K. (2015). Do children with fragile X syndrome show declines or plateaus in adaptive behavior? *American Journal on Intellectual and Developmental Disabilities, 120*(5), 412—432. http://dx.doi.org/10.1352/1944-7558-120.5.412.

Hahn, L. J., Fidler, D. J., Hepburn, S. L., & Rogers, S. J. (2013). Early intersubjective skills and the understanding of intentionality in young children with Down syndrome. *Research in Developmental Disabilities, 34*, 4455—4465. http://dx.doi.org/10.1016/j.ridd.2013.09.027.

Hall, S. S., Frank, M. C., Pusiol, G. T., Farzin, F., Lightbody, A. A., & Reiss, A. L. (2015). Quantifying naturalistic social gaze in fragile X syndrome using a novel eye tracking paradigm. *American Journal of Medical Genetics, Part B: Neuropsychiatric Genetics, 168*(7), 564—572. http://dx.doi.org/10.1002/ajmg.b.32331.

Hall, S. S., Lightbody, A. A., Hirt, M., Rezvani, A., & Reiss, A. L. (2010). Autism in fragile X syndrome: a category mistake? *Journal of the American Academy of Child and Adolescent Psychiatry, 49*(9), 921—933. http://dx.doi.org/10.1016/j.jaac.2010.07.001.

Hall, S. S., Lightbody, A. A., Huffman, L. C., Lazzeroni, L. C., & Reiss, A. L. (2009). Physiological correlates of social avoidance behavior in children and adolescents with fragile X syndrome. *Journal of the American Academy of Child and Adolescent Psychiatry, 48*(3), 320—329. http://dx.doi.org/10.1097/CHI.0b013e318195bd15.

Harris, S. W., Hessl, D., Goodlin-Jones, B., Ferranti, J., Bacalman, S., Barbato, I., … Hagerman, R. J. (2008). Autism profiles of males with fragile X syndrome. *American Journal on Mental Retardation, 113*(6), 427—438. http://dx.doi.org/10.1352/2008.113:427-438.

Hepburn, S. L., Fidler, D. J., Hahn, L., & Philofsky, A. (2011). Social-perceptual and social-cognitive skills in young children with Williams syndrome: evidence for discontinuity. *International Review of Research in Developmental Disabilities, 40*, 181—210.

Hepburn, S. L., Philofsky, A., Fidler, D. J., & Rogers, S. (2008). Autism symptoms in toddlers with Down syndrome: a descriptive study. *Journal of Applied Research in Intellectual Disabilities, 21*, 48—57.

Hessl, D., Glaser, B., Dyer-Friedman, J., & Reiss, A. L. (2006). Social behavior and cortisol reactivity in children with fragile X syndrome. *Journal of Child Psychology and Psychiatry and Allied Disciplines, 47*(6), 602—610. http://dx.doi.org/10.1111/j.1469-7610.2005.01556.x.

Hodapp, R. (2004). Studying interactions, reactions, and perceptions: can genetic disorders serve as behavioral proxies? *Journal of Autism and Developmental Disorders, 34*(1), 29—34. http://dx.doi.org/10.1023/B: JADD.0000018071.02942.00.

Hodapp, R., & Desjardin, J. L. (2002). Genetic etiologies of mental retardation: issues for interventions and interventionists. *Jounral of Developmental and Physical Disabilities, 14*(4), 323—338. http://dx.doi.org/10.1023/A:1020378718237.

Howe, M. L., & Lewis, M. D. (2005). The importance of dynamic systems approaches for understanding development. *Developmental Review, 25*(3—4), 247—251. http://dx.doi.org/10.1016/j.dr.2005.09.002.

Hubley, P., & Trevarthen, C. (1979). Sharing a task in infancy. *New Directions for Child Development*, *4*, 57—80. http://dx.doi.org/10.1002/cd.23219790406/abstract.

Järvinen, A., Korenberg, J. R., & Bellugi, U. (2013). The social phenotype of Williams syndrome. *Current Opinion in Neurobiology*, *23*(3), 414—422. http://dx.doi.org/10.1016/j.conb.2012.12.006.

Järvinen-Pasley, A., Bellugi, U., Reilly, J., Mills, D. L., Galaburda, A., Reiss, A. L., & Korenberg, J. R. (2008). Defining the social phenotype in Williams syndrome: a model for linking gene, the brain, and behavior. *Development and Psychopathology*, *20*(1), 1—35. http://dx.doi.org/10.1017/S0954579408000011.

Jawaid, A., Riby, D. M., Owens, J., White, S. W., Tarar, T., & Schulz, P. E. (2012). "Too withdrawn" or "too friendly": considering social vulnerability in two neuro-developmental disorders. *Journal of Intellectual Disability Research*, *56*(4), 335—350. http://dx.doi.org/10.1111/j.1365-2788.2011.01452.x.

Jones, W., Bellugi, U., Lai, Z., Chiles, M., Reilly, J., Lincoln, A., & Adolphs, R. (2001). Hypersociability: the social and affective phenotype of Williams syndrome. In U. Bellugi, & M. St. George (Eds.), *Journey from cognition to brain to gene: Perspectives from Williams syndrome* (pp. 43—71). Cambridge, MA: MIT Press.

Jones, E. A., Carr, E. G., & Feeley, K. M. (2006). Multiple effects of joint attention intervention for children with autism. *Behavior Modification*, *30*(6), 782—834.

Karmiloff-Smith, A. (1998). Development itself is the key to understanding developmental disorders. *Trends in Cognitive Sciences*, *2*(10), 389—398. http://dx.doi.org/10.1016/S1364-6613(98)01230-3.

Karmiloff-Smith, A. (2006). The tortuous route from genes to behavior: a neuroconstructivist approach. *Cognitive, Affective & Behavioral Neuroscience*, *6*(1), 9—17. http://dx.doi.org/10.3758/CABN.6.1.9.

Karmiloff-Smith, A. (2011). Static snapshots versus dynamic approaches to genes, brain, cognition, and behavior in neurodevelopmental disabilities. *International Review of Research in Developmental Disabilities*, *40*, 1—15.

Karmiloff-Smith, A., & Thomas, M. (2003). What can developmental disorders tell us about the neurocomputational constraints that shape development? The case of Williams syndrome. *Development and Psychopathology*, *15*(4), 969—990.

Kasari, C., Freeman, S., Mundy, P., & Sigman, M. (1995). Attention regulation by children with Down syndrome: coordinated joint attention and social referencing looks. *American Journal on Mental Retardation*, *100*(2), 128—136.

Kasari, C., Freeman, S., & Paparella, T. (2006). Joint attention and symbolic play in young children with autism: a randomized controlled intervention study. *Journal of Child Psychology and Psychiatry, and Allied Disciplines*, *47*(6), 611—620. http://dx.doi.org/10.1111/j.1469-7610.2005.01567.x.

Kasari, C., Mundy, P., Yirmiya, N., & Sigman, M. (1990). Affect and attention in children with Down syndrome. *American Journal on Mental Retardation*, *95*(1), 55—67.

Kasari, C., Sigman, M., Mundy, P., & Yirmiya, N. (1990). Affective sharing in the context of joint attention interactions of normal, autistic, and mentally retarded children. *Jounral of Autism and Developmental Disorders*, *20*(1), 87—100.

Kent, L., Clinic, P., Evans, J., Registrar, S., Centre, O., & Oak, S. (1999). Comorbidity of autistic spectrum disorders in children with Down syndrome. *Developmental Medicine and Child Neurology*, *41*, 153—158.

Laing, E., Butterworth, G., Ansari, D., Gsodl, M., Longhi, E., Panagiotaki, G., … Karmiloff-Smith, A. (2002). Atypical development of language and social communication in toddlers with Williams syndrome. *Developmental Science*, *5*(2), 233—246. http://dx.doi.org/10.1111/1467-7687.00225.

Legerstee, M., & Fisher, T. (2008). Coordinated attention, declarative and imperative pointing in infants with and without Down syndrome: sharing experiences with adults and peers. *First Language*, *28*(3), 281—311. http://dx.doi.org/10.1177/0142723708091045.

Legerstee, M., & Weintraub, J. (1997). The integration of person and object attention in infants with and without Down syndrome. *Infant Behavior and Development, 20*(1), 71—82. http://dx.doi.org/10.1016/S0163-6383(97)90062-X.

Lewis, M. D. (1997). Personality self-organization: cascading constraints on cognition-emotion interaction. In A. Fogel, M. Lyra, & J. Valsiner (Eds.), *Dynamics and indeterminism in developmental and social processes* (pp. 193—216). Mahwah, NJ: Lawrence Erlbaum Associates Publishers.

Lewis, M. (2000). The promise of dynamic systems approaches for an integrated account of human development. *Child Development, 71*(1), 36—43. http://dx.doi.org/10.1111/1467-8624.00116.

Lincoln, A. J., Searcy, Y. M., Jones, W., & Lord, C. (2007). Social interaction behaviors discriminate young children with autism and Williams syndrome. *Journal of the American Academy of Child and Adolescent Psychiatry, 46*(3), 323—331.

Lord, C., Rutter, M., DiLavore, P. C., Risi, S., Gotham, K., & Bishop, S. L. (2012). *Autism diagnostic observation schedule, 2nd edition (ADOS-2) Manual (Part 1): Modules 1—4.* Los Angeles, CA: Western Psychological Services.

Lowenthal, R., Paula, C. S., Schwartzman, J. S., Brunoni, D., & Mercadante, M. T. (2007). Prevalence of pervasive developmental disorder in Down's syndrome. *Journal of Autism and Developmental Disorders, 37*(7), 1394—1395. http://dx.doi.org/10.1007/s10803-007-0374-4.

Marschik, P. B., Bartl-Pokorny, K. D., Sigafoos, J., Urlesberger, L., Pokorny, F., Didden, R., … Kaufmann, W. E. (2014). Development of socio-communicative skills in 9- to 12-month-old individuals with fragile X syndrome. *Research in Developmental Disabilities, 35*(3), 597—602. http://dx.doi.org/10.1016/j.ridd.2014.01.004.

Martins, M. P., & Harris, S. L. (2006). Teaching children with autism to respond to joint attention initiations. *Child & Family Behavior Therapy, 28*(1), 51—68.

Masten, A. S., & Cicchetti, D. (2010). Developmental cascades. *Development and Psychopathology, 22*(2010), 491—495. http://dx.doi.org/10.1017/S0954579410000222.

Mazzocco, M., Pennington, B. F., & Hagerman, R. J. (1994). Social cognition skills among females with fragile X. *Journal of Autism and Developmental Disorders, 24*(4), 473—485.

McCary, L. M., & Roberts, J. E. (2013). Early identification of autism in fragile X syndrome: a review. *Journal of Intellectual Disability Research, 57*(9), 803—814.

Meltzoff, A. N. (1995). Understanding the intentions of others: re-enactment of intended acts by 18-month-old children. *Developmental Psychology, 31*(5), 838—850. http://dx.doi.org/10.1037/0012-1649.31.5.838.

Meltzoff, A. N., & Moore, M. K. (1994). Imitation, memory, and the representation of persons. *Infant Behavior and Development, 17*(1), 83—99. http://dx.doi.org/10.1016/0163-6383(94)90024-8.

Meltzoff, A. N., & Moore, M. K. (1998). Infant intersubjectivity: broadening the dialogue to include imitation, identity and intention. In S. Braten (Ed.), *Intersubjective communication and emotion in early ontogeny* (pp. 47—62). Cambridge: Cambridge University Press.

Mervis, C. B., & Bertrand, J. (1993). Acquisition of early object labels: the roles of operating principles and input. In A. Kaiser, & D. B. Gray (Eds.), *Enhancing children's communication: Research foundations for intervention* (pp. 287—316). Baltimore, MD: Brookes Publishing, Inc.

Mervis, C. B., & Bertrand, J. (1997). Developmental relations between cognition and language: evidence from Williams syndrome. In L. B. Adamson, & M. Romski (Eds.), *Communication and language acquisition: Discoveries from atypical development* (pp. 75—106). New York, NY: Brookes Publishing, Inc.

Mervis, C. B., & Klein-Tasman, B. P. (2000). Williams syndrome: cognition, personality, and adaptive behavior. *Mental Retardation and Developmental Disabilities Research Reviews, 6*(2), 148—158. http://dx.doi.org/10.1002/1098-2779(2000)6:2<148::AID-MRDD10>3.0.CO;2-T.

Mervis, C. B., Morris, C. A., Klein-Tasman, B. P., Bertrand, J., Kwitny, S., Appelbaum, L. G., & Rice, C. E. (2003). Attentional characteristics of infants and toddlers with Williams syndrome during triadic interactions. *Developmental Neuropsychology, 23*(1—2), 243—268.

Moore, D. G., Oates, J. M., Hobson, R. P., & Goodwin, J. (2002). Cognitive and social factors in the development of infants with Down syndrome. *Down's Syndrome, Research and Practice, 8*(2), 43—52. http://dx.doi.org/10.3104/reviews.129.

Mundy, P., Delgado, C., Block, J., Venezia, M., Hogan, A., & Seibert, J. (2003). *A manual for the abridged early social communication scales (ESCS)*. Retrieved from http://www.psy.miami.edu/faculty/pmundy/ESCS.pdf.

Mundy, P., Kasari, C., Sigman, M., & Ruskin, E. (1995). Nonverbal communication and early language acquisition in children with Down syndrome and in normally developing children. *Journal of Speech and Hearing Research, 38*(1), 157—167.

Mundy, P., & Newell, L. (2007). Attention, joint attention, and social cognition. *Current Directions in Psychological Science, 16*(5), 269—274. http://dx.doi.org/10.1111/j.1467-8721.2007.00518.x.

Mundy, P., & Sigman, M. (2006). Joint attention, social competence and developmental psychopathology. *Developmental Psychopathology, 1*, 293—332.

Mundy, P., Sigman, M., Kasari, C., & Yirmiya, N. (1988). Nonverbal communication skills in Down syndrome children. *Child Development, 59*(1), 235—249. http://dx.doi.org/10.2307/1130406.

Murphy, M., & Abbeduto, L. (2005). Indirect genetic effects and the early language development of children with genetic mental retardation syndromes: the role of joint attention. *Infants & Young Children, 18*(1), 47—59. http://dx.doi.org/10.1097/00001163-200501000-00006.

Murphy, M., Abbeduto, L., Schroeder, S., & Serlin, R. (2007). Contribution of social and information-processing factors to eye-gaze avoidance in fragile X syndrome. *American Journal on Mental Retardation, 112*(5), 349—360. http://dx.doi.org/10.1352/0895-8017(2007)112[0349:COSAIF]2.0.CO;2.

O'Brien, G. (1992). Behavioural phenotypes and their measurement. *Developmental Medicine and Child Neurology, 34*(4), 365—367.

Parker, S. E., Mai, C. T., Canfield, M. A., Rickard, R., Wang, Y., Meyer, R. E., … Correa, A. (2010). Updated national birth prevalence estimates for selected birth defects in the United States, 2004—2006. *Birth Defects Research. Part A, Clinical and Molecular Teratology, 88*(12), 1008—1016. http://dx.doi.org/10.1002/bdra.20735.

Pitcairn, T. K., & Wishart, J. G. (1994). Reaction of young children with Down's syndrome to an impossible task. *British Journal of Developmental Psychology, 12*, 485—498.

Plesa-Skwerer, D., Faja, S., Schofield, C., Verbalis, A., & Tager-Flusberg, H. (2006). Perceiving facial and vocal expressions of emotion in individuals with Williams syndrome. *American Journal of Mental Retardation, 111*(1), 15—26. http://dx.doi.org/10.1352/0895-8017(2006)111[15:PFAVEO]2.0.CO;2.

Reilly, C. (2009). Autism spectrum disorders in Down syndrome: a review. *Research in Autism Spectrum Disorders, 3*(4), 829—839. http://dx.doi.org/10.1016/j.rasd.2009.01.012.

Riby, D. M., & Back, E. (2010). Can individuals with Williams syndrome interpret mental states from moving faces? *Neuropsychologia, 48*(7), 1914—1922. http://dx.doi.org/10.1016/j.neuropsychologia.2010.03.010.

Riby, D. M., Bruce, V., & Jawaid, A. (2012). Everyone's friend? The case of Williams syndrome. In B. Oakley, A. Knafo, G. Madhavan, & D. Sloan Wilson (Eds.), *Pathological altruism* (p. 116). New York, NY: Oxford University Press.

Roberts, J. E., Clarke, M. A., Alcorn, K., Carter, J. C., Long, A. C. J., & Kaufmann, W. E. (2009). Autistic behavior in boys with fragile X syndrome: social approach and HPA-axis dysfunction. *Journal of Neurodevelopmental Disorders, 1*(4), 283—291. http://dx.doi.org/10.1007/s11689-009-9028-5.

Roberts, J. E., Mankowski, J. B., Sideris, J., Goldman, B. D., Hatton, D. D., Mirrett, P. L., ... Bailey, D. B., Jr. (2009). Trajectories and predictors of the development of very young boys with fragile X syndrome. *Journal of Pediatric Psychology, 34*(8), 827—836. http://dx.doi.org/10.1093/jpepsy/jsn129.

Roberts, J. E., Mirrett, P., Anderson, K., Burchinal, M., & Neebe, E. (2002). Early communication, symbolic behavior, and social profiles of young males with fragile X syndrome. *American Journal of Speech-Language Pathology, 11*(3), 295—304. http://dx.doi.org/10.1044/1058-0360(2002/034).

Roberts, J. E., Weisenfeld, L. A. H., Hatton, D. D., Heath, M., & Kaufmann, W. E. (2007). Social approach and autistic behavior in children with fragile X syndrome. *Journal of Autism and Developmental Disorders, 37*(9), 1748—1760. http://dx.doi.org/10.1007/s10803-006-0305-9.

Rocha, M. L., Schreibman, L., & Stahmer, A. C. (2007). Effectiveness of training parents to teach joint attention in children with autism. *Journal of Early Intervention, 29*(2), 154—172.

Rosner, B. A., Hodapp, R. M., Fidler, D. J., Sagun, J. N., & Dykens, E. M. (2004). Social competence in persons with Prader—Willi, Williams and Down's syndromes. *Journal of Applied Research in Intellectual Disabilities, 17*(3), 209—217.

Ruskin, E., Kasari, C., Mundy, P., & Sigman, M. (1994). Attention to people and toys during social and object mastery in children with Down syndrome. *American Journal on Mental Retardation, 99*(1), 103—111.

Seibert, J. M., Hogan, A. E., & Mundy, P. (1982). Assessing interactional competencies: the early social-communication scales. *Infant Mental Health Journal, 3*(4), 244—258.

Sigman, M., & Ruskin, E. M. (1999). Continuity and change in the social competence of children with autism, Down syndrome, and developmental delays. *Monographs of the Society for Research in Child Development, 64.*

Singer, J. D., & Willett, J. B. (2003). *Applied longitudinal data analysis: Modeling change and event occurrence.* New York, NY: Oxford University Press.

Slonims, V., & Mcconachie, H. (2006). Analysis of mother — infant interaction in infants with Down syndrome and typically developing infants. *American Journal of Intellectual and Developmental Disabilities, 111*(4), 273—289.

Stern, D. N. (1974). The goal and structure of mother-infant play. *Journal of the American Academy of Child Psychiatry, 13*(3), 402—421.

Strømme, P., Bjørnstad, P. G., & Ramstad, K. (2002). Prevalence estimation of Williams syndrome. *Journal of Child Neurology, 17*(4), 269—271. http://dx.doi.org/10.1177/088307380201700406.

Tager-Flusberg, H. (2005). What neurodevelopmental disorders can reveal about cognitive architecture: the example of theory of mind. In P. Carruthers, S. Laurence, & S. Stich (Eds.), *The innate mind: Structure and contents* (pp. 272—288). New York, NY: Oxford University Press.

Tager-Flusberg, H., Boshart, J., & Baron-Cohen, S. (1998). Reading the windows to the soul: evidence of domain-specific sparing in Williams syndrome. *Journal of Cognitive Neuroscience, 10*(5), 631—639. http://dx.doi.org/10.1162/089892998563031.

Tager-Flusberg, H., & Skwerer, D. P. (2007). *Williams syndrome: A model developmental syndrome for exploring brain-behavior relationships. In human behavior, learning, and the developing Brain: Atypical development.*

Tager-Flusberg, H., Skwerer, D. P., & Joseph, R. M. (2006). Model syndromes for investigating social cognitive and affective neuroscience: a comparison of autism and Williams syndrome. *Social Cognitive and Affective Neuroscience, 1*(3), 175—182. http://dx.doi.org/10.1093/scan/nsl035.

Tager-Flusberg, H., & Sullivan, K. (2000). A componential view of theory of mind: evidence from Williams syndrome. *Cognition, 76*(1), 59—90.

Thelen, E., & Smith, L. B. (2006). Dynamic systems theories. In R. M. Lerner, W. Damon, R. M. Lerner, & W. Damon (Eds.) (6th ed.) *Theoretical models of human development: Vol. 1. Handbook of child psychology.* Hoboken, NJ: John Wiley & Sons Inc.

Thomas, M. S. C., Annaz, D., Ansari, D., Jarrold, C., Karmiloff-Smith, A., & Scerif, G. (2009). Using developmental trajectories to understand developmental disorders. *Hearing Research, 52*(April), 336—359. http://dx.doi.org/10.1044/1092-4388(2009/07-0144).

Thurman, A. J., & Fisher, M. H. (2015). The Williams syndrome social phenotype. *International Review of Research in Developmental Disabilities, 49,* 191—227. http://dx.doi.org/10.1016/bs.irrdd.2015.06.002.

Tomasello, M. (1995). Joint attention as social cognition. In C. Moore, & P. Dunham (Eds.), *Joint attention: Its origins and role in development* (pp. 103—130). Lawrence Earlbaum & Associates.

Tomasello, M., Carpenter, M., & Hobson, R. P. (2005). The emergence of social cognition in three young chimpanzees. *Monographs of the Society for Research in Child Development, 70.* i—152.

Trevarthen, C. (1979). Communication and cooperation in early infancy: a description of primary intersubjectivity. In M. Bullowa (Ed.), *Before speech: The beginning of interpersonal communication.* New York, NY: Cambridge University Press.

Trevarthen, C. (1998). The concept and foundations of infant intersubjectivity. In S. Braten (Ed.), *Intersubjective comunication and emotion in early ontogeny* (pp. 15—46). New York, NY: Cambridge University Press.

Trevarthen, C., & Aitken, K. J. (2001). Infant intersubjectivity: research, theory, and clinical applications. *Journal of Child Psychology and Psychiatry, and Allied Disciplines, 42*(1), 3—48. http://dx.doi.org/10.1111/1469-7610.00701.

Trevarthen, C., & Hubley, P. (1978). Secondary intersubjectivity: confidence, confiding and acts of meaning in the first year. In A. Lock (Ed.), *Action, gesture and symbol* (pp. 183—229). London: Academic Press.

Tronick, E. (1982). *Social interchange in infancy: Affect, cognition, and communication.* University Park Press.

Wetherby, A. M., & Prizant, B. M. (2003). *Communication and symbolic behavior scales (CSBS) manual.* Baltimore, MD: Brookes Publishing, Inc.

Wishart, J. G. (2007). Socio-cognitive understanding: a strength or weakness in Down's syndrome? *Journal of Intellectual Disability Research, 51*(12), 996—1005. http://dx.doi.org/10.1111/j.1365-2788.2007.01007.x.

Wolff, P. H., Gardner, J., Paccia, J., & Lappen, J. (1989). The greeting behavior of fragile X males. *American Journal on Mental Retardation, 93*(4), 406—411.

Yirmiya, N., Solomonica-Levi, D., Shulman, C., & Pilowsky, T. (1996). Theory of mind abilities in individuals with autism, Down syndrome, and mental retardation of unknown etiology: the role of age and intelligence. *Journal of Child Psychology and Psychiatry and Allied Disciplines, 37*(8), 1003—1014. http://dx.doi.org/10.1111/j.1469-7610.1996.tb01497.x/abstract.

Zelazo, P. D., Burack, J. A., Benedetto, E., & Frye, D. (1996). Theory of mind and rule use in individuals with Down's syndrome: a test of the uniqueness and specificity claims. *Journal of Child Psychology and Psychiatry and Allied Disciplines, 37*(4), 479—484. http://dx.doi.org/10.1111/j.1469-7610.1996.tb01429.x/abstract.

Zinck, A. (2008). Self-referential emotions. *Consciousness and Cognition, 17*(2), 496—505. http://dx.doi.org/10.1016/j.concog.2008.03.014.

CHAPTER FIVE

Sleep in Neurodevelopmental Disorders

A.J. Esbensen[*,1], A.J. Schwichtenberg[§]
*Cincinnati Children's Hospital Medical Center, Cincinnati, OH, United States
§Purdue University, West Lafayette, IN, United States
[1]Corresponding author: E-mail: anna.esbensen@cchmc.org

Contents

International Review of Research in Developmental Disabilities, Volume 51
ISSN 2211-6095
http://dx.doi.org/10.1016/bs.irrdd.2016.07.005

© 2016 Elsevier Inc.
All rights reserved.

Abstract

Individuals with intellectual and developmental disabilities (IDD) experience sleep problems at higher rates than the general population. Although individuals with IDD are a heterogeneous group, several sleep problems cluster within genetic syndromes or disorders. This review summarizes the prevalence of sleep problems experienced by individuals with Angelman syndrome, Cornelia de Lange syndrome, Cri du Chat syndrome, Down syndrome, fragile X syndrome, Prader—Willi syndrome, Smith—Magenis syndrome, Williams syndrome, autism spectrum disorder, and idiopathic IDD. Factors associated with sleep problems and the evidence for sleep treatments are reviewed for each neurodevelopmental disorder. Sleep research advancements in neurodevelopmental disorders are reviewed, including the need for consistency in defining and measuring sleep problems, considerations for research design and reporting of results, and considerations when evaluating sleep treatments.

1. INTRODUCTION

Individuals with intellectual and developmental disabilities (IDD) experience sleep problems at higher rates than the general population. Prevalence estimates vary with estimates of reported sleep problems ranging from 34% to 86% (Bartlett, Rooney, & Spedding, 1985; Clements, Wing, &

Dunn, 1986). Although the nature of sleep problems in individuals with IDD has been a focus of research for several decades, less research has been focused on treatment options and often assessed individuals with IDD as a homogenous group with little distinction for developmental changes with age. Several literature reviews in the last decade have drawn attention to sleep problems in specific genetic syndromes or disorders, specific age groups, or targeting issues with assessment and treatment (Churchill, Kieckhefer, Landis, & Ward, 2012; Didden & Sigafoos, 2001; Doran, Harvey, Horner, & Scotti, 2006; Richdale & Baker, 2014; Tietze et al., 2012; van de Wouw, Evenhuis, & Echteld, 2012). Given the prevalence of sleep problems in individuals with IDD, there is growing need to understand the types of sleep problems experienced by this heterogeneous group of individuals with IDD, how measurement of sleep problems impacts findings, and implications for appropriate treatment of sleep problems among individuals with IDD across the life span.

Several studies have compared sleep problems across syndrome groups in an effort to better characterize associated behavioral phenotypes and areas of concern specific to genetic syndromes (Ashworth, Hill, Karmiloff-Smith, & Dimitriou, 2013; Cotton & Richdale, 2006, 2010). These efforts are helpful in identifying potential neurobiological or craniofacial contributions to sleep problems. For example, facial and physical features may contribute to an increased risk for obstructive sleep apnea (OSA) in individuals with Down syndrome (DS) and circadian timing may be altered in individuals with autism spectrum disorder (ASD) (Esbensen, 2016; Glickman, 2010). Additionally, previous studies highlight circadian rhythm problems in some children with Smith—Magenis syndrome (SMS) reporting higher endogenous melatonin levels during the day than at night (De Leersnyder et al., 2001; Potocki et al., 2000). However, the research rigor in studies of sleep problems in individuals with IDD or specific genetic syndromes varies from (1) limited to case series, cohort studies, (2) well-conducted cohort studies or case control, and (3) few high-quality systematic reviews or cohort studies (van de Wouw et al., 2012). Sleep research in individuals with IDD is further hindered by diverse sleep assessment methods, small sample sizes, and heterogeneous groups with respect to disorders and age. This variability impacts the ability to draw conclusions about sleep problems in specific populations and the ability to effectively evaluate sleep treatment efficacy.

This review focuses on common sleep problems among individuals with different genetic syndromes or disorders, in an effort to identify research gaps and methods for improving research replicability and ultimately the sleep of individuals with IDD. Rather than compare the rates of problems across syndromes, we elected to focus on the specific sleep problems experienced within syndromes/disorders. The intention is to highlight sleep problems and commonalities within syndrome to better identify research gaps and inform sleep evaluation and treatment. The following sections will review sleep problems types and sleep assessment methods, review research targeted to specific syndromes and disorders, and identify areas for future research.

2. COMMON SLEEP PROBLEMS

Prior to reviewing specific sleep problems experienced by individuals with IDD, a review of common sleep problems and their definitions is warranted. Prior classification systems for sleep disorders varied, contributing to the use of different terms to describe sleep problems in the research literature. Recent revisions to the International Classification of Sleep Disorders (ICSD-3) and Diagnostic and Statistical Manual of Mental Disorders (DSM-5) provide for more consistent definitions of sleep problems (American Psychiatric Association, 2013; Medicine, 2014). Sleep problems are a heterogeneous set of problems, including difficulties with insomnia, sleep-related breathing disorders, excessive daytime sleepiness (EDS), circadian rhythm sleep disorders, parasomnias, and sleep–related movement disorders.

Insomnia includes difficulties with initiating or maintaining sleep and can be behavioral or physiological. Behavioral insomnias often include bedtime refusals and difficulties settling associated with poor sleep hygiene. These behaviors often delay sleep onset and/or can contribute to difficulties settling back to sleep after a night waking. Stressors may also exacerbate insomnia. Physiological causes of insomnia may include heightened arousal or anxiety prior to bedtime, atypical melatonin profiles, pain, acid reflux, and heart dysfunction.

Sleep-related breathing disorders include a class of insomnia concerns that implicate the respiratory system. They include periodic difficulties with respiration during sleep, like obstructive and central sleep apnea, and sleep–related hypoventilation. OSA is an upper airway obstruction that leads to cessation in breathing for between 20 and 200 s. Specific criteria for defining hypopnea have been developed and are a well–used tool in research (Medicine, 2007). Central sleep apnea is less common and refers to recurrent difficulties with respiratory effort during sleep. These apneas are often related to arousals and fractured sleep.

Excessive daytime sleepiness (EDS) includes hypersomnolence and narcolepsy. EDS can involve an excess of total sleep time (at night or including daytime napping), reduced daytime arousal, and difficulty waking after a nap.

Circadian rhythm sleep disorders involve a repeated pattern of delayed or advanced sleep (generally off by more than 2 h) in relation to the desired sleep—wake schedule. Circadian rhythm sleep disorder can result in symptoms of insomnia and EDS.

Parasomnias include events or arousals that accompany sleep, for example, sleepwalking, sleep terrors, excessive nightmares. While seizures can be associated with parasomnias, they are not in themselves a parasomnia. Nocturnal enuresis (bed-wetting) falls under Other Parasomnias within ICSD-3 criteria, but fall under Elimination Disorders within the DSM-5 (American Psychiatric Association, 2013; Medicine, 2014).

Sleep-related movement disorders include rhythmic or repeated movements of the legs, limbs, jaw, and/or neck during sleep. These disorders commonly include restless leg syndrome, bruxism, or sleep-related leg cramps.

3. MEASUREMENT

In addition to the heterogeneous set of sleep problems that are common concerns in individuals with IDD, there exists heterogeneity in the methods used to measure sleep behaviors and problems in individuals with IDD, which complicates the extraction of knowledge for these specialized populations. Different methods for assessing sleep were recently reviewed in relation to children with ASD (Hodge, Parnell, Hoffman, & Sweeney, 2012). Readers are encouraged to consult Hodge et al. (2012) for a thorough review on how various measures of sleep have been used with this population. Briefly, we review the measurement of sleep and how they have been applied more generally with individuals with IDD.

Polysomnography (PSG) is the gold standard for assessing sleep problems, providing measures of brain, muscle, and heart activity via electroencephalography, electrooculography, electromyography, electrocardiography, and pulse oximetry. PSG has been used to assess sleep in individuals with IDD for almost 50 years (Feinberg, Braun, & Shulman, 1969). However, access to PSG and the ability of all individuals with IDD to successfully complete a PSG is hindered by several characteristics that may present when administered to individuals with IDD. Sensory sensitivity may reduce electrode compliance, and anxiety of being away at home or in a new environment contributes to some children not completing a PSG. Recent advancements in supporting PSG through sensitization techniques, social stories, and preparatory visits have increased the ability of individuals with IDD to successfully complete a PSG. However, accessibility and cost of PSGs likely make them prohibitive for some research studies or study populations (Primeau et al., 2015).

Actigraphy is commonly used as a measure of sleep. It has demonstrated reliability with PSG in the general population (Sadeh, Hauri, Kripke, & Lavie, 1995) and in small studies of children with IDD (Goldman, Bichell, Surdyka, & Malow, 2012). Benefits of actigraphy include the ability to measure sleep in the home setting over several nights, reduced cost, and increased compliance in comparison to PSG. Actigraphy is generally tolerated by children and adults with IDD (Ashworth et al., 2013; Goldman, Bichell, et al., 2012). However, a recent large study of older adults with IDD demonstrated that successful use was only obtained in 35% of adults, with unsuccessful use generally related to intolerance with wearing the device (van Dijk, Hilgenkamp, Evenhuis, & Echteld, 2012). To address sensory sensitivity to actigraphy watches worn on the wrist, their accuracy in measuring sleep has been evaluated when worn on the shoulder or ankle. Generally, actigraphy worn on the shoulder demonstrates high correlation with wrist actigraphy for sleep onset, total sleep time, and sleep efficiency among children with ASD (Adkins et al., 2012). However, shoulder actigraphy demonstrates poor correlations with wrist actigraphy for wake–after–sleep-onset (WASO). Ankle-worn actigraphy for individuals with IDD demonstrates higher rates of compliance and comparable estimates for sleep onset time and total sleep time but this placement does not appear to capture night awakenings well when compared to videosomnography (VSG) (Sitnick, Goodlin-Jones, & Anders, 2008). Given the small samples in each of these studies, additional research is needed to strengthen the use of actigraphy in individuals with IDD, especially when considering shoulder or ankle placement.

Subjective measures of sleep include parent-reported sleep diaries and sleep questionnaires. *Sleep diaries* are often used in conjunction with actigraphy, where parents report on nightly sleep behaviors over a 1 or 2 week period. Parents generally are asked to report on time in bed, time asleep, time awake, and any night awakenings. Parents may also be asked about daytime behaviors, such as napping, and regarding behaviors that may influence sleep hygiene, such as exercise, screen time, and caffeine intake.

Relatively few studies have addressed the accuracy or biases inherent in parent-reported dairies for children or individuals with IDD but a recent study demonstrated that in families raising children with ASD, parent-reported diaries were just as accurate as those from families raising children with no known diagnosis (Schwichtenberg et al., 2016). In general, parents in both groups were accurate reporters of their child's nighttime sleep; however, both groups underestimated daytime sleep (when compared to actigraphy estimates).

Questionnaire measures of sleep have been most commonly used to screen for sleep problems among individuals with IDD. However, sleep questionnaires have often been author designed or generally not standardized for use with individuals with IDD (Rosen, Lombardo, Skotko, & Davidson, 2011). Most commonly, studies have used the Children's Sleep Habits Questionnaire (CSHQ) due to its reliability with and ability to make comparison to typically developing children, however, its psychometric properties have not been established with individuals with IDD (Ashworth et al., 2013). Others measures have been developed or adapted for use with children with IDD, such as the Behavioral Evaluation of Disorders of Sleep Scale (BEDS) and adapted Simonds—Parraga Sleep Questionnaire (Maas et al., 2011; Simonds & Parraga, 1982; Wiggs & Stores, 1996). However, questionnaire reports of sleep generally demonstrate poor reliability with actigraphy. Parent reports of sleep among school-age children with DS or Williams syndrome (WS) correlate well with total sleep time, but not with sleep onset latency, and number and duration of night wakings (Ashworth et al., 2013). While parent reports of sleep problems have been found to correlate with objective measures of restlessness and snoring in children with DS, these objective measures have not then been correlated with sleep quality (Stores & Stores, 2014). Further, among young children with DS, questionnaires based on parent report have demonstrated poor reliability with PSGs (Maris, Verhulst, Wojciechowski, Van de Heyning, & Boudewyns, 2016; Shott et al., 2006), such that the American Academy of Pediatrics recommends all children with DS receive a PSG prior to 4 years of age (Bull & Genetics, 2011).

Meeting *standards* for a sleep condition based on the ICSD-3 or the DSM-5 are also used to document the presence of sleep problems (American Psychiatric Association, 2013; Medicine, 2014). The challenge when comparing the rates of sleep problems across different types of measurement tools is that they often result in different reported rates of sleep problems (Dohnt, Gradisar, & Short, 2012; Espie & Tweedie, 1991).

This challenge is not a new concern or specific to just sleep problems, yet our research community has continued to frequently rely on questionnaire findings rather than diagnostic criteria. Screening tools, such as parent report questionnaires, are often an overestimate of certain sleep problems such as difficulties with sleep onset or cosleeping, and an underestimate of other sleep problems such as motor movement or sleep apneas. Informant report sleep questionnaires are likely restricted to use with adults with IDD with overnight support staff or coresiding family, thus not easily generalized to all adults with IDD. Similarly, self-reports of sleep problems by adults with IDD are not easily generalized to all adults with IDD.

4. SYNDROME/CONDITION-SPECIFIC SLEEP PROBLEMS

4.1 Angelman Syndrome

4.1.1 Prevalence

Among children with Angelman syndrome (AS), sleep problems have been reported among 20—80% of individuals, with a more recent review citing rates of 48—70% (Tietze et al., 2012; Walz, Beebe, & Byars, 2005; Williams et al., 1995). In AS, sleep problems of specific concern include insomnia (sleep initiation and sleep maintenance), parasomnia, daytime sleepiness, and sleep-related breathing problems, with reported rates varying depending on how sleep was measured (Goldman, Bichell, et al., 2012). A study combining actigraphy, rating scales, and PSG reported significant difficulties with sleep latency, frequent and longer night waking, fragmented sleep, and shorter sleep duration (Goldman, Bichell, et al., 2012). Using PSG, the sleep architecture for young children with AS includes poor efficiency, a lower percentage of time in REM sleep, and a higher percentage of time in slow wave sleep (Miano et al., 2004). These sleep problems were replicated on parental rating scales. Parent rating scales also indicated individuals with AS are reliant on sleep facilitators, disoriented when aroused, and awaken easily to loud noises (Walz et al., 2005).

4.1.2 Associated Problems

Sleep problems in individuals with AS are associated with age and potentially to seizures (Goldman, Bichell, et al., 2012). Comparisons across research reports suggest a lessening of severity of sleep problems with age, with improvements noted from preschooler to school-age children. However, these conclusions ignore the persistence of sleep problems in individuals with AS. The relationship between sleep problems in individuals with AS and associated seizures has been mixed. Two studies have suggested that seizures were associated with more severe sleep problems (Clayton-Smith, 1993; Didden, Korzilius, Smits, Curfs, & Dykens, 2004). A more recent study using parental reports did not support an association between seizures and sleep problems (Walz et al., 2005).

Sleep problems in children with AS impact their family environment. Shorter sleep duration in children with AS is associated with more frequent night waking in their parents, variable bedtime is associated with parent stress, and longer sleep latency is associated with parental insomnia and daytime sleepiness (Goldman, Bichell, et al., 2012).

4.1.3 Treatment

The evaluation of treatments to improve sleep among individuals with AS has generally been limited to case reports and case series (Clayton-Smith, 1993; Summers et al., 1992). These treatment trials have included behavioral and combined behavioral treatment with medication. Some researchers have speculated that the longer sleep latency common in children with AS is associated with poor sleep facilitators or poor sleep hygiene, which would be amenable to behavioral sleep interventions or medications to support sleep initiation (Walz et al., 2005). In one survey, 29% of individuals with AS were taking medications to support sleep (Walz et al., 2005). In a small sample of children with AS, 53% were taking melatonin (Goldman, Bichell, et al., 2012). Medication trials have generally been open label and uncontrolled, although demonstrating improvements in sleep latency and motor restlessness (Braam, Didden, Smits, & Curfs, 2008a; Zhdanova, Wurtman, & Wagstaff, 1999). Two small studies specifically assessed the efficacy of medication use of children with AS. The first was an open label trial in 13 children wherein sleep duration increased from baseline levels with melatonin treatment (0.3 mg). However, this study also reported lower overall activity levels (as indexed by an actigraphy) which in and of itself may have affected the actigraphy estimates of sleep. A second study, a randomized double-blind placebo-controlled study, of eight individuals with AS reported several improvements in sleep with melatonin (2.5—5 mg), when compared to baseline and placebo, including shorter sleep onset latencies, earlier sleep onset time, fewer night awakenings, and longer sleep durations (Braam et al., 2008a).

4.2 Cornelia de Lange Syndrome

4.2.1 Prevalence

According to research estimates, 55–72% of children with Cornelia de Lange syndrome (CdLS) have a comorbid sleep problem, the most common of which is insomnia (bedtime settling and night awakenings) (Basile, Villa, Selicorni, & Molteni, 2007; Berney, Ireland, & Burn, 1999; Gualtieri, 1991; Hall, Arron, Sloneem, & Oliver, 2008; Tietze et al., 2012). However, when comparable to a case-controlled sample of individuals with IDD matched for age, gender, degree of intellectual disability (ID), and mobility the rates in CdLS do not appear elevated (Hall et al., 2008). Recent studies using rating scales suggest a high rate of sleep-disordered breathing, with 35% of children demonstrating moderate to severe symptoms, and additional symptoms of insomnia and circadian rhythm disorder (Stavinoha et al., 2011).

4.2.2 Associated Problems

Given the high rate of self-injury present in CdLS, the association between sleep problems and self-injury has been explored, but with no reported relationship (Hall et al., 2008). A higher rate of sleep problems is reported among individuals with CdLS with more severe IDD and among children with CdLS in comparison to adults (Berney et al., 1999; Rajan et al., 2012). Small sample sizes preclude statistical analyses to determine if sleep problems become less prevalent with age but are suggestive that difficulties with sleep onset decline from childhood into adulthood in individuals with CdLS (Rajan et al., 2012).

4.2.3 Treatment

No research was identified that has evaluated treatments for sleep problems among individuals with CdLS. However, in studies of diverse IDD (like those seen in CdLS), a combination of individualized behavioral therapy and medication has been effective (Didden & Sigafoos, 2001).

4.3 Cri du Chat Syndrome

4.3.1 Prevalence

Among children with Cri du Chat syndrome (CDC), sleep problems are reported among 30–50% (Maas et al., 2009; Tietze et al., 2012). Sleep questionnaire reports suggest difficulties with insomnia (bedtime settling, sleep anxiety, night waking, and poor quality sleep) and sleep-disordered breathing (Cornish, Oliver, Standen, Bramble, & Collins, 2003; Cornish & Pigram, 1996; Maas et al., 2009). Snoring is also frequently reported

(Maas, Didden, Korzilius, & Curfs, 2012). Researchers have suggested that the rate of sleep problems in individuals with CDC is not different from that reported among individuals with IDD or other genetic syndromes (Maas et al., 2009, 2012).

4.3.2 Associated Problems
No research was identified that assessed associated problems relative to sleep problems solely among individuals with CDC.

4.3.3 Treatment
In one descriptive survey of a small sample, 13% of individuals with CDC were taking medications to support sleep (Maas et al., 2009). Among those reported to be using medication to support sleep, half of parents indicated that medication was helpful. Parents receiving psychological supports for sleep found it helpful, but those receiving educational or general advice did not find it helpful in supporting the sleep problems in their children with CDC (Maas et al., 2009).

4.4 Down Syndrome
4.4.1 Prevalence
Among children with DS, sleep problems are reported among 31—54% (Stores & Stores, 2013; Tietze et al., 2012). Measurement of sleep problems has included PSGs, actigraphy, sleep diaries, and sleep questionnaires. Sleep problems of specific concern among children with DS include insomnia, OSA, and daytime sleepiness. With actigraphy and/or PSG, children with DS have more fractured sleep, as measured by longer WASO, longer time in bed, lower sleep efficiency, less time in REM sleep, and more movement during sleep as compared to typically developing children (Ashworth et al., 2013; Ashworth, Hill, Karmiloff-Smith, & Dimitriou, 2015; Harvey & Kennedy, 2002). On rating scales, children with DS were noted to have difficulties with insomnia (sleep onset, bedtime settling, sleep anxiety, bedtime resistance, sleep maintenance, and night waking), parasomnias, and sleep-disordered breathing (Ashworth et al., 2013; Breslin, Edgin, Bootzin, Goodwin, & Nadel, 2011; Cotton & Richdale, 2006; Stores, Stores, Fellows, & Buckley, 1998). Night waking is reported to be frequent and for long periods of wakefulness, and to also be related to restlessness during sleep.

OSA is a specific concern in DS, affecting 31—63% of individuals (Marcus, Keens, Bautista, von Pechman, & Ward, 1991; de Miguel-Diez,

Villa-Asensi, & Alvarez-Sala, 2003; Stebbens, Dennis, Samuels, Croft, & Southall, 1991). Slightly, lower rates of OSA are reported in community samples of individuals with DS, affecting 24—59% of individuals (Dahlqvist, Rask, Rosenqvist, Sahlin, & Franklin, 2003; Stebbens et al., 1991). However, both community and clinic samples report risks significantly higher than the 3—7% reported in the general population (Punjabi, 2008). The increased risk of OSA is likely related to certain facial and physical features present in DS, including midfacial hypoplasia, mandibular hypoplasia, glossoptosis (retraction or downward displacement of tongue), an abnormally small upper airway, superficially positioned tonsils, relative tonsillar and adenoidal encroachment, and hypotonia of the upper airway (Churchill et al., 2012; Marcus et al., 1991; Roizen & Patterson, 2003).

4.4.2 Associated Problems

For individuals with DS, several demographic and daytime behaviors have demonstrated relationships with sleep problems. Older age (within school-age children with DS) is related to a decrease in total sleep time, fewer parasomnias and lower sleep anxiety, and bed-wetting. Additionally, males have a higher frequency of parent-reported sleep problems and daytime sleepiness (Ashworth et al., 2013; Breslin et al., 2011; Maris et al., 2016; Stores, 1993). However, age and gender findings have not been replicated in relation to OSA (Maris et al., 2016).

Among children with DS, associations between sleep problems and daytime behaviors and daily life habits are common. Specifically, parent reports of sleep problems were associated with higher scores of irritability, hyperactivity, and stereotypies, but surprisingly not to lethargy, on the Aberrant Behavior Checklist (Stores, 1993). In addition, parent-reported sleep problems were also associated with parent reports of difficulty across 11 domains of functional outcomes, including mealtimes, fitness, personal care, communication, home life, mobility, responsibilities, relationships, community life, school, and recreation (Churchill, Kieckhefer, Bjornson, & Herting, 2014).

Sleep-disordered breathing, specifically OSA, is linked with lower verbal IQ scores and poorer performance on tests of cognitive flexibility among children with DS (Breslin et al., 2014). Further, a higher number of apneas per hour was related to difficulties with visuo-perceptual skills, such as orientation, among young adults with DS, suggesting that the severity of OSA can have a large impact on some cognitive skills (Andreou, Galanopoulou, Gourgoulianis, Karapetsas, & Molyvdas, 2002).

Adults with DS are also at high risk for sleep problems, increased by their additional risk for dementia (Trois et al., 2009). Among adolescents and young adults with DS, several parent-reported sleep problems were associated with poorer executive functioning. Specifically, insomnia was associated with poorer verbal fluency, OSA was associated with poorer verbal fluency and inhibitory control, and daytime sleepiness was associated with poor inhibitory control (Chen, Spanò, & Edgin, 2013). The severity of OSA assessed using PSG was related to younger age and obesity among adults with DS, but findings regarding the relationship to obesity have also been inconsistent (Fitzgerald, Paul, & Richmond, 2007; Shires et al., 2010; Telakivi, Partinen, Salmi, Leinonen, & Härkönen, 1987; Trois et al., 2009).

4.4.3 Treatment

Treatments for sleep problems in individuals with DS are currently tailored to the nature of their sleep problems, particularly OSA. While no clinical trials have been conducted for examining the efficacy of positive airway pressure (PAP) or surgical interventions among individuals with DS, case reviews and pre–post designs suggest modest improvements following adenotonsillectomy among children with DS (Shete, Stocks, Sebelik, & Schoumacher, 2010). However, following surgery, many children with DS continue to need other interventions, such as PAP or surgical revisions (Shott et al., 2006). Children with DS are reported to accept and adhere to CPAP treatment (O'Donnell, Bjornson, Bohn, & Kirk, 2006).

Behavioral treatments for sleep have been evaluated using group-administered formats and educational pamphlets. Minimal improvements in sleep have been noted in group-administered treatment sessions (Stores & Stores, 2004). However, children with DS were not screened for sleep problems prior to study entry, likely limiting the impact of treatment. Research evaluations of melatonin are few, although case series suggest an improvement with melatonin with young children and adolescents with DS (Jan, Espezel, & Appleion, 1994).

4.5 Fragile X Syndrome

4.5.1 Prevalence

The research literature on sleep problems in fragile X syndrome (FXS) is limited, in part because sleep problems generally appear consistent with those experienced by typically developing peers and in part because sleep problems are consistent with their ID and not specifically FXS (Harvey & Kennedy, 2002). However, animal models of FXS document sleep problems with the phenotype and parent reports (although limited) also endorse sleep problems for some individuals with FXS (Zhang et al., 2008). Research studies estimate that 31–77% of individuals with FXS also have a sleep problem, which is consistent with reported rates in other IDD groups (Kronk et al., 2010; Richdale, 2003). Children with FXS do experience shorter sleep duration, difficulties settling to sleep, and increased WASO (Gould et al., 2000; Miano et al., 2008; Richdale, 2003). Children and young adults with FXS demonstrate a high percentage of stage 1 sleep, low percentage of REM sleep, and a low number of REM episodes when compared to typically developing children (Miano et al., 2008). Recent findings suggest that despite having similar sleep problems when examining conventional sleep parameters, individuals with FXS demonstrate disturbances in their sleep microstructure, specifically lower transient slow EEG oscillations within non-REM sleep (Miano et al., 2008).

4.5.2 Associated Problems

According to one FXS study, sleep problems are associated with poor health, listening skills, adaptability, and in those with a higher number of co-occurring conditions (Kronk et al., 2010). Similarly, Richdale (2003) reported an association between sleep problems and child psychopathology. Few studies exist that specifically address FXS outside of its common comorbid conditions (e.g., ASD). For this reason, associated features of sleep problems in FXS may be informed by the ASD and larger IDD literature. For example, sleep problems are associated with more daytime anxiety and sensory sensitivities in children with ASD (Mazurek & Petroski, 2015).

4.5.3 Treatment

Randomized controlled clinical trials of melatonin have been conducted on small samples of children with FXS alone, with the permutation or with co-morbid ASD. Although the sample size for the individual subtypes was small, overall melatonin demonstrated improvements in total sleep time, sleep onset latency, and earlier bedtimes overall for this sample of children (Wirojanan et al., 2009). Additionally, behavioral sleep treatments have been demonstrated as effect in a small group (n = 5) of children with FXS (Weiskop, Richdale, & Matthews, 2005).

4.6 Prader—Willi Syndrome

4.6.1 Prevalence

Common sleep problems reported among individuals with Prader—Willi syndrome (PWS) include difficulties with insomnia (settling, sleep onset, maintenance), early morning waking, and EDS (Cassidy, McKillop, & Morgan, 1990; Cotton & Richdale, 2006; Gibbs, Wiltshire, & Elder, 2013). Among children with PWS, sleep problems are reported among 35—100% and specifically include EDS and snoring (Richdale, Cotton, & Hibbit, 1999; Tietze et al., 2012). In a population study, 20% had a diagnosed sleep disorder (Butler et al., 2002). Using actigraphy, children with PWS are reported to have longer WASO but shorter sleep latency. These findings persist when controlling for body mass index (BMI) (Gibbs et al., 2013). The frequency of night waking and total time asleep is comparable to typically developing children, but children with PWS remain awake for longer and exhibit more daytime sleepiness (Gibbs et al., 2013).

Using PSG, studies have continually replicated shorter sleep latencies in children with PWS but demonstrated variable results regarding sleep latency in adults with PWS (Joo et al., 2010; Verrillo et al., 2009; Vgontzas et al., 1996). PSG studies have also replicated findings of a greater frequency and duration of WASO among children with PWS, but not among adults (Verrillo et al., 2009). Abnormal REM sleep patterns have been reported, with individuals with PWS having REM sleep onset earlier during the night (Manni et al., 2001).

4.6.2 Associated Problems

In contrast to other syndrome groups where age is often associated with decreasing rates of sleep difficulties, among children with PWS, the reported rate of sleep problems is reported to increase with age (Richdale et al., 1999). Given the high rate of obesity among individuals with PWS and the association between obesity and OSA, the rate of OSA has been investigated among individuals with PWS. While some individuals do demonstrate OSA, many do not despite marked obesity (Vela-Bueno et al., 1984). More recent case reviews have suggested a link between BMI, sleep arousals, and hypoxemia during sleep (O'Donoghue et al., 2005).

Sleep problems in children with PWS affect the child and their family. In a parent survey, child's sleep problems were detrimental to the child (87%), adversely impacted other family members (44%), and adversely impacted child and family well-being (32%) (Cotton & Richdale, 2006). Another study identified that the severity of OSA is related to higher parental reports of child impulsivity and inactivity (O'Donoghue et al., 2005).

Several studies of individuals with PWS have investigated the possible link between sleep-disordered breathing and EDS, with mixed findings. Daytime sleepiness is considered to be a central feature of PWS, and not secondary to nighttime sleep disturbances, with hypothalamic dysfunction suspected as contributing to excessive daytime sleepiness (Nixon & Brouillette, 2002).

4.6.3 Treatment

Although sufficient intervention studies have not directly assessed individuals with PWS, treatment recommendations to support the sleep of individuals with PWS have been provided based on treatment recommendations for the general population (Nixon & Brouillette, 2002). Recommended treatments for OSA include adenotonsillectomy, weight loss, PAP, and tracheostomy. The effectiveness of adenotonsillectomy in a small sample suggests that although this surgery improves the obstructive apnea/hypopnea index and oxygen desaturations among children with PWS, postoperative complications are also present (Pavone et al., 2006). A review of studies in PWS suggests the improvements following adenotonsillectomy but with residual OSA postsurgery (Sedky, Bennett, & Pumariega, 2014). Recommendations for treating central apnea include nasal mask, tracheostomy, and weight loss. Recommendations for treating EDS include behavioral treatments (extending total time asleep, supporting sleep onset) and consideration of medication to support sleep.

4.7 Smith—Magenis Syndrome

4.7.1 Prevalence

The physiology of individuals with SMS predisposes them to having disturbed circadian rhythm. Specifically, melatonin rhythms are often inverted, impacting their ability to fall asleep. Among children with SMS, sleep problems are reported in all children (100%) across multiple studies (Tietze et al., 2012). On rating scales, individuals with SMS (infants to adults) demonstrate significant sleep problems in 65—100% of individuals (Greenberg et al., 1996; Smith, Dykens, & Greenberg, 1998). Common sleep problems included insomnia (bedtime settling, frequent and long sleep waking), parasomnias (bed-wetting), EDS (daytime napping), short sleep cycles, and snoring (Smith et al., 1998). As expected, reported rates of bed-wetting were most common among younger children (82% under

10 years of age). Using PSG, over half of a small sample demonstrated abnormalities in REM sleep, primarily reduced REM sleep (Greenberg et al., 1996).

4.7.2 Associated Problems
Using a rating scale to assess sleep problems, relationships were found with older age and earlier morning waking, more frequent naps, more WASO, and shorter sleep duration (Smith et al., 1998).

4.7.3 Treatment
Responses to a survey suggest that 59% of individuals with SMS use medication to facilitate sleep, with higher use of medication among individuals over the age of 10 years (Smith et al., 1998). Several case studies report effectively treating circadian sleep disturbances using melatonin and β1-adrenergic antagonists (Carpizo et al., 2006; Chou, Tsai, Yu, & Tsai, 2002; Van Thillo, Devricndt, & Willekens, 2010). A case series of children with SMS reported a reversal of melatonin patterns with the treatment of β1-adrenergic antagonists during the day and melatonin prior to bedtime (De Leersnyder et al., 2001). In total, these studies reflect the treatment of only 13 children with SMS. However, within a rare disorder such as SMS they present growing evidence that melatonin treatment (coupled with a β1-adrenergic antagonist) may help children with SMS who present with inverted or altered circadian patterns.

4.8 Williams Syndrome
4.8.1 Prevalence
Sleep problems are reported in 36–57% of children with WS with sleep latency as a common concern (Tietze et al., 2012). On rating scales, children with WS were noted to have difficulties with insomnia (initiating sleep, night waking, and sleep anxiety), parasomnias (bed-wetting, limb movement), daytime drowsiness, and sleep duration (Annaz, Hill, Ashworth, Holley, & Karmiloff-Smith, 2011; Ashworth et al., 2013; Goldman, Malow, Newman, Roof, & Dykens, 2009). Among adolescents and young adults, self-reports indicate a high level of daytime drowsiness, with 34% meeting criteria for EDS (Goldman, Malow, et al., 2009). Using actigraphy, studies have replicated that children with WS have long sleep latencies, and that adolescents and young adults with WS have long sleep latencies, poorer sleep efficiency, more WASO, fragmented sleep, and increased motor movements (Ashworth et al., 2015; Goldman, Malow, et al., 2009). More

recently, studies using PSG in children with WS have been conducted, suggesting additional problems with sleep architecture. Children with WS were reported to have poorer sleep efficiency, decreased REM sleep, and increased slow wave sleep (Gombos, Bódizs, & Kovács, 2011; Mason et al., 2011).

4.8.2 Associated Problems
The shorter night sleep experienced by children with WS has been associated with lower language development in preschoolers and possibly with learning performance in school-age children (Axelsson, Hill, Sadeh, & Dimitriou, 2013; Dimitriou, Karmiloff-Smith, Ashworth, & Hill, 2013). In children with WS, less total sleep time is associated with older age (Ashworth et al., 2013). Further, sleep duration is associated with cardiac problems in school-age children with WS, and sleep latency is associated with asthma and allergies (Annaz et al., 2011). In relation to maternal characteristics, frequent night wakings among school-age children with WS are reported to be associated with maternal sleep and mood (Axelsson et al., 2013).

4.8.3 Treatment
No research was identified that has evaluated treatments for sleep problems among individuals with WS.

4.9 Autism Spectrum Disorders
4.9.1 Prevalence
For individuals with ASD parent/caregiver reports of sleep problems are common with estimates of roughly 50—80% (Couturier et al., 2005; Goodlin-Jones et al., 2009; Liu, Hubbard, Fabes, & Adam, 2006; Schreck & Mulick, 2000). Sleep problems in ASD are diverse and include insomnias, parasomnias, and sleep-disordered breathing (Elrod et al., 2016; Hirata et al., 2016). Sleep problems are among the first concerns that parents report in young children later diagnosed with ASD and persist through adolescence and into adulthood (Goldman, Richdale, Clemons, & Malow, 2012; Limoges, Mottron, Bolduc, Berthiaume, & Godbout, 2005; Ozonoff et al., 2009). Sleep problems are not a constant in the development of individuals with ASD but are fairly stable with sleep problems noted across the life course (Cohen, Conduit, Lockley, Rajaratnam, & Cornish, 2014; Croen et al., 2015). Only a few studies directly assess the stability of sleep problems/ behaviors in ASD noting short-term stability for 3—6 months without

intervention (Anders, Iosif, Schwichtenberg, Tang, & Goodlin-Jones, 2011; Goodlin-Jones et al., 2009) but numerous studies document elevated rates of sleep problems in children, adolescents, and adults using cross-sectional designs (Croen et al., 2015). Sleep problems are more common in individuals with ASD who also have comorbid ADHD, anxiety, depression, or gastrointestinal problems (Klukowski, Wasilewska, & Lebensztejn, 2015). Research on comorbid ID and ASD with respect to sleep problems is less consistent. Several studies report elevated rates of sleep problems in individuals with ASD and ID (Giannotti et al., 2008) but at least two studies also demonstrate no significant difference between individuals with ASD without ID and ASD with ID (Johnson, Turner, Foldes, Malow, & Wiggs, 2012; Krakowiak, Goodlin-Jones, Hertz-Picciotto, Croen, & Hansen, 2008).

Insomnia is the most common type of sleep problem in individuals with ASD and may include prolonged sleep onset latency, extended night awakenings, and early morning rise times (Baker, Richdale, Short, & Gradisar, 2013; Richdale & Schreck, 2009; Sivertsen, Posserud, Gillberg, Lundervold, & Hysing, 2012; Souders et al., 2009). Less common but documented sleep problems in ASD also include frequent night awakenings, a free-running sleep rhythm, sleep-disordered breathing, high sleep variability, and several parasomnias (Giannotti et al., 2008; Goldman, Richdale, et al., 2012; Liu et al., 2006; Richdale & Schreck, 2009; Schreck & Mulick, 2000; Tordjman et al., 2012). Individuals with ASD are a heterogeneous group; similarly, their sleep problems are just as diverse.

The highest rates of sleep problems in ASD come from studies utilizing parent-reported indices like the Child Behavior Checklist (CBCL) or the CSHQ. Several studies have substantiated parent-reported sleep problem reports using more objective measures of actigraphy and PSG (Goldman, Richdale, et al., 2012; Malow et al., 2006; Wiggs & Stores, 2004). However, several studies also note parent reports of sleep problems are higher than those specified using behavioral criteria (Goodlin-Jones et al., 2009; Gringras et al., 2014; Schreck & Mulick, 2000). For example, in a study of young children with ASD, other (non-ASD) developmental disabilities (DD), and no known diagnosis, Goodlin-Jones et al. (2009) reported elevated sleep problems via parent report in both the DD and ASD groups but only found elevated behaviorally defined sleep problems (e.g., frequent night awakenings) in the DD group (Goodlin-Jones, Tang, Liu, & Anders, 2009). Similarly, Schreck and Mulick (2000) found that parents of children with ASD reported comparable amounts of sleep in their children when compared to controls but endorsed higher rates of sleep problems. Additionally, behaviorally focused treatments have been effective in reducing parent reports of sleep problems but these changes did not always coincide with actigraphically measured changes in sleep behavior (Johnson et al., 2013).

4.9.2 Associated Problems

Sleep problems are associated with elevated rates of daytime behavior problems in children with ASD and with elevated rates of anxiety and depression in older children and adults (Allik, Larsson, & Smedje, 2006; Goldman et al., 2011; Henderson, Barry, Bader, & Jordan, 2011; Mazurek & Petroski, 2015; Mazurek & Sohl, 2016; Sikora, Johnson, Clemons, & Katz, 2012). Across the life course, sleep problems are associated with more severe ASD symptomology (e.g., higher rates of repetitive behaviors) and GI problems (Klukowski et al., 2015; Schreck, Mulick, & Smith, 2004; Tudor, Hoffman, & Sweeney, 2012). Sleep problems are so common in ASD and they are, at times, considered a phenotype marker (Cohen et al., 2014; Goldman, Surdyka, et al., 2009). Studies following this approach report individuals with ASD and sleep problems display more intellectual disabilities, inattention, hyperactivity, and restricted/repetitive behaviors when compared to individuals with ASD without sleep problems (Elrod & Hood, 2015; Goldman, Surdyka, et al., 2009; Mazurek & Sohl, 2016).

4.9.3 Treatment

Sleep problems in ASD may be biological, medical, or behavioral in nature and treatment of such problems should start with a detailed medical and family history. The three most common sleep treatment approaches in ASD include parent/caregiver education, behavioral, and pharmacological. Studies of *parent/caregiver education* programs focus on providing parents/caregivers with developmentally appropriate sleep information in various forms along with basic behavioral approaches to support optimal sleep. Information provided via pamphlets did not improve parental perceptions or child sleep behaviors (Adkins et al., 2012) but small group information sessions have been effective in improving parental sleep perceptions and child sleep onset delay (Malow et al., 2014; Reed et al., 2009).

Behavioral treatments in individuals with ASD include several cognitive behavioral approaches, various extinction protocols, sleep hygiene, chronotherapy, scheduled awakenings, sleep restriction, visual supports, stimulus fading, and reward programs. Using the standards put forth by Chambless and Hollon, two systematic reviews of behavioral treatments for sleep problems in ASD have been published (Chambless & Hollon, 1998; Schreck, 2001; Vriend, Corkum, Moon, & Smith, 2011). Within these reviews, empirical support is the strongest for standard extinction approaches when treating night awakenings or cosleeping and scheduled awakenings for reducing night terrors. Several small studies of individuals with ASD document improvements in sleep with behavioral therapy (Reed et al., 2009), but without adequate replication these treatment approaches do not meet the standard of "well-established" or "possibly efficacious" treatments. Given the diverse nature of individuals with ASD and their sleep problems, current field recommendations include using an individualized treatment approach that starts with education and behavioral therapy (Malow et al., 2014). If these approaches are not successful, then a combined behavioral and pharmacological treatment plan is recommended (Cortesi, Giannotti, Sebastiani, Panunzi, & Valente, 2012).

Pharmacological treatments for sleep problems in ASD include most commonly melatonin and may also include α-agonists, anticonvulsants, antidepressants, atypical antipsychotics, and benzodiazepines. In a registry study of 1518 children with ASD, Malow et al. (2016) reported that roughly 40% of children with ASD were treated pharmacologically for sleep problems. A full review of pharmacological treatments in ASD is beyond the scope of this review; however, we have included a section on the most commonly used medication—melatonin.

Several studies have assessed the efficacy of melatonin in treating sleep problems in individuals with ASD and associated genetic conditions (e.g., FXS, tuberous sclerosis). Although the dose, duration, and elements of sleep affected by melatonin vary considerably across studies, the cumulative findings provide support for melatonin treatment (Doyen et al., 2011; Guénolé & Baleyte, 2011; Rossignol & Frye, 2011; Schwichtenberg & Malow, 2015). The most consistent finding across studies of individuals with ASD and associated genetic conditions is decreases in sleep onset latency. Findings regarding other elements of sleep are less consistent. For example, some studies report increased night awakenings (Paavonen, Nieminen-von Wendt, Vanhala, Aronen, & von Wendt, 2003) and others report decreased night awakenings (Garstang & Wallis, 2006). Although inconsistency in research findings could stem from differences in dose, melatonin type (fast release or continuous release), administration time, duration of administration, and sleep measurement technique as well as individual differences in melatonin metabolism. Overall, studies of melatonin in individuals with ASD are promising and report relatively few side effects (i.e., headaches, vomiting, upset stomach, dizziness, diarrhea, and daytime sleepiness). Considering the relatively low rate(s) of side effects and the consistent findings regarding sleep onset latency, melatonin treatment for individuals with ASD who struggled with sleep onset is supported by the literature studies. For other types of sleep disturbances (e.g., early morning awakenings, several nighttime awakenings), the research findings are less consistent.

4.10 Idiopathic Intellectual Disability

4.10.1 Prevalence

When examining children with idiopathic IDD, rates of sleep problems ranged from 34 to 86%, with rates varying for specific subtypes of sleep problems (Bartlett et al., 1985; Clements et al., 1986). The variability in reported rates of sleep problems is influenced by how sleep problems are measured in the individual studies, but reported sleep problems persist at the same rate in longitudinal studies (Quine, 1991).

Difficulties with insomnia, both with settling to sleep and staying asleep, in individuals with IDD range from 8 to 34% based upon a systematic review of the literature from 1990 to 2011 (van de Wouw et al., 2012). However, when actigraphy was used to evaluate insomnia (sleep latency and WASO), sleep problems were more common, occurring in 72% of a large community sample (van de Wouw, Evenhuis, & Echteld, 2013). The sleep of older adults with IDD is reported to be fragmented, inconsistent with regard to rhythm, and of lower relative amplitude (more fragmented sleep rhythm) (Maaskant, van de Wouw, van Wijck, Evenhuis, & Echteld, 2013).

4.10.2 Associated Problems

Sleep problems are an increasingly important area of research among individuals with IDD as researchers and clinicians recognize the bidirectional impact of sleep with comorbid medical and psychological conditions, cognition and executive functioning, mood and maladaptive behavior, and medication use. Some researchers have speculated that difficulties with sleep may contribute to a pattern of poorer cognitive outcomes for individuals with IDD (Harvey & Kennedy, 2002). However, sleep problems, as measured by actigraphy and pulse oximetry, were not related to attention tasks among children with genetic syndromes (Ashworth et al., 2015). In contrast, this study did replicate the relationship between sleep problems and attention among typically developing children. This finding may suggest that sleep does not have a significant impact on cognitive and executive functioning, or it may suggest the need for improved outcome measures of cognitive and executive functioning to adequately detect the impact of sleep problems on individuals with IDD (Esbensen et al., 2016).

Consistent with typically developing children, a pattern of findings suggest that sleep problems (e.g., insomnia) are more frequent among younger children (Richdale, Francis, Gavidia-Payne, & Cotton, 2000). More severe levels of ID have been associated with more severe sleep problems, less time in REM, lower REM density, and difficulties with sleep onset (Churchill et al., 2012; Didden, Korzilius, Aperlo, Overloop, & Vries, 2002; Harvey & Kennedy, 2002). Among adolescents with IDD, the timing of sleep (late to bed, late to rise) was associated with the adolescent being overweight or obese, controlling for sleep duration (Vanhelst, Bui-Xuan, Fardy, & Mikulovic, 2013).

While directional interpretations cannot be made due to the cross-sectional nature of many studies, sleep problems are associated with maladaptive behaviors, health and mental health conditions, and medication (Didden et al., 2002; Doran et al., 2006). Among children with IDD, parent ratings of sleep problems were correlated with parental ratings of maladaptive behaviors and with the presence of seizures (Didden et al., 2002; Quine, 1991; Richdale et al., 2000). Sleep problems in school-age children with IDD were also related to more frequent and more intense parenting hassles, parental stress and well-being, parenting behaviors, and parental sleep (Quine, 1991, 1992; Richdale et al., 2000). Among adults with IDD, maladaptive behaviors have consistently been related to sleep problems reported on rating scales or observations of sleep (van de Wouw et al., 2012). Caregiver ratings of sleep problems in adults with IDD are also related to respiratory conditions and visual impairment (Boyle et al., 2010).

Several large studies of aging adults with IDD using actigraphy have identified associations between sleep problems and demographic and environmental variables. Females tended to spend more time in bed but not necessarily asleep (van de Wouw et al., 2013). Older age, severity of ID, motor impairment (bound to wheelchair), living arrangement, and mental health (depression) were also associated with more time in bed (Maaskant et al., 2013; van de Wouw et al., 2013). However, it should be noted that some of these relationships may be related more to caregiver/caregiving needs with supporting the physical needs of aging adults with IDD rather than true difficulties with sleep problems (Richdale & Baker, 2014). Overall, some researchers state that there is no clear evidence for a relationship between sleep problems and demographic variables of age, gender, and level of ID, particularly among adults with IDD (van de Wouw et al., 2012).

Fragmented sleep was associated with lower physical activity, dementia, epilepsy, sensory impairments, and spasticity (Maaskant et al., 2013).

Sleep problems do not only impact the individual with IDD but also others in their household. Parents report that sleep problems in children with IDD disrupt the sleep of other family members (Cotton & Richdale, 2006; Robinson & Richdale, 2004).

4.10.3 Treatment

There is evidence to support that some sleep interventions, that are effective in the general population, are also beneficial for individuals with IDD (Lancioni, O'Reilly, & Basili, 1999). The behavioral sleep treatments of extinction and graduated extinction with preschool and school-age children with IDD have received support, with study designs including case series and randomized control trials (Montgomery, Stores, & Wiggs, 2004; Richdale & Wiggs, 2005; Thackeray & Richdale, 2002). Parental/caregiver instruction has been found to be effective in improving sleep, both with individualized instruction and with educational booklets, with effects being maintained over 6 months (Montgomery et al., 2004). Educational training for staff-supporting adults with IDD has demonstrated improvements in sleep efficiency and declines in time in bed and daytime napping (Hylkema, Petitiaux, & Vlaskamp, 2011).

Among adults, the use of CNS medication is reported to be associated with longer sleep duration and better sleep efficiency (van de Wouw et al., 2013). A meta-analysis of the use of melatonin with individuals with IDD demonstrates that it is consistently related to decreases in sleep latency and night wakings and improvements in total sleep time (Braam et al., 2009).

5. FUTURE RESEARCH

Sleep problems continue to be an area of concern for many individuals with IDD or specific genetic syndromes, with reported rates higher than those in the general population. The literature to date on individuals with IDD, various genetic syndromes or disorders has been able to replicate certain findings relating to associated sleep problems. However, different sleep measurement methodologies contributed to varied prevalence rates and patterns of associated problems. Further, suitable interventions lack strong empirical evidence and implementation in the community. This limited evidence within our research community is due in part to the challenges of gathering sufficient sample sizes of individuals with specific genetic syndromes. While there does exist some variability in sleep problems across syndrome or disorder subgroups of individuals with IDD, there are some commonalities that can be capitalized on when designing future research studies. There are also promising steps that have been or are being taken to advance our understanding and treatment of sleep problems among individuals with IDD.

5.1 Recommendations for Definition and Measurement of Sleep

When studying sleep in individuals with IDD, our field is encouraged to be more consistent in how we define sleep problems and how we measure sleep problems. The definition of sleep problems has varied across studies, in part due to how sleep problems were measured. Given that the DSM-5 criteria for sleep disorders now mirrors more closely the ICSD-3 classification system, the use of common terminology to define sleep is encouraged. Future research needs to be consistent in how sleep problems are defined, in an effort to more clearly evaluate differences across subgroups of individuals with IDD and changes in sleep problems across the age span (Medicine, 2014).

As evidenced by the earlier review of the literature, the prevalence of sleep problems can vary tremendously based on the assessment tool. To establish an accurate measure of sleep problems, our field is strongly encouraged to use a combination of objective tools to assess sleep. Meritorious research in sleep problems in individuals with IDD should use several different methods for assessing sleep (i.e., PSG and actigraphy). While sleep questionnaires and parental reports of sleep problems have not correlated well with PSG in identifying sleep problems, they continue to warrant evaluation for utility in serving as a valid measure of improving sleep outcomes, or for initially screening for sleep problems. When sleep questionnaires are used, research needs to acknowledge the limitations of this selected tool in measuring different types of sleep problems.

Our field is also encouraged to make use of advances in technology to assess sleep in the individual's home environment. Other techniques have been developed to assess sleep. *Portable PSGs* can be used in the individual's own home and technology, which continues to develop with the use of more subtle wiring (i.e., wires embedded in head gear or within clothing). This technology has been used to measure sleep and OSA among children with DS (Breslin et al., 2014). VSG is a sleep-recording method that is growing in popularity and includes indexing sleep from video recordings of sleep in the natural sleep environment. The use of VSG is attractive to researchers and clinicians because of (1) the "stand-off" or no contact requirements, (2) in-home recording options, and (3) its ability to capture dyadic or behavioral sleep associations (Sadeh, 2015). For individuals with ASD or other developmental concerns the electrode or sensor placements associated with PSG or even actigraphy can be distressing and can disrupt sleep. VSG has been used to diagnose sleep problems in a clinical populations (Ipsiroglu et al., 2015) and in numerous research studies of children with ASD, ID, and other developmental concerns (Ariagno et al., 2003; Henderson, France, Owens, & Blampied, 2010; Schwichtenberg et al., 2016; Sitnick et al., 2008). Currently, VSG coding is labor intensive, taking roughly 1 h to code a single night. Recent advancements in video-processing techniques may reduce this time and make the coding process automated.

Several "mass" market devices now provide estimates of sleep using accelerometers (e.g., Basis, Jawbone, Fitbit, smart watches, smart phone apps), respiration sounds/movement (e.g., S+, Mimo), bioimpedance (e.g., Jawbone), optical (e.g., Basis), ballistocardiography (e.g., Beddit), and other proprietary sensors. The accuracy and clinical utility of these devices are inconclusive at this time (Grifantini, 2014). Overall, it appears that many of these devices overestimate sleep duration in adults and children in the general population (Evenson, Goto, & Furberg, 2015; de Zambotti et al., 2016); however, they may have utility in helping track improvements in sleep or changes in typical sleep patterns. Researchers within the field of IDD are encouraged to monitor research advances on these devices and evaluate their utility in assessing sleep in individuals with IDD.

5.2 Recommendations for Research Design

The literature on sleep problems in IDD encompasses different subpopulations, genetic syndromes, and disorders. Given the difficulties of collecting sizable samples of specific genetic syndromes and the similarities of sleep problems across several syndrome groups, our field is encouraged to consider both the genetic syndrome and the specific sleep problems in designing future studies. While combining all individuals with IDD may mask sleep problems more common to a specific genetic syndrome, targeting a specific sleep problem across prespecified syndrome groups may be an appropriate methodology for larger-scale studies targeting a treatment for that sleep problem.

The literature on sleep in IDD has generally encompassed a wide age range. This feature of research is not unusual given the rarity of some genetic syndromes (Rosen et al., 2011). However, it is a concern worth noting in future research. There is a need to consider that sleep problems present in early childhood may vary from those present in school-age children, adolescents, and adults, and that variance may depend on the specific genetic syndrome. In SMS, sleep changes with age may be of less concern as sleep problems are related to inverted melatonin rhythm, which likely persists across age. In contrast, behavioral sleep problems in younger children with DS will differ from sleep problems associated with the onset of dementia or mental health concerns in adults with DS. Thus, future research is cautioned to consider the age of the individuals sampled for sleep problems. Otherwise, studies that span the life span are likely to mask that rates of different sleep problems will vary across the life span of individuals with specific genetic syndromes. Surveys of sleep problems in individuals with IDD are also often cross sectional. Future longitudinal research is warranted to assess changes in sleep problems across specific developmental periods.

There is a need for studies that assess the prevalence of sleep problems to consider treatments already in place. Prevalence estimates can vary based on the previously mentioned syndrome and age heterogeneity in a sample. Prevalence estimates can also vary based on the ongoing use of effective behavioral or pharmaceutical interventions, or previous surgeries that may improve sleep-disordered breathing. Discounting this information can contribute to diverse prevalence estimates in the research literature.

While research advances have recently been heavily focused on children with ASD, there continues to be a need to better understand sleep problems in the heterogeneous population of IDD to provide tailored interventions specific to the sleep problem. Sleep research on specific syndromes is advancing but continually plagued by small sample sizes due to the low prevalence rates of the specific syndromes. Advances have also been made in the reporting of specific syndrome groups within larger heterogeneous samples (Braam, Didden, Smits, & Curfs, 2008b; Didden et al., 2002; Montgomery et al., 2004). However, few studies provide data on these smaller syndrome subgroups relative to syndrome-specific treatment outcomes. Presenting findings on small syndrome samples within a larger study of individuals with IDD, with the use of consistent sleep measures, supports the ability to combine findings across studies. Few studies are randomizing smaller syndrome subgroups to intervention groups (Montgomery et al., 2004). Future studies are encouraged to randomly assign genetic syndromes within their sample (block randomization) to treatment groups, in an effort to support the ability to infer treatment effects.

5.3 Recommendations to Advance Evidence-Based Treatment

The evidence in support of sleep interventions for individuals with IDD or specific genetic syndromes is limited. Extinction and graduated extinction are probably efficacious for common sleep problems in individuals with IDD (Montgomery et al., 2004; Richdale & Wiggs, 2005; Thackeray & Richdale, 2002). Evidence for these behavioral interventions is consistent with the general population, where extinction, graduated extinction, and early intervention/parent education meet criteria for being well-established interventions, and scheduled awakenings for being probably efficacious among children with bedtime refusal and frequent night waking (Kuhn & Elliott, 2003). However, a recent meta-analysis was unable to include many studies evaluating treatment interventions with individuals with IDD due to limited information on outcome measures consistent across studies (Meltzer & Mindell, 2014).

As with any intervention, it is important to ensure that the intervention is tailored to the condition. In the case of sleep problems, while it is beneficial to understand what types of sleep problems are more common in specific genetic syndromes or disorders, it is imperative to match the sleep intervention to the specific sleep problem. In pursuing larger scale randomized control trials of sleep interventions, our field is encouraged to balance the type of sleep problem and underlying contributing cause with the type of genetic syndrome to advance our knowledge of evidence-based treatments. Syndrome groups may be worth including within block randomization to ensure that various syndrome groups are equally allocated to treatment or control groups. By expanding the sample eligible to study interventions and including genetic syndromes within the study design, sufficient samples can be collected to assess efficacy of other sleep interventions.

5.4 Summary

Our understanding of sleep problems in individuals with IDD and specific disorders or genetic syndromes continues to grow, and our field continues to make use of advances in sleep assessment and diagnostic criteria. Although sleep problems contribute to difficulties with learning, attention, affect regulation, memory, and daytime behavior problems, the use of individualized treatment plans that build on established behavioral or medical sleep approaches and approved pediatric medications has improved the lives of many individuals and families. The sleep assessment gold standard, PSG, continues to be a challenge for some individuals with IDD but recent advancements in home-based PSG and no-contact or minimal-contact sleep assessment methods are improving clinical diagnostic options. Studies of sleep and IDD include diverse sleep assessment methods, ages, diagnostic criteria, and treatment approaches. Despite this, findings within and across disorders/syndromes are building consensus. Overall, sleep problems are common and treatable in individuals with IDD and for some syndromes/disorders (e.g., SMS, DS), our understanding of the physiological or anatomical mechanisms have greatly improved treatment approaches. The impact of sleep on outcomes for individuals with IDD cannot be understated and continues to warrant ongoing research to improve how we measure sleep problems, how we report findings to improve comparisons across studies, what are the associated risk factors and outcomes of sleep problems, what are developmental changes in sleep problems over the life span, and what sleep interventions are effective for what specific sleep problems.

ACKNOWLEDGMENTS

This manuscript was prepared with support from the *Eunice Kennedy Shriver* National Institute of Child Health and Human Development (R21 HD082307) and National Institute of Mental Health (R00 MH092431). The content is solely the responsibility of the authors and does not necessarily represent the official views of the National Institutes of Health.

REFERENCES

Adkins, K. W., Goldman, S. E., Fawkes, D., Surdyka, K., Wang, L., Song, Y., & Malow, B. A. (2012). A pilot study of shoulder placement for actigraphy in children. *Behavioral Sleep Medicine, 10*(2), 138–147.

Allik, H., Larsson, J.-O., & Smedje, H. (2006). Sleep patterns of school-age children with Asperger syndrome or high-functioning autism. *Journal of Autism and Developmental Disorders, 36*(5), 585–595.

Anders, T. F., Iosif, A.-M., Schwichtenberg, A., Tang, K., & Goodlin-Jones, B. L. (2011). Six-month sleep–wake organization and stability in preschool-age children with autism, developmental delay, and typical development. *Behavioral Sleep Medicine, 9*(2), 92–106.

Andreou, G., Galanopoulou, C., Gourgoulianis, K., Karapetsas, A., & Molyvdas, P. (2002). Cognitive status in Down syndrome individuals with sleep disordered breathing deficits (SDB). *Brain and Cognition, 50*, 146–149.

Annaz, D., Hill, C. M., Ashworth, A., Holley, S., & Karmiloff-Smith, A. (2011). Characterisation of sleep problems in children with Williams syndrome. *Research in Developmental Disabilities, 32*(1), 164–169.

Ariagno, R. L., Mirmiran, M., Adams, M. M., Saporito, A. G., Dubin, A. M., & Baldwin, R. B. (2003). Effect of position on sleep, heart rate variability, and QT interval in preterm infants at 1 and 3 months' corrected age. *Pediatrics, 111*(3), 622–625.

Ashworth, A., Hill, C. M., Karmiloff-Smith, A., & Dimitriou, D. (2013). Cross syndrome comparison of sleep problems in children with Down syndrome and Williams syndrome. *Research in Developmental Disabilities, 34*(5), 1572–1580.

Ashworth, A., Hill, C. M., Karmiloff-Smith, A., & Dimitriou, D. (2015). The importance of sleep: attentional problems in school-aged children with Down syndrome and Williams syndrome. *Behavioral Sleep Medicine, 13*(6), 455–471.

American Psychiatric Association. (2013). *Diagnostic and statistical manual of mental disorders* (5th ed.). Arlington, VA: American Psychiatric Association.

Axelsson, E. L., Hill, C. M., Sadeh, A., & Dimitriou, D. (2013). Sleep problems and language development in toddlers with Williams syndrome. *Research in Developmental Disabilities, 34*(11), 3988–3996.

Baker, E., Richdale, A., Short, M., & Gradisar, M. (2013). An investigation of sleep patterns in adolescents with high-functioning autism spectrum disorder compared with typically developing adolescents. *Developmental Neurorehabilitation, 16*(3), 155–165.

Bartlett, L., Rooney, V., & Spedding, S. (1985). Nocturnal difficulties in a population of mentally handicapped children. *The British Journal of Mental Subnormality, 31*(60), 54–59.

Basile, E., Villa, L., Selicorni, A., & Molteni, M. (2007). The behavioural phenotype of Cornelia de Lange Syndrome: a study of 56 individuals. *Journal of Intellectual Disability Research, 51*(9), 671–681.

Berney, T., Ireland, M., & Burn, J. (1999). Behavioural phenotype of Cornelia de Lange syndrome. *Archives of Disease in Childhood, 81*(4), 333–336.

Boyle, A., Melville, C. A., Morrison, J., Allan, L., Smiley, E., Espie, C. A., & Cooper, S. A. (2010). A cohort study of the prevalence of sleep problems in adults with intellectual disabilities. *Journal of Sleep Research, 19*(1), 42–53.

Braam, W., Didden, R., Smits, M. G., & Curfs, L. M. (2008a). Melatonin for chronic insomnia in Angelman syndrome: a randomized placebo-controlled trial. *Journal of Child Neurology, 23*(6), 649–654.

Braam, W., Didden, R., Smits, M. G., & Curfs, L. M. (2008b). Melatonin treatment in individuals with intellectual disability and chronic insomnia: a randomized placebo-controlled study. *Journal of Intellectual Disability Research, 52*(3), 256–264.

Braam, W., Smits, M. G., Didden, R., Korzilius, H., Van Geijlswijk, I. M., & Curfs, L. M. (2009). Exogenous melatonin for sleep problems in individuals with intellectual disability: a meta-analysis. *Developmental Medicine and Child Neurology, 51*(5), 340–349.

Breslin, J., Edgin, J., Bootzin, R., Goodwin, J., & Nadel, L. (2011). Parental report of sleep problems in Down syndrome. *Journal of Intellectual Disability Research, 55*(11), 1086–1091.

Breslin, J., Spanò, G., Bootzin, R., Anand, P., Nadel, L., & Edgin, J. (2014). Obstructive sleep apnea syndrome and cognition in Down syndrome. *Developmental Medicine and Child Neurology, 56*(7), 657–664.

Bull, M. J., & Genetics, C. o. (2011). Health supervision for children with Down syndrome. *Pediatrics, 128*(2), 393–406. http://dx.doi.org/10.1542/peds.2011-1605.

Butler, J., Whittington, J., Holland, A., Boer, H., Clarke, D., & Webb, T. (2002). Prevalence of, and risk factors for, physical ill-health in people with Prader–Willi syndrome: a population-based study. *Developmental Medicine and Child Neurology, 44*(4), 248–255.

Carpizo, R., Martínez, Á., Mediavilla, D., González, M., Abad, A., & Sánchez-Barceló, E. J. (2006). Smith–Magenis syndrome: a case report of improved sleep after treatment with β1-adrenergic antagonists and melatonin. *Journal of Pediatrics, 149*(3), 409–411.

Cassidy, S., McKillop, J., & Morgan, W. (1990). Sleep disorders in Prader–Willi syndrome. *Dysmorphology and Clinical Genetics, 4*(1), 13–17.

Chambless, D. L., & Hollon, S. D. (1998). Defining empirically supported therapies. *Journal of Consulting and Clinical Psychology, 66*(1), 7.

Chen, C.-C. J., Spanò, G., & Edgin, J. (2013). The impact of sleep disruption on executive function in Down syndrome. *Research in Developmental Disabilities, 34*(6), 2033—2039.

Chou, I.-C., Tsai, F.-J., Yu, M.-T., & Tsai, C.-H. (2002). Smith—Magenis syndrome with bilateral vesicoureteral reflux: a case report. *Journal Formosan Medical Association, 101*(10), 726—728.

Churchill, S. S., Kieckhefer, G. M., Bjornson, K. F., & Herting, J. R. (2014). Relationship between sleep disturbance and functional outcomes in daily life habits of children with Down syndrome. *Sleep, 38*(1), 61—71.

Churchill, S. S., Kieckhefer, G. M., Landis, C. A., & Ward, T. M. (2012). Sleep measurement and monitoring in children with Down syndrome: a review of the literature, 1960—2010. *Sleep Medicine Reviews, 16*(5), 477—488.

Clayton-Smith, J. (1993). Clinical research on Angelman syndrome in the United Kingdom: observations on 82 affected individuals. *American Journal of Medical Genetics, 46*(1), 12—15.

Clements, J., Wing, L., & Dunn, G. (1986). Sleep problems in handicapped children: a preliminary study. *Journal of Child Psychology and Psychiatry, 27*(3), 399—407.

Cohen, S., Conduit, R., Lockley, S. W., Rajaratnam, S. M., & Cornish, K. M. (2014). The relationship between sleep and behavior in autism spectrum disorder (ASD): a review. *Journal of Neurodevelopmental Disorders, 6*(1), 44.

Cornish, K., Oliver, C., Standen, P., Bramble, D., & Collins, M. (2003). *Cri-du-chat syndrome: Handbook for parents and professionals* (2nd ed.). Earl Shilton: Cri-du-Chat Syndrome Support Group.

Cornish, K., & Pigram, J. (1996). Developmental and behavioural characteristics of Cri du Chat syndrome. *Archives of Disease in Childhood, 75*(5), 448—450.

Cortesi, F., Giannotti, F., Sebastiani, T., Panunzi, S., & Valente, D. (2012). Controlled-release melatonin, singly and combined with cognitive behavioural therapy, for persistent insomnia in children with autism spectrum disorders: a randomized placebo-controlled trial. *Journal of Sleep Research, 21*(6), 700—709.

Cotton, S. M., & Richdale, A. (2006). Brief report: parental descriptions of sleep problems in children with autism, Down syndrome, and Prader—Willi syndrome. *Research in Developmental Disabilities, 27*(2), 151—161.

Cotton, S. M., & Richdale, A. L. (2010). Sleep patterns and behaviour in typically developing children and children with autism, Down syndrome, Prader—Willi syndrome and intellectual disability. *Research in Autism Spectrum Disorders, 4*(3), 490—500.

Couturier, J. L., Speechley, K. N., Steele, M., Norman, R., Stringer, B., & Nicolson, R. (2005). Parental perception of sleep problems in children of normal intelligence with pervasive developmental disorders: prevalence, severity, and pattern. *Journal of the American Academy of Child and Adolescent Psychiatry, 44*(8), 815—822.

Croen, L. A., Zerbo, O., Qian, Y., Massolo, M. L., Rich, S., Sidney, S., & Kripke, C. (2015). The health status of adults on the autism spectrum. *Autism: The International Journal of Research and Practice, 19*(7), 814—823.

Dahlqvist, A., Rask, E., Rosenqvist, C.-J., Sahlin, C., & Franklin, K. A. (2003). Sleep apnea and Down's syndrome. *Acta Otolaryngologica, 123*(9), 1094—1097.

De Leersnyder, H., de Blois, M.-C., Claustrat, B., Romana, S., Albrecht, U., von Kleist-Retzow, J.-C., ... Vekemans, M. (2001). Inversion of the circadian rhythm of melatonin in the Smith—Magenis syndrome. *Journal of Pediatrics, 139*(1), 111—116.

Didden, R., Korzilius, H., Aperlo, B. V., Overloop, C. V., & Vries, M. D. (2002). Sleep problems and daytime problem behaviours in children with intellectual disability. *Journal of Intellectual Disability Research, 46*(7), 537—547.

Didden, R., Korzilius, H., Smits, M. G., Curfs, L. M., & Dykens, E. M. (2004). Sleep problems in individuals with Angelman syndrome. *American Journal on Mental Retardation, 109*(4), 275—284.

Didden, R., & Sigafoos, J. (2001). A review of the nature and treatment of sleep disorders in individuals with developmental disabilities. *Research in Developmental Disabilities, 22*(4), 255—272. Retrieved from http://www.ncbi.nlm.nih.gov/pubmed/11523951.

van Dijk, E., Hilgenkamp, T., Evenhuis, H., & Echteld, M. (2012). Exploring the use of actigraphy to investigate sleep problems in older people with intellectual disability. *Journal of Intellectual Disability Research, 56*(2), 204—211.

Dimitriou, D., Karmiloff-Smith, A., Ashworth, A., & Hill, C. M. (2013). Impaired sleep-related learning in children with Williams syndrome. *Pediatrics Research International Journal, 2013*, 1—10. http://dx.doi.org/10.5171/2013.662275.

Dohnt, H., Gradisar, M., & Short, M. A. (2012). Insomnia and its symptoms in adolescents: comparing DSM-IV and ICSD-II diagnostic criteria. *Journal of Clinical Sleep Medicine, 15*(8), 295—299. http://dx.doi.org/10.5664/jcsm.1918.

Doran, S. M., Harvey, M. T., Horner, R. H., & Scotti, J. (2006). Sleep and developmental disabilities: assessment, treatment, and outcome measures. *Mental Retardation, 44*(1), 13—27.

Doyen, C., Mighiu, D., Kaye, K., Colineaux, C., Beaumanoir, C., Mouraeff, Y., … Contejean, Y. (2011). Melatonin in children with autistic spectrum disorders: recent and practical data. *European Child & Adolescent Psychiatry, 20*(5), 231—239.

Elrod, M. G., & Hood, B. S. (2015). Sleep differences among children with autism spectrum disorders and typically developing peers: a meta-analysis. *Journal of Developmental and Behavioral Pediatrics, 36*(3), 166—177.

Elrod, M. G., Nylund, C. M., Susi, A. L., Gorman, G. H., Hisle-Gorman, E., Rogers, D. J., & Erdie-Lalena, C. (2016). Prevalence of diagnosed sleep disorders and related diagnostic and surgical procedures in children with autism spectrum disorders. *Journal of Developmental and Behavioral Pediatrics, 37*.

Esbensen, A. J. (2016). Sleep problems and associated comorbidities among adults with Down syndrome. *Journal of Intellectual Disability Research, 60*(1), 68—79.

Esbensen, A. J., Hooper, S. R., Fidler, D., Hartley, S. L., Edgin, J. O., d'Ardhuy, X., … Group, O. M. W. (2016). *Outcome measures for clinical trials in Down syndrome* (under review).

Espie, C. A., & Tweedie, F. (1991). Sleep patterns and sleep problems amongst people with mental handicap. *Journal of Mental Deficiency Research, 35*(1), 25—36.

Evenson, K. R., Goto, M. M., & Furberg, R. D. (2015). Systematic review of the validity and reliability of consumer-wearable activity trackers. *International Journal of Behavioral Nutrition and Physical Activity, 12*(1), 1—22.

Feinberg, I., Braun, M., & Shulman, E. (1969). EEG sleep patterns in mental retardation. *Electroencephalography and Clinical Neurophysiology, 27*(2), 128—141.

Fitzgerald, D. A., Paul, A., & Richmond, C. (2007). Severity of obstructive apnoea in children with Down syndrome who snore. *Archives of Disease in Childhood, 92*(5), 423—425.

Garstang, J., & Wallis, M. (2006). Randomized controlled trial of melatonin for children with autistic spectrum disorders and sleep problems. *Child: Care, Health and Development, 32*(5), 585—589.

Giannotti, F., Cortesi, F., Cerquiglini, A., Miraglia, D., Vagnoni, C., Sebastiani, T., & Bernabei, P. (2008). An investigation of sleep characteristics, EEG abnormalities and epilepsy in developmentally regressed and non-regressed children with autism. *Journal of Autism and Developmental Disorders, 38*(10), 1888—1897.

Gibbs, S., Wiltshire, E., & Elder, D. (2013). Nocturnal sleep measured by actigraphy in children with Prader—Willi syndrome. *Journal of Pediatrics, 162*(4), 765—769.

Glickman, G. (2010). Circadian rhythms and sleep in children with autism. *Neuroscience and Biobehavioral Reviews, 34*(5), 755—768.

Goldman, S. E., Bichell, T., Surdyka, K., & Malow, B. (2012). Sleep in children and adolescents with Angelman syndrome: association with parent sleep and stress. *Journal of Intellectual Disability Research, 56*(6), 600–608.

Goldman, S. E., Malow, B., Newman, K., Roof, E., & Dykens, E. (2009). Sleep patterns and daytime sleepiness in adolescents and young adults with Williams syndrome. *Journal of Intellectual Disability Research, 53*(2), 182–188.

Goldman, S. E., McGrew, S., Johnson, K. P., Richdale, A. L., Clemons, T., & Malow, B. A. (2011). Sleep is associated with problem behaviors in children and adolescents with autism spectrum disorders. *Research in Autism Spectrum Disorders, 5*(3), 1223–1229.

Goldman, S. E., Richdale, A. L., Clemons, T., & Malow, B. A. (2012). Parental sleep concerns in autism spectrum disorders: variations from childhood to adolescence. *Journal of Autism and Developmental Disorders, 42*(4), 531–538.

Goldman, S. E., Surdyka, K., Cuevas, R., Adkins, K., Wang, L., & Malow, B. A. (2009). Defining the sleep phenotype in children with autism. *Developmental Neuropsychology, 34*(5), 560–573.

Gombos, F., Bódizs, R., & Kovács, I. (2011). Atypical sleep architecture and altered EEG spectra in Williams syndrome. *Journal of Intellectual Disability Research, 55*(3), 255–262.

Goodlin-Jones, B., Schwichtenberg, A., Iosif, A.-M., Tang, K., Liu, J., & Anders, T. F. (2009). Six-month persistence of sleep problems in young children with autism, developmental delay, and typical development. *Journal of the American Academy of Child and Adolescent Psychiatry, 48*(8), 847–854.

Goodlin-Jones, B., Tang, K., Liu, J., & Anders, T. F. (2009). Sleep problems, sleepiness and daytime behavior in preschool-age children. *Journal of Child Psychology and Psychiatry, 50*(12), 1532–1540.

Gould, E. L., Loesch, D. Z., Martin, M. J., Hagerman, R. J., Armstrong, S. M., & Huggins, R. M. (2000). Melatonin profiles and sleep characteristics in boys with fragile X syndrome: a preliminary study. *American Journal of Medical Genetics, 95*(4), 307–315.

Greenberg, F., Lewis, R. A., Potocki, L., Glaze, D., Parke, J., Killian, J., … Dutton, R. (1996). Multi-disciplinary clinical study of Smith–Magenis syndrome (deletion 17p11.2). *American Journal of Medical Genetics, 62*(3), 247–254.

Grifantini, K. (2014). How's my sleep? Personal sleep trackers are gaining in popularity, but their accuracy is still open to debate. *IEEE Pulse, 5*(5), 14–18.

Gringras, P., Green, D., Wright, B., Rush, C., Sparrowhawk, M., Pratt, K., … Zaiwalla, Z. (2014). Weighted blankets and sleep in autistic children: a randomized controlled trial. *Pediatrics, 134*(2), 298–306.

Gualtieri, C. T. (1991). Behavior in the Cornelia de Lange syndrome. In C. T. Gualtieri (Ed.), *Neuropsychiatry and behavioral pharmacology* (pp. 173–186). New York: Springer.

Guénolé, F., & Baleyte, J. M. (2011). Meta-analysing the effectiveness of melatonin for sleep-disturbed individuals with autism spectrum conditions: should Rett syndrome be included? *Developmental Medicine and Child Neurology, 53*(11), 1063.

Hall, S., Arron, K., Sloneem, J., & Oliver, C. (2008). Health and sleep problems in Cornelia de Lange syndrome: a case control study. *Journal of Intellectual Disability Research, 52*(5), 458–468.

Harvey, M. T., & Kennedy, C. H. (2002). Polysomnographic phenotypes in developmental disabilities. *International Journal of Developmental Neuroscience, 20*(3), 443–448.

Henderson, J. A., Barry, T. D., Bader, S. H., & Jordan, S. S. (2011). The relation among sleep, routines, and externalizing behavior in children with an autism spectrum disorder. *Research in Autism Spectrum Disorders, 5*(2), 758–767.

Henderson, J. M., France, K. G., Owens, J. L., & Blampied, N. M. (2010). Sleeping through the night: the consolidation of self-regulated sleep across the first year of life. *Pediatrics, 126*(5), e1081–e1087.

Hirata, I., Mohri, I., Kato-Nishimura, K., Tachibana, M., Kuwada, A., Kagitani-Shimono, K., ... Taniike, M. (2016). Sleep problems are more frequent and associated with problematic behaviors in preschoolers with autism spectrum disorder. *Research in Developmental Disabilities, 49*, 86—99.

Hodge, D., Parnell, A. M., Hoffman, C. D., & Sweeney, D. P. (2012). Methods for assessing sleep in children with autism spectrum disorders: a review. *Research in Autism Spectrum Disorders, 6*(4), 1337—1344.

Hylkema, T., Petitiaux, W., & Vlaskamp, C. (2011). Utility of staff training on correcting sleep problems in people with intellectual disabilities living in residential settings. *Journal of Policy and Practice in Intellectual Disabilities, 8*(2), 85—91.

Ipsiroglu, O. S., Hung, Y.-H. A., Forson Chan, M. L. R., Veer, D., Soo, S., Ho, G., ... Kloesch, G. (2015). "Diagnosis by behavioral observation" home-videosomnography — a rigorous ethnographic approach to sleep of children with neurodevelopmental conditions. *Frontiers in Psychiatry, 6*, 39.

Jan, J. E., Espezel, H., & Appleion, R. (1994). The treatment of sleep disorders with melatonin. *Developmental Medicine and Child Neurology, 36*(2), 97—107.

Johnson, C. R., Turner, K. S., Foldes, E., Brooks, M. M., Kronk, R., & Wiggs, L. (2013). Behavioral parent training to address sleep disturbances in young children with autism spectrum disorder: a pilot trial. *Sleep Medicine, 14*, 995—1004.

Johnson, C. R., Turner, K. S., Foldes, E. L., Malow, B. A., & Wiggs, L. (2012). Comparison of sleep questionnaires in the assessment of sleep disturbances in children with autism spectrum disorders. *Sleep Medicine, 13*(7), 795—801.

Joo, E. Y., Hong, S. B., Sohn, Y. B., Kwak, M. J., Kim, S. J., Choi, Y. O., ... Jin, D.-K. (2010). Plasma adiponectin level and sleep structures in children with Prader—Willi syndrome. *Journal of Sleep Research, 19*(1p2), 248—254.

Klukowski, M., Wasilewska, J., & Lebensztejn, D. (2015). Sleep and gastrointestinal disturbances in autism spectrum disorder in children. *Medycyna Wieku Rozwojowego, 19*(2), 157—161.

Krakowiak, P., Goodlin-Jones, B., Hertz-Picciotto, I., Croen, L. A., & Hansen, R. L. (2008). Sleep problems in children with autism spectrum disorders, developmental delays, and typical development: a population-based study. *Journal of Sleep Research, 17*(2), 197—206.

Kronk, R., Bishop, E. E., Raspa, M., Bickel, J. O., Mandel, D. A., & Bailey, D. B., Jr. (2010). Prevalence, nature, and correlates of sleep problems among children with fragile X syndrome based on a large scale parent survey. *Sleep, 33*(5), 679—687.

Kuhn, B. R., & Elliott, A. J. (2003). Treatment efficacy in behavioral pediatric sleep medicine. *Journal of Psychosomatic Research, 54*(6), 587—597. Retrieved from http://www.ncbi.nlm.nih.gov/pubmed/12781314.

Lancioni, G. E., O'Reilly, M. F., & Basili, G. (1999). Review of strategies for treating sleep problems in persons with severe or profound mental retardation or multiple handicaps. *American Journal on Mental Retardation, 104*(2), 170—186.

Limoges, É., Mottron, L., Bolduc, C., Berthiaume, C., & Godbout, R. (2005). Atypical sleep architecture and the autism phenotype. *Brain: A Journal of Neurology, 128*(5), 1049—1061.

Liu, X., Hubbard, J. A., Fabes, R. A., & Adam, J. B. (2006). Sleep disturbances and correlates of children with autism spectrum disorders. *Child Psychiatry and Human Development, 37*(2), 179—191.

Maas, A. P., Didden, R., Korzilius, H., Braam, W., Collin, P., Smits, M. G., & Curfs, L. M. (2011). Psychometric properties of a sleep questionnaire for use in individuals with intellectual disabilities. *Research in Developmental Disabilities, 32*(6), 2467—2479.

Maas, A. P., Didden, R., Korzilius, H., Braam, W., Smits, M., & Curfs, L. (2009). Sleep in individuals with Cri du Chat syndrome: a comparative study. *Journal of Intellectual Disability Research, 53*(8), 704—715.

Maas, A. P., Didden, R., Korzilius, H., & Curfs, L. M. (2012). Exploration of differences in types of sleep disturbance and severity of sleep problems between individuals with Cri du Chat syndrome, Down's syndrome, and Jacobsen syndrome: a case control study. *Research in Developmental Disabilities, 33*(6), 1773—1779.

Maaskant, M., van de Wouw, E., van Wijck, R., Evenhuis, H. M., & Echteld, M. A. (2013). Circadian sleep—wake rhythm of older adults with intellectual disabilities. *Research in Developmental Disabilities, 34*(4), 1144—1151.

Malow, B. A., Adkins, K. W., Reynolds, A., Weiss, S. K., Loh, A., Fawkes, D., ... Hundley, R. (2014). Parent-based sleep education for children with autism spectrum disorders. *Journal of Autism and Developmental Disorders, 44*(1), 216—228.

Malow, B. A., Katz, T., Reynolds, A. M., Shui, A., Camo, M., Connolly, H. V., ... Bennett, A. E. (2016). Sleep difficulties and medications in children with autism spectrum disorders: a registry study. *Pediatrics, 137*(Suppl. 2), S98—S104.

Malow, B. A., Marzec, M. L., McGrew, S. G., Wang, L., Henderson, L. M., & Stone, W. L. (2006). Characterizing sleep in children with autism spectrum disorders: a multidimensional approach. *Sleep, 29*(12), 1563.

Manni, R., Politini, L., Nobili, L., Ferrillo, F., Livieri, C., Veneselli, E., ... Tartara, A. (2001). Hypersomnia in the Prader Willi syndrome: clinical-electrophysiological features and underlying factors. *Clinical Neurophysiology, 112*(5), 800—805.

Marcus, C., Keens, T., Bautista, D., von Pechman, W., & Ward, S. (1991). Obstructive sleep apnea in children with Down syndrome. *Pediatrics, 88*, 132—139.

Maris, M., Verhulst, S., Wojciechowski, M., Van de Heyning, P., & Boudewyns, A. (2016). Sleep problems and obstructive sleep apnea in children with Down syndrome, an overview. *International Journal of Pediatric Otorhinolaryngology.* http://dx.doi.org/10.1016/j.ijporl.2015.12.014.

Mason, T. B., Arens, R., Sharman, J., Bintliff Janisak, D., Schultz, B., Walters, A. S., ... Pack, A. I. (2011). Sleep in children with Williams syndrome. *Sleep Medicine, 12*(9), 892—897.

Mazurek, M. O., & Petroski, G. F. (2015). Sleep problems in children with autism spectrum disorder: examining the contributions of sensory over-responsivity and anxiety. *Sleep Medicine, 16*(2), 270—279.

Mazurek, M. O., & Sohl, K. (2016). Sleep and behavioral problems in children with autism spectrum disorder. *Journal of Autism and Developmental Disorders, 46*(6), 1906—1915.

Medicine, A. A. o. S. (2007). *AASM manual for the scoring of sleep and associated events.* American Academy of Sleep Medicine.

Medicine, A. A. o. S. (2014). *International classification of sleep disorders* (3rd ed.). Chicago, IL: American Academy of Sleep Medicine.

Meltzer, L. J., & Mindell, J. A. (2014). Systematic review and meta-analysis of behavioral interventions for pediatric insomnia. *Journal of Pediatric Psychology, 39*(8), 932—948.

Miano, S., Bruni, O., Elia, M., Scifo, L., Smerieri, A., Trovato, A., ... Ferri, R. (2008). Sleep phenotypes of intellectual disability: a polysomnographic evaluation in subjects with Down syndrome and Fragile-X syndrome. *Clinical Neurophysiology, 119*(6), 1242—1247.

Miano, S., Bruni, O., Leuzzi, V., Elia, M., Verrillo, E., & Ferri, R. (2004). Sleep polygraphy in Angelman syndrome. *Clinical Neurophysiology, 115*(4), 938—945.

de Miguel-Diez, J., Villa-Asensi, J. R., & Alvarez-Sala, J. L. (2003). Prevalence of sleep-disordered breathing in children with Down syndrome: polygraphic findings in 108 children. *Sleep, 26*(8), 1006—1009. Retrieved from http://www.ncbi.nlm.nih.gov/pubmed/14746382.

Montgomery, P., Stores, G., & Wiggs, L. (2004). The relative efficacy of two brief treatments for sleep problems in young learning disabled (mentally retarded) children: a randomised controlled trial. *Archives of Disease in Childhood, 89*, 125—130.

Nixon, G. M., & Brouillette, R. T. (2002). Sleep and breathing in Prader—Willi syndrome. *Pediatric Pulmonology, 34*(3), 209—217.

O'Donnell, A. R., Bjornson, C. L., Bohn, S. G., & Kirk, V. G. (2006). Compliance rates in children using noninvasive continuous positive airway pressure. *Sleep, 29*(5), 651—658.

O'Donoghue, F. J., Camfferman, D., Kennedy, J., Martin, A., Couper, T., Lack, L., ... McEvoy, R. D. (2005). Sleep-disordered breathing in Prader—Willi syndrome and its association with neurobehavioral abnormalities. *Journal of Pediatrics, 147*(6), 823—829.

Ozonoff, S., Young, G. S., Steinfeld, M. B., Hill, M. M., Cook, I., Hutman, T., ... Sigman, M. (2009). How early do parent concerns predict later autism diagnosis? *Journal of Developmental and Behavioral Pediatrics, 30*(5), 367—375.

Paavonen, E. J., Nieminen-von Wendt, T., Vanhala, R., Aronen, E. T., & von Wendt, L. (2003). Effectiveness of melatonin in the treatment of sleep disturbances in children with Asperger disorder. *Journal of Child and Adolescent Psychopharmacology, 13*(1), 83—95.

Pavone, M., Paglietti, M., Petrone, A., Crino, A., De Vincentiis, G., & Cutrera, R. (2006). Adenotonsillectomy for obstructive sleep apnea in children with Prader—Willi syndrome. *Pediatric Pulmonology, 41*(1), 74—79.

Potocki, L., Glaze, D., Tan, D.-X., Park, S.-S., Kashork, C. D., Shaffer, L. G., ... Lupski, J. R. (2000). Circadian rhythm abnormalities of melatonin in Smith—Magenis syndrome. *Journal of Medical Genetics, 37*(6), 428—433.

Primeau, M., Gershon, A., Talbot, L., Cotto, I., Lotspeich, L., Hardan, A., ... O'Hara, R. (2015). Individuals with autism spectrum disorders have equal success rate but require longer periods of systematic desensitization than control patients to complete ambulatory polysomnography. *Journal of Clinical Sleep Medicine, 12.*

Punjabi, N. M. (2008). The epidemiology of adult obstructive sleep apnea. *Proceedings of the American Thoracic Society, 5*(2), 136—143.

Quine, L. (1991). Sleep problems in children with mental handicap. *Journal of Intellectual Disability Research, 35*(4), 269—290.

Quine, L. (1992). Severity of sleep problems in children with severe learning difficulties: description and correlates. *Journal of Community & Applied Social Psychology, 2*(4), 247—268.

Rajan, R., Benke, J. R., Kline, A. D., Levy, H. P., Kimball, A., Mettel, T. L., ... Ishman, S. L. (2012). Insomnia in Cornelia de Lange syndrome. *International Journal of Pediatric Otorhinolaryngology, 76*(7), 972—975.

Reed, H. E., McGrew, S. G., Artibee, K., Surdkya, K., Goldman, S. E., Frank, K., ... Malow, B. A. (2009). Parent-based sleep education workshops in autism. *Journal of Child Neurology, 24*(8), 936—945.

Richdale, A. L. (2003). A descriptive analysis of sleep behaviour in children with fragile X. *Journal of Intellectual & Developmental Disability, 28*(2), 135—144.

Richdale, A. L., & Baker, E. K. (2014). Sleep in individuals with an intellectual or developmental disability: recent research reports. *Current Developmental Disorders Reports, 1*(2), 74—85.

Richdale, A. L., Cotton, S., & Hibbit, K. (1999). Sleep and behaviour disturbance in Prader—Willi syndrome: a questionnaire study. *Journal of Intellectual Disability Research, 43*(5), 380—392.

Richdale, A. L., Francis, A., Gavidia-Payne, S., & Cotton, S. (2000). Stress, behaviour, and sleep problems in children with an intellectual disability. *Journal of Intellectual & Developmental Disability, 25*(2), 147—161.

Richdale, A. L., & Schreck, K. A. (2009). Sleep problems in autism spectrum disorders: prevalence, nature, & possible biopsychosocial aetiologies. *Sleep Medicine Reviews, 13*(6), 403—411.

Richdale, A. L., & Wiggs, L. (2005). Behavioral approaches to the treatment of sleep problems in children with developmental disorders: what is the state of the art? *International Journal of Behavioral Consultation and Therapy, 1*, 165—190.

Robinson, A., & Richdale, A. (2004). Sleep problems in children with an intellectual disability: parental perceptions of sleep problems, and views of treatment effectiveness. *Child: Care, Health and Development, 30*(2), 139—150.

Roizen, N. J., & Patterson, D. (2003). Down's syndrome. *Lancet, 361*(9365), 1281—1289.

Rosen, D., Lombardo, A., Skotko, B., & Davidson, E. J. (2011). Parental perceptions of sleep disturbances and sleep-disordered breathing in children with Down syndrome. *Clinical Pediatrics, 50*, 121—125.

Rossignol, D. A., & Frye, R. E. (2011). Melatonin in autism spectrum disorders: a systematic review and meta-analysis. *Developmental Medicine and Child Neurology, 53*(9), 783—792.

Sadeh, A. (2015). III. Sleep assessment methods. *Monographs of the Society for Research in Child Development, 80*(1), 33—48.

Sadeh, A., Hauri, P. J., Kripke, D. F., & Lavie, P. (1995). The role of actigraphy in the evaluation of sleep disorders. *Sleep, 18*(4), 288—302.

Schreck, K. A. (2001). Behavioral treatments for sleep problems in autism: empirically supported or just universally accepted? *Behavioral Interventions, 16*(4), 265—278.

Schreck, K. A., & Mulick, J. (2000). Parental reports of sleep problems in children with autism. *Journal of Autism and Developmental Disorders, 30*, 127—135.

Schreck, K. A., Mulick, J. A., & Smith, A. F. (2004). Sleep problems as possible predictors of intensified symptoms of autism. *Research in Developmental Disabilities, 25*(1), 57—66.

Schwichtenberg, A. J., Hensle, T., Honaker, S., Miller, M., Ozonoff, S., & Anders, T. (2016). Sibling sleep — what can it tell us about parental sleep reports in the context of autism? *Clinical Practice in Pediatric Psychology, 4*(2), 137—152.

Schwichtenberg, A J , & Malow, B. A. (2015). Melatonin treatment in children with developmental disabilities. *Sleep Medicine Clinics, 10*(2), 181—187.

Sedky, K., Bennett, D. S., & Pumariega, A. (2014). Prader Willi syndrome and obstructive sleep apnea: co-occurrence in the pediatric population. *Journal of Clinical Sleep Medicine, 10*(4), 403.

Shete, M. M., Stocks, R. M. S., Sebelik, M. E., & Schoumacher, R. A. (2010). Effects of adeno-tonsillectomy on polysomnography patterns in Down syndrome children with obstructive sleep apnea: a comparative study with children without Down syndrome. *International Journal of Pediatric Otorhinolaryngology, 74*(3), 241—244.

Shires, C. B., Anold, S. L., Schoumacher, R. A., Dehoff, G. W., Donepudi, S. K., & Stocks, R. M. (2010). Body mass index as an indicator of obstructive sleep apnea in pediatric Down syndrome. *International Journal of Pediatric Otorhinolaryngology, 74*(7), 768—772.

Shott, S., Amin, R., Chini, B., Heubi, C., Hotze, S., & Akers, R. (2006). Obstructive sleep apnea: should children with Down syndrome be tested? *Archives of Otolaryngology Head Neck and Surgery, 132*, 432—436.

Sikora, D. M., Johnson, K., Clemons, T., & Katz, T. (2012). The relationship between sleep problems and daytime behavior in children of different ages with autism spectrum disorders. *Pediatrics, 130*(Suppl. 2), S83—S90.

Simonds, J. F., & Parraga, H. (1982). Prevalence of sleep disorders and sleep behaviors in children and adolescents. *Journal of the American Academy of Child Psychiatry, 21*(4), 383—388.

Sitnick, S. L., Goodlin-Jones, B. L., & Anders, T. F. (2008). The use of actigraphy to study sleep disorders in preschoolers: some concerns about detection of nighttime awakenings. *Sleep, 31*(3), 395—401.

Sivertsen, B., Posserud, M.-B., Gillberg, C., Lundervold, A. J., & Hysing, M. (2012). Sleep problems in children with autism spectrum problems: a longitudinal population-based study. *Autism: The International Journal of Research and Practice, 16*(2), 139—150.

Smith, A. C., Dykens, E., & Greenberg, F. (1998). Sleep disturbance in Smith—Magenis syndrome (del 17 p11.2). *American Journal of Medical Genetics, 81*(2), 186—191.

Souders, M. C., Mason, T. B., Valladares, O., Bucan, M., Levy, S. E., Mandell, D. S., … Pinto-Martin, J. (2009). Sleep behaviors and sleep quality in children with autism spectrum disorders. *Sleep, 32*(12), 1566—1578.

Stavinoha, R. C., Kline, A. D., Levy, H. P., Kimball, A., Mettel, T. L., & Ishman, S. L. (2011). Characterization of sleep disturbance in Cornelia de Lange syndrome. *International Journal of Pediatric Otorhinolaryngology, 75*(2), 215—218.

Stebbens, V., Dennis, J., Samuels, M., Croft, C., & Southall, D. (1991). Sleep related upper airway obstruction in a cohort with Down's syndrome. *Archives of Disease in Childhood, 66*, 1333—1338.

Stores, G., & Stores, R. (2013). Sleep disorders and their clinical significance in children with Down syndrome. *Developmental Medicine and Child Neurology, 55*(2), 126—130.

Stores, R. (1993). A preliminary study of sleep disorders and daytime behaviour problems in children with Down's syndrome. *Down Syndrome Research and Practice, 1*, 29—33.

Stores, R., & Stores, G. (2004). Evaluation of a group-administered instruction for parents to prevent or minimize sleep problems in young children with Down syndrome. *Journal of Applied Research in Intellectual Disabilities, 17*, 61—70.

Stores, R., & Stores, G. (2014). The significance of aspects of screening for obstructive sleep apnoea in children with Down syndrome. *Journal of Intellectual Disability Research, 58*(4), 381—392.

Stores, R., Stores, G., Fellows, B., & Buckley, S. (1998). A factor analysis of sleep problems and their psychological associations in children with Down's syndrome. *Journal of Applied Research in Intellectual Disability, 17*, 345—354.

Summers, J. A., Lynch, P. S., Harris, J. C., Burke, J. C., Allison, D. B., & Sandler, L. (1992). A combined behavioral/pharmacological treatment of sleep-wake schedule disorder in Angelman syndrome. *Journal of Developmental and Behavioral Pediatrics, 13*(4), 284—287.

Telakivi, T., Partinen, M., Salmi, T., Leinonen, L., & Härkönen, T. (1987). Nocturnal periodic breathing in adults with Down's syndrome. *Journal of Mental Deficiency Research, 31*(1), 31—39.

Thackeray, E. J., & Richdale, A. L. (2002). The behavioral treatment of sleep difficulties in children with an intellectual disability. *Behavioral Interventions, 17*, 211—231.

Tietze, A.-L., Blankenburg, M., Hechler, T., Michel, E., Koh, M., Schlüter, B., & Zernikow, B. (2012). Sleep disturbances in children with multiple disabilities. *Sleep Medicine Reviews, 16*(2), 117—127.

Tordjman, S., Anderson, G. M., Bellissant, E., Botbol, M., Charbuy, H., Camus, F., … Cohen, D. (2012). Day and nighttime excretion of 6-sulphatoxymelatonin in adolescents and young adults with autistic disorder. *Psychoneuroendocrinology, 37*(12), 1990—1997.

Trois, M. S., Capone, G. T., Lutz, J. A., Melendres, M. C., Schwartz, A. R., Collop, N. A., & Marcus, C. L. (2009). Obstructive sleep apnea in adults with Down syndrome. *Journal of Clinical Sleep Medicine, 5*(4), 317—323. Retrieved from http://www.ncbi.nlm.nih.gov/pubmed/19968008.

Tudor, M. E., Hoffman, C. D., & Sweeney, D. P. (2012). Children with autism sleep problems and symptom severity. *Focus on Autism and Other Developmental Disabilities, 27*(4), 254—262.

Van Thillo, A., Devriendt, K., & Willekens, D. (2010). Sleep disturbances in Smith—Magenis syndrome: treatment with melatonin and beta-adrenergic antagonists. *Tijdschrift voor Psychiatrie, 52*(10), 719—723.

Vanhelst, J., Bui-Xuan, G., Fardy, P., & Mikulovic, J. (2013). Relationship between sleep habits, anthropometric characteristics and lifestyle habits in adolescents with intellectual disabilities. *Research in Developmental Disabilities, 34*(9), 2614—2620.

Vela-Bueno, A., Kales, A., Soldatos, C. R., Dobladez-Blanco, B., Campos-Castello, J., Espino-Hurtado, P., & Olivan-Palacios, J. (1984). Sleep in the Prader—Willi syndrome: clinical and polygraphic findings. *Archives of Neurology, 41*(3), 294—296.

Verrillo, E., Bruni, O., Franco, P., Ferri, R., Thiriez, G., Pavone, M., ... Cutrera, R. (2009). Analysis of NREM sleep in children with Prader—Willi syndrome and the effect of growth hormone treatment. *Sleep Medicine, 10*(6), 646—650.

Vgontzas, A. N., Kales, A., Seip, J., Mascari, M. J., Bixler, E. O., Myers, D. C., ... Rogan, P. K. (1996). Relationship of sleep abnormalities to patient genotypes in Prader—Willi syndrome. *American Journal of Medical Genetics (Neuropsychiatric Genetics), 67*, 478—482.

Vriend, J. L., Corkum, P. V., Moon, E. C., & Smith, I. M. (2011). Behavioral interventions for sleep problems in children with autism spectrum disorders: current findings and future directions. *Journal of Pediatric Psychology, 36*(9), 1017—1029.

Walz, N. C., Beebe, D., & Byars, K. (2005). Sleep in individuals with Angelman syndrome: parent perceptions of patterns and problems. *American Journal on Mental Retardation, 110*(4), 243—252.

Weiskop, S., Richdale, A., & Matthews, J. (2005). Behavioural treatment to reduce sleep problems in children with autism or fragile X syndrome. *Developmental Medicine and Child Neurology, 47*(2), 94—104.

Wiggs, L., & Stores, G. (1996). Severe sleep disturbance and daytime challenging behaviour in children with severe learning disabilities. *Journal of Intellectual Disability Research, 40*(6), 518—528.

Wiggs, L., & Stores, G. (2004). Sleep patterns and sleep disorders in children with autistic spectrum disorders: insights using parent report and actigraphy. *Developmental Medicine and Child Neurology, 46*(6), 372—380.

Williams, C. A., Angelman, H., Clayton-Smith, J., Driscoll, D., Hendrickson, J., Knoll, J., ... Zori, R. (1995). Angelman syndrome: consensus for diagnostic criteria. *American Journal of Medical Genetics, 56*(2), 237—238.

Wirojanan, J., Jacquemont, S., Diaz, R., Bacalman, S., Anders, T., Hagerman, R., & Goodlin-Jones, B. (2009). The efficacy of melatonin for sleep problems in children with autism, fragile X syndrome, or autism and fragile X syndrome. *Journal of Clinical Sleep Medicine, 5*(2), 145—150.

van de Wouw, E., Evenhuis, H., & Echteld, M. (2012). Prevalence, associated factors and treatment of sleep problems in adults with intellectual disability: a systematic review. *Research in Developmental Disabilities, 33*(4), 1310—1332.

van de Wouw, E., Evenhuis, H. M., & Echteld, M. A. (2013). Objective assessment of sleep and sleep problems in older adults with intellectual disabilities. *Research in Developmental Disabilities, 34*(8), 2291—2303.

de Zambotti, M., Baker, F. C., Willoughby, A. R., Godino, J. G., Wing, D., Patrick, K., & Colrain, I. M. (2016). Measures of sleep and cardiac functioning during sleep using a multi-sensory commercially-available wristband in adolescents. *Physiology & Behavior, 158*, 143—149.

Zhang, J., Fang, Z., Jud, C., Vansteensel, M. J., Kaasik, K., Lee, C. C., ... Oostra, B. A. (2008). Fragile X-related proteins regulate mammalian circadian behavioral rhythms. *American Journal of Human Genetics, 83*(1), 43—52.

Zhdanova, I. V., Wurtman, R. J., & Wagstaff, J. (1999). Effects of a low dose of melatonin on sleep in children with Angelman syndrome. *Journal of Pediatric Endocrinology & Metabolism, 12*(1), 57—68.

CHAPTER SIX

Parent Advocacy Across the LifeSpan

M.M. Burke[1], K.A. Patton, C. Lee

University of Illinois at Urbana-Champaign, Champaign, IL, United States
[1]Corresponding author: E-mail: meghanbm@illinois.edu

Contents

International Review of Research in Developmental Disabilities, Volume 51
ISSN 2211-6095
http://dx.doi.org/10.1016/bs.irrdd.2016.07.001

© 2016 Elsevier Inc.
All rights reserved.

Abstract

Services are critical for individuals with intellectual and developmental disabilities (IDD). However, due to complicated and insufficiently funded service delivery systems, parents have to advocate for services for their offspring with IDD. To date, although parents of children with IDD advocate from receiving the initial diagnosis until adulthood, no study has examined parent advocacy across the lifespan. In this paper, we examine studies about parent advocacy with respect to four age periods: early childhood, school-based services, transition services, and adulthood. In each period, we examined the need for advocacy, methods of advocacy used, and effect of advocacy. By examining advocacy across the lifespan, we present the similarities and differences in advocacy in relation to the age of the child. Directions for future research are discussed.

Parent advocacy refers to acting on behalf of a child with a disability to obtain services to meet the child's needs, strengths, and preferences (Trainor, 2010). Across the lifespan, parents advocate to ensure their offspring with

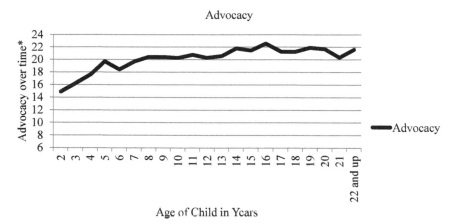

Figure 1 Advocacy over time. *, Advocacy was determined by the frequency in which parents engaged in advocacy activities.

intellectual and developmental disabilities (IDD) receive sufficient services (Haveman, van Berkum, Reijnders, & Heller, 1997). Indeed, services for individuals with IDD are crucial. In early childhood, services can help children forge progress (Guralnick, 2005). Among school-aged children, services can ensure that children make academic progress as well as have access to the general education curriculum and their peers without disabilities (e.g., Hanushek, Kain, & Rivkin, 2002). During adolescence, transition services help streamline the shift from school to adult services (Hanley-Maxwell, Whitney-Thomas, & Pogoloff, 1995). Finally, adult services enable individuals with disabilities to secure employment, housing, recreation activities, and education.

Across the lifespan of the individual with IDD, parent advocacy is needed. Further, it seems that the need for parent advocacy may increase over time. Using a national dataset of over 1500 parents of children with IDD ranging in age from 0 through 28, parents responded to a six-item advocacy scale (Burke & Hodapp, 2016). Over time, parents reported greater advocacy with especially strong advocacy when children transitioned to school-based services (ages 3–5), received transition plans (ages 14–16), and exited the school system for adult services (ages 18–22 and older). See Fig. 1. Although cross-sectional, these data provide some insight in how advocacy increases at certain points in time. In this review, we examine the need for advocacy, methods of advocacy, and outcomes of advocacy in relation to four time periods: early childhood, school-based services, transition, and adult services.

1. NEED FOR ADVOCACY OVER TIME

Although services are critical to individuals with IDD, services are difficult to receive. Indeed, many parents struggle to obtain appropriate services for their offspring with disabilities (Public Agenda, 2002). Because of the difficulty in obtaining needed services, parents need to advocate. However, the need for advocacy may vary with respect to the age of the child and the nature of the needed services. Specifically, the need for parent advocacy may relate to various funding mechanisms, complex and different eligibility systems, waiting lists for services, difficult to navigate service delivery systems, evolving disability policies, and a lag time in proving eligibility for services. Each of these barriers varies depending on the age of the child and, relatedly, the service delivery system. By understanding the need for advocacy with respect to each time period, we can better determine how relevant policies pose unique challenges at different points in the life of the individual with IDD as well as in the parent's life.

2. METHODS OF ADVOCACY OVER TIME

Depending on the need for advocacy, parents may use different methods of advocacy. Notably, there is no agreed upon definition of advocacy. Thus, in this review, we broadly define advocacy as acting on behalf of a child with a disability to obtain services to meet the child's needs, strengths, and preferences (Trainor, 2010). Relatedly, methods of advocacy may include a range of activities including gaining knowledge, attending support groups, asking for services as well as having advocacy experiences and using different strategies to receive services. Of the limited extant literature, the studies which identify methods of parent advocacy do so in relation to a given time period (e.g., school-based services, Trainor, 2010). By understanding the methods of advocacy used with respect to a given time period, we can then identify similar advocacy methods used over the course of the lifespan as well as methods unique to a certain time period. Further, by identifying advocacy methods, future research can operationally define parent advocacy and, subsequently, empirically determine its effect on child, parent, and family outcomes.

3. EFFECT OF ADVOCACY OVER TIME

Finally, it is important to understand the impact of parent advocacy especially with respect to child, parent, and family outcomes. Across the lifespan, it seems that the effect of parent advocacy may be mixed including both positive and negative effects. In a study using focus groups and individual interviews with 104 parents of individuals with IDD of varying ages, Wang, Mannan, Poston, Turnbull, and Summers (2004) found that families perceived advocacy as an obligation and means to improve services. Positive benefits of advocacy included greater coping skills and potentially better and/or more services for individuals with IDD. Negative outcomes included that advocacy related to increased stress, adversarial struggles, and worse family—professional partnerships. By understanding the impact of parent advocacy over time, we can determine whether advocacy is effective as well as whether advocacy has unintended, negative effects.

Although several studies have examined parent advocacy, it is unclear whether there are similarities and differences in advocacy in relation to life stages. It seems that there must be changes in advocacy as the need for advocacy varies across the lifespans of individuals with IDD. Namely, the change in advocacy shifts from early childhood (ages 0—5, wherein services are family-centered) to school-based services (ages 5—22, wherein school services focus on the individual with a disability) to transition services (ages 14—22, wherein the student continues to receive school-based services with an increasing emphasis on post-school outcomes and self-advocacy), and, finally, to adult services (ages 18—22 until the end of the lifespan, wherein services are fragmented across multiple agencies). Notably, although early intervention services are primarily for children aged 0—3, we extended early childhood until age 5 as services continue to be family-centered and children can continue to receive early intervention services until age 5. Adult services begin between the ages of 18—22 as, when individuals with IDD turn 18, they are eligible for many services; however, individuals with IDD may also stay in school until age 22 delaying the utilization of the adult service delivery system. Because the need for advocacy varies across the lifespan, the method of advocacy and its effects may also change over time. By understanding the changes in the need for advocacy, methods of advocacy, and effects of advocacy over time, we can better understand advocacy from a lifespan perspective as well as identify time periods for targeted support or interventions.

In this paper, we discuss parent advocacy across the lifespan of individuals with IDD. We review parent advocacy with respect to early childhood, school-based services, transition services, and adult services. Specifically, we identify the need for advocacy, methods of advocacy, and effects of advocacy. We then discuss similarities and differences in advocacy across the different age periods. We conclude with directions for future research.

4. PARENT ADVOCACY FOR EARLY CHILDHOOD SERVICES

4.1 Nature of Early Childhood Services

In the United States, from birth to age 3, children with disabilities receive services through Early Intervention or Part C of the Individuals with Disabilities Education Act (IDEA). Early intervention services are provided by individual states. A key premise of early intervention services is family-centeredness. Relatedly, children receive an Individualized Family Service Plan (IFSP). In the IFSP, services for the child as well as the family are identified and provided. The purpose of the IFSP is to not only teach skills to the child but also to educate the parents to better support the child's development.

When children turn three, they age into school-based services. Specifically, they receive an Individualized Education Program (IEP). Unlike the IFSP, the IEP details the placement, services, and supports based on the child's unique needs—not the family's. However, for this paper, we refer to early childhood as ages 0—5 for two reasons. First, according to IDEA, children with disabilities can continue to receive early intervention services until age 5. Second, school-based services and, relatedly, IEPs, tend to be family-centered until age 5. See Table 1 for an overview of the nature of services across the lifespan.

4.2 Need for Advocacy

Notably, because of the family-centered nature of early intervention services, parent advocacy may be less needed when the child is between the ages of 0—3 (McWilliam, Maxwell, & Sloper, 1999). Because the IEP is less family-centered than the IFSP, parents may begin to advocate as their children transition from an IFSP to an IEP. But although more family-centered than other services, parents may need to advocate for services during early childhood. Specifically, parent advocacy may begin when children

Table 1 Nature of American Services Across the Lifespan

Type of Services	Age of Recipient	Focus of Services	Service provider
Early childhood	0—5 years of age • Early intervention is primarily for children 0—3 years of age but can extend to age 3 • Early childhood is from 0 to 5	To conduct family-centered practices and encourage progress of young children with disabilities	Individual states for early intervention; schools for school services
School	3—22 years of age	To develop individualized education programs for children with disabilities to forge progress	Schools
Transition	14—22 years of age	To enable young adults with disabilities to be self-determined and have positive post-school outcomes	Schools; when the child turns 18, adult service delivery systems directed by individual states and/or federal programs
Adult	18—22 years of age and older	To ensure adults with disabilities have positive post-school outcomes	Adult service delivery systems directed by individual states and/or federal programs

with IDD first receive their diagnoses. After receiving a diagnosis, parents begin to navigate the service delivery system (Barnett, Clements, Kaplan-Estrin, & Fialka, 2003). Parents report that, upon receiving the diagnosis, physicians explain the type of disability of the child but leave parents without direction about where to acquire needed services (Drake, Couse, DiNapoli, & Banach, 2008). Thus, at an early age, parents need to learn how to advocate for services. Indeed, early childhood marks the beginning of a lifetime of parent advocacy (Smith, Gundler, Casey, & Jones, 2011).

Further, for all children, early childhood (ages 0—5) marks an important developmental period. For children with IDD, this period is especially important. Over 50 years of research demonstrates the importance of early childhood services for children with IDD (Trohanis, 2008). During early childhood, children with IDD receive services enabling them to make progress (Guralnick, 2005). Such services are designed to meet the specific needs of young children with IDD. In a comparative study of parents of kindergartners with (versus without) IDD, Welchons and McIntyre (2015) found that parents of young children with (versus without) IDD reported significantly greater concerns. In addition to more parental concerns, children with (versus without) IDD also experience significantly more problem behaviors, worse child—teacher relationships, poorer social skills, and worse self-regulation skills (McIntyre, Eckert, Fiese, DiGennaro, & Wildenger, 2006). With early childhood services, young children with IDD may develop more appropriate behaviors and skills.

Additionally, minority (versus White) families of young children with IDD face greater barriers in accessing early childhood services (Liptak et al., 2008; Montes, Halterman, & Magyar, 2009; Thomas, Ellis, McLaurin, Daniels, & Morrissey, 2007). For example, in a multistate study, among children with autism spectrum disorder (ASD), compared to White children, minority (specifically, Latino and Asian) children received significantly less services with respect to speech and occupational therapy (Irvin, McBee, Boyd, Hume, & Odom, 2012). African American families also face barriers in securing services for their young children. In a review of the literature about African American families of children with ASD and their unmet needs, Pearson (2015) identified three barriers to accessing services: differential diagnoses, socioeconomic status, and cultural divergence. Differential diagnoses refer to the delayed diagnoses of ASD for African American (versus White) children. Socioeconomic status refers to the fiscal barriers, which particularly impact African American families. Finally, cultural divergence recognizes the disconnect between African American parents and professionals.

Generally, for minority (versus White) families of children with IDD, early education services are limited, inaccessible, and costly (Irvin et al., 2012). In a study comparing White and Latino children diagnosed with ASD, Latino (versus White) children were diagnosed significantly later, received fewer services, and had higher unmet service needs (Magaña, Lopez, Aguinaga, & Morton, 2013). Additionally, White (versus minority) families are more likely to use private services (i.e., services that parents pay-out-of-pocket for) for their young children (Thomas et al., 2007). Thus, minority families may only be relying on formal disability service delivery systems to provide services to their young children, making advocacy even more important.

4.3 Methods of Advocacy

One way that parents of young children learn to advocate is through parent support groups. In support groups, parents may share strategies for advocating for services (Fish, 2006; Spann, Kohler, & Soenksen, 2003). Notably, learning advocacy skills may be in tandem with learning about the child's diagnosis. Using a parent support group format, Banach, Iudice, Conway, and Couse (2010) examined the effectiveness of a parent training intervention which included components regarding understanding the child's diagnosis as well as developing advocacy skills. After receiving the training intervention, parents reported greater knowledge about: the special education process, available resources, special education law, and advocacy strategies for special education meetings. Specifically, parents reported learning about advocacy from hearing other parent participants speaking about their advocacy experiences. Other studies have similarly indicated that parent support groups enable families to learn to advocate (e.g., Guralnick, 2000).

In a case study of a novice special education teacher of children with ASD, the teacher reported working in a school district wherein parents were strong advocates for their children (Boyer & Lee, 2001). To advocate, parents reported concerns to the teacher regarding their child's placement as well as the curriculum and instructional methods. Parents reported primarily advocating within the context of IEP meetings. In addition to the parents being strong advocates themselves, the teacher reported that most parents also brought professional special education advocates to IEP meetings.

Another way parents advocate is by having knowledge about their rights, the child's disability, and available services. In a qualitative study about parents of young children with apraxia, parents reported feeling obligated to advocate for their children (Miron, 2012). Parents reported advocating by questioning professionals, learning about services and their rights, and doing research about service delivery systems and their children's needs. Parents reported advocating by having a greater understanding and awareness of what their children should be receiving and questioning professionals to ensure their children are receiving appropriate services.

Parents also advocated by asking for services, supports, and help from professionals. Rao (2000) conducted a case study with an

African American mother of a four-year old with developmental disabilities. In this study, the mother advocated by requesting assistance from professionals to address the maladaptive behaviors of her child as well as requesting placement in a general education classroom. In both instances, the mother was met with resistance by the school staff. The professionals provided reactive (versus proactive) strategies to address the child's behaviors. Additionally, the school refused to educate the child in the general education setting.

4.4 Effect of Advocacy

4.4.1 Effect on Parents

After advocating, parents reported feeling empowered (Banach et al., 2010; Miron, 2012). Whether parents learned to advocate via support groups (Banach et al., 2010) or self-education about their rights (Miron, 2012), parents reported that advocacy made them feel empowered to question professionals and to ensure their children receive needed services.

4.4.2 Effect on Teachers

Early childhood studies indicated a mixed effect of parent advocacy on teachers. In the case study of a novice special education teacher (Boyer & Lee, 2001), at the end of the first school year, the teacher reported feeling intimidated by parent advocacy. Because of the assertiveness of the advocacy, the teacher reported increased scrutiny of her instruction and the IEPs of her students. Further, the teacher reported feeling emotionally fatigued (e.g., upset, worried, anxious) because of parent advocacy.

Regarding early intervention providers, parents reported wanting their providers to advocate for their children. In a study of parents of young children with hearing impairments and/or deafness, parents reported that they wished early intervention providers had better advocacy skills (Rice & Lenihan, 2005). While parents realized that they needed advocacy training to be empowered themselves, parents also reported relying on early intervention providers to advocate, especially when children transitioned from IFSPs to IEPs. Other studies have similarly reported that providers and clinicians for young children should advocate for children with disabilities to receive services (for a review, see Neeley-Barnes & Dia, 2008). Thus, an effect of parent advocacy is that parents want professionals to also advocate for their children.

5. PARENT ADVOCACY FOR SCHOOL SERVICES

5.1 Nature of School Services

When children with IDD turn three, they age into school-based services (i.e., Part B of IDEA). From age 3 to 22, children with IDD receive special education services, from the school, via an IEP. Annually, the family and school professionals meet to develop the IEP which includes present levels of performance, related and supplementary services, goals and objectives, and placement for the student. Within IDEA, there are six guiding principles (Turnbull, 2005). First, IDEA includes a zero rejection principle by requiring all states to have plans to educate students with disabilities. Second, IDEA has a nondiscriminatory evaluation principle; schools must conduct evaluations of children with disabilities to examine their academic, developmental, and functional performance. Third, students with disabilities are entitled to a free, appropriate public education (FAPE). Fourth, students should be educated in the least restrictive environment, wherein the student is educated to the maximum extent possible with peers without disabilities. Fifth, there are procedural safeguards (e.g., due process) in place to resolve conflicts between families and schools. Finally, the sixth principle indicates that parents should be key members of the decision-making process for their children with disabilities.

5.2 Need for Advocacy

Although IDEA outlines the rights of parents and students with disabilities, 33 out of 50 states are out of compliance with IDEA (Annual Report to Congress, 2015). Thus, parents often feel they need to advocate for their children to obtain services. Specifically, 70% of parents report needing advocacy skills and special education knowledge to ensure that their children with disabilities receive appropriate services; yet, most parents report not understanding their special education rights (Public Agenda, 2002). Barriers to advocacy include lack of parent special education knowledge (Leiter & Krauss, 2004); caution about sharing information (Cartledge, Kea, & Simmons-Reed, 2002); feelings of intimidation (Fish, 2008); and difficulty understanding jargon (Park & Turnbull, 2001). Limited advocacy also relates to attitudinal barriers such as the power differential between schools and parents (Leiter & Krauss, 2004), and parents feeling they lack the legitimacy of an expert (Kalyanpur, Harry, & Skrtic, 2000).

There are several barriers to receiving services; all of these barriers necessitate parent advocacy. A key barrier is cost. Every student with a disability, in accordance with IDEA, is entitled to a FAPE. However, in practice, schools may be considering costs when determining whether to provide services. Such considerations may be due to the limited federal funding for special education expenditures. When IDEA was first passed in 1975 (then called the Education for All Handicapped Children Act), the federal government promised to fund 40% of all special education expenditures; presently, the federal government funds approximately 15% (Council for Exceptional Children, 2014). Thus, schools may struggle to finance services for students with disabilities making parent advocacy necessary but difficult.

Another barrier to obtaining services is the accessibility of understanding one's rights. Annually, at the student's IEP meeting, the school is required to provide parents with their procedural safeguards. From these safeguards, parents are supposed to understand their special education rights as well as options for dispute resolution with the school. However, on average, procedural safeguards are written at a 16th grade reading level making them largely inaccessible to many families (Mandic, Rudd, Hehir, & Acevedo-Garcia, 2012). Other studies have similarly reported that parents want to understand their special education rights; however, procedural safeguards are too dense and cumbersome to educate parents about their options for conflict resolution (Friesen & Huff, 1990; Simon, 2006). Thus, because safeguards are inaccessible, parents need to seek other resources to advocate.

In a national survey of parents of children with disabilities, parents reported needing to advocate under certain conditions (Burke & Hodapp, 2016). Specifically, parents who reported less satisfactory partnerships with the schools and were less satisfied with educational services engaged in greater advocacy activities. Additionally, parents who engaged in the highest levels of advocacy reported negative experiences with the school. For example, parents were more likely to advocate when schools refused to provide services, acted disingenuously, lacked trained personnel, and communicated poorly with parents. Thus, it seems that poor parent—teacher relationships and low-quality services require parent advocacy.

Advocacy may be especially needed and difficult among minority families. Although minority children are over-represented in special education (Albrecht, Skiba, Losen, Chung, & Middleberg, 2011), their voices are the least likely to be heard by professionals (Harry, 2002). Indeed, the expectation of parent advocacy may not be culturally aligned with many families. Specifically, the assumption that parents have access to information and resources and are aware of their rights may not be true for minority families given barriers to accessing information, lack of cultural responsiveness, and limited social and cultural capital (Kalyanpur et al., 2000).

For example, Latino, Spanish-speaking parents of children with disabilities are less likely to receive needed services and more likely to need to advocate (Cohen, 2013). Latino families face added challenges in advocacy because special education documents are only available in English (Shapiro, Monzo, Rueda, Gomez, & Blacher, 2004). Also, Spanish-speaking families often need translators at IEP meetings; because of the jargon in IDEA, most translators do not effectively communicate everything that is said at the meeting and, as a result, Spanish-speaking families are often reduced to listening roles (Hughes, Valle-Riestra, & Arguelles, 2002). Given the need for services as well as the barriers to advocacy, it is clear that minority families have a greater need for advocacy.

5.3 Methods of Advocacy

In a seminal article about parent advocacy, Trainor (2010) conducted focus groups with parents of school-aged children with IDD. Notably, her sample included culturally, socioeconomically, and linguistically diverse families. From the focus groups, Trainor identified four approaches to parent advocacy: intuitive, Strategist, disability expert, and agent of systemic change. Intuitive parent advocates relied on their intimate knowledge of the strengths, weaknesses, and needs of their children to advocate for services. Disability experts used their knowledge of the type of disability and its implications to advocate for services. Strategist advocacy included understanding and applying one's special education rights to ensure appropriate services are received. Finally, agents of systemic change include individuals who advocate for changes not just for their own child but also for more global changes.

Realizing that knowledge of special education rights is crucial to parent advocacy for school-based services, other research has defined advocacy in relation to special education knowledge. Lo (2005) examined parent advocacy by asking 12 true/false questions about special education law to Chinese American parents of elementary school children with disabilities. Similarly, Plunge and Kratochwill (1995) asked parents of children with disabilities to respond to 13 true/false questions about special education knowledge. Additionally, Plunge and Kratochwill asked participants 17 questions about participation in IEP meetings. Thus, it seems special education knowledge and, to a lesser extent, participation in IEP meetings are methods of parent advocacy.

Parent advocacy strategies may also differ with respect to the advocacy experiences of the parent. Balcazar, Keys, Bertram, and Rizzo (1996) conducted a study examining the Partners in Policymaking program, a national program designed for family members of individuals with IDD and self-advocates to develop advocacy skills. In their study, participants reflected three developmental stages of advocacy: beginner, involved, and activist. Beginner advocates belonged to one organization, received few services, and engaged in few advocacy activities. Involved advocates belonged to at least one organization as an active member, obtained services as needed, and engaged in advocacy activities. Finally, activist advocates belonged to several local and state organizations, had leadership roles, and obtained services for others. To determine the stages of advocacy, Balcazar et al. (1996) examined various advocacy actions of the participants: phone calls, office visits or meetings, letters and mass mailings, media reports, and other activities. Thus, another method of parent advocacy may be related to the degree of communication with the school and other agencies.

Minority families may employ different advocacy strategies. For example, Williams (2007) conducted a case study with African American families of children with disabilities. Because of noncompliance with IDEA, the Office for Civil Rights (OCR) visited their school district. Indeed, some parents had contacted OCR to advocate for their children to receive services. Parents advocated for systemic changes because the school had over-referred and segregated African American students in special education settings. Parents also mentioned being ignored in the special education process and having to advocate to participate in IEP meetings. In another study of urban, African American parents, parents reported making unannounced visits to the school and reminding the school to focus on their child's academic skills (not just behavior) (Munn-Joseph & Gavin-Evans, 2008). Parents also reported relying on learning about services and their rights by talking to agencies, family members, and friends. By using social networks, parents reported trying to ensure their children receive appropriate services from the school.

In a qualitative study of rural, African American parents of children with disabilities, various advocacy methods were identified (Stanley, 2015). Parents reported using intuitive advocacy to know and advocate for the best services for their children. Other parents reported being disability experts and educating staff about their child's disability and needed services.

Parents also reported engaging in collective advocacy by presenting their concerns to the School Board on behalf of all children (not just their child). Additionally, parents used resources to educate themselves on their rights and available services. Finally, parents reported that communication with professionals was a key method of advocacy. Specifically, parents reported asking questions, making specific requests, and disagreeing with teachers' recommendations.

5.4 Effect of Advocacy

5.4.1 Effects for the Child

Of the limited studies about the effect of parent advocacy, it seems that parent advocacy has positive effects on children with disabilities. Such effects may be direct or indirect. In a study about advocacy across developmental stages (Balcazar et al., 1996), advocacy directly impacted children by increasing their inclusion in general education settings. Additionally, parent advocacy led to systemic changes including legislative changes restricting the use of punitive measures in school settings; these impacts indirectly impacted children with disabilities.

5.4.2 Effects for the Parent

Given that most advocacy involves some degree of conflict, it is understandable that advocacy relates to stress (Wang et al., 2004). In a national study of mothers of children with IDD, Burke and Hodapp (2014) found that advocacy related to significantly greater stress. Specifically, there was a nonlinear relation between advocacy and stress. Mothers who engaged in even a few advocacy activities (versus those who engaged in no advocacy activities) demonstrated significantly greater levels of stress. Thus, it seems that, for parents, advocacy activities may negatively impact parent well-being.

Additionally, advocacy can impact parents financially. When parents retain an attorney or advocate to assist with their advocacy efforts, parents must pay, out of pocket, for those expenditures. Given that families of individuals with IDD are disproportionately more likely to live in poverty (Emerson, 2007), additional expenses can exacerbate the financial solvency of a family. Additionally, 15 out of 50 states lack reduced-cost or pro bono attorneys for families (Ahearn, 2001). Indeed, only half of state special education directors report that parents of children with disabilities have access to attorney representation even when cost is not a barrier; when parents are unable to afford attorney representation, the number of attorneys further shrinks (Seven & Zirkel, 2002).

Finally, advocacy may make parents feel uncomfortable. Especially at IEP meetings, there is a power differential between the parents and the school (Leiter & Krauss, 2004). To overcome this power differential, parents may advocate more assertively than they feel comfortable doing (Allen & Hudd, 1987; Soodak & Erwin, 2000).

5.4.3 Effects for the School

With respect to legal advocacy methods (e.g., due process and mediation), there are several negative effects for the school. Similar to parents, schools are also negatively impacted by due process hearings. Indeed, for parents and schools, the combined average due process hearing costs $60,000 (Mueller, 2009). Schools may be frustrated with the cost of due process and mediation as the money spent on such safeguards could be re-directed toward instruction (Zirkel, 1994). Further, due process harms family—school partnerships (Burke & Goldman, 2015; Mueller, 2009).

6. PARENT ADVOCACY FOR TRANSITION SERVICES

6.1 Nature of Transition Services

Transition services were part of the 1990 and 1997 IDEA reauthorizations mandating that children with disabilities begin transition planning at 14.5 years of age. In the 2004 IDEA reauthorization, the minimum age requirement for transition services changed to age 16. Transition-age students (aged 16—21) are required to have "appropriate measurable postsecondary goals based upon age—appropriate transition assessments related to training, education, employment, and, where appropriate, independent living skills" (IDEA, 2004, 300.320(b)). Transition planning is part of the development of a student's IEP. Although transition services are provided by the school, transition planning should include adult services.

The transition process should reflect the Taxonomy of Transition Programming which includes five components: (1) Student-focused planning; (2) Student development; (3) Interagency and interdisciplinary collaboration; (4) Family involvement; and (5) Program structure and attributes (Kohler, 1996). Student-focused planning involves individualizing transition plans to meet the needs of the students and including students in decision-making. Student development requires transition plans to include goals related to post-school employment and occupational skills.

Collaborative service delivery entails agencies, namely adult service agencies, working together; such collaboration is necessary for effective transition planning (Mazzotti, Test, & Mustian, 2014). Family involvement indicates that parents should be partners in transition planning. Program structure refers to programmatic features that impact the quality of the transition process.

6.2 Need for Advocacy

During the transition process, parents and adolescents with IDD report being dissatisfied with their special education services (Hetherington et al., 2010). Specifically, such dissatisfaction stems from: insufficient school communication, frustration with stereotypes about the student, lack of individualization of post-school outcomes, and the absence of school accountability. Parent dissatisfaction is problematic because, for transition to be successful, it is crucial to have parent input and participation (Kim & Turnbull, 2004; Turnbull, Turnbull, Erwin, Soodak, & Shogren, 2015). Dissatisfaction not only impacts the effectiveness of transition planning but also causes parents to advocate more frequently.

During transition, adolescents with IDD begin to shift from the school service delivery system to an unfamiliar and complex adult service delivery system (Hanley-Maxwell et al., 1995). Put simply, adolescents begin to shift from an entitlement system (i.e., in accordance with IDEA, schools are required to provide services to individuals with IDD) to an eligibility-based service system (i.e., adult services are only provided when individuals are eligible for services). Transition is often confusing, difficult, and requires tremendous parent advocacy to ensure that appropriate services are received (for a review, see Burke et al., 2016).

Although the onus is placed on parents to advocate for transition services, parents often feel ill-prepared to advocate. The adult service delivery system is new to parents of transition-aged youth. In trying to advocate for services, parents face challenges with not only finding appropriate transition services, but also identifying which adult services are potentially available for their children (Bianco, Garrison-Wade, Tobin, & Lehmann, 2009; Cooney, 2002). In a qualitative study of young adults with disabilities, their parents, and professionals from schools and adult service agencies, Cooney (2002) found that parents were hopeful during the transition process but struggled to understand the various services, procedures, and adult service agencies. Thus, while serving as caregivers for their offspring, parents struggle with also advocating for transition and adult services.

The need for advocacy may intensify with respect to minority and/or low-income families of transition-aged youth with IDD. In a focus group study of 16 low-income Latina mothers of young adults with IDD, Shapiro et al. (2004) reported that parents experienced difficult conditions necessitating advocacy. Specifically, parents reported poor communication with the school due to a lack of written information provided in Spanish. Parents also perceived that teachers and service providers held negative views about their children. Correspondingly, parents reported that the school put in minimal effort when working with their children. Finally, parents reported that professionals were disrespectful to parents. Parents reported that professionals treated parents as "outsiders" during transition planning. Given these difficult conditions, Latino parents (and, more generally, minority and low-income families) may need to advocate for their transition-aged youth with IDD.

6.3 Methods of Advocacy

Through focus groups and individual interviews with 30 parents of young adults with IDD, Timmons, Whitney-Thomas, McIntyre, Butterworth, and Allen (2004) determined that, throughout the transition process, parents viewed their role as a "linchpin" of the overlapping school and adult service systems. Specifically, given that there are multiple service systems and agencies, parents reported that they held everything together by being the only person who could coordinate all of the services between difference agencies.

Serving as a linchpin required persistent advocacy and assertiveness as parents were often confronting challenges with gaining access to needed services for their children. To effectively advocate, parents reported: connecting with other parents of transition-aged youth with IDD; asking professionals for advice about advocacy; and seeking information about adult services. By meeting with other parents and professionals as well as seeking their own resources, parents became informed and were able to advocate for services.

Hetherington et al. (2010) conducted interviews with young adults with IDD and their parents. Similar to Timmons et al., (2004), Hetherington and colleagues found that parents relied on information to advocate for their children to receive services. Parents also reported advocating with the school by "nagging" (p. 168) the school to begin the transition planning earlier. Additionally, parents reported advocating by challenging the school's low expectations for their offspring. Parents reported that schools did not seek out post-school options for their children. Thus, parents independently sought out post-school services and, relatedly, needed school-based services. Then, parents advocated for those services through the school.

Cultural and socioeconomic differences between parents and teachers can also impact parent advocacy. From the Shapiro et al.'s (2004) study, Latina mothers reported advocating in a more confrontational way to ensure that their young adults' transition needs would not be neglected. Parents reported advocating by seeking out services for their children, repeatedly contacting professionals, and requesting services. Parents reported wanting more training about adult services as well as having a parent support group to exchange information and advocacy strategies.

6.4 Effect of Advocacy
6.4.1 Effect for the Young Adult
The focus of parent advocacy during transition is on providing young adults with needed services and supports to help them achieve their desired post-school outcomes (Hetherington et al., 2010; Shapiro et al., 2004; Timmons et al., 2004). Parent advocacy and involvement in transition planning has been shown to positively impact post-school employment and quality of life for young adults in transition (Hanley-Maxwell et al., 1995; Kraemer, McIntyre, & Blacher, 2003). Hetherington et al. (2010) found that some parents reported that their advocacy was the sole reason that their children's transition plans accurately reflect their children's transition needs. Similarly, Timmons et al. (2004) found that parents reported that they were the center of their children's transition planning process. Parents also advocated for needed services, supports, and resources that can benefit young adults during transition (e.g., computer, transportation training, community vocational training) (Hanley-Maxwell et al., 1995; Timmons et al., 2004). By having such needed school-based supports, individuals with IDD may have better post-school outcomes.

6.4.2 Effect for the Parent
Parents reported that their advocacy during the transition process was stressful and exhausting (Hetherington et al., 2010; Shapiro et al., 2004; Timmons et al., 2004). While seen as necessary, parents described advocacy as difficult and frustrating; even when parent advocacy was agreeable between parents and teachers, it was still tiresome (Timmons et al., 2004). Parent advocacy during the transition process may be especially frustrating because the

transition process includes the school *and* adult service delivery systems. Specifically, advocating during transition planning includes advocating not only for needed school-based services to prepare students for life after school, but also advocating for the adult services that individuals with IDD may need after they exit school (Cooney, 2002; Hetherington et al., 2010; Timmons et al., 2004). Thus, parent advocacy entails additional stressors that are different from other stages of the educational system (Hanley-Maxwell et al., 1995).

Parents may also experience stress, as a result of their advocacy, because of the increased pressure to seek services. When parents disagree with teachers about the type of adult service agency or potential employment outcomes they desire for their children, it was often left to parents to find and advocate for services they desire for their children's future (Cooney, 2002). Parents reported having limited information or understanding of needed transition and adult services available to their offspring (Hetherington et al., 2010; Timmons et al., 2004; Young, Morgan, Callow-Heusser, & Lindstrom, 2016). Such limited information lead to increased stress and anxiety when advocating for services (Hanley-Maxwell et al., 1995).

7. PARENT ADVOCACY FOR ADULT SERVICES

7.1 Nature of Adult Services

In adulthood, individuals with IDD may need various services including: supported employment, housing, day programs, healthcare, and leisure activities. Adult services are fragmented as services are provided by a variety of agencies and policies. For example, the Home and Community-Based Services (HCBS) Medicaid waiver is a federal program (administered by individual states) to provide services for adults with IDD. Indeed, the HCBS Medicaid waiver is the primary funding source for services for adults with IDD. Such services can include (but are not limited to) personal support workers, respite, transportation, and educational assistance. Other programs include Vocational Rehabilitation programs, which are operated individually by each state; such programs may assist with education or employment assistance with the intended outcome that adults with IDD will be able to secure and maintain employment. Regarding housing, adults with IDD may be eligible for a Section 8 Housing Voucher—a national program administrated by state and local agencies.

These programs (e.g., HCBS waivers, Vocational Rehabilitation, and Section 8 Housing Vouchers) provide just a glimpse of the different types of services, programs, and agencies that may support adults with IDD.

7.2 Need for Advocacy

Unfortunately, there is limited funding for adult services; furthermore, as individuals with IDD have longer lives, there is an increasing number of individuals with IDD eligible for adult services thus further exacerbating the limited funding for services (Braddock et al., 2014). Because of the limited funding and expanded population of individuals eligible for adult services, many adults with IDD wait for services. Across the United States, more than 73,000 adults with IDD are waiting for HCBS waiver services (Prouty, Smith, & Lakin, 2006). Additionally, 43 states have waiting lists for adults with IDD to receive the HCBS Medicaid waiver (Research and Training Center on Community Living, 2002).

While waiting for services, there may be poor outcomes for individuals with IDD and their parents. In a national study of 796 siblings of adults with IDD, nearly 13% of the individuals with IDD lacked daytime activities (Taylor & Hodapp, 2012). Compared to individuals with IDD with daytime activities, the individuals without daytime activities were more likely to have behavioral and health problems, be underserved by the formal service system, and have parents who were less able to provide caregiving. The lack of services may also negatively impact parents. Gill and Renwick (2007) conducted interviews with families of individuals with IDD; when individuals with IDD lacked services, both the individuals and their parents reported a reduced quality of life. Thus, waiting for services in adulthood can delay the reception of services.

Additionally, unlike the school service system or early intervention, the adult service delivery system is fragmented. There is not a single place or agency to go to for services. Instead, multiple agencies provide services to adults with IDD. Further, some agencies overlap with the services that they provide. For example, adults with IDD can receive employment services from the HCBS Medicaid waiver or the Department of Vocational Rehabilitation Services. Yet, both agencies have different eligibility criteria, services, plans for employment, and supports. Thus, parents of adults with IDD need to advocate for the appropriate agency for their child to secure services.

Additionally, many adult service delivery systems place the onus on parents to apply for services. For example, in the United States, individuals with IDD may be eligible for financial benefits via Supplemental Security Income (SSI). To be eligible for SSI, individuals must undergo a stepwise process including providing medical and vocational information. Unfortunately, parents of individuals with IDD and service coordinators report many barriers to applying for and proving eligibility for SSI (Kessler, 2015) including difficulty understanding the SSI application process and confusion regarding the differences between benefits and services. In addition to a complicated eligibility system, SSI also has a complex relation with other agencies and, accordingly services. For example, to be eligible for HCBS waiver services, an individual with IDD must also be eligible for SSI. Yet, upon receiving employment supports and securing a full-time job with appropriate benefits, an individual with IDD may lose their SSI. Given the difficulty in proving eligibility for adult services, parents need to advocate.

Finally, during adulthood, it is important to recognize the age of the caregiver. As individuals with IDD have longer lives, they are beginning to outlive their parents. Compared to agencies and other individuals, parents provide the most long-term caregiving for their offspring with IDD (Wolff & Kasper, 2006). During adulthood, parents may be facing the growing needs of their offspring with IDD (including worsening health, maladaptive behaviors, and psychopathology) as well as their own declining health. This issue of aging is especially poignant among families of individuals with Down syndrome. As individuals with Down syndrome are living longer, they begin to show aging-related declines by their late 40s (Hodapp, Burke, Finley, & Urbano, 2016). Additionally, compared to parents of individuals without intellectual disabilities and with other types of intellectual disabilities, parents of individuals with Down syndrome are, on average, older. Thus, especially with respect to families of individuals with Down syndrome but also families of adults with other types of IDD, there is a need for parents to advocate not only for current but also future supports for their offspring.

7.3 Methods of Advocacy

To better understand parent advocacy, Bianco et al. (2009) conducted semistructured interviews with nine families of adults with IDD. Compared to when their offspring were children, parents identified new advocacy roles with their adult offspring: collaborators, instructors, trainers, role models, mentors, evaluators, decision-makers, and system change agents. Specifically, parents worked as collaborators with adult service agencies and direct service providers. Through collaborations with these agencies, parents sought to ensure appropriate services for their adult offspring. However, when appropriate services were not available or professionals did not have the skills to help their children, parents reported advocating via different roles such as instructors, trainers, role models, and mentors. For example, parents taught job-related skills to their adult offspring with the hope of obtaining meaningful employment. Also, parents trained service providers to work with their children. Furthermore, parents were mentors for other parents; as mentors, parents helped other parents advocate effectively for their offspring. In addition, in their advocacy pursuits, parents were evaluators and decision-makers monitoring whether their offspring were receiving services to meet their needs. Interestingly, parents also mentioned teaching their offspring to self-advocate. Specifically, parents mentioned trying to balance their own advocacy with their children's self-advocacy.

7.4 Effect of Advocacy

7.4.1 Effects for the Adult Offspring

Among parents of adult offspring with IDD, many parents are concerned about services with respect to employment, independent living, and self-advocacy. As a result of parent advocacy, adults with IDD may have more meaningful employment opportunities (Petner-Arrey, Howell-Moneta, & Lysaght, 2015). Specifically, when parents advocate, their adult offspring may be more likely to find appropriate jobs, secure needed employment supports, and develop social networks in the workplace. By having jobs matched to the strengths of the adult with IDD, individuals may be more likely not only to obtain but also maintain employment. Furthermore, when parents are strong advocates, their adult children with IDD are more likely to understand how to navigate the service delivery system.

Additionally, parent advocacy can create more opportunities for adults with IDD to learn how to self-advocate (Bianco et al., 2009). Especially during adulthood, self-advocacy is considered a necessary life skill for individuals with IDD. Indeed, by having self-advocacy skills, adults with IDD may be better able to secure services especially when their parents are no longer able to advocate. When parents advocate for their adult offspring to be independent and to self-advocate, parents are modeling advocacy skills. Additionally, by witnessing their parents advocate by communicating their wants and needs, adults with IDD may have more opportunities to establish their own communication with professionals.

7.4.2 Effects for the Parent

For parents, advocacy during adulthood can be challenging. During adulthood, individuals should be developing their own livelihoods including finding meaningful employment, leisure activities, and education and training. However, for adults with IDD, this "launching" is not seamless, as adults with IDD often require support especially from their parents. Thus, while adult offspring typically leave their parents to develop their own livelihoods, adults with IDD may rely on their parents for continued advocacy (Petner-Arrey et al., 2015). Thus, parents may struggle with allowing their offspring to gain independence while still supporting their adult offspring by advocating for needed services.

Additionally, parents who are long-time advocates for their children report being frustrated and tired with the advocacy process especially when their offspring reach adulthood (Bianco et al., 2009; Petner-Arrey et al., 2015). Advocacy, in addition to general caregiving responsibilities, may fatigue and unduly stress many parents. With respect to adult services, advocacy may be especially stressful as parents may be confronted with getting their children on waiting lists for those services, often without any knowledge of how long until those services will become available (Hanley-Maxwell et al., 1995). Given that parents of adult offspring are older, combining the fatigue and stress of advocacy with the worsening health of aging parents may further negatively impact their caregiving abilities.

8. DISCUSSION

From these studies, it seems that parents advocate over the course of their offspring's life with varying parent and child outcomes. Although few studies have examined parent advocacy, this review provides an important foundation for understanding advocacy across the lifespan as well as directions for future research. Below, we outline similarities and differences regarding the need for, methods of, and effects of advocacy over the lifespan. Then, we outline directions for future research including conducting research with diverse populations, examining aging and advocacy, and comparing parent versus self-advocacy. See Table 2 for a synthesis of advocacy across the lifespan.

Table 2 Need, Methods, and Effect of Advocacy Across the Lifespan

	Early Childhood	School-Based Services	Transition	Adult Services
Need for advocacy	• Early childhood services are crucial for long-term progress • Individuals with (vs. Without) IDD have more needs and concerns • Transition from an IFSP to an IEP • After receiving a diagnosis, parents feel lost • Inequity in accessing services	• Poor experiences with school • Inaccessibility of safeguards • Cost of services • Lack of cultural responsiveness • Cultural expectations of advocacy • Schools are out of compliance with IDEA	• Dissatisfaction with transition services • Shift from school to adult services • Difficult to find adult and transition services • Poor communication and disrespectful treatment by the school	• Limited funding for adult services • Waiting lists for services lead to no progress for the child • Fragmented service delivery system • Aging parents
Methods of advocacy	• Attend parent support groups • Learn about child's diagnosis • Learn about special education law	• Use intuition • Rely on knowledge of disability • Apply special education rights • Encourage systems change	• Coordinate services • Learn from other parents and professionals • Learn about adult services	• Train providers • Mentor providers • Collaborate with agencies • Evaluate and monitor services

(Continued)

Table 2 Need, Methods, and Effect of Advocacy Across the Lifespan—cont'd

	Early Childhood	School-Based Services	Transition	Adult Services
	• Bring special education advocates • Report concerns • Question professionals • Request assistance from professionals	• Contact the office for civil rights • Make unannounced visits to the school • Engage in collective advocacy • Participate in IEP meetings • Communicate with the school (e.g., phone calls, meetings, letters, media reports)	• Seek out services • Contact professionals • Demand services • Use information and support groups	• Teach child skills • Teach adult offspring to self-advocate
Effect of advocacy	• Increases parent empowerment • Increases intimidation among teachers • Increases parent expectations for professionals to advocate	• Increases inclusion of the child • Increases parent stress • Increases parent and school fiscal costs • Increases parent discomfort • Harms family-school partnerships	• Increases transition services and post-school outcomes for individuals with IDD • Increases parent stress and anxiety	• Increase employment opportunities for adult offspring • Increase self-advocacy opportunities for adult offspring • Increase parent struggle with detachment from adult offspring • Increase frustration and fatigue for parents

8.1 Similarities and Differences Regarding the Need for Advocacy Across the Lifespan

8.1.1 Similarities

Across the lifespan, there is a persistent need for parent advocacy due to the importance of services for individuals with IDD. Regardless of the time period, individuals with IDD may need services to forge meaningful progress whether such progress relates to pre-academic skills (as in early childhood) or post-school outcomes (as in adulthood). Additionally, across each time period, there are barriers to parent advocacy. Indiscriminate of child age, parents face difficult conditions in advocacy related to limited available and accessible information and lack of direction or guidance. Also, for minority and/or low-income families, advocacy is especially difficult across the lifespan. Indeed, such families face even greater barriers with respect to communication, disrespectful treatment, and insufficient information.

8.1.2 Differences

Although the need for advocacy is consistent throughout the life of the individual with IDD, some of the reasons advocacy is needed are different. For example, parents of school-aged children may advocate for services that are expensive. Because each child is entitled to a FAPE, schools may not refuse services due to fiscal costs. Thus, although there is inadequate federal funding of IDEA, schools cannot use cost as a way to refuse services. However, in adult services, cost can be a factor in securing services. For example, parents may advocate for long-term services and supports via the HCBS Medicaid waiver. However, partly because adult services are driven by an eligibility-based system, many states have inadequate funding mechanisms and waiting lists for HCBS services. Indeed, in adult services, cost can be a prohibitive factor in providing services.

Another difference with respect to the need for advocacy relates to where services are housed. For children aged 0–22, services are accorded by IDEA and, primarily, housed within the school system (with the exception of early intervention services which are housed in provider agencies). However, as individuals with IDD transition into adulthood, services are no longer housed within a single agency. Instead, services are scattered among different agencies along with varying eligibility criteria, timelines, services offered, and funding schemes. Thus, as the individual with IDD ages, it becomes more difficult to locate, apply for, and receive appropriate services. The need for advocacy expands to include coordinating services across agencies.

8.1.3 Summary of the Need for Advocacy Across the Lifespan

For individuals with disabilities to receive services, parent advocacy is needed across the lifespan. Further, barriers to advocacy persist across time; some barriers are similar (e.g., lack of communication with professionals, limited access to information), while other barriers vary with age (e.g., funding mechanisms for services and the location of service providers). Not considered, though, is how the need for advocacy varies with respect to the duration of advocacy. Specifically, within a 22-year time span, three time periods were discussed (early childhood, school-based, and transition). Individuals with IDD spend the majority of their lives needing adult services. Yet, the biggest barriers to advocacy (e.g., lack of funding and fragmented service systems) are most—if not only—present in adult services. Given the longevity of adult services as well as the difficult conditions for advocacy and obtaining services, it seems that future research should consider understanding and encouraging parent advocacy for adults with IDD.

8.2 Similarities and Differences Regarding Methods of Advocacy Across the Lifespan

8.2.1 Similarities

Regardless of age, parents reported needing information and knowledge to advocate for services. Parents became informed by attending parent support groups and sharing information with parents and professionals. Specifically, parents sought knowledge about service delivery systems, and available services and agencies. Using this knowledge, parents advocated for services for their offspring.

8.2.2 Differences

Although, throughout the lifespan, parents seek information to advocate for their offspring, in adulthood (versus earlier stages) parents use their knowledge to educate others (not just to educate themselves to advocate). In adulthood, parents advocate by educating providers about their child and related needs and services. Perhaps because early childhood, school-based, and some transition services are primarily housed within one educational policy (i.e., IDEA), some educational professionals may already know the parent and child. Conversely, in the adult system, individuals with IDD (and their parents) are entering the system anew. Adult service professionals have no previous experience with or knowledge of the individual with IDD. Additionally, turnover in adult services is high (Kozak, Kersten, Schillmöller, & Nienhaus, 2013). Thus, when their child ages into the adult service delivery system, parents may need to advocate for services by educating professionals about their child.

Additionally, when the child is transitioning to and receiving adult services, parent advocacy includes collaborating with other agencies and coordinating services. Because services from ages 0–22 are housed within one system, under one policy, parents may not have to advocate across agencies or assist with coordinating services. However, for adulthood, parents need to become familiar with different agencies and learn how to coordinate all of their services.

Another key difference in advocacy relates to the context. In early childhood, school-based, and transition services, parents primarily reported advocating within meetings, namely IFSP and IEP meetings. Such meetings are the primary forums wherein services are discussed. For adult services, there is no clear forum for advocacy. For example, for SSI, parents may not have annual, in-person meetings with the Social Security Administration to discuss financial assistance. Thus, it seems that advocacy for adults with IDD is fragmented.

8.2.3 Summary of the Methods of Advocacy Across the Lifespan

To date, there is no universally agreed upon measure of advocacy. From this study, it is clear that knowledge is essential to parent advocacy regardless of the age of the child. Aside from knowledge, however, few advocacy methods seemed to transcend child age. The lack of uniformity regarding methods of advocacy presents instrumentation challenges. Namely, since advocacy strategies change over time, there may be no accurate, global measure of advocacy. Instead, future research should consider developing an operational definition of advocacy for different time periods of the child. In this way, measures of advocacy may be more sensitive and reliable.

8.3 Similarities and Differences Regarding the Effect of Advocacy Across the Lifespan

8.3.1 Similarities

Parent advocacy seems to have positive outcomes for offspring with IDD. At each stage of life, parent advocacy seems to help the individual with IDD. Such child effects included access to inclusive classrooms, more services, and better post-school outcomes. Thus, it seems that parent advocacy is effective in meeting the needs of individuals with IDD.

Also, with the exception of early childhood, advocacy seems to increase parent stress. Such stress may be due to the fiscal cost of advocacy, parent–school conflict, or, as in adulthood, growing tired and frustrated with advocacy. Thus, while parent advocacy may improve child outcomes, there are some negative outcomes with respect to parent well-being.

8.3.2 Differences

Not until adulthood does advocacy seem to lead to increased self-advocacy outcomes. Given that the transition process is intended to empower and educate the individual with IDD to self-advocate, it seems strange not to see self-advocacy as an outcome of parent advocacy. Extending beyond transition, self-advocacy should always be an outcome of parent advocacy. Borrowing from the disability studies literature, advocacy has been a central tenet in securing civil rights for individuals with disabilities (Shapiro, 1994). Most notably, "nothing about us, without us" is a key message for advocacy in the disability field (Charlton, 1998). Yet, self-advocacy is not mentioned as an outcome until adulthood. It seems that, even beginning in early childhood, opportunities for self-advocacy as a result of parent advocacy should be present.

8.3.3 Summary of the Effect of Advocacy Across the Lifespan

Over time, parent advocacy may have positive outcomes for offspring with IDD but result in greater stress for parents. In tandem with the need to operationally define and measure advocacy, it is also important to empirically measure the effect of advocacy especially with respect to parent and child outcomes. Specifically, research is needed to understand whether advocacy can have such mixed effects for parents and children. If the effect of advocacy increases parent stress but also increases positive outcomes for the child, perhaps advocacy training interventions need to include stress-based reduction components to help alleviate the negative impact on parent well-being.

8.4 Directions for Future Research

8.4.1 Need for Research About Culturally Diverse Families

From this review, it is clear that the need for advocacy and methods of advocacy are different for minority and/or low-income families. Unfortunately, in the special education literature, cultural differences are largely ignored (Burke, 2012). Indeed, special education studies often combine minority families into the category *culturally and linguistically diverse* (Turnbull et al., 2015). However, individual cultures are important. For example, when considering Latino families, *confianza* (social) support (Zuniga, 1992) and familism (Cortés, 1995) may relate to advocacy. For African American families, religiousness, single parenting, and extended family may impact advocacy (McAdoo, 2002; Rogers-Dulan & Blacher, 1995). In addition, Latino and African American families may also encounter similar barriers (e.g., discrimination and socioeconomic status, Spencer, Harpalani, & Dell-Angelo, 2002) to advocacy. Below, we outline the need for further research among African American and Latino families as two sample populations; notably, more research is needed about parent advocacy across all diverse populations.

8.4.2 Research About Advocacy Among African American Families

For decades, African American parents of children with IDD have experienced discrimination (Green & Darity, 2010; McAdoo, 2002). The power differential between African American parents and the school contributes to poor educational experiences and to deficit views of African American families (Burkett, Morris, Manning-Courtney, Anthony, & Shambley-Ebron, 2015). Further, African American (vs. White and Latino) families are more dissatisfied with special education services (Hernandez, Harry, Newman, & Cameto, 2008). Such dissatisfaction may be related to inequity in resources and expectations about parent involvement (Williams, 2007). Given the historical discrimination toward African American families, it is especially crucial to examine parent advocacy within this population with respect to the need for advocacy, methods of advocacy, and effect of advocacy.

8.4.3 Research About Advocacy Among Latino Families

Latino families also face obstacles in advocacy. For example, special education documents are only available in English (Shapiro et al., 2004) and, because of the jargon in IEP meetings, most translators do not accurately interpret the dialogue (Hughes et al., 2002). As a result, Latino families are often relegated to listening roles. Further, Latino (vs. White) families of children with IDD obtain fewer special education services (Magaña et al., 2013). Language proficiency, immigration status, and ethnic identity may also impact how Latino families relate to the educational system (Phinney, 1996). For example, parents who immigrated from Mexico wherein institutionalization of individuals with disabilities is common (Rosenthal, Jehn, & Galvan, 2010) may struggle to advocate within the American educational system which values inclusive education. Such barriers highlight the need to especially examine advocacy among Latino families of individuals with IDD.

8.4.4 Research About Advocacy for Aging Parents

Parents report being tired, frustrated, and stressed due to advocacy. Coupled with their own health and daily caregiving responsibilities for their offspring, advocacy may introduce additional stress to parents. For aging parents who face their own declining health (Hodapp et al., 2016), advocacy and related stress may worsen their caregiving abilities. Thus, future research may be needed to examine the relation between stress and advocacy among aging parents of individuals with IDD.

Additionally, unlike advocacy at earlier stages of life, in adulthood, parents may not only be advocating for current supports but also for future services for their adult offspring. For example, currently, more than 75% of adults with IDD live with their aging parents (Fujiura, 2014). Thus, although housing supports may not currently be needed for individuals with IDD, parents may need to advocate for future housing supports to be in place when the parent can no longer caregive and/or co-reside with the individual with IDD.

There are few studies that have examined advocacy among aging adults. However, from the aging and disability literature, it is clear that future planning is among the highest unmet needs for aging parents (Heller & Factor, 1991). Yet, fewer than half of families report engaging in future planning (Freedman, Krauss, & Seltzer, 1997). Thus, there is a disconnect between desiring to plan for the future and actually planning. Research is needed to understand whether parents are advocating for future supports and, if not, the barriers to advocating for future services.

With respect to aging parents, it is also important to consider siblings and their advocacy role. Many siblings anticipate transitioning to caregiving roles (Burke, Taylor, Urbano, & Hodapp, 2012; Heller & Arnold, 2010). By becoming caregivers for their brothers and sisters with IDD, adult siblings will need to learn how to advocate for services. In a study about sibling advocacy, siblings reported advocating for their brothers and sisters in various ways (Burke, Arnold, & Owen, 2015). However, siblings also reported struggling to understand the adult service delivery system and advocate for adult services. Thus, research is needed to determine how parents can enable their offspring without IDD to advocate for their adult children with IDD.

8.4.5 Research About Parent Versus Self-Advocacy

Finally, research is needed about parent versus self-advocacy. As noted among parents of transition-aged youth and adults with IDD, it is crucial to teach individuals with IDD to self-advocate. However, the ways in which parents teach their family members to self-advocate are unclear. Kim and Turnbull (2004) discussed ways to integrate person–centered planning and family-centered planning to become person–family interdependent planning. Although not the same as advocacy, these two types of planning show that both the individual with IDD and the family need to be a part of the planning process and jointly choose services, exercise their rights, and attain goals. Yet, it is unclear what happens when the individual with IDD and the parent have different choices and preferences.

Although not discussed in special education literature, self-advocacy groups have begun to highlight the potential tension between self-advocates and parents of adults with IDD (Ashkenazy, 2009). For example, parents may advocate within the medical model of disability. Upon receiving a diagnosis from a physician, a parent may identify the "deficits" of the child and advocate for services to address such deficits. Self-advocates, however, may work from a social model of disability. In this framework, disability is socially constructed; disability does not inherently include deficits that need to be addressed by services and intervention. Thus, while parents are advocating for services to address the "needs" of their offspring, self-advocates may advocate for social change and acceptance of disability.

Further, clarity is needed to understand how parents enable their offspring to self-advocate. For many parents, watching their adult offspring with IDD become more independent can be difficult as parents can be overprotective (Beck, Daley, Hastings, & Stevenson, 2004). Indeed, adult siblings of individuals with IDD report that their parents are often overprotective (Burke, Fish, & Lawton, 2015). Research is needed to determine whether and how parents transition their advocacy roles for their children to become self-advocates.

9. SUMMARY

Although parent advocacy has been instrumental in individuals with IDD obtaining services, few studies have examined parent advocacy across the lifespan. In this review, we identified similarities and differences with respect to the need for, methods of, and effects of parent advocacy. Given the limited literature about parent advocacy, it is clear that more research is needed to examine advocacy at different age periods of individuals with

IDD. Research is particularly needed to examine advocacy among underserved families as well as how parent and self-advocacy align. To this end, we offered several directions for future research. We hope that this review serves as a jumping off point to better understand parent advocacy across the lifespan.

REFERENCES

Ahearn, E. M. (2001). *The involvement of lay advocates in due process hearings. Quick turn around (QTA)*. Alexandria, VA: National Association of State Directors of Special Education (ERIC Document Reproduction Service No. ED 458753).

Albrecht, S. F., Skiba, R. J., Losen, D. J., Chung, C., & Middleberg, L. (2011). Federal policy on disproportionality in special education: is it moving us forward? *Journal of Disability Policy Studies, 23*, 14—25.

Allen, D. A., & Hudd, S. S. (1987). Are we professionalizing parents? Weighing the benefits and pitfalls. *Mental Retardation, 25*, 133—139.

Ashkenazy, E. (2009). *Parents in the autism world*. Retrieved from http://autisticadvocacy.org/2009/12/parents-in-the-autism-world/.

Balcazar, F. E., Keys, C. B., Bertram, J. F., & Rizzo, T. (1996). Advocate development in the field of developmental disabilities: a data-based conceptual model. *Mental Retardation, 34*, 341—352.

Banach, M., Iudice, J., Conway, L., & Couse, L. J. (2010). Family support and empowerment: post autism diagnosis support group for parents. *Social Work With Groups, 33*, 69—83.

Barnett, D., Clements, M., Kaplan-Estrin, M., & Fialka, J. (2003). Building new dreams: supporting parents' adaption to their child with special needs. *Infants and Young Children, 16*, 184—200.

Beck, A., Daley, D., Hastings, R. P., & Stevenson, J. (2004). Mothers' expressed emotion towards children with and without intellectual disabilities. *Journal of Intellectual Disability Research, 48*, 628—638.

Bianco, M., Garrison-Wade, D. F., Tobin, R., & Lehmann, J. P. (2009). Parents' perceptions of postschool years for young adults with developmental disabilities. *Intellectual and Developmental Disabilities, 47*, 186—196.

Boyer, L., & Lee, C. (2001). Converting challenge to success: supporting a new teacher of students with autism. *The Journal of Special Education, 35*, 75—83.

Braddock, D., Hemp, R., Rizzolo, M. C., Tanis, E. S., Haffer, L., & Wu, J. (2014). *The state of the states in developmental disabilities, 2014: Emerging from the great recession*. Washington, DC: American Association on Intellectual and Developmental Disabilities.

Burke, M. M. (2012). Examining family involvement in regular and special education: lessons to be learned from both sides. *International Review of Research in Developmental Disabilities, 43*, 187—218.

Burke, M. M., Arnold, C. K., & Owen, A. (2015). The role of advocacy among siblings of individuals with intellectual and developmental disabilities. *Inclusion, 3*, 162—175.

Burke, M. M., Fish, T., & Lawton, K. (2015). A comparative analysis of adult siblings' perceptions toward caregiving. *Intellectual and Developmental Disabilities, 53*, 143—157.

Burke, M. M., & Goldman, S. E. (2015). The associated factors of mediation and due process among families of students with autism spectrum disorder. *Journal of Autism and Developmental Disorders, 45*, 1345—1353.

Burke, M. M., & Hodapp, R. M. (2014). Relating stress of mothers of children with developmental disabilities to family-school partnerships. *Intellectual and Developmental Disabilities, 52,* 13—23.

Burke, M. M., & Hodapp, R. M. (2016). The nature, correlates, and conditions of advocacy in special education. *Exceptionality, 24,* 137—150.

Burke, M. M., Taylor, J. L., & Patton, K. A. (2016). *Family support: a literature review of families of adolescents with disabilities* (under review).

Burke, M. M., Taylor, J. L., Urbano, R. C., & Hodapp, R. M. (2012). Predictors of future caregiving by siblings of individuals with intellectual and developmental disabilities. *American Journal on Intellectual and Developmental Disabilities, 117,* 33—47.

Burkett, K., Morris, E., Manning-Courtney, P., Anthony, J., & Shambley-Ebron, D. (2015). African American families on autism diagnosis and treatment: the influence of culture. *Journal of Autism and Developmental Disorders, 45,* 3244—3254.

Cartledge, G., Kea, C., & Simmons-Reed, E. (2002). Serving culturally diverse children with serious emotional disturbance and their families. *Journal of Child and Family Studies, 11,* 113—126.

Charlton, J. I. (1998). *Nothing about us without us: Disability oppression and empowerment.* University of California Press.

Cohen, S. (2013). Advocacy for the 'abandonados': harnessing cultural beliefs for Latino families and their children with intellectual disabilities. *Journal of Policy and Practice in Intellectual Disabilities, 10,* 71—78.

Cooney, B. F. (2002). Exploring perspectives on transition of youth with disabilities: voices of young adults, parents, and professionals. *Mental Retardation, 40*(6), 425—435.

Cortés, D. E. (1995). Variations in familism in two generations of Puerto Ricans. *Hispanic Journal of Behavioral Sciences, 17,* 249—255.

Council for Exceptional Children. (2014). Retrieved at http://www.policyinsider.org/2014/03/cec-endorsed-legislation-introduced-to-fully-fund-idea.html.

Drake, J., Couse, L. J., DiNapoli, P., & Banach, M. (2008). Interdisciplinary best practice: a case study of family and school support for a young child with ASD. *International Journal of Nursing in Intellectual and Developmental Disabilities, 4,* 1—3.

Emerson, E. (2007). Poverty and people with intellectual disabilities. *Mental Retardation and Developmental Disability Research Reviews, 13,* 107—113.

Fish, W. W. (2006). Perceptions of parents of students with autism towards the IEP meeting: a case study of one family support group chapter. *Education, 127,* 56—68.

Fish, W. W. (2008). The IEP meeting: perceptions of parents of students who receive special education services. *Preventing School Failure, 53,* 8—14.

Freedman, R., Krauss, M., & Seltzer, M. M. (1997). Aging parents' residential plans for adults with mental retardation. *Mental Retardation, 35,* 114—123.

Friesen, B. J., & Huff, B. (1990). Parents and professionals as advocacy partners. *Preventing School Failure, 34,* 31—39.

Fujiura, G. T. (2014). The political arithmetic of disability and the American family: a demographic perspective. *Family Relations, 63,* 7—19.

Gill, T., & Renwick, R. (2007). Family quality of life and service delivery for families with adults who have developmental disabilities. *Journal of Developmental Disabilities, 13,* 13—36.

Green, T. L., & Darity, W. A. (2010). Under the skin: using theories from biology and the social sciences to explore the mechanisms behind the Black-White health gap. *American Journal of Public Health, 100,* 36—40.

Guralnick, M. J. (2000). Early childhood intervention: evolution of a system. *Focus on Autism and Other Developmental Disorders, 15,* 68—79.

Guralnick, M. J. (2005). Early intervention for children with intellectual disabilities: current knowledge and future prospects. *Journal of Applied Research in Intellectual Disabilities, 18,* 313—324.

Hanley-Maxwell, C., Whitney-Thomas, J., & Pogoloff, S. M. (1995). The second shock: a qualitative study of parents' perspectives and needs during their child's transition from school to adult life. *Research and Practice for Persons with Severe Disabilities, 20,* 3—15.

Hanushek, E. A., Kain, J. F., & Rivkin, S. G. (2002). Inferring program effects for special populations: does special education raise achievement for students with disabilities? *Review of Economics and Statistics, 84,* 584—599.

Harry, B. (2002). Trends and issues in serving culturally diverse families of children with disabilities. *The Journal of Special Education, 36,* 131—138.

Haveman, M., van Berkum, G., Reijnders, R., & Heller, T. (1997). Differences in service needs, time demands, and caregiving burden among parents of persons with mental retardation across the life cycle. *Family Relations, 46,* 417—425.

Heller, T., & Arnold, C. K. (2010). Siblings of adults with developmental disabilities: psychosocial outcomes, relationships, and future planning. *Journal of Policy and Practice in Intellectual Disabilities, 7,* 16—25.

Heller, T., & Factor, A. (1991). Permanency planning for adults with mental retardation living with family caregivers. *American Journal on Mental Retardation, 96,* 163—176.

Hernandez, J. E., Harry, B., Newman, L., & Cameto, R. (2008). Survey of family involvement in and satisfaction with the Los Angeles Unified School District special education process. *Journal of Special Education Leadership, 21,* 84—93.

Hetherington, S. A., Durant-Jones, L., Johnson, K., Nolan, K., Smith, E., Taylor-Brown, S., & Tuttle, J. (2010). The lived experiences of adolescents with disabilities and their parents in transition planning. *Focus on Autism and Other Developmental Disabilities, 25*(3), 163—172.

Hodapp, R. M., Burke, M. M., Finley, C. I., & Urbano, R. C. (2016). Family caregiving of aging adults with Down syndrome. *Journal of Policy and Practice in Intellectual Disabilities, 13,* 181—189.

Hughes, M. T., Valle-Riestra, D. M., & Arguelles, M. E. (2002). Experiences of Latino families with their child's special education program. *Multicultural Perspectives, 4,* 11—17.

Irvin, D. W., McBee, M., Boyd, B. A., Hume, K., & Odom, S. L. (2012). Child and family factors associated with the use of services for preschoolers with autism spectrum disorder. *Research in Autism Spectrum Disorders, 6,* 565—572.

Kalyanpur, M., Harry, B., & Skrtic, T. (2000). Equity and advocacy: expectations of culturally diverse families' participation in special education. *International Journal of Disability, Development, and Education, 47,* 119—136.

Kessler, J. M. (2015). Applying for supplemental security income (SSI) for individuals with intellectual and developmental disabilities: family and service coordinator experiences. *Intellectual and Developmental Disabilities, 53,* 42—57.

Kim, K. H., & Turnbull, A. P. (2004). Transition to adulthood for students with severe intellectual disabilities: shifting toward person-family interdependent planning. *Research and Practice for Persons with Severe Disabilities, 29,* 53—57.

Kohler, P. D. (1996). *Taxonomy for transition programming: Linking research and practice.* Champaign: University of Illinois at Urbana-Champaign, Transition Research Institute.

Kozak, A., Kersten, M., Schillmöller, Z., & Nienhaus, A. (2013). Psychosocial work-related predictors and consequences of personal burnout among staff working with people with intellectual disabilities. *Research in Developmental Disabilities, 34,* 102—115.

Kraemer, B. R., McIntyre, L. L., & Blacher, J. (2003). Quality of life for young adults with mental retardation during transition. *Mental Retardation, 41*(4), 250—262.

Leiter, V., & Krauss, M. W. (2004). Claims, barriers, and satisfaction: parents' requests for additional special education services. *Journal of Disability Policy Studies, 15,* 135—146.

Liptak, G. S., Benzoni, L. B., Mruzek, D. W., Nolan, K. W., Thingvoll, M. A., Wade, C. M., & Fryer, G. E. (2008). Disparities in diagnosis and access to health services for children with autism: data from the National Survey of Children's Health. *Journal of Developmental and Behavioral Pediatrics, 29*, 152–160.

Lo, L. (2005). Barriers to successful partnerships with Chinese-speaking parents of children with disabilities in urban schools. *Multiple Voices, 8*, 84–95.

Magaña, S. M., Lopez, K., Aguinaga, A., & Morton, H. (2013). Access to diagnosis and treatment services among Latino children with autism spectrum disorders. *Intellectual and Developmental Disabilities, 51*, 141–153.

Mandic, C. G., Rudd, R., Hehir, T., & Acevedo-Garcia, D. (2012). Readability of special education procedural safeguards. *Journal of Special Education, 45*, 195–203.

Mazzotti, V. L., Test, D. W., & Mustian, A. L. (2014). Secondary transition evidence-based practices and predictors: implications for policymakers. *Journal of Disability Policy Studies, 25*, 5–18.

McAdoo, H. P. (2002). In M. Bornstein (Ed.), *African American parenting in handbook of parenting*. Batlimore, Maryland: Lawrence Erlbaum Associates.

McIntyre, L. L., Eckert, T. L., Fiese, B. H., DiGennaro, F. D., & Wildenger, L. K. (2006). Transition to kindergarten: family experiences and involvement. *Early Childhood Education Journal, 35*, 83–88.

McWilliam, R. A., Maxwell, K. L., & Sloper, K. M. (1999). Beyond 'involvement': are elementary schools ready to be family-centered? *School Psychology Review, 28*, 378–394.

Miron, C. (2012). The parent experience: when a child is diagnosed with childhood apraxia of speech. *Communication Disorders Quarterly, 33*, 96–110.

Montes, G., Halterman, J. S., & Magyar, C. I. (2009). Access to and satisfaction with school and community health services for US children with ASD. *Pediatrics, 124*, 407–413.

Mueller, T. G. (2009). Alternative dispute resolution: a new agenda for special education policy. *Journal of Disability Policy Studies, 20*, 4–13.

Munn-Joseph, M. S., & Gavin-Evans, K. (2008). Urban parents of children with special needs: advocating for their children through social networks. *Urban Education, 43*, 378–393.

Neeley-Barnes, S. L., & Dia, D. A. (2008). Families of children with disabilities: a review of the literature and recommendations for interventions. *Journal of Early and Intensive Behavior Intervention, 5*, 93–107.

Park, J., & Turnbull, A. P. (2001). Quality of partnerships in service provision for Korean American parents of children with disabilities: a qualitative inquiry. *Research and Practice for Persons With Severe Disabilities, 26*, 158–170.

Pearson, J. (2015). Disparities in diagnoses and access to services for African American children with autism spectrum disorder. *DADD Online Journal, 2*, 52–65.

Petner-Arrey, J., Howell-Moneta, A., & Lysaght, R. (2015). Facilitating employment opportunities for adults with intellectual and developmental disability through parents and social networks. *Disability and Rehabilitation, 2*, 1–7.

Phinney, J. S. (1996). Understanding ethnic diversity. *The American Behavioral Scientist, 40*, 143–148.

Plunge, M. M., & Kratochwill, T. R. (1995). Parental knowledge, involvement, and satisfaction with their child's special education services. *Special Services in the Schools, 10*, 113–138.

Prouty, R. W., Smith, G., & Lakin, K. C. (2006). *Residential services for persons with developmental disabilities: Status and trends through 2005*. Minneapolis: Research and Training Center on Community Living, University of Minnesota.

Public Agenda. (2002). *When it's your own child: A report on special education from the families who use it*. New York, NY: (Author).

Rao, S. S. (2000). Perspectives of an African American mother on parent-professional relationships in special education. *Mental Retardation, 38*, 475–488.

Research and Training Center on Community Living. (2002). *Policies and resources related to waiting lists of persons with mental retardation and related developmental disabilities.* Found on September 1, 2014 at http://www.ici.umn.edu/index.php?products/view/367.

Rice, G. B., & Lenihan, S. (2005). Early intervention in auditory/oral deaf education: parent and professional perspectives. *The Volta Review, 105,* 73−96.

Rogers-Dulan, J., & Blacher, J. (1995). African American families, religion, and disability: a conceptual framework. *Mental Retardation, 33,* 226−238.

Rosenthal, E., Jehn, E., & Galvan, S. (2010). Abandoned and disappeared: Mexico's segregation and abuse of children and adults with disabilities. *Disability Rights International & Comision Mexicana de Defensa y Promocion de los Derechos Humanos.* Retrieved from http://www.disabilityrightsintl.org/work/country-projects/mexico/.

Seven, K. H., & Zirkel, P. A. (2002). In the matter of Arons: construction of IDEA's lay advocate provision too narrow? *Georgetown Journal on Poverty Law and Policy, 9,* 193−223.

Shapiro, J. P. (1994). *No pity: People with disabilities forging a new civil rights movement.* Three Rivers Press.

Shapiro, J., Monzo, L. D., Rueda, R., Gomez, J. A., & Blacher, J. (2004). Alienated advocacy: perspectives of Latina mothers of young adults with developmental disabilities on service systems. *Mental Retardation, 42,* 37−54.

Simon, J. B. (2006). Perceptions of the IEP requirement. *Teacher Education and Special Education, 29,* 225−235.

Smith, M. A., Gundler, D., Casey, M., & Jones, T. (2011). Sustaining family involvement in Part C policy and services: successes and challenges moving forward. *Zero to Three, 31,* 39−44.

Soodak, L. C., & Erwin, E. J. (2000). Valued member or tolerated participant: parents' experiences in inclusive early childhood settings. *The Journal of the Association for Persons with Severe Handicaps, 25,* 29−41.

Spann, S. J., Kohler, F. W., & Soenksen, D. (2003). Examining parents' involvement in and perceptions of special education services: an interview with families in a parent support group. *Focus on Autism and Other Developmental Disabilities, 18,* 228−237.

Spencer, M. B., Harpalani, V., & Dell-Angelo, T. (2002). Structural racism and community health: a theory-driven models for identity intervention. *African American Education: Race, Community, Inequality, and Achievement, 259.*

Stanley, S. L. G. (2015). The advocacy efforts of African American Mothers of children with disabilities in rural special education: considerations for school professionals. *Rural Special Education Quarterly, 34,* 3−17.

Taylor, J. L., & Hodapp, R. M. (2012). Doing nothing: adults with disabilities with no daily activities and their siblings. *American Journal on Intellectual and Developmental Disabilities, 117,* 67−79.

Thomas, K. C., Ellis, A. R., McLaurin, C., Daniels, J., & Morrissey, J. P. (2007). Access to care for autism-related services. *Journal of Autism and Developmental Disorders, 37,* 1902−1912.

Timmons, J. C., Whitney-Thomas, J., McIntyre, J. P., Jr., Butterworth, J., & Allen, D. (2004). Managing service delivery systems and the role of parents during their children's transitions. *Journal of Rehabilitation, 70*(2), 19−26.

Trainor, A. A. (2010). Diverse approaches to parent advocacy during special education home- school interactions: identification and use of cultural and social capital. *Remedial and Special Education, 31,* 34−47.

Trohanis, P. L. (2008). Progress in providing services to young children with special needs and their families: an overview to and update on the implementation of the Individuals with Disabilities Education Act (IDEA). *Journal of Early Intervention, 30,* 140−151.

Turnbull, H. R. (2005). Individuals with disabilities education act reauthorization accountability and personal responsibility. *Remedial and Special Education, 26,* 320−326.

Turnbull, A., Turnbull, R., Erwin, E. J., Soodak, L. C., & Shogren, K. A. (2015). *Families, professionals, and exceptionality: Positive outcomes through partnerships and trust* (7th ed.). Upper Saddle River, NJ: Pearson.

Wang, M., Mannan, H., Poston, D., Turnbull, A. P., & Summers, J. A. (2004). Parents' perceptions of advocacy activities and their impact on family quality of life. *Research and Practice for Persons with Severe Disabilities, 29,* 144—155.

Welchons, L. W., & McIntyre, L. L. (2015). The transition to kindergarten for children with and without disabilities: an investigation of parent and teacher concerns and involvement. *Topics in Early Childhood Special Education, 35,* 52—62.

Williams, E. R. (2007). Unnecessary and Unjustified: African-American parental perceptions of special education. *The Educational Forum, 71,* 250—261.

Wolff, J. L., & Kasper, J. D. (2006). Caregivers of frail elders: updated a national profile. *The Gerontologist, 46,* 344—356.

Young, J., Morgan, R. L., Callow-Heusser, C. A., & Lindstrom, L. (2016). The effects of parent training on knowledge of transition services for students with disabilities. *Career Development and Transition for Exceptional Individuals, 39*(2), 79—87.

Zirkel, P. A. (1994). Over-due process revisions for the individuals with disabilities education act. *Montana Law Review, 55,* 403—414.

Zuniga, M. E. (1992). *Latino families: Developing cross cultural competence.* Baltimore, Maryland: Paul H. Brookes.

CHAPTER SEVEN

Victimization of Individuals With Intellectual and Developmental Disabilities Across the Lifespan

M.H. Fisher*[,1], C. Corr[§], L. Morin*
*Michigan State University, East Lansing, MI, United States
§Vanderbilt University, Nashville, TN, United States
[1]Corresponding author: E-mail: fishermh@msu.edu

Contents

International Review of Research in Developmental Disabilities, Volume 51
ISSN 2211-6095
http://dx.doi.org/10.1016/bs.irrdd.2016.08.001

© 2016 Elsevier Inc.
All rights reserved.

Abstract

Compared to those without disabilities, individuals with intellectual and developmental disabilities (IDD) are at increased risk of experiencing victimization across the lifespan. In this chapter, we discuss the progression of victimization from child abuse in early childhood, to bullying during the school-age years, and finally to criminal victimization in adulthood. We begin with a discussion of the notion that victimization is a lifelong concern for individuals with IDD. We then describe the methodological difficulties in establishing reliable definitions and prevalence rates for specific forms of victimization. After noting these limitations, we discuss three types of victimization in greater detail. In terms of child abuse, we discuss the prevalence of abuse among children with disabilities, while also discussing risk factors and potential prevention and intervention strategies. Next, we discuss the experiences of bullying of adolescents with IDD, while providing information on why these students are at increased risk and which prevention and intervention strategies might be implemented to reduce bullying of students with IDD. Finally, we discuss criminal forms of victimization experienced by adults with IDD, while noting specific risk factors that increase risk and the importance of prevention and intervention strategies. We end this chapter with a call for additional longitudinal victimization investigations to better understand the lifespan perspective of victimization and the relation between risk factors and experiences; an emphasis on the relation between disability etiology and experiences of victimization; and a focus on resilience and well-being of individuals with IDD who experience victimization.

1. INTRODUCTION

Although society has made significant progress toward the inclusion of individuals with intellectual and developmental disabilities (IDD) into schools and communities, such inclusion has not always been met with positive social acceptance and experiences (Mikton & Shakespeare, 2014). Indeed, even as fewer children with IDD are placed into institutions, as more students with IDD are taught within inclusive educational settings alongside same-aged peers, and as more inclusive residential, vocational, and post-secondary educational opportunities are developed for adults with IDD, such movement toward social and community participation brings forth risks along with the benefits. Just as inclusion leads to more social interactions, job opportunities, and community participation, it can also lead to victimization.

In this chapter, we tackle the issue of victimization experienced by individuals with IDD across the lifespan. Compared to those without disabilities, individuals with IDD are more likely to experience victimization. Such experiences are pervasive across the lifespan; while victimization may change form throughout life, the impact remains the same. Thus, rather than focusing on one form of victimization (e.g., child abuse, bullying) or one age group (e.g., adulthood), we designed this chapter to raise awareness of the issue of victimization as it is experienced for individuals with IDD throughout their lives. Specifically, we describe how victimization can take multiple forms, occur multiple times, and involve multiple perpetrators throughout the lives of individuals with IDD.

We organize the discussion around the progression of victimization from child abuse in early childhood, to bullying during the school-age years, to criminal victimization in adulthood. We begin by examining the notion that while victimization may change in form, it is a concern for individuals with IDD across the lifespan. We then note the difficulty in developing exact definitions and determining the exact prevalence of victimization. Next, we discuss in more detail three specific forms of victimization with respect to its estimated prevalence, risk factors, and prevention and intervention strategies for individuals with IDD. We end by describing future directions for research.

1.1 Victimization: A Lifespan Perspective

The term "abuse" often leads to the perception of a young child experiencing physical, sexual, or emotional abuse at the hands of a parent or other caregiver. In most situations, such a perception is accurate. For individuals with IDD, however, abuse extends far beyond early childhood and close caregivers. Thus, rather than using the term "abuse" to discuss the experiences of individuals with IDD, we use "victimization" to signify the importance of recognizing that abuse of individuals with IDD does not end when they reach a certain age.

In early childhood, young children with IDD (compared to those without disabilities) are at least 3.4 times more likely to experience child abuse and neglect (Sullivan & Knutson, 2000). As they age, the risk of abuse decreases for children without disabilities, but this is not necessarily the case for children with IDD (Sullivan & Knutson, 2000). Rather, while older children with IDD remain at risk of experiencing abuse at home, they also face the increased risk of experiencing bullying and peer victimization in school. Compared to the national average, students with IDD are at least 1.5 times more likely to experience bullying (Blake, Lund, Zhou, Kwok, & Benz, 2012). Again, while the risk of bullying decreases with age for individuals without disabilities, such risk of victimization does not decrease for youth with IDD. Rather, bullying changes form; from overt verbal bullying to more subtle ways of taking advantage of individuals with IDD, such as peer pressure (Fisher, Moskowitz, & Hodapp, 2012).

Finally, as they enter adulthood, individuals with IDD remain at risk of being taken advantage of. Such victimization comes not only at the hands of peers, but also from acquaintances, paid staff, and even family members (Fisher, Baird, Currey, & Hodapp, 2016). Adults with IDD are at least 12.8 times more likely to be robbed, 10.7 times more likely to be sexually assaulted, and 2.8 times more likely to be physically assaulted (Wilson & Brewer, 1992). Overall then, individuals with IDD are at risk for experiencing many types of victimization, including child abuse and neglect, physical and sexual assault, personal or property crimes, psychological abuse such as bullying or coercion, discrimination, and financial abuse (Fisher et al., 2012; Jawaid et al., 2012; Petitpierre, Masse, Martini-Willemin, & Delessert, 2013; Ticoll, 1994; White, Holland, Marsland, & Oakes, 2003).

1.2 Defining Victimization

Because victimization can take several forms, it is difficult to pin down one definition that truly encompasses all forms of victimization. Additionally, definitions of what constitutes each form of victimization vary among researchers, agencies, states, and other fields of inquiry. Indeed, the criteria used to determine whether abuse or victimization has occurred can vary considerably (Fisher, Hodapp, & Dykens, 2008). For example, the definition of child abuse differs based on whether it is defined by a medical professional, the legal system, or a researcher (Fisher et al., 2008). While doctors have a broader definition of child abuse that allows suspicions of abuse (based on visual evidence) to be reported, the legal system has a more narrow definition that requires further review of the evidence (including testimony) to substantiate the abuse and remove the child from the parents.

Researchers, on the other hand, must decide which definition of abuse they will include in their study: taking either a scoping review of all possible cases of abuse or a more narrow review of only substantiated cases that led to legal action. Choosing the type of reported abuse becomes even more complicated for disability researchers. Specifically, children with disabilities are often unable to report or describe their own abusive experiences leading to fewer substantiated cases of abuse of children with IDD (Fisher et al., 2008). Thus, if a researcher relies on substantiated cases of abuse, the majority of cases of abuse of children with IDD will likely be missed.

Further complicating the definition of victimization is that what some may consider social victimization (e.g., bullying/teasing) might not be a legally defined form of victimization (Luckasson, 1992; Nettelbeck & Wilson, 2001). For example, for most adolescents bullying is not considered a crime; yet, the Office for Civil Rights (OCR) recently indicated that bullying of students with a disability constitutes "disability-based harassment," which can result in legal ramifications (Office for Civil Rights, 2014). For the purposes of this chapter, we focus on types of victimization that fall into three broader forms, including child abuse, bullying, and criminal victimization (see Table 1 for definitions and examples).

Table 1 Definitions and Examples of Child Abuse, Bullying, and Adult Victimization

Type of Victimization	Definition	Specific Forms	Examples of Victimization
Child abuse	A recent act or failure to act on the part of a parent or caretaker, which results in death, serious physical or emotional harm, sexual abuse, or exploitation of a child		
		Physical abuse	Bruises, blisters, burns, cuts and scratches, internal injuries, brain damage, broken bones, sprains, dislocated joints
		Sexual abuse	Fondling or inappropriately touching a child

(Continued)

Table 1 Definitions and Examples of Child Abuse, Bullying, and Adult Victimization—cont'd

Type of Victimization	Definition	Specific Forms	Examples of Victimization
		Neglect	Leaving a child home alone
		Emotional abuse	Ignoring, isolating, terrorizing, or verbally assaulting a child
Bullying	Is the experience of aggressive behavior directed at a child from a peer		
		Physical bullying	Hitting, kicking, or spitting
		Relational bullying	Spreading rumors, threats, public embarrassment
		Verbal bullying	Teasing and taunting, harmful oral or written communication
		Damage to property	Theft, alteration, or damaging property
Criminal victimization	Victimization, including hate crimes that can or does lead to legal action against the perpetrator		
		Physical and sexual assault	Intentional act that causes a person to fear or experience physical harm, sexual contact or behavior without the explicit consent of the recipient
		Property crimes	Burglary, larceny, theft, motor vehicle theft, arson, vandalism

1.3 Determining the Prevalence of Victimization

Because of the unclear or inconsistent definitions of victimization and because not all forms are considered criminal (and are therefore not reported), it is often difficult to determine the true prevalence of specific forms of victimization for those with and without IDD. Further complicating the assessment of prevalence rates is that formal data collection systems do not always indicate whether a victim had a disability or what specific type of disability (Petersilia, 2001). Finally, even criminal victimization of individuals with IDD is not always reported (Petersilia, 2001). Factors influencing reporting to police include communication limitations (e.g., inability to report), dependency on the perpetrator (e.g., caregiver is the abuser), or fear of harm if a report is made (Hughes et al., 2012; Luckasson, 1992; Nosek, Clubb Foley, Hughes, & Howland, 2001).

Within the research literature, most information on victimization is collected through anecdotal accounts, case studies, or small samples (Atkinson & Ward, 2012; Horner-Johnson & Drum, 2006; Nettelbeck & Wilson, 2002). While these studies offer important information related to victimization, they are also limited by poor measurement systems. For example, because individuals with IDD might have a hard time recalling events from the past and rating items on Likert scales, they often have difficulty responding to items on self-report questionnaires (Finlay & Lyons, 2000). Additional concerns are raised, however, when other informants are asked to report abusive situations; caregivers might not know about the abuse or they might actually be the perpetrator of the abuse (Luckasson, 1992). As a result, it is likely that most data are an underestimate of the true prevalence of victimization of individuals with IDD (Nettelbeck & Wilson, 2002).

Still, the data we review in this chapter indicate, time and again, that individuals with IDD are at increased risk of experiencing victimization. It is vitally important that we understand these experiences, the risk factors related to these experiences, what we can do to prevent these situations, and how we can help support those who have been victimized.

2. CHILD ABUSE

Definitions of child maltreatment are largely driven by state law and regulations. The Child Abuse Prevention and Treatment Act (CAPTA),

(42 U.S.C. §5101), as amended by the CAPTA Reauthorization Act of 2010, defines child abuse and neglect as, at a minimum:

> Any recent act or failure to act on the part of a parent or caretaker which results in death, serious physical or emotional harm, sexual abuse or exploitation; or an act or failure to act, which presents an imminent risk of serious harm.

The four categories of child maltreatment include physical abuse, sexual abuse, neglect, and emotional abuse. Children commonly experience co-occurring types of maltreatment (i.e., physical, sexual, etc.), rather than just one form.

Physical abuse. Physical abuse is generally defined as "any nonaccidental physical injury to the child" and can include "striking, kicking, burning, or biting the child, or any action that results in a physical impairment of the child" (Child Welfare Information Gateway, 2014). Biological parents are the most common perpetrators, followed by a mother's boyfriend (defined as biologically unrelated and unmarried to the mother) (Esernio-Jenssen, Tai, & Kodsi, 2011). Perpetrators of physical abuse frequently cite inconsolable crying as a trigger that set off the abusive event (Starling, Holden, & Jenny, 1995). The incidence of physical abuse among children with disabilities happens at a rate 2.1 times the rate of children without IDD (Giardino, Lyn, & Giardino, 2009).

Sexual abuse. Sexual abuse involves any sexual activity with a child below the age of consent (this age varies by state). Sexual abuse includes penetration, touching, and noncontact such as exposure (Berliner, 2000). Girls are at a higher risk for sexual abuse than boys. Typically, the perpetrator involved in sexual abuse engages in a gradual process of sexualizing the relationship over time (Berliner & Conte, 1990). Sexual abuse reports among children with IDD are 1.75 times higher than the rate for children without disabilities (Newman, Christopher, & Berry, 2000).

Neglect. Child neglect represents the largest category of child maltreatment reported to child protective services. Although there is no single cause of child neglect, it exists when a child's basic needs are not being met (Dubowitz et al., 2011), making the assessment of neglect a complex process. Of victims medically neglected, 20.4% were under the age of one (US Department of Health and Human Services, 2010). Neglect is more likely to occur for children with IDD because they require more medical and physical care on a daily basis (Van IJzendoorn et al., 2011).

Emotional abuse. Emotional abuse is considered an injury to the psychological capacity or emotional stability of the child. Emotional abuse includes but is not limited to ignoring, rejecting, isolating, exploiting or corrupting, verbally assaulting, or terrorizing the child. Perpetrators typically include parents or other caregivers who are regularly responsible for the day-to-day care of the child (e.g., teacher, babysitter, etc.) (Garbarino, 1994). Typically, emotional abuse is noted by changes in behavior, emotional responses, or cognition. This can manifest in children as incidents of anxiety, depression, withdrawal, or aggressive behavior (US Department of Health & Human Services, 2016). The prevalence rate of emotional abuse for children without a disability is 18% (range of 11.5–25.8%), whereas for children with IDD the rate of emotional abuse is 27% (range of 11.1–46.0%) (Jones et al., 2012).

2.1 Abuse of Children With Intellectual and Developmental Disabilities

Early childhood (birth through 8 years of age), a period marked by rapid physical, cognitive, and social emotional development for children (Center on the Developing Child, 2007), is considered critical in supporting the overall health and well-being of children. It is also one of the most vulnerable periods for children. In 2014, approximately 3.2 million children were the subjects of at least one report of child abuse (US Department of Health and Human Services, 2016), with the likelihood of a child experiencing abuse decreasing as the child ages (Barnett, Miller-Perrin, & Perrin, 2011). Thus, children experience the highest rates of physical abuse during the first year of life (Reece, 2011); 13.2% of these children experienced abuse when they were less than one week old (US Department of Health and Human Services, 2010).

The connection between development and abuse in the first year of life further emphasizes early childhood as a critical period in which a child's development can be, but is not always, supported. The impact of child abuse is discussed in terms of physical, psychological, behavioral, and societal consequences. In these instances, a child's disability status can be considered both a risk factor and a consequence of experiencing child abuse. In reality, it is difficult to separate the types of impacts child abuse has on developing children (Child Welfare Information Gateway, 2013). Especially, for the youngest victims of child abuse, it is often difficult to determine if the child's disability was a result of abuse or if the abuse was a consequence of the child's preexisting disability.

2.2 Prevalence of Abuse of Children With Intellectual and Developmental Disabilities

In the child welfare system, children are considered to have a disability if they are diagnosed with an intellectual disability, emotional disturbance, visual or hearing impairment, learning disability, physical disability, behavioral problems, or another medical condition. The National Center on Child Abuse and Neglect reported the incidence of child maltreatment was twice as high for children with disabilities than for children without disabilities (US Department of Health and Human Services, 2010). Indeed, it is estimated that between 10% and 25% of children with IDD experience abuse (Sobsey, 1994). While the rates of specific forms of child abuse vary for children with disabilities (physical abuse 16.1%, sexual abuse 9.1%), neglect (71%) is the most common form of maltreatment (Erickson & Egeland, 1996). Similar to children without disabilities, the perpetrator of abuse to the child with IDD is most often a family member, but can also include other caregivers, professionals, and paraprofessionals (Prevent Child Abuse America, n.d.).

Signs of abuse for children with IDD are often the same as indicators of abuse for children in the general population. While identifying child abuse can be difficult to determine in general, identification is even more difficult for children with IDD, as physical signs and child reports are often overlooked or misinterpreted by caregivers in the child's life. For example, children with disabilities may exhibit behavioral indicators of abuse that might be misinterpreted as a manifestation of their disability and thus are not recognized by their caregivers as the child's inability to effectively and convincingly communicate what happened. Alternatively, if a child has visual or physical limitations, injuries resulting from physical abuse may be ignored and or attributed to clumsiness or accidents (Sobsey, 1994). As a result, the prevalence rates of abuse of children with IDD are likely underestimates.

2.3 Risk Factors for Abuse of Children With Intellectual and Developmental Disabilities

A young child's overall health status has been identified as a factor that affects a parent's ability to provide care for the child (Belsky & Vondra, 1989). As such, young children with disabilities are at a higher risk for experiencing abuse and neglect (Klerman, 1985). When a young child has a disability or delay, his or her daily needs can be more intense, resulting in a parent or caregiver feeling overwhelmed (Klerman, 1985; Sullivan & Knutson, 2000). Thus, working with families to help incorporate recommendations into their everyday lives helps families adhere to recommendations and avoid abuse and neglect (Dubowitz et al., 2011).

Overall, children with disabilities are supported by multiple professionals (e.g., education, health-care specialists) throughout the day and therefore there can be more opportunities for abuse or neglect incidents across the day. Some have argued that this exposure to multiple caregivers increases the likelihood that children with IDD are overrepresented in groups that experience neglect (Sullivan & Knutson, 2000). Others have argued that because of their reliance on others, young children with disabilities have more complex needs and therefore are more likely to be neglected (Dubowitz et al., 2011). Because parents and caregivers have access to the child over long periods of time and the care provided is very personal in nature (e.g., changing, bathing, feeding), there are many opportunities for abuse and neglect to take place (Barranti & Yuen, 2008; Nosek, Howland, & Young, 1998). In fact, 44% of child abuse victims had a relationship with their abuser that was directly related to their disability (Davis & Gidycz, 2000).

Family and parent risk factors. In many ways, early childhood is a unique period when children are completely dependent on their parents/caregivers to meet their basic needs (note: the term parents and caregivers includes biological parents, as well as foster parents, child-care providers, babysitters, and relatives who care for young children). During this time, young children depend on their parents/caregiver to meet basic needs such as shelter, food, clothing, and safety.

A family that experiences conflict, coercion, and/or physical abuse creates substantial risk for children to develop significant psychiatric, behavioral, and adjustment difficulties, including aggression, poor interpersonal skills/functioning, and emotional reactivity (Child Welfare Information Gateway, 2013). Caregivers in such families often report using punitive or excessive parenting practices, experiencing frequent anger and hyperarousal among other stressful conditions that can lead to abuse (Child Welfare Information Gateway, 2013). Many abusive parents engage in fewer positive interactions with their children (i.e., playing together, showing affections) (Boyle et al., 2004) and many adults who were abused as children become perpetrators of abuse later in life (Coohey, 2007; Coohey & Braun, 1997).

Less research has investigated abuse against children with IDD, including abuse committed by family members (Barnett et al., 2011). For children with IDD and their families, access to adequate support networks may be limited, leading to families feeling more socially isolated, which can lead to abuse. Furthermore, these families may have difficulties accessing adequate resources and support for a child with IDD, which can affect family stress levels (WHO & UNICEF, 2012).

Child risk factors. Along with specific parent and family risk factors, there are also child-specific factors that could lead to increased risk of abuse. This section is by no means meant to "blame the victim," but is instead intended to highlight certain characteristics that are important to acknowledge and address when working to prevent abuse of children with IDD. For the parents of a child with IDD who displays difficult behavior patterns (e.g., persistent crying or biting), or communication difficulties, parental stress can increase, which in turn can result in the higher likelihood of physical abuse (Sullivan & Knutson, 2000).

Some research suggests that children with IDD may have increased risk of abuse because of society's response to the disability, rather than the disability itself. This can lead to instances when children with IDD are perceived as less valuable or trustworthy about reporting abuse (e.g., adults may assume that the child is easily suggestible) than other children without disabilities, thus perpetuating a cycle of abuse (Sobsey, 1994; Wescott, 1993). Unless a child can convincingly communicate what happened, and "be believed," the indicators of abuse may go overlooked, especially for children with intellectual disabilities (Sullivan, Vernon, & Scanlan, 1987).

Finally, the prevalence of child abuse varies based on the specific form of disability. Maltreatment is most prevalent among children with behavior disorders, speech/language impairments, and intellectual disability (Sullivan & Knutson, 2000). Another population that has an increased risk for maltreatment is children who are deaf, hard of hearing, and or have a severe speech impediment (Fisher et al., 2008; Sullivan & Knutson, 1998; Verdugo, Bermejo, & Fuertes, 1995). Researchers have found conflicting results regarding children with autism spectrum disorders (ASD). For these children, some researchers have documented that ASD can increase the likelihood of child abuse (Mandell, Walrath, Manteuffel,

Sgro, & Pinto-Martin, 2005), while others have noted ASD does not increase the risk for child maltreatment (Spencer et al., 2005).

2.4 Child Abuse Prevention Strategies

Child abuse prevention efforts are intended to strengthen the capacity of parents and communities to care for the well-being of all children. These prevention efforts have focused around three primary goals: (1) reduce the incidence of abuse and neglect; (2) minimize the chance that children who are maltreated will be revictimized; and (3) break the cycle of maltreatment by providing victims the help they need to overcome the negative consequence of abuse or neglect (Daro, 2011). Below we discuss three types of child abuse prevention strategies available for all families: public education and awareness efforts, parent education and support groups, and home visitation programs. We then discuss prevention strategies specific for families with children with IDD.

Child abuse prevention for all families. In recent years, multidisciplinary groups have focused on preventing child abuse and neglect through public awareness efforts. Public awareness campaigns raise awareness in the general public with the hope of making an impact across the overall population. The "Never Shake a Baby" campaign is an example of a successful public awareness and education effort. This campaign was marked by multidisciplinary groups focused on reducing the prevalence of shaken baby syndrome. This campaign included increased media coverage, the availability of a nationwide toll-free information line and referral hotlines, advertisements (on television, radio, and in print), as well as the distribution of information and guidance to all new parents caring for new babies (Daro, 2011). Although it is difficult to know the exact number of shaken baby syndrome cases per year, because many cases are underreported and/or never receive diagnosis (Black, Heyman, & Smith Slep, 2001), this campaign's success focused on raising the public's overall awareness. While these broader campaigns relate to ensuring the safety of all young children, youth with IDD are not specifically targeted or highlighted, but can certainly benefit.

Parent education and support groups. On a more individualized level, education and support services for parents at risk for child abuse range from education and information sharing, to general support, to therapeutic interventions. Typically these programs focus on young children's cognitive and social—emotional development (Layzer, Goodson, Bernstein, & Price, 2001). Components of educational and support services for children aged from birth to eight years include teaching parents emotional communication skills; helping parents acquire positive parent—child interaction skills; and providing parents opportunities to demonstrate and practice skills while observed by professionals (Fortson, Klevens, Merrick, Gilbert, & Alexander, 2016).

Many families find it difficult to sustain participation in these programs. Barriers to enrollment and sustained participation include lack of reliable transportation, scheduling, and limited access to dependable child care (Daro, 1993). Furthermore, while these educational and support services aim to share information about healthy child development and growth, specific information tailored to children with IDD is often not included in these programs (Fisher, 2009). The inability to tailor these programs to families with varying needs reduces their effectiveness for children with IDD (Daro & McCurdy, 2006).

Home visitation programs. Seeking to reduce child abuse, professionals have promoted home visitation programs for new parents. Such programs are guided by the belief that home visitation can reduce the risk of child maltreatment by strengthening the early parent—child bonds and linking parents to new information and needed resources (Daro, 2009). Home visitor programs serve as gatekeepers to community resources spanning health, education, and housing (Daro, 2011). When these programs are used in child abuse and maltreatment prevention efforts, pregnant women and new parents are targeted for services and meet specific risk factors (e.g., low socioeconomic status, teenage parents). These programs intend to increase a parent's ability, confidence, and competence in providing safe and nurturing environments for children.

Many states have invested in such home visitation models as Parents as Teachers, Healthy Families America, Early Head Start, Parent Child Home Program, SafeCare, HIPPY, and Nurse Family Partnership to insure services are of high quality and integrated into the broader systems of early intervention and support (Johnson, 2009). While home visitation programs can produce positive effects on mother—child interactions (Bull, McCormick, Swann, & Mulvihill, 2004), the home visitors in these programs do not often have knowledge of disabilities or atypical child development. Thus, more research is needed to determine the effectiveness of abuse prevention for children with disabilities involved in home visitation programs.

Child abuse prevention for families with children with IDD. Part C of the Individuals with Disabilities Education Act mandates the provision of special education services (i.e., early intervention) to young children with disabilities (birth—3 years). Depending upon state eligibility standards, children qualify for these services by either being at risk for or identified with a developmental delay or disability. These services include but are not limited to physical therapy, occupational therapy, developmental therapy, and speech language therapy and are delivered to the child and family in their most natural environment (e.g., home, child care, etc.). While, early intervention services were not developed to prevent child abuse and neglect, the scope (family/child outcomes), structure (family-centered), and delivery (natural environments/homes) of these services provide great potential for promoting positive parent—child interactions as well as preventing child abuse for young children with disabilities.

Specifically, early intervention services are family-centered and strength-based, meaning families drive the service delivery and early intervention professionals focus on building off a family's strengths. Early intervention services are uniquely tailored to children who have disabilities and their families. However, these professionals are not trained in supporting young children with disabilities who have experienced abuse and neglect. Therefore, even though young children with disabilities who have experienced abuse are receiving early intervention services, their unique needs may not be specifically addressed by the early intervention or child welfare systems (Corr & Danner, 2014; Hibbard & Desch, 2007; Kenny, 2004; Manders & Stoneman, 2009).

2.5 Child Abuse Intervention Strategies

A variety of intervention approaches are used to help parents who are at risk for or have abused or neglected their children. Effective treatments frequently address parenting skills, distorted cognitions/attributions, development of adaptive and nonviolent coping strategies, and development of regulation (Runyon & Urquiza, 2011). Three empirically tested interventions with some evidence for supporting parents with children with IDD are Parent—Child Interaction Therapy (PCIT); Alternatives for Families: A Cognitive—Behavioral Therapy (AF-CBT); and Combined Parent—Child Cognitive Behavioral Therapy (CPC-CBT).

First, PCIT is a parent training program founded on social learning principles. PCIT focuses on promoting intense positive interaction by incorporating parents and children within the session and using live coaching to change dysfunctional parent—child relationships. PCIT emphasizes parent—child interactions but does not directly address the child's emotional distress. Compared to parents who have received other intervention programs, parents receiving PCIT have significantly fewer physical abuse recurrences and report significantly reduced stress levels (Kennedy, Kim, Tripod, Brown, & Gowdy, 2016).

Bagner and Eyberg (2007) used PCIT for families with young children (3—6 years) who had an identified intellectual disability and comorbid oppositional defiant disorder. Thirty families were randomly assigned to an immediate PCIT treatment or waitlist control group. Mothers who received PCIT treatment interacted more positively with their children after treatment comparatively to those who did not receive treatment. Mothers and their children who received PCIT treatment were also more compliant after treatment. Overall, compared to mothers who did not receive the PCIT treatment, mothers receiving PCIT reported fewer disruptive behaviors at home and lower parenting stress related to difficult child behavior. Despite these positive effects, there is still a lack of research about the effectiveness of PCIT for children with IDD.

Second, AF-CBT is designed to intervene with families of children (5—15 years) referred for conflict or coercion, verbal or physical aggression by caregivers (including the use of excessive physical force or threats), behavior problems in children/adolescents, or child physical abuse. AF-CBT comprehensively addresses both the risk factors and the consequences of physical, emotional, and parental verbal aggression (Child Welfare Information Gateway, 2013). AF-CBT is recommended for use with families that exhibit any or all of the following: caregivers whose disciplinary or management strategies range from mild physical discipline to physically aggressive or abusive behaviors, or who exhibit heightened levels of anger, hostility, or explosiveness; children who exhibit significant externalizing or aggressive behavior (e.g., oppositionality, antisocial behavior), with or without significant physical abuse-/discipline-related trauma symptoms (e.g., anger, anxiety, post-traumatic stress disorder (PTSD)); and/or families who exhibit heightened conflict or coercion or who pose threats to personal safety.

While this program may be a good option for parents with children with IDD, use in this population may require more simplified services or translations of some of the more complicated treatment concepts (Kolko, 1996; Kolko, Iselin, & Gully, 2011). For example, discussions about emotions may require a simplification of vocabulary, visual supports, and/or concrete examples. Some modifications have been used for families of children with

IDD, but few researchers have documented the overall effectiveness (Grosso, 2012).

Finally, CPC-CBT is used with families with young children (3–18 years) and a history of physical abuse and inappropriate physical discipline/coercive parenting strategies. Goals of CPC-CBT are to help the child heal from the trauma of the physical abuse, to empower and motivate parents to modulate their emotions and use effective noncoercive parenting strategies, and to strengthen parent–child relationships while helping families stop the cycle of violence. CPC-CBT has not been used regularly with children with IDD; however, there is reason to believe this population could benefit from the same goals of addressing trauma, motivating parents, and strengthening parent–child relationships. To understand how CPC-CBT could be effective for specific populations, future CPC-CBT research studies should include children with IDD.

While adaptations for the PCIT, AF-CBT, and CPC-CB have been noted for working with children with IDD, these interventions were not specifically designed to be responsive to children with IDD (Charlton & Tallant, 2003). Still, emerging research indicates these programs may be successful for families with children with IDD. Future research should focus on how PCIT, AF-CBT, and CPC-CB can be adapted and implemented with families with children with IDD.

3. BULLYING

Bullying is a public health concern among school-aged youth (Espelage, Low, Polanin, & Brown, 2013). The United States Department of Education, Centers for Disease Control and Prevention, and Health Resources and Services Administration recently partnered with bullying experts to develop a uniform definition of bullying for research and surveillance. This definition states that bullying is any unwanted aggressive behavior(s) by another youth or group of youths (who are not siblings or current dating partners) that *involves an observed or perceived power imbalance and is repeated multiple times or is highly likely to be repeated. Bullying may inflict harm or distress on the targeted youth including physical, psychological, social, or educational harm* (Gladden, Vivolo-Kantor, Hamburger, & Lumpkin, 2014, p. 7).

Bullying is most prevalent during the middle school years and leads to detrimental short- and long-term emotional outcomes, including anxiety, depression, and low self-esteem (Cook, Williams, Guerra, Kim, & Sadek, 2010; Hawker & Boulton, 2000; Swearer, Espelage, Vaillancourt, & Hymel, 2010). More alarmingly, extreme bullying has led to behavior problems (Olweus, 1994), self-harm (McMahon, Reulbach, Keeley, Perry, & Arensman, 2010), suicidal ideation (Klomek, Marrocco, Kleinman, Schonfeld, & Gould, 2008), and suicide (Nansel et al., 2001).

Bullying can take direct and indirect forms. Direct forms of bullying include aggressive attacks on the victim when the victim is present. Indirect forms of bullying can include subtle attacks that are not directly communicated to the victim, such as rumor spreading (Espelage & Swearer, 2003; Gladden et al., 2014). Both direct and indirect bullying incidents can be classified into four categories: physical bullying, relational bullying, verbal bullying, and damage to property (Gladden et al., 2014).

Certain variables have been identified as likely to increase the risk of bullying for all students. Specifically, victims of bullying often have poor social skills, few friends, are rejected by peers, have observable differences, and have low self-esteem (Cook et al., 2010; Kumpulainen et al., 1998; Nansel et al., 2001; Whitney, Nabuzoka, & Smith, 1992). Additionally, some victims of bullying are described as having problems with internalizing and externalizing behaviors and maintaining interpersonal relationships (Kumpulainen et al., 1998). Given these risk factors, it is apparent that individuals with IDD might possess several such factors, thus leading to increased risk of bullying. Indeed, compared to the national average, students with disabilities are at least 1.5 times more likely to be bullied (Blake et al., 2012).

3.1 Bullying of Adolescents With Intellectual and Developmental Disabilities

While investigations related to the prevalence and nature of bullying are not new, attention has only recently shifted toward adolescents with IDD. This more recent research sheds light on the importance of understanding the prevalence and risk factors of bullying of adolescents with IDD and aids in the advancement of prevention and intervention strategies. Still, when considering the literature related to bullying of adolescents with IDD, important measurement factors must be taken into consideration.

First, a recent review of the literature found that studies employ various methods for measuring experiences of bullying, including parent and teacher report questionnaires, self-report questionnaires, and student interviews

(Schroeder, Cappadocia, Bebke, Pepler, & Weiss, 2014). Such various methods of data collection make it difficult to compare results across studies (e.g., reports through qualitative interviews cannot be compared to prevalence rates from a national questionnaire study).

Second, the majority of the bullying research relies on reports from other informants, such as parents and teachers, without accounting for the perspective of the individual with IDD. More recent research suggests, however, that informant reports may not capture the totality of bullying experiences (Adams, Fredstrom, Duncan, Holleb, & Bishop, 2014; Chen & Schwartz, 2012; Fisher & Taylor, 2016; van Roekel, Scholte, & Didden, 2010; Rowley et al., 2012; Zeedyk, Rodriguez, TipTon, Baker, & Blacher, 2014). For example, parents and teachers might not be aware of certain experiences of youth with IDD, leading to underreporting of bullying. Alternatively, teachers and parents may be able to provide insight into instances of victimization that students with IDD do not recognize as bullying or choose not to disclose (Pellegrini, 1998; Theriot, Dulmus, Sowers, Johnson, 2005). These insights could provide a valuable description of the nature of bullying of students with IDD.

Alternatively, of those studies that do include self-reports from adolescents with IDD, most assess bullying through questionnaires developed and normed for adolescents without disabilities (Begeer, Fink, van der Meijden, Goossens, & Olthof, 2015; Kowalski & Fedina, 2011; Rieffe, Camodeca, Pouw, Lange, & Stockman, 2012; van Roekel et al., 2010; Shtayermman, 2007). Use of questionnaires that are not validated for adolescents with disabilities could result in underreporting of bullying, as adolescents might not understand the items on the questionnaires or they might experience disability-specific bullying that is not addressed on questionnaires developed for adolescents without disabilities. For example, students with IDD may not be able to abstractly relate their disability-specific bullying experiences to the examples provided on generic bullying questionnaires (Fisher & Taylor, 2016). Thus, rather than considering one reporter as the most accurate informant of bullying, multiple informants should be assessed to form a more complete picture of victimization (van Roekel et al., 2010).

Finally, although this field has explained several correlates of bullying of adolescents with IDD—including educational, social, emotional, and behavioral problems—the direction of the relationship between these characteristics and bullying experiences is not yet known. While it is possible that bullying has led to increased educational, social, emotional, and behavioral problems, it is also possible that these problems increased the risk of being bullied (Zeedyk et al., 2014). Despite the concerns with the current literature, findings consistently report that, compared to those without disabilities, youth with IDD experience increased rates of bullying. It is vitally important to understand these experiences. Thus, in the following sections we discuss what we know about the prevalence and correlates of bullying, before discussing prevention and intervention programs.

3.2 Prevalence of Bullying of Adolescents With Intellectual and Developmental Disabilities

Compared to those without disabilities, adolescents with IDD are more likely to experience bullying (Blake et al., 2012); indeed, estimates of victimization range from 19% to 94% (Christensen, Fryant, Neece, & Baker, 2012; Doren, Bullis, & Benz, 1996; Little, 2002; Rose, Monda-Amaya, & Espelage, 2011). Although few studies have examined the prevalence of specific forms of bullying for students with IDD, it appears that they are at heightened risk of experiencing all forms (Rose et al., 2011).

While early research examined the prevalence of bullying among students with IDD as a heterogeneous group (regardless of type of IDD; e.g., see Rose & Espelage, 2012), more recent research has begun to explore specific subgroups of individuals with IDD (Rose et al., 2011). Findings indicate that students with disabilities may differentially experience bullying, based on the disability condition. First, some examined the risk of bullying based on whether the student had what was considered an observable versus invisible disability. For example, a child who has cerebral palsy, muscular dystrophy, spina bifida, hemiplegia is considered to have an observable disability; whereas, individuals with intellectual disability, emotional impairment, and attention deficit hyperactivity disorder (ADHD) have an invisible disability (Christensen et al., 2012; Carter & Spencer, 2006; Doren et al., 1996; Rose et al., 2011). At least 50% of students with an observable disability reported being bullied at least once within the past year and 30% reported experiences of frequently recurring bullying; in contrast 21% of students with an invisible disability reported experiencing bullying within the past year, and 14% reported consistent bullying (Carter & Spencer, 2006; Dawkins, 1996).

Other research has examined bullying by the specific type of disability. For example, students with intellectual disability (57%), learning disabilities (49%), and emotional and behavioral disorders (30%) are all reported to experience high rates of victimization (Rose & Espelage, 2012; Sterzing, Shattuck, Narendorf, Wagner, & Cooper, 2012). Compared to typically developing peers, adolescents with intellectual disability report significantly higher rates of verbal bullying, including being picked on and called names in school and other public places like the bus (Sheard, Clegg, Standen, & Cromby, 2001). Students with learning disabilities reported higher rates of property theft, threats, and physical bullying (i.e., school fights) (Mishna, 2003).

Finally, the most research has been conducted on students with ASD. Although estimates vary greatly, parents report that nearly half (46.3%) to almost all (94%) students with ASD are victims of bullying (Little, 2002; Sterzing et al., 2012). Most often, individuals with ASD report experiencing verbal or relational bullying (Cappadocia, Weiss, & Pepler, 2012; Mishna, 2003), and they less often report experiences of physical bullying (Adams et al., 2014). Parent reports, on the other hand, have described incidents where students with ASD have been punched in the mouth, pushed to the ground, and had dirt thrown on them (Pfeffer, 2012).

3.3 Risk Factors for Bullying of Adolescents With Intellectual and Developmental Disabilities

Several risk factors have been identified as potentially leading to victimization of individuals with IDD. Recent research has shown that factors such as internalizing and externalizing behaviors, social communication problems (e.g. difficulty making and maintaining friendships; recognizing social cues), low or below average academic skills, and physical and environmental differences can all increase risk of bullying for students with IDD (Bear, Mantz, Glutting, Yang, & Boyer, 2015; Kaukiainen et al., 2002; Zeedyk et al., 2014). Most of these factors can also be considered both a cause and a consequence of bullying; however, more longitudinal research is needed to identify the directional relations.

Internalizing and externalizing behaviors. Students who display internalizing and externalizing behavior problems are more likely to experience bullying. Internalizing behavior problems have been identified as both a risk factor for and a result of victimization (Zeedyk et al., 2014). Specifically, such internalizing behavior problems, as anxiety, depression, withdrawal, and low self-esteem are predictive of experiences of bullying and continual victimization (Cappadocia et al., 2012; Mahady Wilton, Craig, & Pepler, 2000; Zeedyk et al., 2014). Such risk is likely because internalizing behavior problems can lead to poor peer relations, peer rejection, and loneliness (Nolan,

Flynn, & Garber, 2003), which are also predictors of bullying. Alternatively, bullying experiences can lead to the internalization of negative thoughts, withdrawal, and interpersonal and emotional problems (Adams et al., 2014; Reiter & Lapidot-Lefler, 2007). Peer rejection and social difficulties (e.g., relational bullying) can lead to anxiety and depression (Cappadocia et al., 2012; Mazurek & Kanne, 2010).

Students with IDD who display externalizing behavior problems are also at risk for bullying. Cappadocia et al. (2012) reported that students with ASD who displayed more externalizing behavior problems were more likely to be categorized in the high victimization group (vs low or no victimization). These students are sometimes considered "provocative victims," as they often display aggressive reactions toward bullies, or display bullying characteristics themselves (Kumpulainen et al., 1998). Several studies, in fact, have found that students with IDD who display externalizing behavior problems are more likely to be bully victims (Reiter & Lapidot-Lefler, 2007). Such students are not only victims of bullying, but they are also more likely to be the perpetrator of bullying.

Social communication. The lack of developed social skills can be described as the inability to recognize social cues, engage in reciprocal conversations, and distinguish another's emotions (Cappadocia et al., 2012). These deficits can make it difficult to establish and maintain friendships. Compared to their typical peers, adolescents with IDD report that they are not included in social activities, do not have as many friendships, and are lonely (Cappadocia et al., 2012; Heiman, 2000; McVilly, Stancliffe, Parmenter, & Burton-Smith, 2006; Zeedyk et al., 2014). Individuals with IDD are also more likely to be left out of the popular peer group and instead included in the unpopular or cast-off group. Children associated with the unpopular group are victimized at a higher rate than other peer groups (Yude, Goodman, & McConachie, 1998).

School friendships play a crucial role in adolescence and can provide safety for individuals while in school. Indeed, individuals who have friendships are less likely to be bullied. This protection could be related to higher self-confidence displayed by the adolescent or because of the protective connection to others (Larkin, Jahoda, MacMahon, & Pert, 2012). For example, the association to at least one friend is shown to decrease anxiety and loneliness, which can then decrease risk of bullying (Mazurek & Kanne, 2010).

Academic skills. Compared to their typical peers, adolescents with IDD who struggle with the academic workload have reported a higher rate of bullying. Students with IDD who have higher distractibility, hyperactivity, and/or struggle with attention may attract more negative attention from peers, which could then lead to verbal bullying. Additionally, individuals with learning disabilities may receive differentiated instruction, setting them apart from their typical peers (Mishna, 2003). Finally, students who have experienced bullying may be afraid to go to school, or might not participate (raise hand or seek support) while at school, impacting their overall grades and motivation (Gietz & McIntosh, 2014; Mishna, 2003).

Physical and environmental school differences. Placement in a special education classroom may increase risk for bullying of students with IDD. As such, students are at increased risk of experiencing bullying when they attend different or separate schools as well as resource classrooms within the student's regular school building (Mishna, 2003; Norwich & Kelly, 2004). Such risk might be related to the lack of socialization between students with IDD and students without disabilities (Rose et al., 2011). Alternatively, high rates of bullying impact students with IDD who attend class in the general education classroom (Zablotsky, Bradshaw, Anderson, & Law, 2013). Specifically, despite the movement to include students with IDD in general education classrooms, these students are often still isolated and rejected by students without disabilities (Pivik, McComas, & LaFlamme, 2002; Saylor & Leach, 2009). Rejection of students with IDD in the general education classroom has been related to their different appearance (both physical and behavioral), the presence of a one-on-one aide in the classroom, and because typically developing students do not understand students with IDD or the reasons for their differences (Humphrey & Lewis, 2008). As such, risk arises when students with IDD are included in the classroom but are not properly integrated into social groups or provided the social skills to be successfully socially included (Rose et al., 2011).

3.4 Bullying Prevention Strategies

In response to the escalated victimization of students with IDD, the Department of Education's Office of Special Education and Rehabilitative Services (OSERS) recently issues a *Dear Colleague Letter* to all school districts across the United States. That letter provided an overview of a school district's responsibilities toward addressing bullying of students with disabilities (OSERS, 2013). Specifically, the letter stated that if a student with a disability does not receive a meaningful education as a result of bullying, this is considered a denial of a free appropriate public education under the Individuals with Disabilities Education Improvement Act. The letter further stated, "A student must feel safe in school in order to fulfill his or her full academic potential…We also encourage States and school districts to reevaluate their policies and practices addressing problematic behaviors, including bullying" (OSERS, 2013, p. 10). One year later, the Office for Civil Rights (OCR) issued follow-up *Dear Colleague Letter* to further explain that bullying of students with a disability constitutes "disability-based harassment." Schools were urged to work proactively to ensure a safe school environment for all students, including those with disabilities (Office for Civil Rights, 2014).

Despite the call for bullying prevention programs from OSERS and OCR, few school-based bullying prevention programs have been developed specifically for students with IDD. Thus, we will first review bullying prevention programs designed for all students, before discussing promising practices that could lead to the reduction of bullying for students with IDD.

Bullying prevention for all students. Bullying prevention typically begins with a whole-school approach, in which anti-bullying interventions are implemented for all students. While the effects of these programs vary, a recent meta-analysis reported these programs generate an overall reduction in bullying of 17–23% (Ttofi & Farrington, 2011). The most effective program elements include parent involvement (e.g., parent training/meetings, information for parents), enhanced playground supervision, strict disciplinary methods in response to bullying, classroom management and clear classroom rules, teacher training, a school-wide anti-bullying policy, and school conferences. Programs that were longer and more intense were also more successful (Farrington & Ttofi, 2009; Ttofi & Farrington, 2011).

In addition to school-wide bullying prevention programs, other researchers have attempted to reduce bullying by targeting the risk and protective factors associated with bullying. For example, school-based social–emotional learning programs could lead to the reduction of bullying by addressing social and emotional skills (e.g., empathy and communication). One such program, Second Step: Student Success Through Prevention (SS-SSTP; Committee for Children, 2008), has been examined for its impact on bullying (Espelage, Low, Polanin, & Brown, 2015). Although this program was not shown to produce overall reductions in victimization (Espelage et al., 2015), there is some promise that it leads to reductions in physical bullying and sexual harassment in middle school (Espelage et al. 2013, 2015).

Bullying prevention for students with IDD. Although no school-wide bullying prevention programs have yet been developed to specifically target reduction of bullying of students with IDD, programs addressing specific risk factors of victimization might help protect students with IDD. Such programs could focus on working to reduce risk factors displayed by students with IDD or working to improve attitudes and behaviors of students without disabilities toward students with IDD.

First, social skills interventions often target social communication, including social skills and conflict resolution. For example, the Program for the Education and Enrichment of Relational Skills (PEERS) program, developed for students with ASD and other IDD, focuses on improving social competence and friendship (Laugeson & Frankel, 2010). Although the reduction of bullying is not a primary goal of the program, lessons do cover such topics as choosing appropriate friends, handling teasing, bullying and bad reputations, and rumors and gossip (Laugeson, Frankel, Gantman, Dillon, & Mogil, 2012). Each aspect could lead to improved relationships and reduced bullying experiences. Future research should examine the impact of peers on victimization rates of individuals with IDD.

Second, to enhance the social experience of students with IDD, it is important to promote acceptance and understanding of students with disabilities (Gus, 2000; Humphrey. 2008). As Betts, Betts, and Gerber-Eckard (2007) stated, "a little understanding and knowledge can go a long way to show other students how to assist easily, rather than ignore or taunt a student with [disabilities]" (p.143). Schools have begun to bridge the gap between inclusion and peer acceptance in various ways, with one of the most successful techniques being peer-mediated interventions (Carter & Kennedy, 2006; National ASD Center, 2009) and providing education about IDD to the students without disabilities (Humphrey & Lewis, 2008). As these programs aim to increase acceptance and enhance the social networks of students with IDD through the development of positive social relationships, they could help to decrease bullying experiences.

Specifically, peer-mediated interventions address the risk of educational setting, as they remove students with disabilities from more restrictive environments and into general education classrooms. By providing students with the social supports they need to enhance social integration into the classroom, peer-mediated interventions address the individual risk factors of peer rejection and isolation of students with IDD. At the same time, these programs promote disability awareness and acceptance to the students without disabilities who serve as peer mentors. In fact, peer supports participating in peer-mediated interventions report feeling more comfortable advocating for students with IDD, intervening to stop other students from teasing students with IDD, and modeling acccptance of students with disabilities for other peers to see (Copeland et al., 2004). Such positive attitudes are then transferred to other students in the school who did not actively participate as peer supports (Copeland et al., 2004; Owen-DeSchryver, Carr, Cale, Blakeley-Smith, 2008). Given such positive results, it is possible that attitudes and acceptance toward students with IDD could increase school-wide and bullying of students with IDD could decrease.

3.5 Bullying Intervention Strategies

Bullying can have a detrimental effect on the health and mental health of the victim. The experience of bullying can lead to undue stress, anxiety, depression, health concerns, as well as impact school concentration and work completion. Such symptoms, in turn, can lead to poor academic outcomes for the victim (Dawkins, 1996; Mishna, 2003). Adolescents who experience internalizing behavior problems as a result of bullying may benefit from counseling (individual or group) sessions regarding social anxiety and stress reduction. Such session may provide a safe place for individuals to discuss their personal experiences and meet others who have had similar experiences (Hillier, Fish, Siegel, & Beversdorf, 2011; Zeedyk et al., 2014). A therapeutic intervention would also be beneficial if it addressed self-esteem and other coping skills, such as assertiveness training (Craig, 1998; Smith, Shu, & Madsen, 2001). Throughout treatment, adolescents should be continually monitored for how they are coping with their bullying experience. Adults should follow-up and inquire about how the student is navigating school and if bullying has continued (Bourke & Burgman, 2010).

4. CRIMINAL VICTIMIZATION

In adulthood, the definition of victimization can encompass several different aspects, as more legal implications are involved. In 1994 "disability" was added to the list of protected categories considered under the Hate Crimes Statistics Act (28 U.S.C. § 994; McMahon, West, Lewis, Armstrong, & Conway, 2004). This act states that data must be collected annually on crimes that *manifest evidence of prejudice based on race, gender and gender identity, religion, disability, sexual orientation, or ethnicity, including where appropriate the crimes of murder, non-negligent manslaughter; forcible rape; aggravated assault, simple assault, intimidation; arson; and destruction, damage, or vandalism of property.*

With this addition, crimes against adults with disabilities are considered a hate crime if the offense is committed against a person or property and is believed to be the result of bias toward the individual (e.g., a negative attitude). As a result, individuals with disabilities are now considered a protected group and crimes against them can be considered a federal offense (McMahon et al., 2004). At the same time, what is legally defined as victimization or a hate crime does not encompass all forms of victimization experienced by adults with IDD.

With the transition to adulthood, individuals with IDD often experience a decrease in services and systems of supports (Newman, Wagner, Cameto, & Knokey, 2009). Specifically, upon high school graduation, where services were mandated for all school-age children with IDD, the service delivery system changes to an eligibility system (Hanley-Maxwell, Whitney-Thomas, & Pogoloff, 1995). Thus, although individuals with IDD were eligible for services in childhood, they may find they are ineligible in adulthood or they may find themselves on long waitlists to access the limited funds intended to support a growing number of individuals (Braddock et al., 2014).

As a result of the limited resources of the adult service system, adults with IDD often face limited employment options (Wagner, Newman, Cameto, & Levine, 2005), segregation, and social isolation (Chambers, Hughes, & Carter, 2004). Such negative experiences can lead to even more detrimental outcomes, as adults with IDD find themselves living in low-income housing, often located in dangerous areas (McMahon et al., 2004; Petersilia, 2001) supervised by staff who are not adequately trained to meet their unique needs (Keesler, 2014; White et al., 2003). Indeed, as personal risk factors are coupled with a lack of services, adults with IDD are at increased risk of victimization.

While less research has been dedicated to the study of victimization of adults with IDD, a growing body of evidence highlights the importance of examining the prevalence and risk factors of abuse of adults with IDD and developing ways to prevent such situations from occurring (Fisher et al., 2016). In fact, the most recent survey of crime victims in the United States found that adults with IDD experienced victimization at least twice as often as adults without disabilities (Harrell, 2015), and 1.4% of all hate crimes reported in 2012 involved adults with disabilities (US Department of Justice, 2013).

4.1 Criminal Victimization of Adults With Intellectual and Developmental Disabilities

While the risk of abuse and bullying generally decreases as the typical population ages, this is not the case for the IDD population. Just as when they are children and adolescents, adults with IDD (compared to those without disabilities) experience increased rates of victimization (Harrell, 2015). In the following sections, we first examine the prevalence of specific forms of victimization experienced by adults with IDD, we discuss the risk factors for victimization of adults with IDD, including both societal and demographic characteristics. Finally, we address prevention and intervention strategies to reduce victimization and support adults who have been victimized.

4.2 Prevalence of Criminal Victimization of Adults With Intellectual and Developmental Disabilities

The Bureau of Justice Statistics' National Crime Victimization Survey (NCVS) is the largest survey used to assess the prevalence of victimization among adults with disabilities. This survey examines several forms of victimization encompassed within simple assault and serious violent crime (e.g., rape/sexual assault, robbery, aggravated assault). In 2013, compared to other disabilities, individuals with IDD experienced the highest rate of violent victimization (67 per 1000), and they were at least twice as likely to experience simple assault (42 per 1000) (Harrell, 2015). Compared to those without disabilities, adults with IDD are also more likely to experience multiple types of victimization, multiple instances of victimization, and victimization by multiple perpetrators (Fisher et al., 2016; Mansell, Beadle-Brown, Cambridge, Milne, & Whelton, 2009). While few studies examined the prevalence and experiences of each form of victimization for adults with IDD, in the sections that follow we provide an overview of the currently available research related to physical and sexual assault and other criminal victimization.

Sexual and physical assault. The largest amount of research has been dedicated to examining the sexual assault of adults with IDD, including both forceful sexual victimization and psychologically coerced sexual assault. Sexual assault rates of adults with IDD are estimated to be two to five times those in the general population (Lin, Yen, Kuo, Wu, & Lin, 2009). More specifically, current estimates of the prevalence of sexual assault vary considerably, with a recent review of the literature (Fisher et al., 2016) reporting rates ranging from 5.4% of the sample (Pan, 2007) to 80% of the sample (Stromsness, 1993). Overall, women with IDD (versus men) are more likely to experience some form of sexual victimization in their lifetime (Nettelbeck & Wilson, 2002).

Adults with IDD also experience high rates of physical assault. Specifically, results from a recent meta-analysis reported that 9.9% (range 2.2–22.3%) of individuals with IDD experienced physical violence (Hughes et al., 2012). Additional research indicates that simple assault is the most common form of victimization (42% of all victimization) experienced by adults with IDD, followed by intimidation (41%) (McMahon et al., 2004).

Other criminal victimization. Adults with IDD are also at increased risk of experiencing other forms of criminal victimization, including property crimes (e.g., breaking-and-entering, household property theft; Wilson & Brewer, 1992) and financial victimization (Fisher et al., 2012; Luckasson, 1992). In a seminal article examining victimization of adults with IDD, Wilson and Brewer (1992) reported that, compared to population norms, adults with IDD were one and half times more likely to experience household victimization, including theft and robbery. More recent research indicates that such criminal victimization is still prevalent, as McMahon et al. (2004) reported 16% of their sample experienced property destruction, vandalism, or property damage, and Fisher et al. (2012) reported nearly 35% of their sample experienced money or property theft.

Finally, a small but important body of research highlights that adults with IDD are at increased risk of financial victimization, including misappropriation of benefit payments, swindling, fraud or scams, and friends "borrowing" money without offering a repayment (Fisher et al., 2012; Greenspan, Loughlin, & Black, 2001; Luckasson, 1992; Nettelbeck & Wilson, 2001). In fact, financial abuse encompassed 14.6% of referrals to Adult Protective Services (Mansell et al., 2009).

4.3 Risk Factors for Criminal Victimization of Adults With Intellectual and Developmental Disabilities

Several factors have been identified as related to the increased risk of victimization of adults with IDD. While some factors highlight characteristics displayed by individuals with IDD, others highlight societal issues that could increase vulnerability.

Societal factors. Throughout early childhood and the school-age years, individuals with IDD are guaranteed specific safeguards and support services. With the transition to adulthood, however, adults with IDD often experience a sharp and sudden decrease in services and supports (Newman et al., 2009). Loss of such support could lead to less supervision and oversight, increasing the chances of victimization going unnoticed and unreported. For example, adults who continue to live with family members are at lower risk of victimization than are those who live alone (Fisher et al., 2012; Wilson & Brewer, 1992).

An additional concern involves the cultural attitudes that often prevent individuals with IDD from learning strategies to detect and avoid vulnerable situations. For example, individuals with IDD are often excluded from sex education courses, or are even presumed to be asexual. As a result, they are not taught appropriate ways to engage in or express interest in sexual activities (Keesler, 2014; Kempton & Kahn, 1991; Rosen, 2006). Additionally, they do not learn ways to differentiate between appropriate and inappropriate touching or how to report events of sexual abuse.

As another example, as children, individuals with disabilities are often taught to be compliant and cooperative with parents and other caregivers. While such instruction might be necessary for success in school, it could lead to difficulties for adults with IDD who need to discriminate between situations and determine when it is okay to defend themselves against unwelcome advances (Rosen, 2006; Westcott & Jones, 1999). Finally, compared to those without disabilities, adults with IDD often experience less privacy and increased dependency on caregivers. Such lack of control over their own lives, bodies, and finances could increase the risk of abuse by caregivers or service providers (Hughes et al., 2012).

Individual characteristics. In addition to societal factors, research has also identified specific characteristics of individuals with IDD that could increase risk of victimization. Again, we highlight that we are not blaming the victim, but are instead working to understand how these characteristics relate to risk so that important intervention and prevention programs can be designed to specifically target these risk factors.

Research consistently indicates that the presence of intellectual disability (in general) is a risk factor for victimization (Brown, Stein, & Turk, 1995; Fisher et al., 2012; Horner-Johnson & Drum, 2006; Hughes et al., 2012). In fact, in their recent meta-analysis, Hughes et al. (2012) reported that intellectual disability was the only factor significantly related to risk of violence. Compared to those without disabilities and with other forms of disability (e.g., physical), adults with intellectual disability have the highest population rates of violence (Harrell, 2015; Hughes et al., 2012).

Gender is associated with risk for sexual victimization but not for other forms of victimization. Specifically, women (versus men) are more likely to experience sexual abuse (Cambridge, Beadle-Brown, Milne, Mansell, & Whelton, 2011; Furey, Niesen, & Stauch, 1994; Mansell, Sobsey, & Calder, 1992; McCarthy & Thompson, 1997; Sobsey & Doe, 1991; Stromsness, 1993; Turk & Brown, 1993). Men and women are equally at risk, however, of experiencing other forms of victimization (Fisher et al., 2016; Harrell, 2015).

The presence of friendships remains an important protective factor, as lack of friendship predicts increased levels of social vulnerability for adults with IDD (Fisher et al., 2012). Few friendships might also highlight the poor social competence often experienced by adults with IDD. Poor social competence could make it more difficult for an adult with IDD to recognize abusive situations or to realize when he or she is being taken advantage of (Doren et al., 1996; Greenspan et al., 2001; Keelser, 2014; Nettelbeck, Wilson, Potter, Perry, 2000; Wilson, Seaman, & Nettlebeck, 1996). Finally, behavioral characteristics are related to increased risk of victimization. Individuals with IDD who have been victimized are more likely to display angry or aggressive behaviors toward perpetrators (Nettelbeck et al., 2000) and externalizing behavior problems (Fisher et al., 2012).

4.4 Criminal Victimization Prevention Strategies

While the evidence clearly points to increased risks for and experiences of victimization, less research has been dedicated to the development of prevention programs to reduce this risk. Mikton, Maguire, and Shakespeare (2014) recently recommended that IDD researchers assume a public health approach to preventing victimization of adults with IDD. Such an approach, they describe, begins with understanding the magnitude and consequences of victimization, as well as identifying the risk and protective factors related to victimization of adults with IDD. These first two steps have clearly been addressed in the literature reviewed above. The most important next step, then, is to develop and evaluate programs to prevent victimization. Promising programs should then be scaled-up and evaluated for their impact and cost-effectiveness (Krug, Dahlberg, Mercy, Zwi, & Lozano, 2002; Mikton & Shakespeare, 2014). While there is still much work to be done, some abuse prevention programs have been developed and evaluated for their effectiveness. The majority of these programs consist of two forms:

behaviorally based abuse prevention programs and cognitively based abuse prevention programs (Lund, 2011).

Behaviorally based prevention programs. Behaviorally based prevention strategies have been used to teach adults with IDD to resist lures from strangers and to avoid potentially abusive situations (see Lumley & Miltenberger, 1997; Mechling, 2008 for reviews). Abuse prevention skills are taught through behavior skills training, in which the adult with IDD learns to resist a lure through instruction, modeling, rehearsal (in the training or natural environment), and feedback. Participants are taught to recognize a potentially abusive situation (e.g., lure from a stranger, unwanted sexual advance) and then taught to say "no," leave the situation, and report the event to a staff member or authority figure. Skill acquisition is assessed in situ during which the adult with IDD is unaware that the situation is a test and that the individual is being observed for correct or incorrect responding (Bergstrom, Najdowski, & Tarbox, 2014; Collins, Schuster, & Nelson, 1992; Egemo-Helm et al., 2007; Fisher, 2014; Fisher, Burke, & Griffin, 2013; Gunby & Rapp, 2014; Haseltine & Miltenberger, 1990; Lumley, Miltenberger, Long, Rapp, & Roberts, 1998; Miltenberger et al., 1999).

While the results of these studies are promising, specific considerations must be taken into account. First, the assessment of skill acquisition must be weighed against the potential risk for the psychological harm that could develop from multiple in situ assessments (Lund, 2011). Second, skill maintenance should be considered, as participants will typically have few opportunities to practice after the conclusion of the study. Finally, although these studies successfully demonstrated skill acquisition for the majority of participants, more mixed results were reported for the generalization of behaviors to untrained settings and situations (Mechling, 2008).

Cognitively based prevention programs. A different approach to teaching abuse prevention has been to teach adults with IDD to respond appropriately to a wide range of abuse situations through effective decision-making strategies. Through a series of studies, Khemka et al. (Hickson, Khemka, Golden, & Chatzistyli, 2015; Khemka, 2000; Khemka, Hickson, & Reynolds, 2005) developed and established the validity of *An Effective Strategy-Based Curriculum for Abuse Prevention and Empowerment* (ESCAPE) to teach adults with IDD to make decisions based on evaluations of their personal goals and consideration of the potential consequences (Khemka, 2000). Through this curriculum, adults learn to distinguish between healthy and abusive situations and to then respond using a step-wise decision-making strategy. The curriculum also teaches participants to prioritize self-protective goals and to recognize the feelings associated with health and abusive situations. Compared to a control group, participants who complete the ESCAPE curriculum displayed increased use of effective decision-making responses to vignettes depicting hypothetical abuse situations. Although these studies clearly demonstrated positive effects for the intervention group, considerations for this research must also be taken into account. Specifically, skill acquisition was not assessed in situ, so it is not clear if participants would apply the decision-making skills in real life situations.

Finally, adults with IDD need to be taught about sex and appropriate and inappropriate sexual activities. Unfortunately, sex education is often taught reactively, after a situation has occurred, rather than as a way to prevent problems and to provide adults with IDD with tools to experience healthy sexual relationships (Abbott & Howarth, 2007; Schaafsma, Kok, Stoffelen, & Curfs, 2015). A recent meta-analysis identified 20 articles that have examined the effectiveness of sex education programs or sex education—related materials for adults with IDD (Schaafsma et al., 2015). The authors found indications that skills and knowledge can be increased and attitudes toward sex can be improved through proactive sex education programs. But few details are available to determine the most effective programs to meet these goals.

4.5 Victimization Intervention Strategies

Exposure to abuse and victimization can lead to the development of significant mental health concerns, including depression, anxiety, post-traumatic stress disorder, drug and alcohol abuse, antisocial personality disorder, and borderline personality disorder (Sequeira & Hollins, 2003; Turner, Finkelhor, & Ormrod, 2006). Thus, it is vitally important that adults with IDD have access to supports and that they receive appropriate services after an experience of victimization (Hughes et al., 2010; Nosek, Foley, Hughes, & Howland, 2001).

Community-based domestic violence and sexual assault programs are often accessible to and used by women with IDD (Lund, 2011). At the same time, employees in these programs have expressed a need for disability-related training and resources to provide more comprehensive and informed services (Chang et al., 2003). Alternatively, Centers for

Independent Living are often the first point of contact for adults with IDD who have experienced abuse; yet, these programs report that staff lack abuse-related training and are often unable to provide effective support services (Swedlund & Nosek, 2000). These concerns highlight the need for cross-training among agencies, but such training is often impossible due to budget constraints (Lund, 2011).

To meet the needs of adults with IDD who have experienced victimization, agencies and practitioners must be able to adapt strategies to address the needs of this unique population. For example, while strategies are needed to help individuals manage distress (Wilczynski, Connolly, Dubard, Henderson, & McIntosh, 2015), adults with IDD may also need help navigating ways to leave abusive relationships (Ballan et al., 2014).

For those who have experienced victimization, group therapy may be beneficial to help them process their experience. Barber, Jenkins, and Jones (2000) examined the impact of a survivor's group for six adults with IDD who had experienced sexual abuse. Throughout the 10 weekly sessions, participants learned assertiveness, self-protection, and coping skills to process their experiences and to avoid future abusive situations (Barber et al., 2000). While participants displayed improvements in self-esteem and personal assertiveness, the impact did not maintain over time and there was no effect on depression and anxiety. Still, participants rated the intervention positively and as helpful. Although these results are promising, more research is needed to determine the most effective way to support adults with IDD who have experienced victimization.

5. FUTURE DIRECTIONS

Throughout this chapter we have focused on the prevalence and correlates of victimization of individuals with IDD across the lifespan, while also offering promising prevention and intervention strategies. The research clearly indicates that individuals with IDD are at heightened risk of experiencing various forms of abuse and victimization, and that this risk does not decrease with age. Despite these findings, there is still a pressing need for more research concerning victimization of individuals with IDD. In this final section, we offer suggestions for future research in three specific areas: longitudinal investigations of victimization, etiology-specific research, and resilience and well-being.

5.1 The Need for Longitudinal Research

Various risk factors have been linked to all forms of victimization of individuals with IDD, including child abuse, bullying, and criminal victimization. The often-used retrospective and cross-sectional designs, however, preclude exploration of whether IDDs were a cause or a consequence of victimization. Perhaps this is most clear in the case of child abuse. Investigations of child abuse are often conducted retrospectively through reports to state agencies or through whole population databases of multiple reporting agencies (Fisher et al., 2008; Horner-Johnson & Drum, 2006). While these studies provide important information about the correlates of abuse, it is still difficult to discern whether disability was a cause or consequence of child abuse.

Similarly, several correlates of bullying and students with IDD have been identified; yet, while cross-sectional investigations indicate specific characteristics are related to bullying of students with IDD, the direction of the relationship between these characteristics and bullying experiences is not yet known. While it is possible that victimization leads to increased educational, social, emotional, and behavioral problems, it is also possible that these problems increased the risk of being bullied (Zeedyk et al., 2014).

Longitudinal investigations of the social and emotional development of individuals with IDD will help to establish the causal relation of specific variables and experiences of victimization. Such investigations will also shed light on whether specific risk factors are more or less related to specific forms of victimization (e.g., child abuse vs bullying), and if individuals who experience one form of victimization (e.g., bullying) are then more likely to experience another form (e.g., adult criminal victimization). Finally, longitudinal investigations will help to identify critical ages when prevention and intervention programs should be implemented.

5.2 The Importance of Etiology

While research clearly shows that individuals with IDD are at increased risk of victimization, less attention has been given to whether specific types of disabilities are more or less at risk. There are several hundred identified etiologies, or causes, of IDD that can occur pre- (e.g., genetic disorders, fetal alcohol spectrum disorder, accidents in utero, etc.), peri- (e.g., prematurity, anoxia, and other birth-related complications. etc.), or postnatally (e.g., sickness such as meningitis and accidents such as head trauma, etc.).

Many specific forms of disability present with unique behavioral characteristics, or a behavioral phenotype. These behavioral characteristics, including cognitive, linguistic, personality, adaptive, or maladaptive functioning, may be differentially related to increased risk of victimization. They might also change risk based on specific forms of victimization. For example, compared to children with other forms of IDD, children with Prader—Willi syndrome show higher rates of temper tantrums and obsessive—compulsive disorders (Dykens, Leckman, & Cassidy, 1996; Walz & Benson, 2002) that could increase the risk of child abuse; on the other hand, individuals with Williams syndrome are indiscriminately social, which could increase the risk of sexual victimization in adulthood (Thurman & Fisher, 2015).

These differences in behavioral phenotypes could shed important light on etiology-specific risk factors for victimization across the lifespan. Thus, future research should move beyond examining disability as a heterogeneous group or grouping disability into generic categories, and should instead examine risk for specific forms of disability.

5.3 A Focus on Resilience and Well-Being

While it is important to understand the risk factors related to child abuse and victimization of people with IDD, it is also important to focus on the protective factors. Such factors might not only protect individuals from experiencing victimization, but they might also help individuals cope and heal in the face of victimization.

Even as the majority of individuals with IDD might experience victimization, there are, of course, many individuals who go through life unscathed. Future research should examine these individuals to determine what factors protect them from victimization. Further, those who do experience victimization react in different ways. It will be important to find those individuals who are more resilient to victimization, so that intervention programs can work to enhance those aspects in other individuals who experience victimization.

Finally, "well being" represents the quality of life for a child or person. This includes (1) physical health, development, and safety; (2) psychological and emotional development; (3) social development and behavior; and (4) cognitive development and educational achievement (Pollard & Lee, 2003). There are two broad approaches to defining and measuring child well-being. The first approach is to consider well-being as a multidimensional concept. Researchers decide on the important life dimensions and populate these dimensions with indicators. The second approach is to directly ask individuals about how they view their well-being (Fattore, Mason, & Watson, 2007; Pollard & Lee, 2003). Historically, the measurement of well-being has focused on deficits (i.e., children with behavior problems, disorders, and disabilities) rather than attempting to measure a continuum of well-being for all children. To better understand how to support the well-being of children and adults with IDD, future research should focus on strength-based approaches for assessing, measuring, and ensuring the well-being of children and adults with IDD.

6. CONCLUSION

We end this chapter with a call for action. We believe children and adults with IDD have the right to develop within healthy and safe environments; however, decades of research indicate that individuals with IDD experience alarmingly high rates of victimization. Despite the evidence, few prevention and intervention programs have been developed to address the needs of this vulnerable population. It is not enough to simply describe risk and victimization; as researchers and educators, we must translate these findings into practice. As we now understand the risk factors related to child abuse, bullying, and adult criminal victimization, it is time to focus on prevention and intervention programs to meet the unique needs of individuals with IDD. Moving forward, we encourage general prevention and intervention programs that focus on child abuse, bullying, and criminal victimization to more purposefully consider, include, accommodate, and support children and adults with IDD.

REFERENCES

Abbott, D., & Howarth, J. (2007). Still off-limits? Staff views on supporting gay, lesbian, and bisexual people with intellectual disabilities to develop sexual and intimate relationships. *Journal of Applied Research in Intellectual Disabilities, 20*, 116—126.

Adams, R. E., Fredstrom, B. K., Duncan, A. W., Holleb, L. J., & Bishop, S. L. (2014). Using self- and parent-reports to test the association between peer victimization and internalizing symptoms in verbally fluent adolescents with ASD. *Journal of Autism and Developmental Disabilities, 44*, 861—872.

Atkinson, J. P., & Ward, K. M. (2012). The development of an assessment of interpersonal violence for individuals with intellectual and developmental disabilities. *Sexuality and Disability, 30*, 301—309.

Bagner, D. M., & Eyberg, S. M. (2007). Parent-child interaction therapy for disruptive behavior in children with mental retardation: a randomized controlled trial. *Journal of Clinical Child and Adolescent Psychology, 36*, 418—429.

Ballan, M. S., Freyer, M. B., Marti, C. N., Perkel, J., Webb, K. A., & Romanelli, M. (2014). Looking beyond prevalence: a demographic profile of survivors of intimate partner violence with disabilities. *Journal of Interpersonal Violence, 29*, 3167–3179.

Barber, M., Jenkins, R., & Jones, C. (2000). A survivor's group for women who have a learning disability. *British Journal of Developmental Disabilities, 46*, 31–41.

Barnett, O., Miller-Perrin, C., & Perrin, R. D. (2011). *Family violence across the Lifespan: An introduction* (3rd ed.). Newbury Park, CA: Sage Publications.

Barranti, C. C. R., & Yuen, F. K. O. (2008). Intimate partner violence and women with disabilities: toward bringing visibility to an unrecognized population. *Journal of Social Work in Disabilities and Rehabilitation, 7*, 115–130.

Bear, G. G., Mantz, L. S., Glutting, J. J., Yang, C., & Boyer, D. E. (2015). Differences in bullying victimization between students with and without disabilities. *School Psychology Review, 44*, 98–116.

Begeer, S., Fink, E., van der Meijden, S., Goossens, F., & Olthof, T. (2015). Bullying-related behaviour in a mainstream high school versus a high school for autism: self-report and peer-report. *Autism: International Journal of Research and Practice.* http://dx.doi.org/10.1177/1362361315597525 (online).

Belsky, J., & Vondra, I. (1989). Lessons from child abuse: the determinants of parenting. In D. Cicchetti, & V. Carlson (Eds.), *Child maltreatment* (pp. 153–202). Cambridge: Cambridge University Press.

Bergstrom, R., Najdowski, A. C., & Tarbox, J. (2014). A systematic replication of teaching children with autism to respond appropriately to lures from strangers. *Journal of Applied Behavior Analysis, 47*, 861–865. http://dx.doi.org/10.1002/jaba.175.

Berliner, L. (2000). What is sexual abuse? In H. Dubowitz, & D. DePanfilis (Eds.), *Handbook for child protection practice* (pp. 18–22). Thousand Oaks, CA: Sage.

Berliner, L., & Conte, J. R. (1990). The process of victimization: the victims' perspective. *Child Abuse and Neglect, 14*, 29–40.

Betts, S. W., Betts, D. E., & Gerber-Eckard, L. N. (2007). *Asperger syndrome in the inclusive classroom: Advice and strategies for teachers.* London: Jessica Kingsley Publishers.

Black, D. A., Heyman, R. E., & Smith Slep, A. M. (2001). Risk factors for child physical abuse. *Aggressive Violent Behavior, 6*, 121–188.

Blake, J. J., Lund, E. M., Zhou, Q., Kwok, O., & Benz, M. R. (2012). National prevalence rates of bully victimization among students with disabilities in the United States. *School Psychology Quarterly, 27*, 210–222.

Bourke, S., & Burgman, I. (2010). Coping with bullying in Australian schools: how children with disabilities experience support from friends, parents and teachers. *Disability and Society, 25*, 359–371.

Boyle, M. H., Jenkins, J. M., Georgiades, K., Cairney, J., Duku, E., & Racine, Y. (2004). Differential-maternal parenting behavior: estimating within- and between-family effects on children. *Child Development, 75*, 1457–1476.

Braddock, D., Hemp, R., Rizzolo, M. C., Tanis, E. S., Haffer, L., & Wu, J. (2014). *The state of the states in developmental disabilities, 2014: Emerging from the great recession.* Washington, DC: American Association on Intellectual and Developmental Disabilities.

Brown, H., Stein, J., & Turk, V. (1995). The sexual abuse of adults with learning disabilities: report of a second two-year incidence study. *Mental Handicap Research, 8*, 3–24.

Bull, J., McCormick, G., Swann, C., & Mulvihill, C. (2004). *Ante- and post-natal home visiting programs: A review of reviews. UK.*

Cambridge, P., Beadle-Brown, J., Milne, A., Mansell, J., & Whelton, B. (2011). Patterns of risk in adult protection referrals for sexual abuse and people with intellectual disability. *Journal of Applied Research Intellectual Disabilities, 24*, 118–132.

Cappadocia, M. C., Weiss, J. A., & Pepler, D. (2012). Bullying experiences among children and youth with autism spectrum disorders. *Journal of Autism and Developmental Disorders, 42*, 266–277.

Carter, E. W., & Kennedy, C. H. (2006). Promoting access to the general curriculum using peer support strategies. *Research and Practice for Persons with Severe Disabilities, 31*, 284–292.

Carter, B. B., & Spencer, V. G. (2006). The fear factor: bullying and students with disabilities. *International Journal of Special Education, 21*, 11–20.

Center on the Developing Child. (2007). *The impact of early adversity on child development (Inbrief)*. From www.developingchild.harvard.edu.

Chambers, C. R., Hughes, C., & Carter, E. W. (2004). Parent and sibling perspectives on the transition to adulthood. *Education and Training in Developmental Disabilities, 39*, 79–94.

Chang, J. C., Martin, S. L., Moracco, K. E., Dulli, L., Scandlin, D., Loucks-Sorrel, M. B., … Bou-Saada, I. (2003). Helping women with disabilities and domestic violence: strategies, limitations, and challenges of domestic violence programs and services. *Journal of Women's Health, 12*, 699–708.

Charlton, M., & Tallant, B. (2003). *Trauma treatment with clients who have dual diagnoses: Developmental disabilities and mental illness*. Aurora, CO: Intercept Center, Aurora Mental Health Center. From www.NCTSNnet.org.

Chen, P.-Y., & Schwartz, I. S. (2012). Bullying and victimization experiences of students with autism spectrum disorders in elementary schools. *Focus on Autism and Or Developmental Disabilities, 27*, 200–212.

Child Abuse Prevention and Treatment Act. (1974, as amended). *P.L. 93-247. 42 USC 5101 et seq; 5116 et seq*. From http://www.acf.hhs.gov/programs/cb/laws_policies/cblaws/capta/.

Child Welfare Information Gateway. (2013). *Parent-child interaction therapy with at-risk families*. Washington, DC: U.S. Department of Health and Human Services, Children's Bureau.

Child Welfare Information Gateway. (2014). *Definitions of child abuse and neglect*. Washington, DC: U.S. Department of Health and Human Services, Children's Bureau.

Christensen, L. L., Fryant, R. J., Neece, C. L., & Baker, B. (2012). Bullying adolescents with intellectual disability. *Journal of Mental Health Research in Intellectual Disabilities, 5*, 49–65.

Collins, B. C., Schuster, J. W., & Nelson, C. M. (1992). Teaching a generalized response to the lures of strangers to adults with severe handicaps. *Exceptionality, 3*, 67–80.

Committee for Children. (2008). *Second step: Student success through prevention program*. Seattle, WA: Committee for Children.

Coohey, C. (2007). Social networks, informal child care & inadequate supervision by mothers. *Child Welfare, 86*, 53–66.

Coohey, C., & Braun, N. (1997). Toward an integrated framework for understanding child physical abuse. *Child Abuse and Neglect, 21*, 1081–1094.

Cook, C. R., Williams, K. R., Guerra, N. G., Kim, T. E., & Sadek, S. (2010). Predictors of bullying and victimization in childhood and adolescence: a meta-analytic investigation. *School Psychology Quarterly, 25*, 65–83.

Copeland, S. R., Hughes, C., Carter, E. W., Guth, C., Presley, J. A., Williams, C. R., & Fowler, S. E. (2004). Increasing access to general education: perspectives of participants in a high school peer support program. *Remedial and Special Education, 25*, 342–352.

Corr, C., & Danner, N. (2014). Court-appointed special advocates strong beginnings: raising awareness across early childhood and child welfare systems. *Early Childhood Development and Care, 184*, 1436–1446.

Craig, W. (1998). The relationship among aggression types, depression, and anxiety in bullies, victims, and bully/victims. *Personality and Individual Differences, 24*, 123–130.

Daro, D. (1993). Child maltreatment research: implications for program design. In D. Cicchetti, & S. Toth (Eds.), *Child abuse, child development, and social policy* (pp. 331–367). Norwood, NJ: Ablex Publishing Corporation.

Daro, D. (2009). Science and child abuse prevention. A reciprocal relationships. In K. Dodge, & D. Coleman (Eds.), *Community prevention of child maltreatment* (pp. 9–28). Guilford Press.

Daro, D. (2011). Home visitation. In E. Zigler, W. Gilliam, & S. Barnett (Eds.), *The preschool education debates* (pp. 169–173).

Daro, D., & McCurdy, K. (2006). Interventions to treat child maltreatment. In L. S. Doll, S. E. Bonzo, J. A. Mercy, D. A. Sleet, & E. N Haas (Eds.), *The handbook of injury and violence prevention*. New York: Springer.

Davis, M. K., & Gidycz, C. A. (2000). Child sexual abuse programs: a meta-analysis. *Journal of Clinical Child Psychology, 2,* 257–265.

Dawkins, J. L. (1996). Bullying, physical disability, and the pediatric patient. *Developmental Medicine and Child Neurology, 38,* 603–612.

Doren, B., Bullis, M., & Benz, M. R. (1996). Predictors of victimization experiences of adolescents with disabilities in transition. *Exceptional Children, 63,* 7–18.

Dubowitz, H., Kim, J., Black, M. M., Weisbart, C., Semiatin, J., & Magder, L. S. (2011). Identifying children at high risk for a child maltreatment report. *Child Abuse and Neglect, 35,* 96–104.

Dykens, E. M., Leckman, J. F., & Cassidy, B. (1996). Obsessions and compulsions in Prader-Willi syndrome. *Journal of Child Psychology and Psychiatry and Allied Disciplines, 37,* 995–1002.

Egemo-Helm, K. R., Miltenberger, R. G., Knudson, P., Finstrom, N., Jostad, C., & Johnson, B. (2007). An evaluation of in situ training to teach sexual abuse prevention skills to women with mental retardation. *Behavioral Interventions, 22,* 99–119.

Erickson, M., & Egeland, B. (1996). The quiet assault: a portrait of child neglect. In J. Briere, L. Berliner, S. Bulkley, C. Jenny, & T. Reid (Eds.), *The handbook of child maltreatment* (pp. 35–89). Newbury Park, CA: Sage Publications.

Esernio-Jenssen, D., Tai, J., & Kodsi, S. (2011). Abusive head trauma in children: a comparison of male and female perpetrators. *Pediatrics, 127,* 649–657.

Espelage, D. L., Low, S., Polanin, J. R., & Brown, E. C. (2013). The impact of a middle school program to reduce aggression, victimization, and sexual violence. *Journal of Adolescent Health, 53,* 180–186.

Espelage, D. L., Low, S., Polanin, J. R., & Brown, E. C. (2015). Clinical trial of second step© middle-school program: impact on aggression and victimization. *Journal of Applied Developmental Psychology, 37,* 52–63.

Espelage, D. L., & Swearer, S. M. (2003). Research on school bullying and victimization: what have we learned and where do we go from here? *School Psychology Review, 32,* 365–383.

Farrington, D. P., & Ttofi, M. M. (2009). School-based programs to reduce bullying and victimization: a systematic review. *Campbell Systematic Reviews, 6.* http://dx.doi.org/10.4073/csr.2009.6.

Fattore, T., Mason, J., & Watson, E. (2007). Children's conceptualisation(s) of their well-being. *Social Indicators Research, 80,* 5–29.

Finlay, W. M., & Lyons, E. (2000). Methodological issues in interviewing and using self-report questionnaires with people with mental retardation. *Psychological Assessment, 13,* 319–335.

Fisher, M. H. (2009). Literature analysis to determine the inclusion of children with disabilities in abuse interventions. *Child Abuse and Neglect, 33,* 326–327.

Fisher, M. H. (2014). Evaluation of a stranger safety training programme for young adults with Williams syndrome. *Journal of Intellectual Disability Research, 58,* 903–914.

Fisher, M. H., Baird, J. V., Currey, A. D., & Hodapp, R. M. (2016). Victimization and social vulnerability of adults with intellectual disability: a review of research extending beyond Wilson and Brewer. *Australian Psychologist, 51,* 114—127.

Fisher, M. H., Burke, M. M., & Griffin, M. M. (2013). Teaching young adults with intellectual and developmental disabilities to respond appropriately to lures from strangers. *Journal of Applied Behavior Analysis, 46,* 528—533.

Fisher, M. H., Hodapp, R. M., & Dykens, E. M. (2008). Child abuse among children with disabilities: what we know and what we need to know. *International Review of Research in Mental Retardation, 35,* 251—289.

Fisher, M. H., Moskowitz, A. L., & Hodapp, R. M. (2012). Vulnerability and experiences related to social victimization among individuals with intellectual and developmental disabilities. *Journal of Mental Health Research in Intellectual Disabilities, 5,* 32—48.

Fisher, M. H., & Taylor, J. L. (2016). Let's talk about it: peer victimization experiences as reported by adolescents with ASD. *Autism: International Journal of Research and Practice, 20,* 402—411. http://dx.doi.org/10.1177/1362361315585948. Fisher & Taylor, 2015.

Fortson, B. L., Klevens, J., Merrick, M. T., Gilbert, L. K., & Alexander, S. P. (2016). *Preventing child abuse and neglect: A technical package for policy, norm, and programmatic activities.* Atlanta, GA: National Center for Injury Prevention and Control, Centers for Disease Control and Prevention.

Furey, E. M., Niesen, J. J., & Stauch, J. D. (1994). Abuse and neglect of adults with mental retardation in different residential settings. *Behavioural Interventions, 9,* 199—211.

Garbarino, J. (1994). Can most child maltreatment be prevented? Yes. In E. Gambrill, & T. J. Stein (Eds.), *Controversial issues in child welfare* (pp. 49—52). Boston: Allyn & Bacon.

Giardino, A. P., Lyn, M. A., & Giardino, E. R. (2009). Child abuse and neglect. In *A practical guide to the evaluation of child physical abuse and neglect.* New York, NY: Springer Publishing.

Gietz, C., & McIntosh, K. (2014). Relations between student perceptions of their school environment and academic achievement. *Canadian Journal of School Psychology, 29,* 161—176.

Gladden, R. M., Vivolo-Kantor, A. M., Hamburger, M. E., & Lumpkin, C. D. (2014). *Bullying surveillance among youths: Uniform definitions for public health and recommended data elements, version 1.0.* Atlanta, GA: National Center for Injury Prevention and Control Centers for Disease Control and Prevention and US Department of Education.

Greenspan, S., Loughlin, G., & Black, R. S. (2001). Credulity and gullibility in people with developmental disorders: a framework for future research. In L. M. Glidden (Ed.), *24. International review of research in mental retardation* (pp. 101—135).

Grosso, C. (2012). Children with developmental disabilities. In J. A. Cohen, A. P. Mannarino, & E. Deblinger (Eds.), *Trauma CBT for children and adolescents* (pp. 149—174). NY: Guildford.

Gunby, K. V., & Rapp, J. T. (2014). The use of behavioral skills training and in situ feedback to protect children with autism from abduction lures. *Journal of Applied Behavior Analysis, 47,* 856—860.

Gus, L. (2000). Autism: promoting peer understanding. *Educational Psychology in Practice, 16,* 461—468.

Hanley-Maxwell, C., Whitney-Thomas, J., & Pogoloff, S. M. (1995). The second shock: a qualitative study of parents' perspectives and needs during their child's transition from school to adult life. *Research and Practice for Persons with Severe Disabilities, 20,* 3—15.

Harrell, E. (2015). *Crime against persons with disabilities, 2009—2013 — Statistical tables. Bureau of Justice Statistics.* From http://www.bjs.gov/index.cfm?ty=pbdetail&iid=5280.

Haseltine, B., & Miltenberger, R. G. (1990). Teaching self-protection skills to persons with mental retardation. *American Journal on Mental Retardation, 95,* 188—197.

Hate Crimes Statistics Act. (2010, as amended). *P.L. 28 U.S.C.* § *994.* From https://www. fbi.gov/about-us/cjis/ucr/hate-crime/2012/resource-pages/hate-crime-statistics-act/ hatecrimestatisticsact_final.

Hawker, D. S. J., & Boulton, M. J. (2000). Twenty year's research on peer victimization and psychosocial maladjustment. A meta-analytic review of cross sectional studies. *Journal of Child Psychology and Psychiatry, 41,* 441—455.

Heiman, T. (2000). Quality and quantity of friendship: students' and teacher perceptions. *School Psychology International, 21,* 330—339.

Hibbard, R. A., & Desch, L. W. (2007). Maltreatment of children with disabilities. *Pediatrics, 119,* 1018—1025.

Hickson, L., Khemka, I., Golden, H., & Chatzistyli, A. (2015). Randomized controlled trial to evaluate an abuse prevention curriculum for women and men with intellectual and developmental disabilities. *American Journal of Intellectual and Developmental Disabilities, 120,* 490—503.

Hillier, A. J., Fish, T., Siegel, J. H., & Beversdorf, D. Q. (2011). Social and vocational skills training reduces self-reported anxiety and depression among young adults on the autism spectrum. *Journal of Developmental and Physical Disabilities, 23,* 267—276.

Horner-Johnson, W., & Drum, C. E. (2006). Prevalence of maltreatment of people with intellectual disabilities: a review of the recently published research. *Mental Retardation and Developmental Disabilities, 12,* 57—69.

Hughes, K., Bellis, M. A., Jones, L., Wood, S., Bates, G., Eckley, L., ... Officer, A. (2012). Prevalence and risk of violence against adults with disabilities: a systematic review and meta-analysis of observational studies. *Lancet, 379,* 1621—1629.

Hughes, R. B., Robinson-Whelen, S., Pepper, A., Gabrielli, J., Lund, E., Legerski, J., & Schwartz, M. (2010). Development of a safety awareness program for women with diverse disabilities. *Rehabilitation Psychology, 55,* 263—271.

Humphrey, N. (2008). Autistic spectrum and inclusion: Including pupils with autistic spectrum disorders in mainstream schools. *Support for Learning, 23,* 41—47.

Humphrey, N., & Lewis, S. (2008). 'Make me normal': the views and experiences of pupils on the autistic spectrum in mainstream secondary schools. *Autism, 12,* 23—46.

Jawaid, A., Riby, D. M., Owens, J., White, S. W., Tarar, T., & Schulz, P. E. (2012). 'Too withdrawn' or 'too friendly': considering social vulnerability in two neurodevelopmental disorders. *Journal of Intellectual Disability Research, 56,* 335—350.

Johnson, K. (2009). *State-based home visiting: Strengthening programs through state leadership.* New York: National Center for Children in Poverty, Columbia University.

Jones, L., Belilis, M., Wood, S., Hughes, K., McCoy, E., Eckley, L., ... Officer, A. (2012). Prevalence and risk of violence against children with disabilities: a systematic review and meta-analysis of observational studies. *Lancet, 380,* 899—907.

Kaukiainen, A., Salmivalli, C., Lagerspetz, K., Tamminen, M., Vauras, M., Mäki, H., & Poskiparta, E. (2002). Learning difficulties, social intelligence, and self-concept: connections to bully-victim problems. *Scandinavian Journal of Psychology, 43,* 269—278.

Keelser, J. M. (2014). A call for the integration of trauma-informed care among intellectual and developmental disability organizations. *Journal of Policy and Practice in Intellectual Disabilities, 11,* 34—42.

Kempton, W., & Kahn, E. (1991). Sexuality and people with intellectual disabilities: a historical perspective. *Sexuality and Disability, 9,* 93—111.

Kennedy, S. C., Kim, J., Tripod, S., Brown, S., & Gowdy, G. (2016). Does parent-child interaction therapy reduce future physical abuse? A meta analysis. *Research on Social Work Practice, 18,* 1049731514543024.

Kenny, M. (2004). Teachers' attitudes toward and knowledge of child maltreatment. *Child Abuse and Neglect, 28,* 1311—1319.

Khemka, I. (2000). Increasing independent decision-making skills of women with mental retardation in simulated interpersonal situations of abuse. *American Journal on Mental Retardation, 105*, 387—401.

Khemka, I., Hickson, L., & Reynolds, G. (2005). Evaluation of a decision-making curriculum designed to empower women with mental retardation to resist abuse. *American Journal on Mental Retardation, 110*, 193—204.

Klerman, L. V. (1985). Interprofessional issues in delivering services to chronically ill children and their families. In N. Hobbs, & J. M. Perrin (Eds.), *Issues in the care of children with chronic illness: A sourcebook on problems, services and policies* (pp. 420—440). San Francisco: Jossey-Bass.

Klomek, A. B., Marrocco, F., Kleinman, M., Schonfeld, I. S., & Gould, M. S. (2008). Peer victimization, depression, and suicidality in adolescents. *Suicide and Life-Threatening Behavior, 38*, 166—180.

Kolko, D. J. (1996). Individual cognitive- behavioral treatment and family therapy for physically abused children and their offending parents: a comparison of clinical outcomes. *Child Maltreatment: Journal of the American Professional Society on the Abuse of Children, 1*, 322—342.

Kolko, D. J., Iselin, A. M., & Gully, K. (2011). Evaluation of the sustainability and clinical outcome of alternatives for families: a cognitive-behavioral therapy (AF-CBT) in a child protection center. *Child Abuse and Neglect, 35*, 105—116.

Kowalski, R. M., & Fedina, C. (2011). Cyberbullying in ADHD and Asperger syndrome population. *Research in Autism Spectrum Disorders, 5*, 1201—1208.

Krug, E. G., Dahlberg, L. L., Mercy, J. A., Zwi, A., & Lozano, R. (2002). *World report on violence and health*. Geneva: World Health Organization.

Kumpulainen, K., Räsänen, E., Henttonen, I., Almqvist, F., Kresanov, K., Linna, S., ... Tamminen, T. (1998). Bullying and psychiatric symptoms among elementary school-age children. *Child Abuse and Neglect, 22*, 705—717.

Larkin, P., Jahoda, A., MacMahon, K., & Pert, C. (2012). Interpersonal sources of conflict in young people with and without mild to moderate intellectual disabilities at transition from adolescence to adulthood. *Journal of Applied Research in Intellectual Disabilities, 25*, 29—38.

Laugeson, E. A., & Frankel, F. (2010). *Social skills for teenagers with developmental and autism spectrum disorders: The PEERS treatment manual*. New York, NY: Routledge.

Laugeson, E. A., Frankel, F., Gantman, A., Dillon, A. R., & Mogil, C. (2012). Evidence-based social skills training for adolescents with autism spectrum disorders: the UCLA PEERS program. *Journal of Autism and Developmental Disorders, 42*, 1025—1036.

Layzer, J. I., Goodson, B. D., Bernstein, L., & Price, C. (2001). *National evaluation of family support programs: Vol. A the meta analysis*. Cambridge, MA: Abt Associates.

Lin, L.-P., Yen, C.-F., Kuo, F.-Y., Wu, J.-L., & Lin, J.-D. (2009). Sexual assault of people with disabilities: results of a 2002—2007 national report in Taiwan. *Research in Developmental Disabilities, 30*, 969—975.

Little, L. (2002). Middle-class mothers' perceptions of peer and sibling victimization among children with Asperger's syndrome and non-verbal learning disorders. *Issues in Comprehensive Pediatric Nursing, 25*, 43—57.

Luckasson, R. (1992). People with mental retardation as victims of crime. In R. W. Conley, R. Luckasson, & G. N. Bouthilet (Eds.), *The criminal justice system and mental retardation: Defendants and victims* (pp. 209—220). Baltimore, MD, England: Paul H. Brookes Publishing.

Lumley, V. A., & Miltenberger, R. G. (1997). Sexual abuse prevention for persons with mental retardation. *American Journal on Mental Retardation, 101*, 459—472.

Lumley, V., Miltenberger, R., Long, E., Rapp, J., & Roberts, J. (1998). Evaluation of a sexual abuse prevention program for adults with mental retardation. *Journal of Applied Behavior Analysis, 31*, 91—101.

Lund, E. M. (2011). Community-based services and interventions for adults with disabilities who have experienced interpersonal violence: a review of the literature. *Trauma Violence and Abuse, 12*, 171—182.

Mahady Wilton, M. M., Craig, W. M., & Pepler, D. J. (2000). Emotional regulation and display in classroom victims of bullying: characteristic expressions of affect, coping styles and relevant contextual factors. *Social Development, 9*, 226—245.

Mandell, D. S., Walrath, C. M., Manteuffel, B., Sgro, G., & Pinto-Martin, J. A. (2005). The prevalence and correlates of abuse among children with autism served in comprehensive community-based mental health settings. *Child Abuse and Neglect, 29*, 1359—1372.

Manders, J. E., & Stoneman, Z. (2009). Children with disabilities in the child protective services system: an analog study of investigation and case management. *Child Abuse and Neglect, 33*, 229—237.

Mansell, L., Beadle-Brown, J., Cambridge, P., Milne, A., & Whelton, B. (2009). Adult protection incidence of referrals, nature and risk factors in two English local authorities. *Journal of Social Work, 9*, 23—38.

Mansell, S., Sobsey, D., & Calder, P. (1992). Sexual abuse treatment for persons with developmental disabilities. *Professional Psychology: Research and Practice, 23*, 404—409.

Mazurek, M. O., & Kanne, S. M. (2010). Friendship and internalizing symptoms among children and adolescents with ASD. *Journal of Autism and Developmental Disorders, 40*, 1512—1520.

McCarthy, M., & Thompson, D. (1997). A prevalence study of sexual abuse of adults with intellectual disabilities referred for sex education. *Journal of Applied Research in Intellectual Disabilities, 10*, 105—124.

McMahon, E. M., Reulbach, U., Keeley, H., Perry, I. J., & Arensman, E. (2010). Bullying victimisation, self harm and associated factors in Irish adolescent boys. *Social Science and Medicine, 71*, 1300—1307.

McMahon, B. T., West, S. L., Lewis, A. N., Armstrong, A. J., & Conway, J. P. (2004). Hate crimes and disability in America. *Rehabilitation Counseling Bulletin, 47*, 66—75.

McVilly, K. R., Stancliffe, R. J., Parmenter, T. R., & Burton-Smith, R. M. (2006). 'I get by with a little help from my friends': adults with intellectual disability discuss loneliness. *Journal of Applied Research in Intellectual Disabilities, 19*, 191—203.

Mechling, L. C. (2008). Thirty year review of safety skill instruction for persons with intellectual disabilities. *Education and Training in Developmental Disabilities, 43*, 311—323.

Mikton, C., & Shakespeare, T. (2014). Introduction to special issue on violence against people with disability. *Journal of Interpersonal Violence, 29*, 3055—3062. http://dx.doi.org/10.1177/0886260514534531.

Mikton, C., Maguire, H., & Shakespeare, T. (2014). A systematic review of the effectiveness of interventions to prevention and respond to violence against persons with disabilities. *Journal of Interpersonal Violence, 29*, 3207—3226.

Miltenberger, R., Roberts, J., Ellingson, S., Galensky, T., Rapp, J., Long, E., & Lumley, V. (1999). Training and generalization of sexual abuse prevention skills for women with mental retardation. *Journal of Applied Behavior Analysis, 32*, 385—388.

Mishna, F. (2003). Learning disabilities and bullying: double jeopardy. *Journal of Learning Disabilities, 36*, 1—15.

Nansel, T. R., Overpeck, M., Pilla, R. S., Ruan, W. J., Simons-Morton, B., & Scheidt, P. (2001). Bullying behaviors among US youth: prevalence and association with psychosocial adjustment. *Journal of the American Medical Association, 285*, 2094—2100.

National ASD Center. (2009). *National standard's report*. Randolph, MA: National ASD Center.

Nettelbeck, T., & Wilson, C. (2001). Criminal victimization of persons with mental retardation: the influence of interpersonal competenceL. M. Glidden (Ed.). *International Review of Research in Mental Retardation, 24*, 137—169.

Nettelbeck, T., & Wilson, C. (2002). Personal vulnerability to victimization of people with mental retardation. *Trauma, Violence, and Abuse, 3*, 289—306.

Nettlebeck, T., Wilson, C., Potter, R., & Perry, C. (2000). The influence of interpersonal competence on personal vulnerability of persons with mental retardation. *Journal of Interpersonal Violence, 15*, 46—62.

Newman, E., Christopher, S. R., & Berry, J. O. (2000). Developmental disabilities, trauma exposure, and posttraumatic stress disorder. *Trauma, Violence, and Abuse: A Review Journal, 1*, 154—170.

Newman, L., Wagner, M., Cameto, R., & Knokey, A. M. (2009). *The post-high school outcomes of youth with disabilities up to 4 years after high school*. Menlo Park, CA: SRI International.

Nolan, S. A., Flynn, C., & Garber, J. (2003). Prospective relations between rejection and depression in young adolescents. *Journal of Personality and Social Psychology, 85*, 745—755.

Norwich, B., & Kelly, N. (2004). Pupils' views on inclusion: moderate learning difficulties and bullying in mainstream and special schools. *British Educational Research Journal, 30*, 43—65.

Nosek, M. A., Foley, C., Hughes, R. B., & Howland, C. A. (2001). Vulnerabilities for abuse among women with disabilities. *Sexuality and Disability, 19*, 177.

Nosek, M. A., Howland, C. A., & Young, M. E. (1998). Abuse of women with disabilities: policy implications. *Journal of Disability Policy Studies, 8*, 158—175.

Office for Civil Rights. (October 21, 2014). *2014 dear colleague letter: Responding to bullying of students with disabilities*. From http://www2.ed.gov/about/offices/list/ocr/letters/colleague-bullying-201410.pdf.

Office of Special Education and Rehabilitative Services. (August 20, 2013). *2013 dear colleague letter: Bullying among students with disabilities*. From https://www2.ed.gov/policy/speced/guid/idea/memosdcltrs/bullyingdcl-8-20-13.pdf.

Olweus, D. (1994). Bullying at school: basic facts and effects of a school based intervention program. *Journal of Child Psychology and Psychiatry, 35*, 1171—1190.

Owen-DeSchryver, J. S., Carr, E. G., Cale, S. I., & Blakeley-Smith, A. (2008). Promoting social interactions between students with autism spectrum disorders and their peers in inclusive school settings. *Focus on Autism and Other Developmental Disabilities, 23*, 15—28.

Pan, S.-M. (2007). Prevalence of sexual abuse of people with intellectual disabilities in Taiwan. *Intellectual and Developmental Disabilities, 45*, 373—379.

Pellegrini, A. D. (1998). Bullies and victims in school: a review and call for research. *Journal of Applied Developmental Psychology, 19*, 165—176.

Petersilia, J. R. (2001). Crime victims with developmental disabilities: a review essay. *Criminal Justice Behavior, 28*, 655—694.

Petitpierre, G., Masse, M., Martini-Willemin, B., & Delessert, Y. (2013). A complementarity of social and legal perspectives on what is abusive practice and what constitutes abuse. *Journal of Policy and Practice in Intellectual Disabilities, 10*, 196—206.

Pfeffer, R. D. (2012). *Autistic and at-risk: The public and personal safety of children with autism spectrum disorders* (Doctoral dissertation, Northeastern University).

Pivik, J., McComas, J., & LaFlamme, M. (2002). Barriers and facilitators to inclusive education. *Exceptional Children, 69*, 97—107.

Pollard, E., & Lee, P. (2003). Child well-being: a systematic review of the literature. *Social Indicators Research, 61*, 59—78.

Prevent Child Abuse America (n.d.). Fact Sheet: Maltreatment of Children with Disabilities. Retrieved March 3, 2016 from http://preventchildabuse.org/resource/maltreatment-of-children-with-disabilities-2/

Reece, R. M. (2011). Medical evaluation of physical abuse. In J. E. B. Myers (Ed.), *The APSAC handbook on child maltreatment* (3rd ed., pp. 183—194). Thousand Oaks, CA: Sage.

Reiter, S., & Lapidot-Lefler, N. (2007). Bullying among special education students with intellectual disabilities: differences in social adjustment and social skills. *Intellectual and Developmental Disabilities, 45*, 174—181.

Rieffe, C., Camodeca, M., Pouw, L. B. C., Lange, A. M. C., & Stockman, L. (2012). Don't anger me! Bullying, victimization, and emotion dysregulation in young adolescents with ASD. *European Journal of Developmental Psychology, 9*, 351–370.

van Roekel, E., Scholte, R. H. J., & Didden, R. (2010). Bullying among adolescents with autism spectrum disorders: prevalence and perception. *Journal of Autism and Developmental Disorders, 40*, 63–73.

Rose, C. A., & Espelage, D. L. (2012). Risk and protective factors associated with the bullying involvement of students with emotional and behavioral disorders. *Behavioral Disorders, 37*, 133–148.

Rose, C., Monda-Amaya, L., & Espelage, D. (2011). Bullying perpetration and victimization in special education: a review of the literature. *Remedial and Special Education, 32*, 114–130.

Rosen, D. B. (2006). Violence and exploitation against women and girls with disability. In F. L. Denmark, H. H. Krauss, E. Halpern, S. Esther, & A. Jeri (Eds.), *Violence and exploitation against women and girls* (pp. 170–177). Malden: Blackwell Publishing.

Rowley, E., Chandler, S., Baird, G., Simonoff, E., Pickles, A., Loucas, T., & Charman, T. (2012). The experience of friendship, victimization, and bullying in children with an autism spectrum disorder: associations with child characteristics and school placement. *Research in Autism Spectrum Disorders, 6*, 1126–1134.

Runyon, M. K., & Urquiza, A. J. (2011). Child physical abuse: Interventions for parent who engage in coercive parenting practices and their children. In J. E. B. Myers (Ed.), *The APSAC handbook on child maltreatment* (3rd ed., pp. 183–194). Thousand Oaks, CA: Sage.

Saylor, C. F., & Leach, J. B. (2009). Perceived bullying and social support students accessing special inclusion programming. *Journal of Developmental and Physical Disabilities, 21*, 69–80.

Schaafsma, D., Kok, G., Stoffelen, J. M. T., & Curfs, L. M. G. (2015). Identifying effective methods for teaching sex education to individuals with intellectual disabilities: a systematic review. *Journal of Sex Research, 52*, 412–432.

Schroeder, J. H., Cappadocia, M. C., Bebke, J. M., Pepler, D. J., & Weiss, J. A. (2014). Shedding light on a pervasive problem: a review of research on bullying experiences among children with autism spectrum disorders. *Journal of Autism and Developmental Disorders, 44*, 1520–1534.

Sequeira, H., & Hollins, S. (2003). Clinical effects of sexual abuse on people with learning disability: critical literature review. *British Journal of Psychiatry, 182*, 13–19.

Sheard, C., Clegg, J., Standen, P., & Cromby, J. (2001). Bullying and people with severe intellectual disability. *Journal of Intellectual Disability Research, 45*, 407–415.

Shtayermman, O. (2007). Peer victimization in adolescents and young adults diagnosed with Asperger's syndrome: a link to depressive symptomatology, anxiety symptomatology and suicidal ideation. *Issues in Comprehensive Pediatric Nursing, 30*, 87–107.

Smith, P. K., Shu, S., & Madsen, K. (2001). Characteristics of victims of school bullying: developmental changes in coping strategies and skills. In J. Juvonen, & S. Graham (Eds.), *Peer harassment in school: The plight of the vulnerable and victimized* (pp. 332–352). New York: Guilford Press.

Sobsey, D. (1994). *Violence and abuse in the lives of people with disabilities: The end of silent acceptance?* Baltimore: Paul H. Brookes Publishing Co.

Sobsey, D., & Doe, T. (1991). Patterns of sexual abuse and assault. *Sexuality and Disability, 9*, 243–259.

Spencer, N., Devereux, E., Wallace, A., Sundrum, R., Shenoy, M., Bacchus, C., & Logan, S. (2005). Disabling conditions and registration for child abuse and neglect: a population-based study. *Pediatrics, 116*, 609–613.

Starling, S. P., Holden, J. R., & Jenny, C. (1995). Abusive head trauma: the relationships of the perpetrators to their victims. *Pediatrics, 95*, 259–262.

Sterzing, P. R., Shattuck, P. T., Narendorf, S. C., Wagner, M., & Cooper, B. P. (2012). Bullying involvement and autism spectrum disorders: prevalence and correlates of bullying involvement among adolescents with an autism spectrum disorder. *Archives of Pediatrics and Adolescent Medicine, 166*, 1058–1064.

Stromsness, M. M. (1993). Sexually abused women with mental retardation: hidden victims, absent resources. *Women and Therapy, 14*, 139–152.

Sullivan, P. M., & Knutson, J. F. (1998). Maltreatment and behavioral characteristics of youth who are deaf and hard-of-hearing. *Sexuality and Disability, 16*, 295–319.

Sullivan, P. M., & Knutson, J. F. (2000). Maltreatment and disabilities: a population-based epidemiological study. *Child Abuse and Neglect, 24*, 1257–1273.

Sullivan, P., Vernon, M. C., & Scanlan, J. (October 1987). Sexual abuse of deaf youth. *American Annals of the Deaf*, 256–262.

Swearer, S. M., Espelage, D. L., Vaillancourt, T., & Hymel, S. (2010). What can be done about school bullying? Linking research to educational practice. *Educational Researcher, 39*, 38–47.

Swedlund, N. P., & Nosek, M. A. (2000). An exploratory study on the work of independent living centers to address abuse of women with disabilities. *Journal of Rehabilitation, 66*, 57–64.

Theriot, M. T., Dulmus, C. N., Sowers, K. M., & Johnson, T. K. (2005). Factors relating to self-identification among bullying victims. *Children and Youth Services Review, 27*, 979–994.

Thurman, A. J., & Fisher, M. H. (2015). The Williams syndrome social phenotype: disentangling the contributions of social interest and social difficulties. *International Review of Research in Developmental Disabilities, 49*, 191–227.

Ticoll, M. (1994). *Violence and people with disabilities: A review of the literature*. Ottawa, Ontario: National Clearinghouse on Family Violence.

Ttofi, M. M., & Farrington, D. P. (2011). Effectiveness of school-based programs to reduce bullying: a systematic review and meta-analytic review. *Journal of Experimental Criminology, 7*, 27–56.

Turk, V., & Brown, H. (1993). The sexual abuse of adults with learning disabilities: results of a two year incidence survey. *Mental Handicap Research, 6*, 193–216.

Turner, H. A., Finkelhor, D., & Ormrod, R. (2006). The effect of lifetime victimization on the mental health of children and adolescents. *Social Science and Medicine, 62*, 13–27.

US Department of Health & Human Services, Administration for Children and Families, Administration on Children, Youth and Families, Children's Bureau. (2016). *Child maltreatment 2014*. From http://www.acf.hhs.gov/programs/cb/research-data-technology/statistics-research/child-maltreatment.

US Department of Health & Human Services, Administration for Children and Families, Administration on Children, Youth and Families, Children's Bureau. (2010). *Child maltreatment 2008*. From http://www.acf.hhs.gov/programs/cb/stats_research/index.htm#can.

US Department of Justice, Federal Bureau of Investigation. (2013). *Hate crimes statistics*. From https://www.fbi.gov/about-us/cjis/ucr/hate-crime/2012/Hate%20Crime%20Statistics%20Overviews.zip.

Van IJzendoorn, M. H., Palacios, J., Sonuga-Barke, E. J. S., Gunnar, M. R., Vorria, Y., McCall, R., & Juffer, F. (2011). Children in institutional care: delayed development and resilience. *Monographs of the Society for Research of Child Development, 76*, 8–30.

Verdugo, M. A., Bermejo, B. G., & Fuertes, J. (1995). The maltreatment of intellectually handicapped children and adolescents. *Child Abuse and Neglect, 19*, 205–215.

Wagner, M., Newman, L., Cameto, R., & Levine, P. (2005). *Changes over time in the early post-secondary outcomes of youth with disabilities.* Menlo Park, CA: SRI International.

Walz, N. C., & Benson, B. A. (2002). Behavioral phenotypes in children with Down syndrome, Prader-Willi syndrome, or Angelman syndrome. *Journal of Developmental and Physical Disabilities, 14,* 307—321.

Westcott, H. (1993). *Abuse of children and adults with disabilities.* London: NSPCC.

Westcott, H. L., & Jones, D. P. H. (1999). Annotation: the abuse of disabled children. *Journal of Child Psychology and Psychiatry and Allied Disciplines, 40,* 497—506.

White, C., Holland, E., Marsland, D., & Oakes, P. (2003). The identification of environments and cultures that promote the abuse of people with intellectual disabilities: a review of the literature. *Journal of Applied Research in Intellectual Disabilities, 16,* 1—9.

Whitney, I., Nabuzoka, D., & Smith, P. K. (1992). Bullying in schools: mainstream and special needs. *Support for Learning, 7,* 3—7.

WHO & UNICEF. (2012). *Care for child development: Improving the care for young children.* Geneva: WHO and UNICEF.

Wilczynski, S. M., Connolly, S., Dubard, M., Henderson, A., & McIntosh, D. (2015). Assessment, prevention, and intervention for abuse among individuals with disabilities. *Psychology in the Schools, 52,* 9—21.

Wilson, C., & Brewer, N. (1992). The incidence of criminal victimisation of individuals with an intellectual disability. *Australian Psychologist, 27,* 114—117.

Wilson, C., Seaman, L., & Nettlebeck, T. (1996). Vulnerability to criminal exploitation: influence of interpersonal competence differences among people with mental retardation. *Journal of Intellectual Disability Research, 40,* 8—16.

Yude, C., Goodman, R., & McConachie, H. (1998). Peer problems of children with hemiplegia in mainstream primary schools. *Journal of Child Psychology and Psychiatry, 39,* 533—541.

Zablotsky, B., Bradshaw, C. P., Anderson, C. M., & Law, P. (2013). The association between bullying and the psychological functioning of children with autism spectrum disorder. *Journal of Developmental and Behavioral Pediatrics, 34,* 1—8.

Zeedyk, S. M., Rodriguez, G., TipTon, L. A., Baker, B. L., & Blacher, J. (2014). Bullying of youth with autism spectrum disorder, intellectual disability, or typical development: Victim and parent perspectives. *Research in Autism Spectrum Disorders, 8,* 1173—1183.

CONTENTS OF PREVIOUS VOLUMES